10-12-92

... all oppressions are related and all people must fight together to free all human potential.

—from a statement issued in the spring of 1987 by the Congress of Pink Democrats, an interracial coalition of South African lesbian and gay groups

COMING ■ OUT ■

An Anthology of International Gay and Lesbian Writings

EDITED BY STEPHAN LIKOSKY

PANTHEON BOOKS

NEW YORK

Copyright © 1992 by Stephan Likosky

All rights reserved under International and Pan-American
Copyright Conventions. Published in the United States by
Pantheon Books, a division of Random House, Inc., New
York, and simultaneously in Canada by Random House of
Canada Limited, Toronto.

Acknowledgments to reprint previously published materials
begin on p. xi

Library of Congress Cataloging-in-Publication Data

Coming out: an anthology of international gay writings/edited
by Stephan Likosky.
    p.   cm.
  Includes bibliographical references.
  ISBN 0-679-74054-6
  1. Homosexuality—Miscellanea.   2. Gays—Identity.
3. Coming out (Sexual identity).   I. Likosky, Stephan.
HQ76.25.C66   1992
305.9'0664—dc20   91–50834

Design by Maura Fadden Rosenthal

Manufactured in the United States of America
First Edition

This book is dedicated to
the memory of my parents Izzie and Nettie,
Paul Marx,
and to a Future Without Bigotry

COMING
■ OUT ■

An Anthology of International
Gay and Lesbian Writings

EDITED BY STEPHAN LIKOSKY

PANTHEON BOOKS

NEW YORK

Acknowledgments to reprint previously published materials
begin on p. xi

Library of Congress Cataloging-in-Publication Data

Coming out: an anthology of international gay writings/edited
by Stephan Likosky.
    p.   cm.
  Includes bibliographical references.
  ISBN 0-679-74054-6
  1. Homosexuality—Miscellanea.   2. Gays—Identity.
3. Coming out (Sexual identity).   I. Likosky, Stephan.
HQ76.25.C66   1992
305.9'0664—dc20   91–50834

Design by Maura Fadden Rosenthal

Manufactured in the United States of America
First Edition

This book is dedicated to
the memory of my parents Izzie and Nettie,
Paul Marx,
and to a Future Without Bigotry

. . . all oppressions are related and all people must fight together to free all human potential.

—from a statement issued in the spring of 1987 by the Congress of Pink Democrats, an interracial coalition of South African lesbian and gay groups

CONTENTS

CHAPTER THREE:
FORMS OF STRUGGLE

CHAPTER FOUR: ISSUES

SEPARATISM

TRANSVESTISM AND
TRANSSEXUALISM

AIDS

THE GAY GHETTO

IDENTITY POLITICS .

MAN-BOY LOVE

PERMISSIONS/ACKNOWLEDGMENTS

Grateful acknowledgment is made to the following for permission to reprint previously published material:

Alyson Publications, Inc.: Excerpts from *The Spiral Path: A Gay Contribution to Human Survival* by David Fernbach, 1981.

Being Alive: "From the Yucatán to Being Alive" from *Being Alive,* September 1990. Anonymous.

Black Rose Books: Excerpts from "The Jaques Murder" from *The Regulation of Desires: Sexuality in Canada* by Gary Kinsman, 1987.

Jared Braiterman: "Fighting AIDS in Brazil" by Jared Braiterman from *Gay Community News,* vol. 17, no. 39, April 15–21, 1990. Copyright © 1990 by Jared Braiterman.

Colectivo Sol: Excerpts from *Política Sexual: Cuadernos del Frente Homosexual de Acción Revolucionaria,* vol. 1, no. 1, 1979.

Connexions: "Argentina: Shrouded in Silence" from *Connexions* no. 3, Winter 1982. "The Decade Has Been Good for Us" from *Connexions* no. 17/18, Summer/Fall 1985.

Emmanuel Cooper: "Happy Families? Pedophilia Examined" by the Gay Left Collective in *Gay Left* no. 7, Winter 1978–79.

Herbert Daniel: "Above All, Life" from *Vida Antes Da Morte = Life Before Death* by Herbert Daniel, 1989.

Debat Gai: "Common Platform" by the Coordinated Homosexual Liberation Fronts of the Spanish State.

GMP Publishers Ltd.: Excerpts from "Perverts in Paradise" by João S. Trevisan. Copyright © 1986 by João Silverio Trevisan. Translation copyright by Martin Foreman. "The Rad Drag Queens" from *Men in Frocks.* Copyright © 1984 by Kris Kirk and Ed Heath. Excerpts from *Homosexuality and Liberation: Elements of a Gay Critique* by Mario Mieli, translation by David Fernbach. Copyright © 1980 by Guili o Einaudi editori s.p.a., Turin. Translation and English edition copyright by Gay Men's Press.

Masha Gessen: "We Have No Sex: Soviet Gays and AIDS in the Era of *Glasnost*" from *OUT/LOOK* no. 9, Summer 1990.

Clyde M. Hall-"Owlfeather": "Children of Grandmother Moon" by M. Owlfeather (Clyde M. Hall) from *Living the Spirit* edited by Will Roscoe.

Gerald Hannon: "No Sorrow, No Pity: The Gay Disabled" from *Flaunting It! A Decade of Journalism from "The Body Politic."* Vancouver, B.C.: New Star Books, 1982.

The Haworth Press, Inc.: "Gay Leader's Coming Out" and "Jose's Coming Out" from *Journal of Homosexuality,* vol. 17, no. 3/4. Copyright © 1989 by The Haworth Press. "Lesbian Struggle Against a Pillow or a Wall" by Gail Pheterson and Leny Jansen from *Gay Life in Dutch Society* edited by A. X. van Naerssen. Copyright © 1987 by Harrington Park Press.

Homosexual Liberation Front of Argentina: "Sex and Revolution."

Inaczej: "Notes of a Malcontent: Remember the Butt" by Sławek Starosta from *Inaczej,* no. 10 and "In Reply to the Malcontent" by "Carpentarius" from *Inaczej,* no. 12.

Indiana University Press: "The Harlequin and the Faun" by J. A. W. from *Gay Voices from East Germany,* interviews by Jürgen Lemke, 1991.

El Instituto Obregón "Stigma Transformation and Relexification: 'Gay' in Latin America" from *Male Homosexuality in Central and South America* (GAI Saber Monograph 5) by Stephen O. Murray, © 1987, with the permission of El Instituto Obregón.

Peter A. Jackson: Excerpts from *Male Homosexuality in Thailand* by Peter A. Jackson. Copyright Peter A. Jackson, Canberra, Australia, 1989.

Lampião: "Well Then, Why So Much Repression?" from *Lampião,* no. 12, May 1979.

La Pluma: "Transvestites and Transsexuals: Introduction to a Specific Type of Oppression" from *La Pluma* nos. 2 and 3. "Contradictions and Miseries of the Gay Ghetto," by Dario, from *La Pluma* no. 5.

Alison J. Laurie: "From Kamp Girls to Political Dykes" by Alison J. Laurie from *Finding the Lesbians* edited by Julia Penelope and Sarah Valentine,

1990, The Crossing Press, Freedom, CA. Originally published in issues 134 & 135 of *Broadsheet* Magazine, Nov. & Dec. 1985, New Zealand.

Tim McCaskell: "Out in the Basque Country" from *Flaunting It!* Reprinted by permission of Tim McCaskell, *The Body Politic*, A Magazine for Gay Liberation.

N.V.I.H. COC (Nederlandse Vereniging tot integratie van homoseksuali teit COC) "Cuba: We Cannot Jump Over Our Own Shadow" by Henk Van den Boogaard and Kathelijne van Kammen from *IGA Pink Book 1985*.

Penguin USA Inc.: Excerpts from *Homosexual: Oppression and Liberation* by Dennis Altman. Copyright © 1971 by Dennis Altman. Used by permission of the publisher, Dutton, an imprint of New American Library, a division of Penguin Books USA Inc.

Plenum Publishing Corporation: "Male Homosexuality in Contemporary Mainland China" by Fang-fu Ruan and Yung-mei Tsai from *Archives of Sexual Behavior*, vol. 17, no. 2, 1988.

Routledge: "Separatism" by Jane Dixon from *Radical Records* edited by Bob Cant and Susan Hemmings. "Zerrin" from *Inventing Ourselves*, Hall Carpenter Archives. "Zahid Dar" from *Walking After Midnight*, Hall Carpenter Archives.

Makeda Silvera: "Man Royals and Sodomites" from *Lesbians in Canada* edited by Sharon Dale Stone, 1990.

Semiotext(e): "To Destroy Sexuality" by Guy Hocquenghem from *Semiotext(e)* vol. 4, no. 1, 1981.

Simon & Schuster, Inc. Excerpt from *Lesbian Nation* by Jill Johnston. Copyright © 1973 by Jill Johnston.

Rex Wockner: "Homosexuality in the Arab and Moslem World" originally published in *Outlines, BLK, The Weekly News* (Miami), and *Capital Gay* (London).

Women's Press: "Turning Platform" from *The Aerial Letter* by Nicole Brossard, translated by Marlene Wildeman, 1988.

Verlags-Und Gaststattengesellschaft MBH: "Don Poofke," from *Schwuchtel,* June–August 1976, no. 4.

EDITOR'S
ACKNOWLEDGMENTS

I would like to thank The New York Public Library's Emily E. F. Skeel Fund, whose generosity and support made this project possible, and Richard Newman of The New York Public Library's Publications Office for his enthusiasm and confidence in me in this endeavor.

Harold Averill of the Canadian Gay Archives in Toronto offered invaluable help in my research, as did Mimi Bowling, Curator of the Manuscripts and Archives Collection at The New York Public Library, as well as other staff members of its Research Division. Many thanks also to Jim Kepner of the International Gay and Lesbian Archives and W. Dorr Legg of One, Incorporated, for the many insights I obtained from our discussions.

I would also like to thank translators Jolanta and Alicja Benal, Marilyn Kayser-Lilly, Sam Larson, and Kevin M. Mathewson for their fine work, performed often under pressure, as well as Linda Jones and Carlos Torres for their long hours at the word processor and their patience.

Tom Carroll and Harriet Gottfried provided me with personal support and encouragement, for which I am most grateful. And, of course, this work would not have been possible without the expertise and help given by Erroll McDonald, Yoji Yamaguchi, and Liza Wolsky at Pantheon Books, and Susan Herner and Sue Yuen at the Susan Herner Rights Agency.

INTRODUCTION

The determination of lesbians and gay men no longer to be victims of history but to help mold it can no longer be ignored. In over fifty countries around the globe, persons with homoerotic inclinations are "coming out" publicly, organizing movements for recognition and human rights, and, by doing so, challenging the authority of the traditional family, religious doctrine, and state power. It is indeed a revolution which is taking place, for its aims and practices are radically transforming outdated precepts and everyday custom in order to accommodate historically new ways of seeing and being.

The gay movement has much in common with other great freedom movements of the twentieth century: With the anti-apartheid and American civil rights movements, it shares the goals of political empowerment for the disenfranchised and an end to legal and social discrimination; with the feminist movement, it challenges sex role oppression and seeks to democratize a world where political, cultural, and social institutions have been for too long the sole domain of heterosexual men. The gay revolution, however, is unique in at least one important way. It has the potential of liberating the homoerotic component repressed in all of us, and in doing so, transforming social relations as never before experienced in history. The vision of a world peopled by polysexual individuals and freed of rigid sex roles is today no longer confined to sci-fi literature. Rather, it is a vision for which, in conjunction with that of racial and male-female equality, many of us around the globe find it necessary to struggle if the human family is to be preserved.

In spite of the rapid growth in publication of lesbian and gay writers in recent years, there has appeared little that is international in scope. This is especially true of nonfiction. It is my purpose to address this need with an anthology that demonstrates the variety and richness of what has been and is currently being written.

The time for such an endeavor seems appropriate, given not only the wealth of literature being produced, much of which remains inaccessible to the American public, but also the present "globalization" of the lesbian and gay movements. There are now such movements in tens of countries throughout the world,* in addition to several international organizations, such as the International Lesbian and Gay Association (ILGA) and the International Lesbian Information Service (ILIS), which monitor rights, sponsor international conferences, and lend support to new lesbian and gay movements as they evolve.

I have chosen to limit the inclusion of materials to those written post-Stonewall—that is, since 1969. This was the year in which gays, many of them Third World transvestites, took to the streets of New York to battle the police, who had raided the Stonewall Inn, a neighborhood bar. The period since Stonewall has witnessed a resurgence of militant struggle by lesbians and gay men for open recognition, a guarantee of civil rights, and social change. The Stonewall Rebellion is recognized as a watershed in gay history, as witnessed by its commemoration every June in Gay Pride events throughout the world. The literature that has emerged since Stonewall reflects the various changes lesbians and gay men have experienced, both on a collective or organizational plane and in terms of individual consciousness. Generally speaking, the militancy of the late sixties and early seventies, which tied the gay struggle to the call for a radical transformation of society and which is reflected in a preponderance of political manifestos and leftist-oriented social analyses, has recently given way to more concrete and localized struggles, focusing on issues such as legal reform and discrimination, advocacy regarding persons with AIDS, and the position of minority gays within the larger lesbian and gay communities.

In selecting materials for an anthology of international lesbian and gay writings, I have had to consider several important questions concerning what constitutes "gay." Here it is important to note

* The second *ILGA Pink Book* (1988) lists thirty-six countries with a gay and/or lesbian movement, as well as sixteen others where movements are being established.

that the term "homosexual," to denote a self-identified community of people, came into usage only in the second half of the nineteenth century. Homosexual subcultures can be documented as existing only as far back as the twelfth century. Homosexual behavior, on the other hand, has existed in many cultures all throughout recorded history. A critical difference between what might be termed anthropological or historical homosexuality, and the makings of a more modern gay or lesbian consciousness, is delineated by Barry D. Adam in his work *The Rise of a Gay and Lesbian Movement*. Anthropological or historical homosexuality, according to Adam, is characteristic of societies where homosexuality is obligatory and universally practiced, such as those where sexual relations between older and younger males are part of the socialization process into manhood (e.g., in Melanesia, central Africa, Amazonia, and western Egypt), or those where biological males or females fulfill the gender role expectations of the opposite sex (e.g., in Polynesia, Siberia, and among the native peoples of the Americas). The "modern" lesbian and gay worlds, in contrast, share the following characteristics:

1. Homosexual relations have been able to escape the structure of the dominant heterosexual kinship system. 2. Exclusive homosexuality, now possible for both partners, has become an alternative path to conventional family forms. 3. Same-sex bonds have developed new forms without being structured around particular age or gender categories. 4. People have come to discover each other and form large-scale social networks not only because of already existing social relationships but also because of their homosexual interests. 5. Homosexuality has come to be a social formation unto itself, characterized by self-awareness and group identity.[1]

I have limited my materials to those reflecting the ideas and experiences of the "modern" gay worlds. To complicate the issue, however, as modern gay communities have emerged, there are those theorists, especially in Europe and the Americas, who have argued strongly for the abolishment of the very concepts of "homosexual" and "heterosexual." Here a more universal sexual desire is acknowledged, while its breakdown into homosexual and heterosexual components is seen only as a means of social control by authoritarian social/political systems. I have chosen articles that presuppose and reflect a modern gay consciousness, as well as those that object to its existence in calling for a more general sexual liberation. Both ideological stances have had an enormous influence on the gay political movement and its struggles. Lesbians and gay men speak for themselves here, but there are also instances where authors are included who do not identify themselves in terms of sexual orientation but do make extensive use of testimony by lesbians and gay men. Due to scant resources, I have also included a small number of articles wherein gay life in one culture is viewed through the prism of an outsider. Again, however, I have tended to select those articles that contain quoted materials from indigenous informants.

One last note: I have sometimes used the word "gay" to indicate both lesbians and gay males, as both have at times experienced a shared history and common goals. Whenever this has not been the case, the more specific terms "lesbian" and "gay male" have been employed. In concluding, I would like to say that as self-evident as the need is for understanding the cultural context for any given selection, it is, practically speaking, out of the question, in compiling an anthology such as this, to provide more than a brief note on an article's background. To a large degree, however, the authors speak out in universal terms, whether in decrying the injustices of police repression, pleading for more tolerance, or sharing aspects of their personal lives. I would hope each reader remain aware of the difficulties of translation and the limitations of trying to identify another person's experiences with one's own over cultural boundaries. Still, if I have succeeded in piquing the reader's curiosity to investigate further the exciting varieties and commonalities of gay experience emerging throughout the world, I feel I shall have accomplished a large part of my goal.

NOTE

1. Barry D. Adam, *The Rise of a Gay and Lesbian Movement* (Boston: Twayne Publishers, 1987), p. 6.

CHAPTER ONE

OPPRESSIONS

If one were to take even a cursory survey of the instruments of oppression used to subjugate lesbians and gay men, it would be difficult not to stand in awe at the range of perversities and depths of degradation to which human behavior can sink. Since 1900 alone, the arsenal has included: denial of our existence, forced labor and physical extermination in concentration camps, denial of civil rights, assassinations at the hands of both right-wing and left-wing death squads, censorship, imprisonment, castration, forced internment in psychiatric institutions, the barring of parents from raising their children, state hangings, dismissals from jobs and the military, family rejection, shock therapy, forced registration by the state, government-sanctioned torture, prison rape, threats of eternal damnation from religious leaders, evictions from houses of worship, and random street beatings.

Most of the actions, whether physical or psychological in nature, have been sanctioned by governments, usually utilizing the police and military as implements of policy. Mainstream religions have not only provided the ideological framework for these ignoble actions; in many instances their worldly representatives have been directly responsible for instigating them. There is hardly a nation-state in existence today, whatever its economic or political system, or a major religion, be it Christianity, Judaism, or Islam, that has a clean slate in this regard.

The everyday impact of such virulent repression on the lives of lesbians and gay men is also telling: For the vast majority, whether living in Beijing, Omaha, or Buenos Aires, it has meant self-denial, loneliness, double lives, alienating sexual encounters, and fear of discovery; for large numbers we can add suicide, alcoholism and other substance abuse, and mental trauma.

In the following selections we find reflected some of the many patterns in which gay oppression manifests itself. It is important to remember that very few governments give official sanction or support to their gay minorities. Only 5 of the 182 countries surveyed by the International Lesbian and Gay Association in its 1988 *Pink Book,* for example, have laws prohibiting discrimination against lesbians and gay men.* Fifty-five countries, on the other hand, make same-sex relations illegal. Generally speaking, countries with a heritage of British law and those with theocratic traditions are the most repressive, some with penalties of long prison terms and even death. In countries where homosexuality is not illegal, other laws are often used to suppress gays. A common charge employed throughout much of Latin America to detain gays or close down their establishments is that of "offenses against morality." In England, Canada, and the United States, censorship laws and obscenity charges are often employed.

There is also little predictability in what we might expect to find. Among Western-style democracies, the United States is relatively repressive, with twenty-five states and the District of Columbia still prohibiting certain sexual activities between consenting adults, whereas Holland and Denmark are markedly tolerant. In what has until recently been called the "socialist camp," the Soviet Union has been and Cuba still is repressive on the legislative level, whereas the East German government was not.

The Judeo-Christian tradition has been one of the most enduring causes of lesbian and gay oppression, and its negative impact on traditional cultures where homosexuality was tolerated or accepted, such as in large parts of the Americas, Asia, and Africa, cannot be overestimated. In Muslim countries, historically, there have been strong traditions of tolerance toward homosexuality; today, however, antigay legislation in many of these same countries is among

---

* A total of 182 countries were surveyed, of which 124 reported concerning legal data on gays.

the most extreme anywhere. In Southeast Asia, homosexuality has rarely been criminalized or regarded as "sinful," and there is little of the blatant intolerance or violence against gays we find in the West. However, a strong religious-based emphasis on marriage and the family makes it difficult for the majority of gays to lead open lives or develop a supportive community based on their sexual orientation.

THAILAND

In Thailand, with its Buddhist tradition, homosexual love is not regarded as sinful, criminalized by the state, or judged unnatural, as has so often been the case in societies with a Judeo-Christian or Islamic tradition. However, there is a strong social pressure on the individual to behave in an expected or "appropriate" manner, and this means marrying and parenting.

Following is a selection, taken originally from a popular Thai magazine, wherein readers turn for advice to "Uncle Go" concerning matters of the heart. In the first two letters, feelings of shame and the compelling desire to reconcile personal feelings with social expectations come to light. In the third, which includes some explanatory comment, we learn that antigay violence is not uncommon in Thailand, even though embarrassment and fear of police intimidation can often prevent its being reported.

"Letters to Uncle Go," from *Male Homosexuality in Thailand: An Interpretation of Contemporary Thai Sources* by Peter A. Jackson (1989).

LETTER 2: CHIT

*Sawatdee Khun Go,**

I've been following your column for a long time. I have a problem and don't know who to turn to for help except you, Uncle. I've been trying not to get involved in these matters, but it's been torturing and weighing on me for ages. Please help me relieve my suffering, Uncle.

Even when I was a kid I realized I liked staring at good-looking men. I used to remember how they moved, and think about it later to amuse myself. But it wasn't sexual, because I was still too young. If a boy would come and talk with me I'd feel warmer than when a girl would try to get close.

Toward the end of primary school I started to love another boy, but we never did anything more than love each other, and miss each other when we were away. My father has been separated from my mother since I was small and I can't remember him. When I started growing up I didn't get interested in girls like my friends.

I like guys, but I've never let on to anyone about it because I'm ashamed. I'm always looking at handsome men, but I never stare till they know I'm looking. Everyone thinks I'm a complete man, because I give that impression.

I've tried going out with girls and not mixing with guys, so that I can forget it, but as soon as I'm alone it comes back to torment me. Sometimes when I mess with girls I have to think they're guys. I need to come in their back gate to get any pleasure. When I go to the movies and see a handsome movie star I keep thinking of him

---

* *Khun* is a Thai term of address used before first names for both men and women; a general term of respect.

over and over again until I have to help myself.* But I've never had a male friend like that at all—probably because I'm ashamed, and afraid that people will know. I think I'm going to have a nervous breakdown soon.

Uncle, I've read a lot but I only get more confused. I hope you won't throw my letter away. I want you to advertise for a friend for me, too. He shouldn't be open or hard to get along with. He should be between twenty-five and thirty-five years old, and over 160 cm tall. I say this because, when we meet, I don't want us to be too different. I'm twenty-four, 164 cm tall and weigh 60 kg. I have fair skin and reasonable looks.

LETTER 10: SA-NGOP

Revered *Go,*

I have always followed your column, and hold you in high regard. At this time I have a vexing and quite disturbing problem that is fraying my nerves and upsetting everything I do.

But before anything else, please let me introduce myself. I'm thirty-two, of Chinese extraction, and have my own business. My personality and appearance are appropriate, and I have a bachelor's degree. If I didn't have mental problems it could probably be said I should be quite happy, because I have both qualifications and a pleasant appearance. But nobody knows that I experience only suffering, loneliness, sadness, and anxiety.

Let me start talking about my vexing problem. I'm now fairly old and have often mixed with women who've put out feelers but, by and by, I've always knocked back their advances. However, my mother and father now want me to marry once and for all and are always giving me different reasons why I should. I tell them directly that I'm not ready yet.

---

* To help myself *(chuay yua-eng)* means to masturbate.

I've never had any interest in or feeling for the opposite sex, and if I married it would only add to my problems. I'd have to put on a show my whole life, and I doubt that I could keep it up. But if I don't marry, how can I lead a single life so that I will be happy toward the end of things? Is it possible that one could love someone of the same sex and have happiness till one died? What would my friends think, and how would they look upon me?

Thinking of these things I only get anxious, and my mind goes round in circles because I see no way out. My friends and associates generally praise me and envy me but they don't know the truth, that I'm like someone lost in the middle of a forest unable to find the way out. Elder Brother Go, please help me, in this life I've yet to find one iota of happiness.

My deepest desire is to be free of my family and this overwhelming pressure that binds me. I want just one person who can really advise and help me get out of the mental hell I'm now living in.

I want to run away to some other society where I could look for someone who understood and could give me happiness, to show me the light I want so much. Then I'd probably not be lonely and my mental health would improve, and I think that then I might be able to marry. Do you think I'm right? But it's all so difficult.

I have some questions, Elder Brother Go:

1. How should I lead my life so as to be happy?

2. This happiness I want, to have someone of the same sex to be close to, so that we could help and understand each other and make a special world of our own, do you think such a thing is possible?

3. Each time I feel sorrow or feel hurt I want to throw in all my responsibilities and follow my desires. Should I do that, or should I stay put, tired of everything and anxious, bearing this suffering for the sake of my family?

4. If I don't marry, how else could I lead my life, or should I force myself to marry?

I'm quite old already but I acknowledge I'm still stupid. I await your reply with anxiety and with hope.

LETTER 38 (FROM MITHUNA JUNIOR):
*GAYSORN**

I would like to relate some sexual experiences of mine that occurred last year [1983]. If I must say so, I'm still really pretty much of a kid and don't know much about the world. I just like going out with my friends now and then. Each Saturday night I usually meet with my friends and we go to the [gay] bars around Silom Road.

One Saturday night we'd all agreed to go out as usual. This particular time there were five of us and we all went dressed as women, wearing makeup and wigs and putting on skirts. That night I wore a white skirt and blouse and put on a pair of shoes with three-inch heels. When the bars closed we all agreed to spend the night together at a certain friend's house in Thonburi † and caught a taxi, getting out at the entrance to the laneway leading into the house. By the time we got there it was already 3:00 A.M.

But as soon as we got out we came face to face with a group of about seven teenagers sniffing thinners. As we walked past them they teased, "Where are you hurrying off to? Come sit and talk with us a bit." My friends and I were all afraid and all of us hurried on, but then one guy dashed in front of us and barred the way,

---

* *Gaysorn* is a loanword from Pali, with a wide range of meanings. In poetic language it may denote the eyebrows or fibers, especially the tail of the yak, which is used in making the chowries or fly flappers that are part of the Indian-derived regalia of the Thai king. But *gaysorn* also means "pollen," and in addition is used to denote both the male and female reproductive parts of flowers (i.e., stamen and pistil). This pen name thus has both homonymic associations with the English term "gay" and despite its botanical usage also has a bisexual connotation not dissimilar to the popular conception of the *kathoey* as a cross-gendered being. *Gaysorn* is also the name of a street in the Ratchdamri area opposite the Erawan Hotel in Bangkok, a traditional locale of Bangkok *kathoeys* until the late 1960s. The term *gaysorn* would thus seem an especially apt pen name or nickname for a Thai *kathoey*.
† Thonburi is the urban area opposite Bangkok on the west bank of the Chao Phraya River.

pulling out a knife. He made us go under a nearby bridge. All his friends followed us, pushing us apart from each other. It was very dark under the bridge and teeming with mosquitoes. They made us perform oral sex on them and we had to do it out of fear. But after a moment a flashlight shone at us and a voice shouted out, "Stop! Don't run away!" Everyone knew for sure it was the police and everyone started running in all directions, some even jumped into the canal. I started running toward a temple and my friends followed me, but when I turned to look back I saw the police pulling them away by the collars. I kept on running with no thought for life or limb even though I still had on the three-inch heels and the skirt as well.

I ran and hid inside the temple compound, terribly afraid. Just then a *saamlor* [motorized tricycle] happened by and I told the driver to take me to my home. He agreed without any hesitation. But he didn't take me home but to a deserted house, where he forced me to use my mouth and perform oral sex again. When that driver had satisfied his desires he then took me home. As soon as I got home I hurried to have a bath and wash off all the filth.

I've never told this story to anyone. As for my friends they all had to pay fines and were then allowed to go home. Every one of us has kept this secret. Even when we are together as a group nobody mentions it for fear someone else will overhear us. After the events of that night my friends and I didn't go out late again for a long time because we were afraid of history repeating itself. I'd like to ask all my friends [readers of *Mithuna*] who like going out late at night to be wary and to be careful.

COMMENTS

Sexual Violence Against *Kathoeys*

This account by Gaysorn exemplifies the strong anti*kathoey* or anti–effeminate-homosexual attitudes of many Thai men and also, by extension, their antifemale attitudes. *Kathoeys* in Thailand are often regarded as "fair game." It might seem incongruous that the *saamlor* driver would use force to obtain sexual favors from Gaysorn and then still drive him home, but in fact he had little to fear. Gaysorn was very unlikely to report the incident because of shame, and in any event the driver may have observed the arrest of Gaysorn's friends and known Gaysorn was escaping the law and so was even less likely to report the events.

But even if Gaysorn had reported the incident, he might not have been taken seriously by the police. *Kathoeys* are almost universally regarded as prostitutes and, unless severe violence was involved, the incident would in all likelihood be shrugged off by the police: "What? A prostitute complaining about sex?" This is indicated by the fact that even though Gaysorn's friends were forced with threats of violence to fellate the teenagers high on thinners, it was they and not the louts who were arrested and fined by the police. They were probably charged with soliciting, or some related law periodically used against prostitutes whose madams or brothel owners have not kept up their graft payments to the "dark forces" *(amnaat meut)* who have so much influence in Thailand. *Kathoeys* are thus at risk both from toughs and from the law and, together with female prostitutes, probably represent one of the most vulnerable sections of Thai society.

BRAZIL

Two Brazilian lesbians here challenge the commonly held notion that being a lesbian is easier than being a gay male in a *machista* society. Excerpted from a 1979 issue of *Lampião,* Brazil's best-known gay liberation periodical, the two accounts illustrate the victimization gay women can experience at the hands of both family and the psychiatric establishment.

"Well Then, Why So Much Repression?" translated by Kevin M. Mathewson, from *Lampião* (May 1979).

"It's easier to be lesbian than a faggot," a lot of people say, because women can hold hands in the street, and even go arm in arm; because families let girls sleep with their girlfriends, but for boys, it's forbidden. Nevertheless, it's always difficult for anyone to express homosexuality. But it seems evident that male homosexuals have won a bigger space for themselves than female homosexuals— at least a bigger space for themselves in public. But this magazine *Lampião (Streetlight)* is our public space, our streetlight, which will not let us tell lies. It is only after a year of struggle, with a few letters serving as exceptions to the rule of silence, that a few women homosexuals begin to appear. Repression is repression. It comes in different forms, and different people experience it differently. We don't mean to say that we suffer more than men because we are women, and because of our sexual preference (we have our counterparts, it's important to remember). We've picked two testimonies to show how repression works in the lives of women homosexuals. These are real-life stories.

—M., twenty-six years old, secretary and student at the Universidade de São Paulo

I had a very repressed sexual upbringing. When I was fourteen, I hadn't had any experience. My first kiss was with a man, when I was thirteen, and it was all very secret. At fourteen, I fell in love with a boy. I was very strictly controlled by my mother, who forbade me to see him. I ended up losing touch with him. At fifteen I was enjoying high society dances, always getting taken by my mother, who stayed there with me the whole time. This was a kind of repression that made me feel ashamed. When it came to my virginity, my mother was watching like a hawk.

In 1968, when I was fifteen, I met Miriam at school. Little by little we became friends. She spent her time reading, studying music, learning about politics, and getting into other things—it blew my mind how differently we lived. I wasn't happy with my own life, but I couldn't see any way out. Anyway, that's what all the other girls were doing in those days, going to dances, getting set up with boyfriends, and getting married. I really wanted to get it on, but my fear was even greater. I was ashamed of being a virgin, but also really afraid of getting pregnant. My friendship with Miriam became more intense. We went to school together, took the same classes, went home together, spending every afternoon watching television, drinking. By and by the loneliness was all gone, and we became inseparable. At the end of 1969, always together, we started to become closer and closer—we caressed each other, we got really excited, and one afternoon she kissed me, and there wasn't any heavy feeling of guilt or anything. That kiss drove us crazy, but all that came of it was an increased affection between us. We became more and more affectionate, and I thought I wasn't becoming emotionally involved. I knew I liked her a lot, but I never thought I could fall in love with a woman because it wasn't right or even possible. It seemed like I'd found the ideal situation: sex without pregnancy, and with no one coming to punish me, since we were just friends and even my family approved of that.

In a way, I was simply using her for my own satisfaction but that didn't bother me, since I was being used, too: It was an exchange, what we did. I didn't feel the slightest guilt. I knew things wouldn't stop there, but I also thought no one would ever know. Until her mother saw us. We were only kissing, but it was enough for us to be called lesbians, and the speeches started. We agreed then to stop with that kind of playing around, because it was wrong, and wouldn't amount to anything, and because her mother seemed just about fit to die over the whole thing. We made a deal not to touch each other anymore. It seemed like a deal, very serious, and we thought we'd stick to it. But it didn't last an hour, we ended up agreeing the whole idea was silly and started everything all over again.

A few days later, without ever having seen anyone have sex, without even knowing how it was done, without ever having had any information about lesbianism, we started to do it. It was delirious. Sex took us to the peak of satisfaction. We made love constantly. I don't remember ever feeling any regret or guilt even for an instant, or feeling like I was the only one in the world. Never crossed my mind. I always felt everyone had a right to be free; I didn't make a big deal of it, but just let things happen.

We scarcely took any precautions to keep it a secret. We were lovers, and that was all there was to it. Because of this, of course they found out about it. It was a disaster. When I was seventeen years old, I had to begin to face all kinds of repression. From our families' (futile) efforts to keep us apart, to taking me out of school, getting cursed out, house arrest, telephone surveillance, and all the rest of it. We always found a way to meet. Instead of being driven apart, we found ourselves getting closer and closer. I was in love, and was no longer interested in men. We had a big struggle ahead of us, and I was completely dependent on my family. Apart from the moral repression I suffered, I was subject to a number of physical attacks: My mother tried to strangle me, and only failed because her hands weren't strong enough. My father once held a knife to my throat, during one of our fights; I got slapped around a lot and I got my face all cut up. When I tried to leave the house, my mother imprisoned me, claiming to the police that I was running off with a minor—I was eighteen and Miriam was sixteen. We were also kicked out of school, where we were starting high school.

But the family repression was always the worst. Each day the whole thing got harder to take, it was murder. I kept getting thrown out of the house with the memorable line "If you want to be free, the door is that way. Any daughter of mine who leaves home, I'm not even going to phone. Might as well be dead." After I'd heard enough of that, I decided to leave home in 1971. From the beginning of that year I started working—it was off the books, and minimum wage. I didn't have to work, but they put me there to try to separate me from Miriam. Since we were both out of school, we decided to take an English class, but kept it secret from our families so we could get together. After a while we realized we were being watched —by my mother, and by someone who was hired to follow us and report where and when we met. We were surrounded.

For one whole week, I left the house dressed in extra layers of clothes, without anyone catching on. When I felt I had enough clothes, I left. Miriam couldn't go with me, since she was a minor, and I'd already been arrested for that. I decided to go to Rio de Janeiro, it was close and I could always come see her, and I knew people I could stay with until I found a job. Eighteen years old, no profession, no working papers, with 380 cruzeiros in my pocket. I was sure of our love and sure that the separation from my family was final.

But my parents acted immediately. They went to the police precinct and sent a telex to Rio with an APB for the city cops to apprehend an abnormal (mentally defective) person who had escaped from her home. The next day, they'd already located me, and the day after that, my father came to get me. He had a politician with him to sign an agreement between us, giving his word and professional honor to guarantee that my parents could live up to the terms they agreed to. I was saying that I wanted to be accepted as I am, to stop the persecution, and let me be with Miriam, not get locked up, and so on. My father agreed at once. Even though I didn't believe a word of what we had agreed, I decided to go back, willing to stand my ground if it came to a fight. I wouldn't give an inch.

When I got back, I was acting normal, and I couldn't wait to see Miriam and talk to her, but I figured the whole deal with my family would fall apart. We met almost a week later, afraid and in secret. Little by little we saw each other more and more, to see how far the tolerance went. And we ended up being able to open ourselves completely. No one ever spoke of it again. It was and is as if nothing had ever happened. I started to work as a secretary, I went back to school, and we were through with our family problems. My parents ended up falling in love with her, they think of her as a daughter. My mother defends her from everyone, and says she couldn't bear to see us fighting, no, not for the world.

—**T., twenty-two years old, works with computers, and is a student at Universidade de São Paulo, Pontificie Universidade Católica.**

I was twelve or thirteen when I discovered my homosexuality. I only had girlfriends, and I just liked them more and more. Now I know I was in love. I'd be walking down the street thinking, "I'm crazy about her; she must be crazy about me." But I knew she couldn't like me because I was a woman. And I began to see that I wasn't like my mother, who was married to a man. So I figured I also had to get myself a boyfriend, just like my friends, who went walking with them at school and in the street, and at church. That's when I had my first crush. I masturbated a lot. I didn't enjoy it, it actually hurt, but I didn't understand that I was masturbating. I even did it in front of my father, under a blanket while I was watching television. It was only much later, in the hospital, that I realized that everyone knew what I was doing, everybody was onto me, but no one ever said anything.

It was on a television quiz show that I first saw this remarkable woman. She was answering questions about Kennedy on *The Silvio Santos Show.* I did all I could to get close to her, I dreamed up schemes, because she was so far away. She was on TV, and I was on the couch. Suddenly she seemed such an intelligent woman, so brilliant. I couldn't take my eyes off her. Nearby there was only my mother, teachers, and my friends, but no one you could really talk to. At school, I was the tallest, the most intelligent, but on the other hand I was clumsy, dropped things all the time, I couldn't keep track of my hands and feet. I wound up thinking whatever I did couldn't involve anything physical, I'd have to study, be a teacher, anything related to books, so I wouldn't have to move at all. Besides, at my house there was a lot of pressure to study. My father was taught to read by my fourth-grade teacher in a literacy program. My mother's a dressmaker whom I taught to read myself. She told me to study, because she didn't want me to grow up to wash dishes and do laundry for anyone as poor as my father, but instead to marry a doctor. I didn't know a single brilliant woman, not even in movies and soap operas. When that woman appeared on television, I went after her.

I decided to become a contestant on *The Silvio Santos Show,* answering questions about the great Brazilian aviator Santos Dummont. I was only planning to stay a week, but I ended up staying five months. We met every Thursday, the lady and I, and talked a lot. She had a girlfriend who never left her side, they were inseparable. She never told me what was going on, but I figured it out. I also figured out that if she could have a girlfriend, so could I. The only problem was, I didn't have anyone, not her, not anyone else. I started to feel more and more ugly and poor all the time. When she left the show, I left, too, the week after. At home I was beaten because I didn't win any prize money on the show. But I hadn't really gone to be a game-show contestant anyway, that was just a trick. Anyway, I was always getting beaten when I was a kid.

When I was in primary school. In junior high, I went on getting beaten. It was when I fell in love with a woman that I saw the difference: Before, I was beaten so I wouldn't do housework, because I was clumsy, because I got into fights at school; afterward, because they wanted me to do housework, to go out with the girls, go to dances. It was when I got close to that woman on television that I saw the difference: I was not equal to other women. I continued to like her a lot for a long time after that. I started going to church all the time, working on my catechism. But I never confessed my love, or told it to anyone—since I'd had no sex, there was no problem.

Later, I went to high school. I got another job (I had to leave the first one because of the quiz show). Instead of an office, the new job was in a factory that did the finishing work on water tanks. At the time, I had a faggot friend I could talk to, tell about how I was in love, and so on. He lent me a few magazines from which I learned computer terminology. I had gotten to be well known in my section, because I was very young and clumsy, but I was a good worker. My boss wanted to transfer me to the office, but I didn't want to. He took me to the manager, and I said I wanted to work on the quality control computer. So I had to show that I knew how to work with computers, since I had no diploma, and had learned it all by myself, and I was only fourteen years old. I took a test and started to work with computers. Then I went to a technical school to improve. That's where I met my second love, Lucia, who was very rich and very beautiful.

At the time, I knew there was a way for two women to get it on. I didn't know how, but I wanted to find out. Lucia and I became good friends, and things started to get difficult, because I began to feel desire, and this didn't mix well with the Church, which for me meant chastity, charity, and poverty. So I had problems on three fronts: In my family, my salary had tripled and I was making more than my father—that couldn't be, because he had worked all his life, and I was young and a woman. At school, there was Lucia. At work, there were only men in the department, the women just did clerical dirty work, typing, the lower-level jobs. Then the men began to say that I was very masculine (my mother made big clothes to hide my profile); they started to put my computer program in last place to be run; they started giving me all the problems. I was competition: They wanted to get rid of me.

That's when I read Kafka's *Metamorphosis*. Someone had given me a present of practically everything he ever wrote. I read it and started to think I was the character Gregor Samsa, that I was going to turn into a cockroach like him. One day I really did become one: I saw my body was all brown. I stayed in bed two weeks without getting up, without speaking or eating anything. I had turned into a cockroach. My mother took me then to the public health clinic. The clinic sent me to the psychiatrist. On the day of the interview, he treated my mother very badly, and I noticed it—I had moments of lucidity, and other moments when I didn't know anything. And since even cockroaches have mothers, I had a violent fit, cursed out the psychiatrist, broke everything. He had me sedated and I slept for three days. He ordered my mother to take me to another psychiatrist, and I went to a clinic. That's when the worst part of the repression started.

The treatment began with three weeks of sleep therapy. Then I had three sessions of analysis, without saying a word, since I was still a cockroach. They carried me on a stretcher, in a wheelchair, and finally kicking and screaming, because the psychiatrist decided they would have to give me shock treatment. I wasn't going to say a word. Meanwhile, there were drug treatments, shock treatments, hot and cold baths, etc. One day I spoke, and the psychiatrist wanted me to go back and remember so I could start to work through my nervous breakdown. The first thing that came to mind was Lucia. She was all there was before this phase started of being afraid I was turning into a cockroach. The psychiatrist, always very aggressively, made me see that I was homosexual; and he taught me what it meant to be a homosexual: to suffer a lot, to be wretched as I was, with no security, no stable love, because everything was against me and would always be awful. He kept repeating that, even when I said I was never going to get it on with her, that she was never going to come live with me. Because for me, the idea of marriage was very strong, everyone got married. That's also why my love did not require sex.

But he was evoking in me a much greater guilt with the treatment, because he said I wasn't sick, I was just faking it all so I wouldn't have to accept my homosexuality. That's why I turned into a cockroach. The question, then, was to accept it, or choose to change, free myself of homosexuality, find affection with a man. I chose to stop being homosexual. He said there were various ways to achieve this. His treatment consisted of the following: I took injections to induce nausea, and felt like throwing up, I spent long hours in an armchair with him projecting slides. They were women undressed from the front, from the back, in profile. He wanted me to say something about it. I spoke of their hair, their faces, their noses; he asked me about their breasts, their vaginas; he wanted me to talk about each part I didn't want to see. And I didn't want to because I'd never seen these things, it was at odds with the Church, and so on. He started to vary the slides, he wanted me to see it all with indifference. But I came to see it with hatred instead of naturally. I hated the fact that somebody, a man, was with me, looking at what was just like me, and which I didn't even know. And I asked him to stop, I started saying I was suffering a lot, that I was unhappy, that I really wasn't going to get it on.

Then he began to reverse the treatment. He stopped giving me pills to induce vomiting and started giving me sedatives. I felt that was worse. I hated vomiting after the sessions, but it was a moment in which I could let loose, spitting it all out. With the sleep therapy everything was kept in, to be started all over again at the next session (three times a week). Once I managed to stay awake despite the injection. First thing, I hit myself against the wall a lot, then fell down. But then I began to turn things over in my mind, with a lot of hatred, and dreamed up a song and dance to put an end to the whole treatment. I started saying exactly what he wanted to hear. I began to comment on the photographs, and his role as a psychiatrist.

In a week the sessions were over, and I was out. He knew I was playing along, but he also had to know that if I could play along with him, I could play along with other people on the outside.]

I left and went back to work; also back to school. I couldn't see Lucia anymore. I ran away from her, because I felt like throwing up. I couldn't look at myself naked when I took a bath. I discovered myself as a woman and knew what it was, according to the doctor, to be homosexual. I started to channel all my energy into my work, and continued regular sessions of analysis for four years. I took a lot of courses, met a lot of people, including a woman who became interested in me and helped me with my professional training. She was homosexual, but I never got it on with her, never even kissed her. She wanted to, but every time she spoke to me about it, I stopped seeing her and spent two or three months avoiding her. Next thing I knew she was dead. She had an argument with me. And she killed herself. When she died, everything broke inside me: family, Church, school, work. My hate was broken up as well: I discovered that I loved her, and went to pieces. And then I tried to do things differently so that nothing like this could ever happen again. Nothing I did, no matter how wrong, could be as cruel as her killing herself. I decided to switch to men.

Then I went to college, when I was seventeen or eighteen. I decided to switch to men, but the first woman I saw there was the person I fell for. We had similar problems—she had been raped, hadn't ever made love to anyone. We spent a year just taking care of each other. It took six months for us to kiss, and about another six months for us to go to bed together. Old habits die hard: We made love in our clothes, just rubbing together, in order not to expose our bodies. It took a long time for us to take off our clothes. Each step forward was a bitter struggle. And I was getting more and more rough with her. Our problems didn't disappear. Then, when we broke up, I began another affair, and it was no different from before. Could it be that being homosexual simply meant being unhappy? Until the first affair, I had no idea, I'd never lived my homosexuality. And I was miserable. Then the second affair was over before it even got started. I was really miserable. My mother suffered, everybody suffered. But why did I have to suffer differently from other people? That's something the psychiatrist never bothered to explain to me.

CHINA

China, throughout much of its long history, has had a rich and varied tradition of same-sex love. It was only with the arrival of British colonialism in recent times that the stigmatization of homosexuality appeared and prudery began to reign. During the time of Mao, homosexuality was either ignored or viewed, in accordance with orthodox Communist ideology, as a remnant of bourgeois decadence. Today it is considered a misfortune to be a homosexual, although Chinese doctors by and large believe the condition is curable by means of shock treatment.

In the following selection, an analysis is made of the responses to an article on homosexuality, the first of its kind, that appeared in a 1985 Chinese health magazine. Gays from all strata of society express the pain, isolation, fear, and self-doubt they experience as an unrecognized minority in their society.

"Male Homosexuality in Contemporary Mainland China" by Fang-fu Ruan, M.D., and Yung-mei Tsai, Ph.D., from *Archives of Sexual Behavior* (April 1988).

Through a unique circumstance described in the text we have sixty letters (of which fifty-six were from a gay population) concerning homosexuality in contemporary China. Though the sample is not randomly selected, it is the first of its kind. An analysis of these letters shows some interesting results and patterns. Among these are (1) a widespread distribution of gay people in China in terms of their geographic locations, ages, and occupations; (2) the pain and mental anguish they suffer from being unable to openly and legally seek homosexual partners and the contradiction experienced from living in two worlds; (3) their wishes and demands for a better and more reasonable treatment; and (4) their hope that they will be provided a place or some mechanism so they can converse and interact freely. To better reflect what they think and feel about themselves, their problems, and their hopes, we have used quotations from these letters extensively. It is our belief that at this initial exploratory stage of the study on Chinese homosexuality, it is best to let the respondents speak for themselves.

INTRODUCTION

There have been numerous records, including some that glorified homosexuality in the traditional Chinese literature (Pan 1947; Van Gulik 1961; Chou 1971; Bullogh 1976; Ruan and Tsai 1987). Thus it is reasonable to assume that gay life exists in China today. However, the existing literature on gay life in contemporary China is scarce. In Weinberg and Bell's (1972) 550-page book *Homosexuality: An Annotated Bibliography,* for example, not a single study or recording on Chinese homosexual life is listed. In Parker's (1971; 1977; 1985) three-volume edition of bibliography on homosexuality in which a total of 9,924 items were included, only two articles from gay publications on Chinese homosexuality were listed.

This scarcity of literature on Chinese homosexuality is due at least partially to the prohibition and treatment of homosexuality, especially among male homosexuals in contemporary China. Gays are frequently punished and treated as "sodomites." They understandably cannot reveal their identity. As a result, it is extremely difficult to obtain realistic and objective information on gay life in China today.

Through a unique and unexpected circumstance, the senior author obtained fifty-six letters from the gay population in China recently. In these letters were descriptions about life, problems, and personal confessions and aspirations about Chinese homosexuality.

Though hardly a random and representative sample, we believe this is the first and only information of this kind on contemporary Chinese gay life ever obtained by any scholar. As can be seen later, these fifty-six letters represent all walks of life from all regions of China, indicating substantial amounts of variance. A sociological analysis on these letters should fill in some of the void on contemporary Chinese gay life.

DATA AND METHOD

Since 1949, data on homosexuality have been almost nonexistent in the People's Republic of China. Despite some of the changes and improvement on gay rights throughout the world in the past twenty years, information about gay life outside of China was rarely reported inside China. On the rare occasions when gay lives of the outside world were reported, they were primarily used to propagate the "decline and the evil of Western civilization."

In 1985 the senior author, using the pen name Jin-ma Hua, published an article titled "Homosexuality: An Unsolved Puzzle" in a widely circulated health magazine in China, *To Your Good Health,* outlining the fact that homosexuality exists in all nations, all social strata, and all historical periods in human history. It pointed out that in some countries in some historical periods homosexuals were severely punished and prosecuted, even with the death penalty. The article stated that this perhaps was an example of how majorities subjugated minorities in human societies. The article went on to editorialize that homosexuals should not be prosecuted for failing to reproduce; that the number of homosexuals in a society was substantial and more than lay people expected; that homosexuals' problems should not be ignored and that their status should be a reasonable one in society; that homosexuals were no different from heterosexual people in intelligence, physical strength, creativity, etc.; and that two homosexuals can love each other and maintain a stable life and relationship as well as other couples and therefore should not be punished (Hua 1985).

The publication of this article attracted a great deal of attention and social response. Specifically, two things happened. First, many of the readers of *To Your Good Health,* mostly gays, wrote to the editor of the magazine, responding to the article. Second, five months after the publication, the most popular and widely read magazine in China, *Reader's Digest,* reprinted the article almost in its entirety. By April 1986 a total of sixty letters were received and forwarded to the senior author through the editor of *To Your Good Health.* Judging from the fact that gay life is prohibited by law and morally and socially condemned in China and is held in strict and utmost secrecy, this response rate, though small in number, is substantial. Many of these readers actually revealed their real names, geographic locations, and even current occupations.

Following is a report of a content analysis of these sixty letters. For convenience of reporting the results of the analysis and to maintain anonymity of these people we use a number—for example, letter #25—to indicate the source of a statement, quotation, etc. The major focus is to provide a collective portrait based on these letters. We hope that through this analysis we will provide some initial insight into gay life in contemporary China.

RESULTS

For ease of presenting results, we have grouped them in several aspects. The purpose is to provide a profile and is not meant to be a representative sample of the population.

Approval Versus Disapproval

Of the sixty letters received, fifty-six came from gay people. They all approved the editorial of the article for obvious reasons and thanked the author, Dr. Hua, the senior author of this article. Of the remaining four letters, two disapproved of the article's editorial position; the third suggested a way to convert gays back to heterosexual life; and the last letter was written by a transsexual. Since all sixty letters were written by men, our report is limited to males only. The following samples of opinions were expressed by these authors.

> Hua's article on homosexuality provides me with a soothing sense of relief never before experienced in my life. It also gives me hope about my life and my future. [#11]

> I am extremely grateful to Hua's objective, humane, scientific, and fair critique on homosexuality. [#24]

> The publication of this article is a great event to the medical field. It is a salvation of thought, a fruit of progressive advancement. To homosexuals, it is a true "good news." We admire your courage and scientific attitude toward this matter. [#25]

> This article is truly great. It gives us, a small number of homosexuals, a spiritual uplift. It gives me the second life and takes me to the spring of my life. [#28, a college student who attempted suicide as a result of his homosexuality]

Two letters disapproved of homosexuality. One came from a medical college in the northwest region of China (#57) and the other came from a teacher in a factory training center in northeastern China (#58), who wrote the following:

> Hua's article is attempting to legitimize homosexual life and is not an objective treatment of the subject matter. [#57 and #58]

> Homosexuality is an evil product of capitalistic society. Homosexuality brings with it bad influence on our socialist society. It is our obligation to point out our view in stopping this product of spiritual pollution. [#57]

Speaking in the same critical tone as during the period of the Cultural Revolution, #58 stated:

> We should absolutely prohibit homosexuality. . . . Widespread homosexuality will lead to epidemic deterioration of our racial spirit and destroy our society. . . . The reasons why people despise, prohibit, punish, and persecute homosexuals are precisely because the behavior is evil, ugly, antihuman morality, an insult to human dignity, promoting crime among youth, ruining their mental and physical health, leading to the destruction of our race and civilization. . . . It is imperative that we not only expose homosexuality lest it create a flood sweeping away our marital, moral, legal, and customary dam and destroy our socialist civilization. [#58]

Sociological Analysis

The following analysis, based on the fifty-six letters, reflects part of the true picture of male homosexuality in contemporary China. We begin with a description of some demographic characteristics of these people.

Of the fifty-six letters, thirty-four indicated the writer's age. Among these thirty-four, three are twenty years or younger, twenty-five are between twenty-one and thirty, three between thirty-one and forty, two between forty-one and fifty, and one between fifty-one and sixty.

Forty-six letters indicated geographic locations. It seems that Shanghai has the highest concentration. However, the letters have come from almost every region of the nation.

Judging from the writing style, it appears that all have at least some high school education. Eleven indicated that they either are attending or have graduated from college; one is pursuing a master's degree, and one a doctoral degree.

Among the occupations listed are college professor, instructor,

high school teacher, actor, soldier, factory worker, government bu-
reaucrat, and student in high school, college, and graduate school.

Gay Life and Its Pains

As indicated earlier, homosexuality is prohibited and condemned
morally and socially. However, to our surprise, forty-three gays
indicated their true identities. It was a general sentiment that they
trusted the editor and the author of the article. Thus one stated
that "if the magazine and the author are courageous enough and
willing to risk the consequences . . . speaking for homosexuals in a
fair and objective manner . . . they would not double-cross us"
(#52). Twenty solicited names and addresses of other gay people.
They apparently thought that the magazine and the author could
serve as their go-between or facilitators of their network. Generally
they asked the editor and the author to protect their confidentiality.
"Please keep this in utmost secret. I would not know how to face
others if my identity is known" (#19). "If this is known by the
public my future would be ruined" (#24).

Twenty-two indicated their marital status: Twelve were not married; eight were currently married, including six with children; two
were divorced. Among those currently married, all indicated that
they married because of family and social pressures. They are not
sexually interested in their spouses. Sexual relationships with their
wives seldom occur. They are still strongly homosexually oriented.
They see no choice but to live in lies. Their wives have absolutely
no knowledge of their sexuality. They feel extremely guilty over not
being able truly to love and give love to their spouses. They are
constantly under tremendous pain as a result of living in two worlds
at the same time. They resent their hypocrisy. For example, #1
writes:

> I am a 29-year-old young man. . . . I am not interested in the
> female sex at all. I do not even want to have any physical contact
> with them. However, among the men that I encountered some

of them would occupy my body and soul. . . . I am particularly interested in one of them and my love for him is beyond description. He is a little smaller than I but I fall for him in every respect I can think of. This feeling deepens every day. It has been ten years but my feeling for him has not been changed. Of course, I wish I could live with him, be with him even just sitting quietly with him, I would be very happy. Of course I wish to have a sexual relationship with him but my mind stops and controls me from doing this. I regard him as my spiritual supporter. I obtain my spiritual satisfaction through him. Frequently when I thought of him I would masturbate to fulfill my sexual desire. This strong persistent monogamous and inner-directed everlasting devoted feeling toward him for over ten years is unmatched even among normal heterosexual relationships. . . . During the last ten years or so, my life had an interesting twist. When I was twenty-five years old, a woman fell deeply in love with me. I could not tell her about my true feeling. She insisted on marrying me no matter what. I could not do anything to discourage her. Finally I gave in and married her. I was living in a completely different world. I seldom had sexual relations with her. But on one of those very rare occasions I impregnated her. She knows nothing about my deep secret. This relationship has created pain in my heart and my life. I have been in love and devoted my love to him all this time. I think my love for him will never change for the rest of my life. However, the love is a deep secret. He would not understand nor would he be aware of this. My heart is full of contradiction and pain. I pretended to be happy in front of others but when I was alone I cried with pain.

Those who are not married seem to suffer from the same deep-seated pain:

The pain that homosexuals suffer most lies not in homosexuality but in their inability to find suitable lovers. All homosexuals lock their feelings in their heart. They are so afraid of being discovered that it makes it impossible to live their life. [#10]

In this vast world where can I find that 5 to 10% true heart? [#47]

I am longing to love others (homosexuals) and to be loved. I have met some other homosexuals but I have doubt about this type of love. With all the pressure I was afraid to reveal myself and ruined everything. As a result, we departed without showing each other homosexual love. As I am growing older my homosexual desire increases. This is too troublesome and too depressing for anyone. I thought about death many times. When you are young you cannot fall in love and when you are old you will be alone. Thinking of this makes the future absolutely hopeless. [#8]

To the gays in contemporary China, the source of their pains derives from the fear of societal punishment, including arrest, sentence, labor reform camp, and prison terms. The mental pressure and anguish for fear of their true identity being found out are often unbearable. Those currently in prison serving their sentences for homosexuality cannot possibly have a chance to read Hua's article, much less the responses from the gay population to this article. However, letter #22 described a prison inmate's testimony about being jailed as a homosexual. This prisoner was a very fine physics teacher and was the director of academic affairs in a high school. This inmate's homosexual relationship was voluntary and was initiated by others. He was arrested in September 1983 and sentenced to a five-year prison term for his homosexual acts. Since the publication of Hua's article, his colleagues and friends and relatives were reported to have changed their negative view toward him. His superior actually went to the prison to see him, but his prison term remains unaltered. Today he is still serving his sentence.

The social pressure and pain exerted on homosexuals have led to numerous attempted suicides and constant inner conflicts among gay people. Of the fifty-six letters received from gays, fifteen mentioned suicide attempts. One related his suicide experience:

I am an agriculture college student. I will be graduating this year. In 1981 I fell in love with a senior student, I was only seventeen then and had no understanding at all about homosexuality. The mental anguish was so unbearable that I was eventually diagnosed as having a "reactive psychosis." I took a year's leave of absence. In 1983, still quite confused about homosexuality, I mistakenly overdosed myself with sleeping pills and was hospitalized for four days before getting out of danger. [#28]

Wishes and Demands

Generally speaking, three types of wishes and demands stand out. One is the human rights issue—that society should accept homosexuals and their right to express their sexuality and that they should not be persecuted legally and morally. The second is the issue of freedom to interact with other homosexuals. They wish that society could provide them with mechanisms to facilitate contacts and relationships. The third is the wish that objective and scientific studies be done to improve societal understanding of their life and treatment. Seventeen letters demanded protection of homosexual rights. Statements such as the following reflect their common sentiments.

There should be open discussion about the issue [of homosexual rights] and homosexuals should be given legal status. [#10]

A special column should be established to discuss the homosexual problems in comprehensive and in-depth fashion in order for society, especially the public security, judicial departments, party and governmental propaganda organizations, to have an accurate perspective and provide a more reasonable treatment for the homosexuals. [#25]

Homosexual sex is one form of sexual behavior. Because of the problem of population explosion we are facing today, homosexual sex is one effective way of population control. Why do we insist on having a homosexual man marry a woman? Without love marriage is a mere reproductive machine. Mentally one suffers from the constant disharmony of family life. Physically, one is constantly confronted with the unpleasant experience of contradiction. Without a homosexual companion how can one have motivation for his career? Homosexuals should be granted the same right as heterosexuals to fulfill their sexual needs. We are a very populous nation; we need to improve homosexuals' status and be concerned with their problems and pains. [#32]

Twenty letters wished that the magazine and/or the author, Dr. Hua, could help them establish a network for homosexuals. In the article, two cases of gay life in Hubei and Shanghai were described. Those twenty letters' authors all requested the real names and addresses of these two in order to establish contact with them. They expressed their wishes in a very earnest manner. For example,

The greatest pain for us, the homosexuals, is our inability to express our deepest inner sorrow. We have to hide our feelings in front of others. I therefore beg you to fulfill my wish by giving me the names and addresses of other homosexuals. This may help me to want to continue my life. The pain in my heart makes me extremely despair. [#43]

I hope to contact other homosexuals through your magazine in order to work out ways to deal with our future. [#10]

I hope you can become homosexuals' go-between and provide a bridge for the great many homosexuals (to contact one another) and bring them hope and happiness. [#25]

Some letters hoped to establish a clublike organization, although the word for club was not used. For example:

I fantasized that there would be a place where homosexuals can converse and interact freely. I fantasized having a lover. But fantasy is not real. In reality, homosexuals do not automatically love all other homosexuals. They choose their partners just like heterosexuals. But where can I find them? In this wide world all homosexuals hide their true identity. It is so much more difficult for a homosexual to find his ideal partner than a heterosexual. I sometimes was tempted to openly seek a homosexual friend. But how can I? I do not think a homosexual person will do any harm to the country and other people. But why can't we openly discuss this [homosexuality]? We should provide ways for exclusive homosexuals to contact one another. I sincerely wish that our country and related governmental agencies could openly show their concern about our problems. [#8]

There were eighteen letters stressing the wish that studies on homosexuality be carried out. Twenty-one letters asked about ways to heal their problems (signifying that half of these homosexuals wished to be converted to heterosexuality to lessen their dilemma). Four letters mentioned some of the "underground" (not open or approved) studies being done about homosexuals in China. One twenty-four-year-old indicated that he helped a sixty-year-old professor, who had been gay over several decades, at a university in Beijing to collect data on homosexuals. As part of his work he had traveled to eighteen cities and provinces throughout China. He found homosexuals everywhere he went. Thus he stated:

Among those places, Beijing, Shanghai, Guangzhow, Wuhan, Nanjing, Shenyang, Fuzhow, Changsa were most notable [in having a large number of homosexuals]. Among those [homosexuals], intellectuals seemed the most numerous. Others include workers, public security officers, etc. It appeared that the number had increased substantially in the last few years . . . many of those were unfamiliar faces. [#26]

A reader from Jiangsy wrote:

I hope you [the magazine] could invite famous sociologists, doctors, even homosexuals as a team to do an in-depth study on the extent and current condition of homosexuals in our country and to find reasonable ways to deal with them. If you want my humble service on this I would be more than happy to do my best. [#25]

Sexual Psychology and Sexual Behavior

There were very few discussions about concrete sexual behaviors in their letters, but some did relate personal experiences:

I am a genuine male. I am twenty-seven years old. I have been seeking homosexual love for many years. I have yet experienced heterosexual love and am not interested in it at all. When I saw some healthy bearded men (I myself am bearded) my member would automatically erect. I was always tempted to touch others' penises in a crowded bus, in a dark movie theater, a bathhouse . . . but my rationality stopped me. . . . In those lonely and sleepless nights I wish I had a strong man lie right next to me. [#27]

I am a sixteen-year-old masculine-appearing high school student. I am not into girls at all. However, I am very moved by males, especially those handsome and strong ones. When I talked with one of them I was so happy. When I was with one of those I liked I would be elated. I would snuggle up to him. When I saw a suitable man in movies, television, and even in a picture magazine I would experience the elating experience of the preejaculation state. [#36]

I am twenty-six years old. I have been married for two years and have a child. But I only like muscular, well-built men. I love to see their well-built naked bodies. The more I see them the more elated I get. Sometimes I reach an orgasmic state and ejaculate. This orgasmic feeling was quite clear and was much better than with my wife. My wife is very tender to me. She often rubbed my body very softly while we were in bed and sometimes until I fell asleep. She could not arouse my sexual interest in her. During sexual intercourse with my wife I sometimes got erected by thinking of some beautiful young man I met but frequently I had to stop halfway. [#54]

I am a twenty-nine-year-old man. When I was fifteen I was a very nice-looking man. Many people liked me. There was a seventeen-year-old man I met. We fell in love. We kissed, embraced, and finally we had sex. I played the woman's role. We met every day and frequently had sex. I felt great and ejaculated myself. [#1]

There is a man from Szechwan province who has a nickname "cute little fellow" and who was sometimes called "buttocks queen." In his letter he introduced homosexual health-hygiene knowledge. He felt that with proper hygienic attention homosexual sex was safe. He related his own experience in the following manner:

I am a male homosexual. I like the well-built and deeply tanned young men with large members. When I saw them I felt like they had already entered me. I felt extremely elated and eventually erected and ejaculated. I dreamed about this dream often. My buttocks had been entered more than a thousand times by more than two hundred men. [#32]

Some letters express their displeasure about women. For example, a homosexual from Hunan province states:

I was forced to marry a woman partially because of the obligation to have a child and partially to stop the gossip. I have a child but I have been seeking homosexuals for more than twenty years. I felt very distasteful toward some women's bad behaviors such as irrationality, gossiping, cursing, dependency, etc. I dislike sex life with women. [#41]

A homosexual from Beijing relates his story:

I first felt homosexual desire when I was sixteen. I had had several homosexual encounters. In 1984 I got married. I thought this marriage would gradually change my sexuality but it did not happen. I seldom initiated sexual relations with my wife, if and when I did it was to comfort her. In reality I resent any part of a woman's body (including breasts). Their (women's) body shape and muscles are not as beautiful as men's. It has been more than a year (since I got married) and I am still yet to feel anything while having sex with a woman. [#35]

DISCUSSION

Although there is no specific statement concerning the status of homosexuals in the current *Criminal Law of the People's Republic of China,* homosexuals face an extremely difficult position in their everyday life. Criminal Law 106 states: "All revolting behaviors should be subjected to arrest and sentence." The homosexual behavior, sodomy, has been included in "revolting behaviors."

One of the most famous attorneys in China today, Mr. Dun Li, was asked to express his opinion concerning homosexuality and stated:

> Homosexuality, though, exists in different societies and cultures, with some minor exceptions is considered abnormal and disdained. It affects social order, invades personal privacy and rights, and leads to criminal behavior. As a result, homosexuals are more likely to encounter and be penalized administratively and criminally. (Ruan 1985, p. 186)

One of the common reactions toward homosexuality in China is to deny its existence. Thus, for example, a newspaper reporter-editor of a famous magazine in China, Z. G. Lui, who is quite familiar with how Chinese authorities deal with special problems and who after two years of study in Chicago published his book *Two Years in the Melting Pot,* had the following to say:

One group on campus, calling itself the gay and lesbian Illini, met every week. I was enormously curious about this group which concerned itself with issues of homosexuality, but I never ventured to go to any of their meetings. I inquired of friends, however, to find out who these people were and what they did. One of my friends argued that love between those of the same sex is natural and has existed throughout history—during the Roman Empire, it was even made legal, he said. I disagree, saying that wouldn't be good for society to open up this issue. In old China, homosexuality was practiced by a few rich people, but the general public didn't approve. (Liu 1984, pp. 93–94)

This, we think, is a typical Chinese interpretation. This clearly is contradictory to the facts and is not based on any objective research. It is dogmatic. The quotations presented throughout this paper should make explicit that homosexuality does exist in contemporary China, among the rich as well as the poor, the young and the old, and among people in all walks of life.

Some letters with rigorous ideological overtones, such as #57 and #58, consider homosexuality a corrupt Western behavior, an imported "spiritual pollutant." A formal testimony to this appeared in an official newspaper, *Beijing Daily News,* which equated homosexuality as one of the "Western social diseases." It declared that homosexuality was originated from "Western ideology and thoughts" (United Press, February 4, 1987, from Beijing). These people appear quite ignorant of historical facts. We had pointed out in our previous article (Ruan and Tsai 1987) that even during the glorious days of the West Han dynasty, all ten of the emperors had at least one homosexual lover or had a homosexual tendency, including the well-respected Emperor Han Wu Ti.

Homosexuality clearly is not imported from Western capitalistic civilization. Many of the letters quoted in the paper came from those who were under thirty years of age, who were born after the socialist revolution in 1949. They are clearly native products of China.

This paper has let these gay people speak for themselves through their letters. There is little doubt that further study needs to be conducted to present a more complex picture of homosexuality in China. It is not clear how representative these letter writers may be as far as the gay population in China is concerned. Although the diversity in terms of age, geographic distributions, and occupations gives us some confidence about the sample, it is possible that many of the less educated and illiterate may not be represented in this group. We have not learned anything about the relationship between sociocultural background and sexuality. As we know more about the Chinese case we may be able to move one step farther to compare the Chinese gay experience with that of other societies. It is our hope that we have made the first step toward this goal.

ACKNOWLEDGMENTS

The authors express their appreciation to Professor Louis Crompton and to George Lowe for their assistance.

REFERENCES

Bullough, V. L. 1976. *Sexual Variance in Society and History*. New York: Wiley.

Chou, E. 1971. *The Dragon and Phoenix*. New York: Arbor House.

Hua, J. M. 1985. Homosexuality: An unsolved puzzle. *Zhu Nin Jiankang (To Your Good Health)* 3: 14–15.

Liu, Z. R. 1984. *Two Years in the Melting Pot*. San Francisco: China Books and Periodicals.

Pan, G. D. 1947. Translator's Notes and Appendix to *Psychology of Sex* by H. Ellis. In *Psychology of Sex* Chinese ed., trans. G. D. Pan. Shanghai: Commercial Press, pp. 249–55, 380–406.

Parker, W. 1971. *Homosexuality: A Selective Bibliography of 3,000 Items*. Metuchen, N.J.: Scarecrow Press.

————. 1977. *Homosexuality Bibliography: Supplement, 1970–1975.* Metuchen, N.J.: Scarecrow Press.

————. 1985. *Homosexuality Bibliography: Second Supplement, 1976–1982.* Metuchen, N.J.: Scarecrow Press.

Ruan, F. F. (ed.). 1985. *Handbook of Sex Knowledge.* Beijing: Scientific and Technological Literature Publishing House.

Ruan, F. F., and Y. M. Tsai. 1987. Male homosexuality in the traditional Chinese literature. *J. Homsex.* 14:21–33.

Van Gulik, R. H. 1961. *Sexual Life in Ancient China.* Leiden, Neth.: E. J. Brill.

Weinberg, M. S., and A. P. Bell. 1972. *Homosexuality: An Annotated Bibliography.* New York: Harper & Row.

CANADA

With keen insight, Gary Kinsman analyzes a shameful episode in Canadian history, whereby the murder of a young boy in Toronto in 1977 served as a catalyst in a campaign of repression and terror against the gay community. "Bawdy-house" legislation and obscenity laws were employed to justify mass arrests, the closing of gay bars and baths, and attacks on the gay press. Kinsman shows how the furthering of private economic gain and political opportunism were prime motivators in the unfolding of events following the murder. He illustrates how the instruments of state power, including the mass media, can work to repress basic human rights in what is generally considered a liberal Western-style democracy.

"The Jaques Murder Case," from *The Regulation of Desire: Sexuality in Canada,* by Gary Kinsman (1987).

The police and other agencies have played an important role in this backlash. A new police policy regarding the Toronto gay community was signaled by the "clean up Yonge street" campaign in the mid-1970s, and particularly by the moral panic organized through the media after the sex-related murder of Emanuel Jaques, a twelve-year-old boy, by a number of men in a Yonge Street establishment in the summer of 1977. Such groups as Renaissance and Positive Parents have made continual use of the socially constructed image of gays as "child molesters" and "murderers" that were established as part of this moral campaign. A look at that media coverage of the Jaques murder should provide us with insight into the anatomy of moral panic.

Yvonne Chi-Ying Ng contends that to fully understand what happened, this murder must be situated in its historical and social context.[1] A similar murder of a nine-year-old boy in 1973 had not set off a moral panic. What were the circumstances that prompted such a reaction to the Jaques murder? she asks. The answer lies in the particular alignment of social and political forces at the time of the murder.

> It is through the specific social context and historical conjuncture, not the incidents themselves, that we begin to understand why the social control apparatus chose to blame Yonge Street for the death of Jaques.

The key to the response to the Jaques murder is the "clean up Yonge Street" campaign.

Proposals to clean up the Yonge Street strip had first been advanced by politicians and "legitimate" business interests in 1972. Initially they received little support, and much opposition. It is important to examine the economic and social process behind these requests. With the large corporate investment in the Eaton Centre development on Yonge in the early 1970s, the Yonge Street strip became ripe for speculation. The price of land shot up, and small businesses simply couldn't afford to stay. The sex industry, which was able to afford the higher rents, moved in. The Downtown Business Association (to become the Downtown Business Council in 1973), in an effort to reestablish the conditions for the return of "legitimate" small business to the area, submitted a brief to Mayor Crombie. He took up their cause, but without much success for a number of years.

This "clean up Yonge Street" campaign was defined by a number of social, moral, economic, and political interests. This included the business interests who wanted to reestablish themselves in the area, politicians like Crombie who felt it was best for the moral character of the city and plans for redevelopment, and the police who wanted the chance to clamp down on prostitutes and massage parlors. This intersected with a debate over the character of the city, particularly its downtown core. These forces came together in their desire to clear the main street of the sex trade, prostitutes, and visible homosexuals.

Then, in 1975, the provincial election campaign of Bill Davis' ruling Conservative Party focused on "law and order," which included support for cleaning up Yonge Street, the main street of Ontario's principal city. This campaign mobilized antipermissive sentiments, the police having linked the Yonge Street strip to organized crime by associating the sex industry, prostitution, and homosexuality with the criminal underworld.

A special committee of Toronto City Council was established to prepare a report on the strip in February 1977. This report was released in June of the same year. The media was generally favorable to the proposals for a clean-up but there was still some hesitation.

Then, on August 1, 1977, the horrible Jaques murder occurred, and was immediately framed by the media through the interpretive schema already established by the "clean up Yonge Street" campaign. The press treated the murder as a primary news story, playing up its most extraordinary features. The *Star* and the *Sun* juxtaposed articles on the murder with articles on the clean-up campaign. This particular association was established through statements by Premier Davis, Mayor Crombie, and others. Ng explains that this highlights "the crucial role played by . . . government and state officials in defining what is the significant issue involved in the murder of Jaques." The *Globe and Mail* associated the murder with the strip and with the "sexual permissiveness" that had begun in the 1960s.

Through its selective representation of reality, the media plays a clear ideological role. The mass media relies on accredited sources, and thus the perspective of agencies of social regulation are part of the formulation of "objective" news accounts. Such media practices served to neutralize opposition and to create a public consensus for the clean-up campaign.

The sex industry, prostitutes, and particularly homosexuals were presented as "folk devils." [2] Coverage of the "homosexual murder" served to focus hostility against the whole gay community.[3] Demonstrations by the Portuguese community, of which Jaques had been a member, influenced by the media, called for cleaning up Yonge Street, for granting more power to the police, and for capital punishment for homosexuals. The media portrayed the child molester or child murderer as a homosexual stranger to be found lurking in seedy parts of the city."The relationship between homosexual behavior, pedophilia, and murderous acts became a cluster of images that cemented in the public mind."

The moral panic thus created would have a lasting effect, defining the political terrain for discussions of the character of the city, Yonge Street, sexual permissiveness, prostitution, and homosexuality for years to come.

By focusing on an unusually violent crime, the media obscured the common occurrence of sexual abuse and violence against children and young people in the family setting—which clearly points to the application of the public/private distinction in the social regulation. Sexual violence in the private sphere does not attract the same police or media attention (although it may attract the attention of social workers), even though the violence may exceed that of the Jaques case. The provincial government, for instance, prevented the release of a study of fifty-four child abuse deaths in Ontario during that same year, 1977.

The Jaques case and the "clean up Yonge Street" campaign signaled a shift in the Toronto social climate for lesbians and gay men. The "clean-up" campaign provided fertile ground for the growth of sentiments against the visibility of the gay ghetto, particularly in the Yonge Street area. The Jaques murder has reappeared as ammunition in right-wing propaganda; it also resurfaced in mass media coverage of the 1981 bath raids and male prostitution on Yonge Street.

THE EMPIRE STRIKES BACK!

The mid-1970s were the beginning of harder times for gay men all over Canada. In 1975, thirty-five men were arrested as "found-ins" in a "bawdy-house" (police language for a gay bath) in Montreal. In 1976, as part of the clean-up campaign preceding the Montreal Olympics, police raided the Club baths and the Sauna Neptune, charging more than 144 men. The same year twenty-eight men were charged in a raid on the Ottawa Club baths. In 1977, 146 men were charged as "found-ins" during a raid on the Truxx bar in Montreal, provoking a large demonstration of gay resistance in the downtown.[4] The police have been the central force regulating the sexual and community life of gay men, and to a different extent that of lesbians.

The Toronto police continued their policy of harassment and entrapment.[5] As an extension of the "clean up Yonge Street" campaign, the gay men's community became a more specific target. *The Body Politic* was raided in December 1977 and charges were laid in January 1978.[6] The next year the Barracks bath was raided, initiating the late 1970s–early 1980s wave of bath raids in the city.

In Montreal, Ottawa, Toronto, and later Edmonton, the police began to use the bawdy-house law systematically against gay establishments. The raid on the Truxx bar in Montreal was one of the first contemporary uses of this law to mass arrest gay men. The Canadian bawdy-house legislation had originally been drafted to deal with houses of prostitution as part of the movement for sexual purity and defense of marriage. In 1917 the law was broadened to include any place existing "for the practice of acts of indecency," putting massage parlors on the same footing as bawdy-houses.[7] Section 179 of the criminal code currently defines a bawdy-house as "a place that is kept or occupied or resorted to by one or more persons for the purposes of prostitution or the practices of acts of indecency."

This section invites the police to label gay baths, and even private residences, as places habitually resorted to for the performance of acts of indecency and, therefore, "common bawdy-houses." "Indecency" is currently defined as what the contemporary Canadian community is not prepared to tolerate—which, the police and Crown attorneys argue, includes homosexual acts in private rooms in bathhouses.

The assaults on the gay bath in Toronto broke with a policy of "grudging acceptance"[8] or negotiated deals between the police and the bath owners, which had existed for decades with only occasional interruptions like the late-1960s raid on the International Steam Bath. The initial Barracks raid can be seen as the initiation of a new operational policy, and, as Thomas Fleming suggests, as a way to gauge community reaction before proceeding with further police activity.[9] The police and the media attempted to associate the bath and its patrons with sadomasochistic practices and sexual paraphernalia, conjuring up images of sexual sleaziness, deviance, and violence.[10] The association of gay sex with dirt was also made clear in the code name "Operation Soap" given the 1981 police war on the gay community, incorporating an image of dirty gay sex being cleansed from the social body by police action. In 1979 the Hot Tub Club was raided by fifty police officers.[11] Worse was to follow.

The fall 1980 Toronto municipal elections witnessed the defeat of John Sewell, a supporter of gay civil rights and critic of police abuse, and aldermanic candidate George Hislop, a prominent gay figure, and the emergence of a vocal antigay right wing, which had the tacit backing of the police. These results were interpreted by the police as a green light for attacks on gays. On February 5, 1981, 150 police officers were deployed against the city's four major gay baths. Two hundred and eighty-nine men were charged as "found-ins" and twenty as "keepers" of a common bawdy-house. On April 23, 1981, the police laid twenty-two new charges of conspiracy against George Hislop, gay activist Peter Maloney, and four other men. These charges once again associated gay leaders, and the gay community, with criminality.

The police have consistently identified gay baths with organized crime. In testimony before the House of Commons Committee on Justice and Legal Affairs, Guy Lafrance of the Montreal police stated:

> Areas of this country are already blighted by the presence of homosexual bawdy-houses, disguised as "bath" establishments, sex clubs, and operating from apartments and private homes . . . such problems cannot be considered to be of a local or isolated nature; rather, they have international implication and many connections with organized crime.[12]

Donald Banks, then with the Intelligence Bureau of the Metro Toronto police force, and one of the key figures in organizing the 1981 raids, stated before the same committee:

> . . . evidence was brought back to me relating to these premises operating as common bawdy-houses with an international flavor —directors and such of international finance—and monies leaving Canada into the United States from the operations of some places.[13]

Canadian money going to the United States. How unusual, and how criminal!

In July 1981 the police raided two of the remaining baths in Toronto, arresting another twenty-one men on bawdy-house charges. And in 1983 the Back Door was raided again, in a smaller, more sanitized operation.

This police offensive was an attempt at moral crusading, an attempt to regulate the gay male community, and our sexuality, by applying criminal categories—in this case, the bawdy-house legislation to cover gay men's sex. As ideological justification for their crusade, the police made use of media, political, and moral terms of reference established during the "clean up Yonge Street" campaign. They promised to crack down on prostitution, the involvement of minors in "indecent" activity, and the alleged connection with organized crime. Says Thomas S. Fleming, "The charges of prostitution function as a moral key allowing the police entry to the baths."[14] No prostitution, involvement of minors, or evidence of organized crime, however, was documented by the police or demonstrated in court. Nearly ninety percent of the men dragged through the courts were acquitted. Yet the police continue to justify their actions with the few guilty pleas entered and by stating that their internal police complaints bureau received no complaints.[15] The police make use of a schema which divides the population between "the public" and "the scum."

> What distinguishes the scum from the public is that the scum are structurally in conflict with, and are enemies of, the public. The scum are . . . "in essence" troublemakers, while the public are "in essence" their victim. In distinguishing between the scum and the public as two classes who oppose each other as enemies, the police culture makes available to the police a social theory that they can use in the context of their work to define situations and to construct a course of action in response to them. This theory enables the police to transcend the situated features of encounters by relating them to a broader social context which identifies the "real troublemakers" and "real victims."[16]

The "public" here is heterosexual and the "scum" is gay.

The reason for the bath raids and the police campaign against the gay community has been the subject of some dispute.[17] A full understanding would require a more detailed historical study than can be attempted here; however, a few of the elements which inform it can be sketched in. Police organization must be investigated in order to show how the criminal code has directed the police against gays.

Two particular processes are at work. Firstly, Toronto is a city of growing racial, ethnic, and now sexual minorities. The provincial and municipal establishment foresee the need for a fairly militarized police force—which is not accountable to these minorities—to decrease their public visibility and to keep them contained.

Secondly, sectors of the ruling apparatus fear the visibility and concentration of gays in the downtown core. This is the social context in which the "clean up Yonge Street" campaign and the bath raids can be located. In the 1970s and early 1980s, the increasing visibility of the gay community interacted with plans for the redevelopment of the Yonge Street area and the downtown. Police policy sought to limit growth of the gay community.

These police campaigns have not been successful. The attempt to create a moral panic around the 1981 bath raids failed because of resistance by thousands of gays and our supporters. The police had clearly not expected such unprecedented anger and rebellion. Indeed, the raids served to politicize, radicalize, and define the gay community. Support came from feminists, unions, civil liberties and religious groups, and progressive members of City Council. The White and Sheppard Report documented the brutality of the bath raids,[18] and even the mainstream media adopted a critical attitude toward the police. City Council voted for a provincial independent inquiry into the bath raids, and established the city's own Bruner investigation into police/gay relations when the province refused to establish such an inquiry.

By documenting police harassment, the Bruner Report reflected the gains won by gay resistance[19] and it made many progressive recommendations, including sexual orientation protection and the recognition of gays as a legitimate minority. Its central recommendation, however, was for the establishment of dialogue between the gay community and the police:

> It has been obvious throughout the study, and particularly in the complaints and countercomplaints between the police and the gay community and the attitude that each has toward the other, that the relationship suffers from an almost total lack of effective communication. . . . It is my view that regular dialogue is key to improved relations between the police and gay community.[20]

This recommendation presents the main problem as a lack of communication. This assumption is not grounded in the experience of gays and lesbians. The gay movement knew perfectly well what the police were about, and the police, through their surveillance activities, had a profound understanding of the gay movement. The central problem was not a lack of communication. As well, Bruner's approach tended to place the gay community and the police on the same level, whereas it is the police who have the power to arrest, raid, and to regulate sexual life.

A dialogue committee would manufacture gay consent for police activity. In a situation wherein no community has control over the police, wherein there is no police accountability to democratic bodies, and wherein antigay laws remain on the books, discussion of "problem areas"[21] like sexual activity in "public washrooms" or parks would only involve the gay community or its representatives in a process of policing ourselves. This could cause serious division in the community and make campaigns against police harassment very difficult given the apparently consensual relations established with them. Such a dialogue committee could also provide the police with detailed information which could later be used against us.

While the Bruner Report contains many recommendations which legitimize our struggle, it also suggests a new means of regulation of the gay community and same-gender sex which had to be resisted. Gay movements can use the progressive demands of such reports to push forward our struggles while at the same time pushing beyond the boundaries of social regulation they suggest.

The 1980s battles between the gay movement and the police are a manifestation of the social struggles over the State-defined distinction between public and private. The police are trying to establish that gay baths and male sex in parks and washrooms is public sex and therefore subject to their direct intervention. The very institutions of the gay community would thus be rendered "public." This debate takes place in the context of the boundaries drawn by the 1969 reform and contradictory developments to which it has led.

The movement has argued that gay institutions are part of the private sphere and therefore off-limits to the police. It has used the liberal notion of "right to privacy" not only as a defense in court; it has also turned the public/private distinction against State agencies by redefining and shifting the terms of the debate. This strategy not only includes the gay community and its institutions in the private realm; it also shifts the notion of privacy from the language of State discourse and places it in the social practices of everyday life. This notion of right to privacy builds upon the idea of privacy as a realm of individual choice, consent, and morality. But privacy is no longer only territorially defined; if you have sex in this place it is "public," in that place "private." Instead, it focuses on the actual social practice in which people engage. "Right to privacy" is not used in a narrow, individualist sense, but in a collective sense—which requires that one look at sex and social life from the standpoint of gays and which moves beyond the boundaries of State-defined categories. It is quite possible to engage in a private act in a place defined by the State as public (for example, a washroom, with no one else present or a deserted or secluded part of a park).

> . . . privacy is something that is socially constructed in this society. . . . Indeed, in the middle of the night, when it is absolutely pitch black, a park might in fact be a very private place.[22]

The Toronto movement used right to privacy as a vehicle for defending gay men against the police. The dominant public/private strategies of regulation were thus put into question. It should be pointed out, though, that there can also be grave dangers in accepting a narrow State-defined notion of privacy.[23] Conservative gays in the United States have used the ideas of privacy in this limited sense to win the support of anti-gay Republicans. This approach fundamentally accepts State definitions of public and private and the sexual policing that goes with them.

The mass response to the bath raids in Toronto at least temporarily closed off options for the police. Their tactics have therefore changed. The police began to regularly lay overcrowding charges against gay bars in 1981–82. Surveillance, entrapment, and the arrest of men allegedly engaged in sexual acts in washrooms and parks increased significantly. In 1982–83, more than six hundred men were arrested in washrooms for homosexual "offenses." More than six hundred "indecent act" arrests took place in Toronto in 1985.[24]

In 1983–85 police action was extended across southern Ontario, with arrests in Orillia, Welland, Oakville, Peel region, Guelph, Kitchener/Waterloo, and St. Catherines. In most instances, the local police have used video surveillance equipment provided by the Ontario Provincial Police.[25] In many cases the local media have published the arrested men's names. More than 250 men have been charged across southern Ontario and at least one man has killed himself as a result.

Washroom arrests are hard to fight, particularly in small towns, because of the social stigma attached to the offense, the difficulty in mounting a legal defense, and because many of these men do not consider themselves gay. Of the southern Ontario centers, only in Guelph was there a protest against the video surveillance arrests. A "Stop Policing Sexuality" demonstration was held, support activities for the men charged were organized, and legal challenges were launched.[26] Legal defense requires that our right to privacy be extended to include private sexual acts which take place in "public" places like washrooms. Two men having sex in a cubicle in a deserted washroom, for instance, having clearly taken measures to ensure their privacy, are performing a private act.[27] This is, however, a difficult argument to make in court and in political organizing.

The police focused their attentions more specifically against gay institutions. Obscenity charges were brought against Glad Day Bookstore and new obscenity charges were laid against *The Body Politic* in May 1982. Obscenity legislation, which censors sexual presentations on the basis of "the undue exploitation of sex," does not treat all sexual images and texts equally. The law applies more harshly to same-gender presentations.

In the Glad Day trial in 1983, presentation of lesbian and gay sexuality were seen as more "indecent" and "offensive" to community standards than similar heterosexual portrayals. Judge Vanek, in his judgment, referred to the 1970 case of *Regina* v. *Prairie Schooner,* in which the Manitoba Court of Appeal found that "lurid scenes of lesbianism" "went beyond what the community was prepared to tolerate." Vanek referred to the 1969 criminal code reform which decriminalized only homosexual acts between adults in private and which defined a public place as existing when "two or more persons are present or if it is a public place." Vanek stated that in the case of the two magazines which Glad Day was charged with selling, the photographer must have been present, making the acts "public." Again referring to the 1969 reform, he stated that the acts depicted in the magazines "are made public by representing them graphically in a pictorial magazine, which sometimes depicts a third person."[28] Vanek was unable to determine any lowering of Canadian community standards since this earlier case had been heard.[29]

The 1969 reform therefore retained the idea that same-gender sex is more "indecent" and "obscene" than similar heterosexual acts. Obscenity legislation works to keep lesbian and gay sexuality in a subordinate position while generally buttressing heterosexual hegemony. This legislation lets the police regulate the lesbian and gay community and images of same-gender sex more generally. It helps establish proper images of sex, seriously limiting what lesbians and gays can view, read, discuss, and produce.

In the mid-1980s, Canada Customs escalated its seizure of lesbian and gay materials. Using a new internal memorandum that labels depictions of "buggery/sodomy" as "obscene," they have refused entry to numerous materials destined for Little Sister's in Vancouver and Glad Day Bookshop in Toronto. Books and magazines seized include *The Joy of Gay Sex, Lesbian Sex,* and the lesbian sex magazines *Bad Attitude* and *On Our Backs.* A number of sex videos made for lesbians have also been seized.

New federal proposals announced in June 1986 would ban all depictions of "anal intercourse" and many other sex acts as prohibited forms of "pornography," thereby further institutionalizing sanctions against presentations of lesbian and gay sex.[30]

NOTES

1. Yvonne Chi-Ying Ng, "Ideology, Media and Moral Panics: An Analysis of the Jaques Murder," Centre for Criminology, University of Toronto, M.A. thesis (November 1981). The quotes in these sections, and this account, unless otherwise cited, are from this very insightful thesis.

2. Stan Cohen, *Folk Devils and Moral Panics* (London: MacGibbon and Kee. 1972).

3. See *The Body Politic* (September 1977), pp. 1–24.

4. See the Canadian Lesbian and Gay Rights Coalition, *Forum* (Winter 1979) Vol. 4, No. 1.

5. See Lesbian and Gay History Group of Toronto, "A History of the Relationship Between the Gay Community and the Metropolitan Police," submission to the Bruner Study, 1981.

6. Ed Jackson and Stan Persky, eds., *Flaunting It: A Decade of Gay Journalism from The Body Politic* (Vancouver and Toronto: New Star and Pink Triangle, 1982), pp. 146–47.

7. See Stuart Russell, "The Offence of Keeping a Common Bawdy-House," *Ottawa Law Review,* Vol. 14, No. 2 (1982), p. 275.

8. Phil Scraton uses this expression in his work on the police to describe a negotiated tolerance between police and working-class "criminal" practices like street gambling. Also see Scraton, *The State of Police* (London and Sydney: Pluto. 1985).

9. Thomas S. Fleming, "The Bawdy-House Boyd: Some Notes on Media, Sporadic Moral Crusades, and Selective Law Enforcement," *Canadian Criminology Forum,* Vol. 3 (Spring 1981), p. 109.

10. See Gerald Hannon, "Making Gay Sex Dirty," *The Body Politic* (May 1981), No. 73, pp. 6–10; and Fleming, op. cit., p. 112.

11. See *Action!* publication of the Right to Privacy Committee, Vol. 1, No. 3.

12. Mr. Lafrance, Justice and Legal Affairs Committee, Issue No. 81 (May 5, 1982), p. 8.

13. Ibid., p. 23.

14. Fleming, op. cit., p. 105.

15. See Justice and Legal Affairs Committee, Issue No. 81 (May 5, 1982), pp. 24, 26.

16. Clifford D. Shearing. "Subterranean Processes in the Maintenance of Power: An Examination of the Mechanisms Coordinating Police Action," *Canadian Review of Sociology and Anthropology* 18:3 (August 1981), p. 288.

17. See especially George W. Smith, "Policing the Gay Community," unpublished paper. Department of Sociology in Education, OISE (1986), for an excellent analysis of the textually mediated character of police campaigns against the gay community.

18. D. White and P. Sheppard, "Report on the Police Raids on the Gay Steambaths," prepared by Alderman David White and Pat Sheppard, 1981.

19. Arnold Bruner, "Out of the Closet: Study of Relations Between the Homosexual Community and the Police," Report to Mayor Arthur Eggleton and the Council of the City of Toronto (September 24, 1981). This report deals mostly with gay men. "Women in Gay Society" is a total of three pages, pp. 61–63.

20. Ibid., pp. 159–60.

21. Ibid., p. 162.

22. George Smith, "In Defence of Privacy." *Action!* Vol. 3, No. 1.

23. See Scott Tucker, "Our Right to the World," *The Body Politic* (July/August 1982) No. 85, pp. 20–33: Loe Casey, "Sexual Politics and the Subversion of the Public Sphere: A Defense of Feminism and Gay Liberation" in Itala Rutter, ed., *Perspectives on Lesbian and Gay Liberation and Socialism* (New York Democratic Socialist of America, early 1980s), pp. 8–16; and Scott P. Anderson, "Privacy: An Issue for the 80s?" *The Advocate,* Issue 360, pp. 23–25.

24. These statistics are from the important work of Gay Court Watch in Toronto in providing support for the people arrested on homosexual-related charges.

25. On how local police request assistance from the Ontario Provincial Police and for an account of

washroom sex in police language, see "Guelph Sex Video Policing: Internal Cop Documents." *Rites*, Vol. 3, No. 2 (June 1986), p. 7.

26. See Yanni Vassilas, "Guelph Fights Police Busts," *Rites*, Vol. 2, No. 4 (September 1985), p. 4.

27. See Gary Kinsman, "1984—The Police Are Still with Us," *Rites*, Vol. 1, No. 1, pp. 10–11; Gary Kinsman and Doug Wilson. "Police Entrapment Fighting Back with Court Watch," *Rites*, Vol. 1, No. 6, pp. 9–11; and George Smith, "In Defence of Privacy," op. cit.

28. Judge Vanek's judgment in the Glad Day trial (March 4, 1983).

29. In 1984 the conviction against Kevin Orr, who worked at Glad Day, was overturned when the appeal judge agreed with the defense lawyer that Vanek had partially relied on the obsolete Hicklin obscenity test—which defined obscenity as anything that "depraves or corrupts."

30. See Bill C-114 introduced in June 1986. A modified version of this bill is to be introduced in spring 1987.

SOVIET UNION

Denial of recognition of sexual minorities, open discrimination, and criminalization of homosexual behavior between consenting male adults was the mainstay of Soviet social policy for decades. The consequences for individual gays in Soviet society, even in the days of *glasnost,* translated into social isolation, fear of discovery, loss of jobs and membership in the Communist Party, and even imprisonment. Lesbianism, as is the case in many of the world's nations, is not mentioned in criminal codes, and the lesbian for all practical purposes remains even more "invisible" than the gay male in public life. The following article was written by Masha Gessen, a political refugee from the Soviet Union now living in the United States.

From "We Have No Sex: Soviet Gays and AIDS in the Era of *Glasnost*," by Masha Gessen, from OUT/LOOK (Summer 1990).

During the first U.S.-Soviet "telebridge" about five years ago, the Soviet participants were asked about the treatment of gay people in their country. "We don't have homosexuality,"[1] came the confident response of a woman in the Soviet audience. While the speaker's compatriots nodded their agreement, a giggle swept through the American audience and the camera shifted to the U.S. side, where a woman was knowingly shaking her head "no."

Back then the Russian word for openness—*glasnost*—was not yet a household word in the United States, and sex was still a taboo subject in the Soviet Union. Members of Phil Donahue's first Soviet audience would just as sincerely have denied that their fellow citizens were sexual at all. Their choice not to engage in a discussion of matters sexual was wise for many reasons, not the least of which is that such a discussion could not possibly have been conducted in language suitable for television. There is no socially acceptable vocabulary in Russia for discussing sexuality: The only sexually descriptive words belong to *mat-,* a set of words that, its connoisseurs proudly point out, are more vulgar than words found in any other language. And even this lexicon is of little help in a conversation about homosexuality.

The lack of a sexually descriptive Russian vocabulary stems in part from the censorship of any and all sex-related material from books, movies, and periodicals distributed in the Soviet Union during the seven decades preceding *glasnost*: "Soviet literary authorities," writes Yelena Gessen, a former Soviet editor and translator, "desperately want to forget that a person comes into this world endowed with sexual organs."[2] Gessen describes a foreign-fiction anthology that lost an already-approved short story to censorship because in the words of the editor, "it contained too much sex—and totally unjustified sex. One would be unable to explain why it was necessary."

The notion that a person's every action must be motivated by necessity is central not only to the peculiar art form known as Socialist Realism but to the study and execution of anything that can be fitted with ideological underpinning—including, of course, the study of human sexuality.

The few Soviet scientists and laypeople who have chosen to study sexual orientation are no exception. The Soviet Union may be the only country in the world where almost everyone who has thought about it believes the same factor is at the root of homosexuality. Among Soviet citizens, explains Russian lexicographer Vladimir Kozlovsky, the preeminent theory is that homosexuals get that way in the labor camps. He also notes, however, that in his studies of the Soviet gay subculture he met no one who had been incarcerated.[3]

WE HAVE LITTLE SEX

Laughable as the level of Soviet discourse about sex is, publication of even the most repressive articles about sexuality would have been unthinkable just a few years ago. In the spirit of *glasnost,* however, Soviet citizens have begun not only to chip away at the censorship establishment's portrayals of the Soviet Union as a sex-free zone but to laugh at it. There is even a popular new souvenir on the shelves of Soviet stores: a plaque with two hammer-and-sickle-decorated stick figures who have no genitals, with a double entendre caption: "We have no sex."

Regrettably, most of the Soviet media's attempts to break through the sexual denial have been no more informative or graceful than these clay souvenir plaques. Last year, for example, the national monthly magazine for adolescents undertook the ambitious task of educating pubescent boys and girls about the changes taking place in their bodies. The first article for boys dealt with masturbation. Purporting to denounce the old stigma attached to masturbation, the author—a psychiatrist—assured her readers that their perfectly natural masturbatory urges would pass before too long, with the benefit of a little willpower, a lot of exercise, and plenty of studying.[4] Clearly, if the discipline of sex education in the Soviet Union continues to progress at the same pace, teenagers will begin learning about homosexuality sometime in the middle of the next century.

Like the masturbation article, a majority of recent controversial publications in Soviet periodicals have broken only halfway through any given taboo, almost never reaching far enough even to mention homosexuality. While the Soviet media have brought back to the Soviet reader the work of several authors who are known to be gay, lesbian, or bisexual, the accompanying commentaries have never explicitly mentioned the authors' sexuality. The works of André Gide were brought back from a fifty-year literacy exile, together with articles that mentioned Gide's unflattering comments about the Soviet Union following his 1936 visit—but omitted the fact that these comments concerned the country's treatment of homosexuals.[5] When the poetry of Sophia Parnok saw print last winter, she was introduced to Soviet readers as "a friend" of the poet Marina Tsvetayeva, when she was, in fact, her lover.[6] And a true feat of denial was accomplished when Soviet periodicals published interviews with and carefully chosen excerpts from the works of Eduard Limonov, probably the most controversial Russian-language writer, who gained notoriety with an autobiographical novel that included descriptions of his sexual acts, with both men and women. Soviet journalists simply stated that Limonov was a "scandalous" writer who "exposed himself" in his first book.[7,8]

A different form of censorship has affected photographs and artwork showcased in Soviet periodicals. Here editors have opted for showing without telling. An essay on a female students' dormitory consists of half a dozen photographs, each with a detailed caption—except for the lone picture of two women under a blanket thrown over two single beds that have been pushed together.[9] An article about the artist Kuzma Petrov-Vodkin is accompanied by reproductions of his paintings, each of which is analyzed in the text —except for one undeniably homoerotic painting of two naked pubescent boys.[10]

Of course, the only thing really new about the current censorship of gay-related material in the Soviet Union is that it has lessened somewhat. But even before the most recent thaw, and despite the systematic persecution of homosexuals throughout most of the last two centuries, the country has sustained a homosexual subculture.

REPRESS! OPPRESS!...

In czarist Russia voluntary participation in "the unnatural vice" between two men was punishable by incarceration for four to five years, but the law was rarely, if ever, applied. The perpetration of the act upon a minor or a mentally incompetent or unwilling partner upped the sentence to ten to twelve years. The prerevolutionary government considered extending the law to heterosexuals but ended up deciding against it, and it entertained but took no action on a liberalization proposal made by politician Vladimir Nabokov (the writer's father). Ultimately, all laws of the empire were abolished in one fell swoop by the October Revolution of 1917.[11]

The sodomy laws stayed off the books in Soviet Russia until 1933. But while this fact has often been cited in the West as an indication of the early Bolshevik government's lenient view of homosexuality, there is no evidence that the absence of antigay laws was intentional: After all, the new government did not even institute laws against murder, rape, and incest until five years after the revolution. At the same time, like their predecessors, members of the postrevolutionary governments briefly flirted with the idea of sexual liberation. Between 1921 and 1930, Soviet delegations attended the first four congresses of the World Society for Sexual Reform. But the government's commitment to sexual reform apparently faltered in 1931, with the cancellation of the fifth congress, slated for the discussion of "Marxism and the Question of Sex" in Moscow. (The gathering finally took place in Brno, Czechoslovakia, in 1932).[12]

By the early 1930s there was not a trace of liberalism left in any printed references to homosexuality. In an article on fascism published simultaneously in the country's two major dailies in 1934, Maxim Gorky, hailed as Soviet Russia's "writer of the proletariat," summed up the spirit of intolerance that had set in: "I will note that in the country bravely and successfully led by the proletariat, homosexuality, which destroys the youth, is seen and punished as the antisocial crime it is. Meanwhile, in the so-called 'cultured country' of great philosophers, scientists, and musicians, it is allowed to run rampant. Hence the saying: 'Eliminate homosexuality, and you will make fascism disappear.' "[13]

In January 1934 at least four major Soviet cities—including

Moscow and Leningrad—became sites of mass arrests of gay men. According to Kozlovsky, former prisoners estimate that gay men in the GULAG labor camps in the 1930s numbered in the thousands. They were jailed under Article 121 of the 1933 law, which provided for a prison sentence of up to five years for men convicted of voluntarily engaging in sex with other men and up to eight years for having sex with a male minor or with a person who was physically or mentally forced to participate.[14]

Since then the law regarding gay sex remained essentially unchanged. There are no available statistics as to how often this law is invoked, although legal expert Valery Chalidze reports that "the number of such cases was by no means small: Men convicted of gay sex comprised 0.1 percent of all criminal convictions in 1966."[15] Kozlovsky suggests that the number of men arrested under the provisions of Article 121 is far greater, but that the police and the KGB often prefer to make informers, rather than convicts, out of these detainees. According to a number of sources, local law enforcement authorities keep comprehensive lists of individuals believed to be gay.[16]

While neither Article 121 nor any other part of the Criminal Code prohibits lesbian sex, authorities apparently find ways to persecute the few lesbians who are part of the gay subculture. "Say, for example, they'll take me in for speculation [the sale and resale of goods, especially foreign-made clothes, at inflated prices]," explains "Vera," a twenty-year-old Moscovite. "So they'll give me time for that, plus add a little because I'm a lesbian."[17]

... YOU WILL NEVER SUPPRESS IT!

In spite of the government's persecution and the larger society's complete intolerance of homosexuality and all other kinds of nonconformity, gay men and, to a far lesser degree, lesbians have managed to create and maintain a subculture, complete with gathering places, identifying gestures, and a versatile vocabulary. Every major city has what is known as the *marshrut* ("circuit")—a set of streets along which a gay man is likely to spot another. In Moscow the *marshrut,* which circles the center of the city, has its heart in the square in front of the Bolshoi Theater. There gay men, often recognizable by mascara and usually tight jeans, mix with a handful of lesbians, a few hippies, and scores of speculators who buy and sell foreign goods. The gay men and the speculators compete for the attentions of foreign actors and tourists—a scene also found in the lobbies of Moscow's hotels.

Moscow, like other cities around the world, boasts a number of public toilets where men meet and have sex with other men. The omnipresent *banyas*—public baths—are also reportedly popular places for gay men to make contact with other gay men. And while there are no gay bars per se, there is always an eatery or two along the *marshrut* that particularly attracts the circuit regulars.

Like members of the American gay subculture of the 1950s, *marshrut* men and women differentiate heavily between "passive" and "active" homosexuals. It appears, however, that these distinctions are more meaningful in describing social and cultural identities than actual sexual behavior. According to a gay man interviewed by Kozlovsky, most gay men are "synthetic"—what his American counterparts would call *kiki,* neither top nor bottom.[18]

The *marshrut* lifestyle carries a set of hazards that make it best suited for strong and healthy men. The Russian climate and Soviet law enforcement authorities make outdoor social life extremely unfriendly. In addition to the sodomy law, the police use laws against prostitution, speculation, and loitering to harass *marshrut* regulars. Extralegal assistance is provided by street hooligans, who bash gays regularly, sometimes on their own initiative and sometimes at the suggestion of the police. Many who have done the Moscow circuit can recall being lured into an alley by a basher, or narrowly escaping—or not escaping—a gang of attackers. Not surprisingly, the *marshrut* is dominated by young people, many of whom stay around only long enough to find a partner.

Like their American counterparts, Soviet lesbians and gay men seem to believe that the women among them are more likely to form permanent relationships than the men are. But, as in most places, both men and women form committed partnerships, sometimes even with the blessing of a Russian Orthodox priest. Many couples exchange rings, which, according to Kozlovsky's "Vera," are worn on the left hand, as opposed to the right, where Soviet heterosexuals wear their wedding bands.

THE TACTFUL INTELLIGENTSIA

What Gorky did not foresee when he extolled the virtues of the country "bravely and successfully led by the proletariat" was that the gap between the proletariat and the intelligentsia would only grow wider with the development of Soviet society. But even though no one is supposed to be "more equal" than anyone else, completely separate cultures exist in different socioeconomic spheres. Because the solidarity among members of the homosexual minority is not nearly strong enough to bridge this gap, the gay culture in intellectual circles has almost nothing in common with the working-class *marshrut*. A gay mathematics instructor I interviewed from a large Soviet city put it this way: "How am I supposed to know what the people think of homosexuality? I am not one of the people!"

While heterosexual intellectuals rarely tolerate open discussion of homosexuality, every one of the interlocking circles that make up this class has a member or two who are known to be "that way." While gay men are acknowledged in their midst, the intelligentsia would swear on its libraries that lesbians simply do not exist outside labor camps. In contrast to the *marshrut* gay men, who wear makeup and use only feminine forms of verbs and adjectives, then, gay men of the intelligentsia are paragons of discretion, and its lesbians are simply invisible.

When a gay intellectual gets in trouble with the law, his case does not become a *cause célèbre,* as is the case with the trials of some dissidents. Instead, his social circle will quietly come to his aid. In the early 1980s, for example, members of the Moscow elite welcomed with open arms a Ukrainian theater director whom they knew had changed his place of residence in order to stall his prosecution on sodomy charges. For over a year the man received legal aid, money, and housing from people with whom he shared nothing other than his social status and education level.

But while the intellectuals may rush to the aid of an artist in trouble, it would be a mistake to attribute this sympathy to enlightened attitudes toward sexuality. Like their working-class compatriots, Soviet intellectuals use the words for "homosexual" and "pederast" interchangeably, refuse to recognize homosexual unions, and consider homosexuality a tragic but disgusting illness. In other words, gay members of the intelligentsia are safe as long as they keep the glass doors of their closets firmly shut.

A RUDE AWAKENING

With the inauguration of *glasnost* in 1986, Soviet journalists set out to identify and expose the societal ills they had so diligently ignored for the preceding sixty years. After tackling murders, drug addiction, and prostitution, the press was ready for homosexuality by early 1987. The honor fell to *Moskovskiy Komsomolets,* a second-tier daily published by the KOSMSOMOL, the Communist Party branch for fourteen- to twenty-eight-year-olds.

The newspaper confronted the issue head-on, declaring that homosexuality was on the increase in the Soviet Union. The article quoted Vyacheslav Maslov, a specialist in sexual psychology, who cited the case of a man whose mother and grandmother had made him gay by "dressing him like a doll." The rising divorce rate, Maslov declared, forced children to grow up with role models from one sex, which he claimed increases children's chances of growing up gay. The article ended with a call to arms. "If there is freedom for homosexuality, that means it would automatically spread. It would be the same as advertising it." The only way to prevent the spread of the scourge, the authors concluded, is to make sure that the laws against gay sex are enforced even more rigidly.

This and similar articles triggered the painful process of dragging homosexuality out of the collective unconscious, and gay men in the Soviet Union found themselves in a new and uncomfortable position. With the majority of the population in a permanent state of denial on matters of sexuality, gay men had never found it necessary to work on being invisible: They just were. "You could go into a public restroom, or a bathhouse, and just look, or even cruise, and no one would be suspicious, because homosexuality is just not part of their vocabulary."

"Vlad," the mathematics instructor, agrees. "No one used to pay attention to the fact that I wasn't married and lived with another man," he recalls wistfully. "Now I hear people talking about it in the corridors at work, and the questions are beginning to come up."

Additional difficulties for gay men have been created by the rising moralistic fervor that has accompanied the appearance of comparatively sexually explicit articles and films—such as the movie *Little Vera,* which caused almost as much of a stir in the United States as it did in the USSR. In the resulting backlash Soviet citizens have asserted moral views that may seem illogical in a country where the average woman has eight abortions, countless couples live together without registering their marriage, and the divorce rate among those who do marry is 30 percent.[19]

Ogonyok, the magazine that exposed the gay poet Gennady Trifonov, has been transformed from an unremarkable weekly into the main mouthpiece of *glasnost* and *perestroika* proponents, and has broken new ground in Soviet journalism by undertaking public-opinion polls. A recent poll "on issues of family and marriage" showed that 84.5 percent of Soviet citizens believe that every person has an obligation to marry and build a family.[20]

When the magazine screened a video entitled *Risk Group* and asked thirteen viewers their opinion of it, the most tolerant view was expressed by a forty-five-year-old female architect:

> Perhaps nowadays it's more interesting for a man to be with a man: there aren't any details that complicate communication, there is greater mutual understanding. This phenomenon did not start yesterday. More likely, it appeared when millions and millions of people were sent to labor camps, forced to spend long periods of time away from the normal and natural lifestyle. I can neither justify nor judge these people. We created these groups ourselves.[21]

A counterargument was provided by a male medical student:

> If a man cohabits with another adult man—well, what can you do, it's an illness. But when a homosexual on the prowl begins to recruit adolescents, then that is complete perversion. So we must be cruel. We must take the Taras Bulba approach: "I gave birth to you, and I will kill you." Because our society does not need people like that.

Since *Ogonyok* attracts probably the most reform-minded members of the reading public, the predominant attitude toward homosexuality in the Soviet Union is likely even harsher than the above quotes suggest. In 1987 *Literaturnaya Gazeta* printed a letter from a woman who described what happened to her son, a promising young engineer who decided to "come out of the underground"—perhaps the only written account of the consequences of coming out published in the Soviet Union. Within days, wrote the woman, her son was expelled from the Communist Party by order of a specially convened meeting of the local committee. Immediately thereafter he was fired from his job. Months later he still had not found employment.[22]

It is no wonder that few if any Soviet homosexuals choose to confront such dire consequences. Many would probably prefer a return to the era of silence. But in the era of AIDS more and more of them no longer have the luxury of choosing the closet.

EPILOGUE

At the time this article was written, in February 1990, the Soviet Union's first open gay and lesbian organization was inaugurated at a press conference for Western journalists held by about twelve people at an apartment on the outskirts of Moscow. Two years later, this organization and the ones that have followed have made more progress than even the most optimistic observers would have predicted.

Several organizations are working and occasionally fighting among themselves in Moscow, St. Petersburg, several Siberian cities, and elsewhere in Russia, as well as other areas in the territory of the Commonwealth of Independent States, and in the Baltics. The Moscow Union of Lesbians and Gay Men represents a radical queer agenda that prioritizes visibility, while ARGO, as the Association for the Equality of Homosexuals is known, employs more conservative political tactics. Two St. Petersburg groups, the Tchaikovski Foundation for Cultural Initiative and the Defense of Sexual Minorities and *Kryla* (Wings) mirror this conflict. But in September, representatives of these and other groups attended the founding meeting of the Russian Union of Lesbians and Gay Men in Moscow—and this time, over thirty people were willing to disclose their names.

A gay and lesbian newspaper called *Tema* (a slang word for homosexuality, literally meaning *theme*) is publishing every two months in Moscow with a press run of 15,000. Several other publications, including the magazine *RISK* (an acronym for *equality, sincerity, liberty, and compromise*) in Moscow, the newspaper *SV* in Siberia, and others offer *Tema* some competition, though they are not yet publishing regularly. Preparations are under way for an ambitious high-production-quality cultural journal called *Ty* (You).

The nongay media have printed a steady stream of articles on lesbians and gay men, responding quickly, if not always positively, to actions of gay and lesbian activists—interviewing *Tema* editor and MULGUM president Roman Kalinin, for example, when he declared his candidacy for Russian president opposite Boris Yeltsin in the spring of 1991. Gay and lesbian visibility reached a high point in July and August 1991, when Russian activists and the San Francisco-based International Gay and Lesbian Human Rights Commission sponsored a gay and lesbian conference in St. Petersburg and Moscow. Russia's first lesbian and gay rights demonstration took place in front of the Bolshoi Theatre in conjunction with the conference.

Neither laws nor public opinion change overnight, however. Article 121 has not been repealed, and though it is not included in the draft of the new penal code, activists worry that the authorities will continue to enforce sexual-assault laws selectively against homosexuals and that lesbians will continue to be subjected to unwanted psychiatric treatment. A 1990 poll showed that a third of the population of the Soviet Union believed that homosexuals should be exterminated, a third believed we should be isolated from society, and only 10 percent believed we should be left alone.

Antigay violence has soared along with other kinds of crime, effectively shutting down the *marshrut* in Moscow. And while more and more lesbians and gay men are willing to come out publicly, many prominent gays apparently believe that coming out would do irreparable damage to their careers. The Ukrainian theater director mentioned in the article has gone on to prominence in Moscow, and though the "homosexual esthetic" has been discussed extensively by theater critics, he has not come out. One of the country's most prominent scholars of sexuality has spoken out forcefully against the pathologizing of homosexuality, but he too has not acknowledged publicly that he is gay.

Gay and lesbian activists in Russia have a long road ahead of them. But this epilogue has to end on a more optimistic note than the article it follows: Not only have hate movements failed to take over the country, but the progress Russia and its gays and lesbians have made in the last two years just might prove irreversible.

Masha Gessen

February 1992

NOTES

1. This and all other quotations in this article have been translated by Masha Gessen.
2. Yelena Gessen, "Taboos and Loopholes," *Obozreniye*, No. 2 (1983). Gessen is the author's mother.
3. Vladimir Kozlovsky, *The Slang of the Russian Gay Subculture: Research Materials* (Benson, Vt.: Chalidze Publications, 1986), p. 13.
4. Dr. Yulia Gellermankt, "The Age of Transition," *Pioner*, No. 3 (March 1989).
5. "Andre Gide's Works to Be Published," *Moskovskiye Novosti* (July 10, 1989).
6. "The Poems of Sophia Parnok," *Literaturnoye Obozreniye*, No. 11 (March 1990). The relationship between Tsvetayeva and Parnok is described in Sophia Polyakov's book *The Sunset Days of Yore: Tsvetayeva and Parnok* (Ann Arbor, Mich.: Ardis, 1983).
7. Victor Yerofeyey, "A Conversation with 'A Normal Writer,' " *Ogonyok*, No. 7 (February 1990).
8. Dmitri Yakushin, "This Is He, Eddie," *Moskovskiye Novosti* (August 6, 1989).
9. *Smena* (April 3, 1989).
10. *Ogonyok*, No. 13 (March 1989).
11. Kozlovsky, pp. 147–50.
12. Ibid., p. 151.
13. *Collected Works of M. Gorky* (Moscow, 1953), Vol. 27, p. 238. This article was published in both *Pravda* and *Izvestiya* (May 23, 1934).
14. Article 121, Criminal Code of the RSFSR [Russian Soviet Federated Socialist Republic].
15. Valery Chalizde, *Criminal Russia* (New York: Xronika, 1977), p. 149.
16. Kozlovsky, pp. 155–56.
17. Ibid., p. 221.
18. Ibid., p. 218.
19. Statistics from 1990 issues of *Argumenty i Fakty*.
20. "For and Against," *Ogonyok*, No. 47 (November 1989).
21. Irina Malyarova, " 'Risk Group': Thirteen Opinions," *Ogonyok*, No. 49 (December 1988).
22. Letter recounted by Yelena Gessen.

ARGENTINA

Of all Latin American countries, Argentina has been one of the most repressive in regard to gays. In the 1970s, in their struggles against the military dictatorship, many members of the gay groups, as others, were arrested, tortured, and "disappeared." What is less known, perhaps, is how policies of gay oppression continue even today with a viciousness hardly equaled anywhere else in Latin America. A case in point is CHA (Comunidad Homosexual Argentina), an organization of gays that is in the forefront of a gay rights campaign and AIDS education program. In 1990 the Argentine government, citing the Catholic Church, protection of the family, and medical opinion, denied the group official status. As a consequence, it will no longer be able to represent itself or raise funds.

The following article, from *Connexions* in 1982, surveys Argentina's sad and brutal history regarding lesbians and gays and demonstrates to us the very real effects government repression can have on the lives of lesbians as well as others under suspicion of being different.

**"Shrouded in Silence," from *Connexions*
(Winter 1982).**

I have so many brothers and sisters
that I can't count them
and a very beautiful sister
who is called freedom.
                    —Atahualpa Yupanki

BUENOS AIRES, PLAZA SAN MARTÍN, 1978

The Plaza San Martín is a typical downtown park, a pleasant place
with trees and monuments where tourists, couples, children, families, secretaries, and businessmen congregate.

My friend and I were there one summer afternoon at five o'clock.
We weren't holding hands or embracing or touching at all; we were
simply talking. As we talked, we noticed a group of people in the
distance, approaching. Among them were several boys, two older
men, a woman and two middle-aged men. Several of them were
making signs to each other. One of them walked away, accompanied
by the boys.

Meanwhile, we were laughing, thinking that maybe they were a
group of evangelists, who were very common in Buenos Aires. As
two of the men came toward us, we thought for sure they were
going to offer us some pamphlet or something. Instead, they showed
us their identification as federal police.

We didn't know what to think or say, even though, given the
political situation, the police and army regularly detained and questioned people everywhere.

They took us each to different parts of the park, asked for our
identification documents, and began the routine questions—where

do you live, where do you work, etc. The interviews were conducted in a very aggressive way, with the officers acting very macho. They also searched our bags to see if we had any "subversive material," as they called it.

Indignant, one of us asked one of the cops for an explanation. He answered that this was their "job" and that, besides, *we seemed different from other women, since at this hour it was normal to be with a boyfriend and it was strange to see two women together.*

Fortunately, this harassment went no further. The police silently returned our documents and they left, for some reason taking the six or seven boys with them.

Each of us went home, terrified lest anyone should approach or even look at us, trying to imagine what our encounter with the police could mean. A few days later, we read in a newspaper that the federal police had begun an operation called "League of Morality."

This is how things were at the end of 1978.

This oppression, exercised by police and other security forces, should be understood within the context of a society that is traditionally erotophobic. Machismo is deeply rooted in the national identity. The tango, which is the best-known element of *porteña* culture [*porteña* refers to the city of Buenos Aires—meaning either a resident of that city or that which characterizes the city], originated as a dance in which only men participated; it remains a glorification of masculinity. Homophobia is also encouraged by the doctrines of the Catholic Church, which is extremely powerful in Argentina and much more traditional and conservative than it has come to be in other parts of Latin America. Magazines, newspapers, television, radio, and even the shorts seen at movie theaters make it very clear, usually without even mentioning homosexuality, that morality consists of living within an extremely traditional family— and that any other lifestyle is immoral. Besides being immoral, alternative lifestyles for women are nearly impossible, both economically and because women are generally expected to remain in the

home until they marry. There are, of course, exceptions, often
among upper-class women, but the options are not numerous for
any woman.

At the institutional level, the homophobia and sexism of daily life
represent an attempt to prevent—through the use of force—the
deterioration of antiquated social codes.

A LITTLE HISTORY

Historically, there is much more information on male homosexuality
than there is on lesbianism. During the 1940s, male homosexuality
was the subject of several scandals. The first to receive wide attention was the discovery that young students in a military high school
were participating in "homosexual orgies." It was in the late 1940s
and early 1950s that the legal sanctions against homosexuals were
introduced.

For decades, Argentinians have lived with a series of short-lived
governments—both civil and military. Always there has been some
form of institutionalized repression of homosexuality. One civil government (in the late 1950s and early 1960s) perpetrated sweeping
campaigns against "immorality," which included the detention of
heterosexual couples for kissing in the parks, raids on hotels, the
closing of public bathrooms, and the systematic detention of lesbians
and gay men. When a military government took power in 1966, an
identical policy was continued.

Tolerance of homosexuals increased slightly in the early 1970s,
when through police payoffs, a few discreet bars were permitted to
operate, although always under the threat of a raid. This easing of
repression coincided with the formation of the FLH (Homosexual
Liberation Front), a movement which focused on consciousness-
raising among lesbians and gay men. The organization was never
able to grow beyond its underground status.

Between 1973 and 1975, the atmosphere in Argentina became

increasingly chaotic as certain groups of both the left and the right took up arms. During this period, right-wing terrorist groups for the first time began to threaten homosexuals directly. In July 1973, a poster appeared throughout Buenos Aires, bearing the slogan: "Against the ERP [People's Revolutionary Army, an armed left-wing group], homosexuals, and drug addicts." The left responded with the slogan: *No somos putos, no somos faloperos"* (We aren't faggots, we aren't junkies). Physically attacked by the right, getting little support from the left, the FLH continued to exist, and there was some measure of solidarity among lesbians and gay men.

In March 1976, another military coup took place, bringing with it the most repressive regime that has existed in Argentine history. General Videla was named "President." A state of siege was declared; the police and military were given nearly unlimited powers. The immediate and extreme repression that followed extended, of course, to the lives of lesbians and gay men. Some women's experiences at the time of the coup and after are recounted below.

LOOKING FOR A PLACE

During the months that preceded the coup, there were heated discussions among the large groups of people who gathered in downtown Buenos Aires to read the news of the moment on official bulletin boards in front of the offices of the major daily newspapers. People argued over the pros and cons of the coup, which was known to be imminent, and about what would happen afterward.

It was in just such a crowd of people discussing the news of the day that Sara and Mónica first met. Both women worked in offices downtown. They soon discovered they had more to talk about than just the news, the humidity, and their jobs. A beautiful love grew between them, flourishing from one conversation to the next.

Mónica lived with her family on the outskirts of the city. Her parents, conservative Catholics clinging to local customs, hoped that their daughter would marry a nice, good-looking, hardworking Catholic boy.

Sara had come to the capital from the interior of the country after she finished high school. Like many young people, she sought a better intellectual and economic situation, hoping both to help out her family and to make a life for herself. Sara brought with her a certain uneasiness as well. She lived in a pension for young ladies in Flores [a district of Buenos Aires]. She knew she was not like the other women there—always in curlers or waiting for their boyfriends to call at eight o'clock.

As everyone expected, the coup occurred—in the wee hours of the night of March 24. In spite of many difficulties, Sara's and Mónica's romance, and their daily lives, continued.

One Friday evening they met after work and decided to go to dinner. Until this point, almost nothing physical had happened between them—a kiss or two in the bathrooms of cafés or at the movies. But love is stronger than fear. That night they began to wander, looking for a place that would shelter them. They didn't notice the military and police patrols, or that there were still tanks in front of the government buildings. They kissed on a deserted corner in a traitorous darkness. Without their noticing, a man began to follow them.

They arrived at the neighborhood of Buenos Aires that abounds in family hotels—"decent" places that only require that patrons be of age and have their documents. Mónica and Sara anticipated no difficulties when they went into one of these hotels. Without questions, they were given a room. It seemed a perfect place to know each other completely, leaving behind taboo and prejudice. Then came a knock on the door. It was the owner of the hotel. They got dressed quickly, and found that they wouldn't be permitted to stay there. They asked why, since they had paid, but the owner gave little explanation—only that a policeman had spoken with him. The cop was now outside, standing on the corner.

They didn't realize the danger. They only wanted to be left in peace. They crossed the street and entered another hotel, which faced the first. A few seconds later, the plainclothes cop came in. He identified himself and asked for their documents. "Come with me," he said, "because you're under arrest." Again, the familiar question: "Why?" The immediate response: "A police patrol saw you kissing on a street corner. They told me; I followed you."

Nervous though she was, Mónica began talking. She told the cop that her father was a retired member of the Federal Police. This news seemed to soften the cop, Rodríguez, a little. Nonetheless, they kept walking. They came to a plaza, and the three of them sat down. What would happen? The cop kept saying what they were doing was prohibited, and he repeated all the familiar prejudices, slogans, and official edicts against homosexuals. Mónica retorted that heterosexuals weren't as perfect as they might appear.

Rodríguez offered a further argument. He said that because of the situation in the country at that moment, the street was dangerous; everyone is suspect.

Mónica answered, "Us suspect? How? We're not mixed up in politics; we don't go to the university. . . ." [University students are automatically considered suspect, since they are frequently involved in political activity. This means that there are many students among the disappeared.]

Sara, meanwhile, remained silent. She spoke only when the cop asked her something. She thought of the scandal at the pension when they found out she was in jail. Both she and Mónica would lose their jobs. Despite these bleak prospects, there was something that brought the two women closer together with no regrets.

At that moment, a police van pulled up and a lot of heavily armed, uniformed police got out and went into a restaurant on a nearby corner.

"Look at that," said Rodríguez. "Lucky thing for you it was me that got you, 'cause if one of those uniformed guys stops you, he won't think twice about beating you with his billy club, and he'll rape you to boot."

No one spoke for a few moments. Then the cop asked where they lived, saying he'd take them home in a taxi. This change of attitude was a great relief. Sara preferred to go with Mónica, who lived further away.

It was very late when they got to Mónica's house. Her family was furious, but nothing mattered after what they'd been through. They made love, forgetting Rodríguez and the rest of the nightmare. It was not until the next day that they realized how difficult it is to find a place for oneself. There was danger lying in wait, and relentless paranoia, wherever they might be.

REPRESSION SINCE 1976

Buenos Aires still has the appearance of an occupied city: Two heavily armed policemen stand on every street corner, there are innumerable plainclothes agents belonging to a variety of different organizations, and the streets are incessantly patrolled.

In order to crush guerrillas, the left, and all political and social opposition, the government has constructed a gigantic security apparatus which has come to be used for the strict control of the population in general. This powerful political-military machine seems to have a life of its own. Once its primary enemies have been exterminated, it turns to less obvious victims, creating a constant daily terror. It now operates against everything and everyone it considers suspect.

Since 1976, homosexuals have been a target for systematic persecution. The ideological repression is severe. Any reference by the media that might be interpreted as an apology for homosexuality, contraception, or extramarital relations is strictly prohibited by law. In the radio and television industry, a list circulates which prohibits or discourages the presentation of notorious homosexuals. Censorship extends to printed material as well. These controls are part of the "morality" campaign to which the regime is committed—an extreme version of what it calls "Western Christian" ideology.

In 1977, in the Conference on Social Pathology at the University of Buenos Aires, homosexuality was defined as a congenital disease. This definition sets the tone for all published texts and other material to be considered "permissible."

A clear example of how repression works against the homosexual community was the "housecleaning" that took place in 1978 when the World Cup Soccer Championship was played in Argentina. Since this was an international event, with a huge public-relations budget, the police carried out an operation for the removal of all "undesirable" people from public view. With sophisticated electronic equipment, the police were able to identify numerous people they considered suspicious, including lesbians and gay men.

The existence of gay bars and discos was always more or less illegal in Argentina. In 1978 these were shut down, and they are virtually unknown today, even as clandestine gathering places. Their existence before 1978 was always dependent upon monetary "arrangements" between their owners and certain police and military factions, which "protected" them Mafia-style. After a short period of tolerance, a bar would usually be raided by the police or army, who took prisoner everyone they found there. In this context, all socializing becomes very risky, and even holding a private party becomes a bold action.

Uniformed police and plainclothes agents of the Department of Morality, in charge of sexual offenses, relentlessly patrol all parts of the city, looking for people who appear to be lesbian or gay. Often, when making arrests, they justify these by citing "subversion" or possession of drugs.

In the lectures given at schools (directed at the parents of high school students), the refrain is often repeated, "Subversion is not only planting a bomb or distributing a pamphlet; subversion is everything that seeks to subvert the norm; premarital sex, abortion, drugs, homosexuality, etc."

In its zeal to eradicate such "subversion," the federal police force provides special courses for its officers, teaching them to recognize gay men and women (through gestures, etc.) on the street. What is worse, policewomen and -men also learn to impersonate lesbians and gay men and then infiltrate the already tenuous community. This introduces an element of paranoia and distrust in every social interaction, impeding the growth of a basic respect for one's fellow human. It is an atmosphere which promotes false mannerisms and attitudes in the constant effort to cover a deeper lesbian or gay identity.

Lesbians face many problems not shared by their gay brothers. It is women who find few, if any, models with which to identify. The sensational press regularly features articles about crimes of passion among gay men, arrests at parties and corruption of minors, etc. In *porteño* slang and humor, there is no problem in mentioning relations between men.

But lesbianism is shrouded in silence. Each woman faces her feelings alone, uncertain whether any other women share her needs and desires. Not knowing what may reveal one's "difference" to the rest of the world, Argentine lesbians must be cautious in the smallest details—clothing, gestures, speech, and even gait. There have been cases where women recognized as lesbians have been fired from their jobs (under other pretexts). In a country with high unemployment, economic problems are the most severe for women, especially for those who choose independence from men.

It must be remembered also that psychological theorists and practitioners are far more ready to condemn lesbianism, and female sexuality in general, than any variation of male sexual behavior. This is also true of the Church and of society in general.

CONCLUSION

In spite of this gloomy climate, woman do form strong bonds, work together in groups, and resist the regime that seeks to crush them. The Mothers of the Plaza de Mayo work tirelessly on behalf of their daughters and sons who "disappeared" after being kidnapped or arrested and tortured during the waves of repression. These women work publicly, with the support of many international organizations.

Other organizations of women, such as the DIMA (Equal Rights for Argentine Women) and the Argentine Feminist Organization, recently presented publicly a document that calls for the removal of the law of Patria Potestad, which gives fathers complete authority over their children, wresting from the mother all such rights.

There are also groups of lesbians, although these women must do their work underground, who collaborate on small publications and work toward achieving a true community of lesbian women in the future. Gay men also help in this struggle for human survival.

In addition to the military regime's flagrant violations of human rights, Argentina today has a staggering rate of inflation, unprecedented unemployment figures, and a bankrupt national economy.

It is because of these conditions that we need the cooperation of all sisters and brothers, and of everyone who wishes to join this struggle and who, because of the political and historical circumstances in which they happen to live, are able to express their ideas more freely than we. The right to love and the right to freedom must not continue to be ignored or withheld.

CUBA

Cuban policy on homosexuality has been and continues to be the focus of a long-standing debate. Many who support the Cuban revolution are willing to ignore or justify the official government policy, which clearly infringes on the rights of gays, while many in the anti-Castro camp utilize Cuban policy as ammunition to condemn roundly everything Cuban that has appeared on the island since Batista's fall from power. In the following article, taken from the IGA (International Lesbian and Gay Association) *Pink Book 1985,* the authors take a coolheaded look at the history of Cuban policy regarding gays and, as importantly, recent developments that point to a possible softening in the official stance.

"We Cannot Jump Over Our Own Shadow," by Henk van den Boogaard and Kathelijne van Kammen, from *IGA Pink Book 1985.*

"I have never judged people on the grounds of their sexual preference, but I have also never realized that because of their sexual preference people are discriminated. I was aware of discrimination against poor people, this made me fight against hunger and illiteracy. During the past time I have become more aware of the suffering of and the discrimination against homosexuals." Professor Lajonchere, member of the Cuban National Committee on Sexual Education (G.N.T.E.S.), during a visit to the Netherlands in June 1984.[1]

By now it has become a matter of common knowledge that homosexuals have a hard life in Cuba. Much has been said and

written on this subject.[2] Before we discuss the positive changes
that may continue to be developing in the future, we would like
to take a look at the past and the present situations.

TROPICAL CUBA: 1959–84

Cubans themselves often explain the negative attitude toward homosexuality by referring to the situation before 1959. Cuba, a sunny
island near the coast of the United States of America, was very
popular with Americans as a holiday resort. Tourism was linked
closely with existing prostitution, pornography, and gambling. Even
today many Cubans connect homosexuality with prostitution and
American exploitation. To us this view seems to be too simple.

In the first place, it is probable that heterosexual and homosexual
behavior was more evident in urban, tourist-linked surroundings
than in the rest of Cuba, which in this respect is still characterized
by restraint and sense of shame. That does not alter the fact that
homosexuality was of course also part of everyday practice in "normal" Cuban society, albeit much more on the sly, or if you wish, in
a more discreet way.

In the second place, there is almost no factual data with respect
to the existence and shape of a homosexual subculture before 1959,
in contrast with the existence of data on heterosexual prostitution
in those days. Thus, referring to the present discrimination of homosexuals on the basis of the past in the fifties is nothing more than
a partial explanation.

Sometimes it is said that after the triumph of Castro the situation
deteriorated drastically for homosexuals. It is dubious to represent
the situation as if the Revolution had immediately developed and
pursued a consistent policy concerning homosexuality. Its leaders
had different priorities, such as setting up a public health service,
fighting illiteracy, and defending the country against resistance present at home and abroad. That does not alter the fact that in a

climate which was hostile to homosexuals, a number of leaders were not stopped when they tried "to solve" what they considered to be the "gay problem." Thus, in 1961 the Secretary of State for Home Affairs, Ramiro Valdés, set up a police raid under the name of "Operación P"; prostitutes, pimps, and pederasts were taken off the streets in the red-light districts. " 'Operación P' was the first wide-scale, socialist raid of the Cuban Revolution"[3] according to Carlos Franqui, who was one of the activists within the Revolution at that time. His book is one of the few testimonies which shed light on the views concerning homosexuality held by revolutionary leader-ship. According to Franqui, Valdés' action was taken for the purpose of curtailing the influence of homosexuals in the fields of art, cul-ture, and education. This influence was considered to be at variance with revolutionary morals. The fact that the revolution did not stand in the way of such actions signified an important break with the situation before 1959: "Prejudice typically surfaced; form of cruel jokes; words, but not actions. To laugh at a homosexual, yes, but to arrest or to torment him, no."[4]

These acts against homosexuals can be considered part of action taken against anything that was thought to be at variance with socialist morals. In 1961 the movie *PM,* directed by Orlando Jiménez Leal, was prohibited on these grounds as well. The movie, which had nightlife in Havana as its subject, was thought to be sensational and to contribute nothing to the Cuban development. Recently Nestor Almendros, formerly the film critic of *Bohemia,* stated in an interview[5] that he was fired at the time because of an enthusiastic article he had written about the movie. In connection with this movie, Fidel Castro said his "Words for the Intellectuals": "Within the Revolution, complete freedom; against the Revolution, none."[6] The speech was intended to put an end to the cultural confusion which was a result of the recent Revolution as well. However, confusion about what was and what was not allowed in the area of culture remained. Thus, even while the Italian movie *La Dolce Vita* was being shown in Cuban cinemas in 1963, it was considered in Western Europe a symbol of sexual liberation.

Within the framework of the same campaign against behavior considered to be at variance with socialist morals, prostitutes were sent to reeducation camps; since May 1965, purges *(depuraciónes)* had been carried out at universities; and finally, in September of the same year, Umap camps ("Unidades Militares para el Aumento del la Producción") were set up. These were at first established with a view to furnishing employment and reeducating youth, who though liable to military service, turned out to be unfit for the army because of their "moral views of life." In reality, however, undesirable persons, such as homosexuals, were interned.

At home and abroad protests were made against this treatment of homosexuals and the existence of the camps. The French philosopher Sartre described the Cuban situation as follows: "Cuba does not have Jews, but has homosexuals." Shortly after the Cuban Union of Writers and Artists (Uneac) had protested to Castro about the camps, in consequence of the fact that a few artists had to report themselves, the camps were closed. In 1967, during an interview with the American journalist Lee Lockwood, Fidel Castro said: "It would be wrong indeed, if a person was treated badly for something he could not do anything about" and "All of this shows the future need to take a closer look at problems concerning sexual relationships." [7]

Although in 1971 the Minister of Labor, Risquet, was still talking about "institutions for bums, thieves, or homosexuals," it is unclear whether he was referring to reeducation camps. [8] Much remains to be clarified with respect to the existence of such camps in the seventies.

Only now in the eighties are sexual relationships included in official policy. Attempts at defeating homosexuality continued to be the order of the day. Note, for instance, the position taken by the participants in the First National Congress on Education and Culture, organized in 1971. In the final statement it was pointed out with regard to homosexuality that "homosexual deviation depends on social pathology. Our principle is that we do not allow these manifestations in whatever way; one should prevent these manifestations from spreading. . . . Homosexual groups should be dispersed and in certain cases measures should be taken, but always for the purpose of prevention and aimed at reeducation."[9] In the end it was agreed that homosexuals were no longer allowed to work at places where they could come in contact with minors, and as well, "persons whose morals were at variance with the prestige of the revolution should be prevented from becoming members of delegations consisting of artists who are sent abroad."[10] According to Margaret Randall, a North American who knows Cuba thoroughly, the prejudices of the participants were determined especially by the fact that their education had not been very extensive, or as she called it "on a low cultural level." Nevertheless, the government acted upon proposals adopted by the congress. Homosexual teachers and students were removed from schools and universities. At training schools for educators special attention was paid to posture and looks during the selection of new students. As late as 1980 the headmistress of the training college for teachers Enrique José Varona in Havana said in an interview that "students with typical deviations, homosexuals, those with improper social behavior are not allowed. Given the characteristics of this profession—one has to be well balanced, emotionally speaking, stable, working educatively, working with adolescents at boarding schools—one has to proceed in a way which is particularly selective, this means that homosexuality cannot do. . . . Being homosexual itself is not the issue, but the influence they could have on minors."[11]

In the same year, 1980, together with others, more than 10,000 homosexual men and women left their country by way of the harbor of Mariel after a temporary stay on the site of the Peruvian embassy.[12] The official Cuban comment, which was printed in the daily newspaper Granma, ran as follows: "Even though in our country homosexuals are not persecuted or harassed, there are quite a few of them in the Peruvian embassy, aside from all those involved in gambling and drugs, who find it difficult to satisfy their vices here."[13] This gave rise to fierce homophobic reactions among the populations. Fierce homophobic reactions were also the result of the movie *Escoria* (Scum), which was shown in public cinemas. In this account of the situation on the site of the Peruvian embassy, the presence of homosexuals was hinted at very clearly by showing men who posed in a way thought to be unmasculine. It can be proved that reactions among the population led to "the harassment and persecution" of homosexuals. In a society in which polarization is so strong, with on the one hand the threat perceived as posed by homosexuals and on the other hand the aggression of the population, the government cannot follow a wait-and-see policy. In such a situation a wait-and-see policy is a definite policy.

ANTIHOMOSEXUALITY: RELIGION

How can the presence of such a strong hostility to homosexuals in Cuba be explained? As we have already seen, an explanation which only refers to the period before 1959 is not conclusive. Another part of the explanation is the influence of religion. Although the Roman Catholic Church has never been as powerful here as in other countries on this continent, its influence on sexual culture is evident. In this connection it is ironic that the original Cuban population, the Indians, were exterminated by Catholic Spanish conquerors who used arguments that were not all that different from those some Cubans use against their homosexual countrymen. "In order to justify the extermination [of the Indians] they accused the Indians of everything: They were homosexuals and promiscuous, awkward, and endowed with other vices so horrible that many of them are too wicked to be named." [14] The view that sexuality can only be seen in terms of procreation, the severe ban on masturbation, and threats of hell and damnation with respect to homosexuality, left their traces even four hundred years later. The message of the Protestant sects concerning sexuality was not any less puritanical. And then add to this the influence of beliefs which belonged to the imported slaves. "There are no basic contradictions between African and Spanish notions of sexual roles. A factor introduced by African culture seems to be the machismo of the Abakúa religion. The Abakúa believed in the inferiority of women and emphasized many of the traits associated with virility: pride, honor, bravery." [15]

ANTIHOMOSEXUALITY: MACHISMO

To a large extent these views determine present ideas concerning gender roles and the social organization of the sexes. This leads to a society marked by machismo, with its emphasis on dual morals for men and women. The macho society only knows men and women, and a man who does not behave according to prevailing ideas is not appreciated as a man. He is ridiculed by the community. The distinction between hetero-homo, as developed next to the distinctions made between men and women in Western European culture during the last hundred years, has not followed the same development in Cuba. Hence, the position of a Cuban homosexual (somebody whose masculinity is called into question) differs in several respects from the position of a Western European homosexual (a man who is homosexual and has a homosexual lifestyle).

Nevertheless, it seemed that the fate of traditional machismo would be sealed by the victory of the guerrillas in 1959 and the policy with respect to the sexes which has been pursued ever since. Present Cuban society advocates the equality of men and women, which implies that dual morals have to be given up. For women possibilities to work outdoors have been increased by better education and the development of institutions which replace the family, such as day nurseries. Moreover, in 1975, by adopting the Family Act, the government advocated equal division of household duties between husband and wife. However, the above concerns radical changes taking place within the heterosexual norm. The heterosexual norm as such was not brought up for discussion. Marriage and the family are considered as basics of the Revolution. The family is presented as the social unit for the satisfaction of "deeply rooted needs both in social respects and in terms of the affections of the individual." [16] On the basis of this line of thought, Article 34 of the Constitution says: "The State protects the family, motherhood, and marriage." [17]

Changing the traditional gender roles takes much time and effort, as can be seen in the Western countries. Although a final change in traditional gender roles does not necessarily imply the liberation of homosexual men and women, it can make a contribution to such liberation, as developments in the Western world have shown as well.

It is questionable how far Cuban socialism will go in the direction of this development. Like the heritage of religion, present-day views, which are suggested by socialism, put a clear mark on the social organization of sexuality. Since its coming into existence in the previous century, scientific socialism has never been friendly toward homosexuals, to put it mildly. Moreover, its starting point was that questions concerning sexuality would not come up for discussion until later; the class struggle had priority. In this sense, the situation in socialist Cuba is not exceptional, although it remains noteworthy to see that people who are willing to work for a society without oppression and discrimination maintain and advocate the very same oppression and discrimination when homosexuals are concerned. "This is not the persecution of homosexuals, but rather the destruction of their position, their influence. This is revolutionary hygiene." [18]

The Communist Party (PCC) and the Communist Youth Organization (UJC) do not allow membership to people whom they know or suspect to be homosexual. One has to be recommended by the "masses," and it seems that the population never recommends homosexuals. Apart from that, homosexuals are not welcome. Thus, "moral purity in public and private life" is required from every youth member. He or she is "to fight against every form of antisocial behavior, moral instability, and bad habits from the past." [19] Some observers point out that within the party there are tendencies to take a milder attitude toward homosexuals, but members are apprehensive of alienating themselves from the traditional attitude of the Cuban population, other Communist parties, and nations in the Third World. In this case definitely not a vanguard position!

MEDIA, CRIMINAL LAW, AND
SOCIAL ORGANIZATIONS

As the education of the masses is carried out by the media, in criminal law, and by social organizations, it is important to make some observations about them as well. The mass media are considered to be of utmost importance. They "form an integral part of the social system existing in the country. Their functions are of an educative, informative, organizational, mobilizing, orientative, and recreative nature." [20] As the already used example, the movie *Escoria* showed, the media does not attempt to stay antigay sentiments as they are felt by the population. In the course of 1979 and 1980, a series of articles written by Mario Kuchilan Sol appeared in the widely read magazine *Bohemia,* in which homosexuals were depicted as counterrevolutionaries. "They [homosexuals] all want to go to California, the most important residence of Ronald Reagan and a paradise for the sissies who not only have great economic power, but substantial political power as well, enough to influence the forthcoming presidential election." [21] In this way homosexuals are mentioned in one and the same breath with exploitation and North American imperialism. This testifies to irresponsible reporting in a country which is threatened so directly by the United States of America. Conscientious observers of the Cuban press could give many such instances.

CRIMINAL LAW

The way in which the government—as in other countries—defines, categorizes, and regulates sexuality is apparent in the penal code.[22] The Cuban society is based on the so-called family model: "The right to punish, entitled to the State, has made way for the duty of society to reeducate its criminal members and to reintegrate them in the community."[23] When combating criminal behavior, attention is paid to the personality of the individual in particular, as he or she is the cause of crime; for Cuba is "a society in which it is assumed that structural causes of crime have been removed."[24] This also means that of a lawyer—if he or she is needed and willing to take up the case of a homosexual—it is required that "his or her interferences with criminal procedures will contribute positively to the socialist education of the Cuban nation in general and the parties or suspects in particular."[25]

According to the letter of the law, homosexuality is not a penal offense, although public manifestations of homosexuality are punishable. Homosexuality is mentioned in Articles 353–59 of the Penal Code, which deal with "the offenses against the normal development of sexual relationships." Article 354 punishes "anyone who commits active pederastic acts, using violence or intimidation or taking advantage of the fact that the victim is not in full possession of reason or understanding or is not able to resist or is younger than 16 years," with a sentence of 5–20 years of imprisonment or capital punishment. Article 358 speaks of "public scandal." It mentions "imprisonment of 3–9 months and fines for among others anyone who (a) makes a public show of his homosexual condition or bothers others or incites to homosexual behavior; (b) commits homosexual acts in public or in private, where others could observe them involuntarily; (c) offends public decency by shameless manifestations or any other disgraceful act." Anybody who has been a witness can give notice of a "public scandal." This article makes behavior that can be interpreted as homosexual behavior a criminal offense. It will be clear to those who know Cuban street life that it is not always put into effect. Nevertheless, the threat is always present. Articles 367 up to and including 375 refer to minors of 16 years or younger. Thus, inciting or opportuning homosexual behavior with persons younger than 16 years is a criminal offense. Educators who do not prevent homosexual acts from occurring with children or who do not report them to the authorities are liable for punishment as well. Article 375 refers to those who have been convicted among other things on the basis of the above articles and excludes them from "educating or leading youth."

Especially the articles concerning "disruption of public order," Articles 76 up to and including 94 of the Penal Code are the "hatstand articles" upon which convictions for homosexuality are hung, although homosexuality is not mentioned explicitly. Article 77F considers "anyone to be disrupting public order through anti-social behavior, who violates or endangers the rules of the socialist society or interferes with the rights of others or frequently disturbs the order of the community usually by means of violent acts or words or gestures, or by other provocative or threatening means or his behavior in general." According to Cuban homosexuals in Cuba and abroad, it is particularly on the basis of this article that homosexuals are imprisoned for a period of 1–4 years. Moreover, a particular feature of the legislation concerning antisocial behavior is that it gives the government the opportunity to take action before an offense has been ascertained. It is clear that the Penal Code contains many possibilities to punish homosexuality under all circumstances.

Besides the Cuban Penal Code, there are also other official regulations against homosexuality. Thus, according to Ministerial Resolution 10 of 1978, homosexuals are not allowed to be doctors,[26] and Act 1166 of the labor legislation states that those who are involved in homosexuality at their place of work should be dismissed on the spot. During particular periods in Cuban history people were very actively persecuted, one method being police raids. It appeared that in certain cases the police made use of provocateurs as well.[27] It might be important to examine whether there is a connection between the harshness of action against homosexuals in Cuba and periods in which external threats increase.

SOCIAL ORGANIZATIONS

Social organizations play an active part in persecuting homosexuals, the Committees for the Defense of the Revolution (CDR) in particular. These committees, which were set up in every neighborhood, in every row of houses on the whole island, have to monitor all activity which could possibly be directed against the Revolution. The fear of counterrevolutionary activities, the threat of Northern American aggression, and the goals of the Revolution have as their consequence that anything which somewhat deviates from the usual can be considered to be against the Revolution. Particularly this social control influences the everyday life of homosexuals. When a CDR official "exposes" a homosexual the police can be called in or, on the basis of criminal law, preventive measures can be taken. Article 82 mentions reeducation and therapy in this respect. It seems that CDRs differ in the extent to which they persecute homosexuals. There are instances of neighborhoods where homosexuals live at peace with their committee; in others, the CDRs are extremely alert. That the CDRs play a key role in the persecution of homosexuals was also apparent in 1980. During the period of the exodus via the harbor of Mariel, those very committees reported homosexuals to the authorities with the intention of removing them from the neighborhoods.

LIFESTYLES FOR CUBAN HOMOSEXUALS

Homosexual men and women are extremely vulnerable due to leg-islation and the mentality of the major part of the population. Hence most of them lead "a double life" or are married in order to avoid suspicion. In most cases parents, friends, colleagues at school or at work do not know about their homosexuality, and it has to be concealed at the risk of complete isolation. According to some, homosexuals in the arts have less difficulty within their surround-ings. Perhaps this is true to a certain extent. It used to be—and to a less extent it still is—the case in the Western countries as well. "Culture was the place to go and the way out." [28] Some well-known homosexual writers, actors, ballet dancers, and sculptors, among others Alfredo Guevarra, former manager of the film institute Icaic, and the painter Portecarrero, are accepted officially. Homosexuals who are less artistically endowed or less politically protected still run the gauntlet.

Cubans living outside Cuba, such as Reinaldo Arenas, Herberto Padillo, Guillermo Cabrera Infante, Carlos Franqui, and Martha Frayde, talk about this subject in the documentary Mauvaise Conduite [Improper Conduct], financed by the French government. This movie was made by Nestor Almendros and Orlando Jiménez Leal, who have already been mentioned. The Cuban government rejected the documentary, because it was said that homosexuals were not discriminated against by the government in Cuba, and the movie was intended to discredit Cuba. [29] Something which might suggest that this documentary should be viewed with caution is the fact that its producers left Cuba a considerable time ago, do not report on recent developments, and certainly did not have the intention to draw a well-shaded picture of Cuba. Moreover, it is important to take seriously a remark made by Steve Jensen in his article "The Anger of Exiles": "The film focuses so narrowly on its exile-witnesses that the Cuba it describes exists in a vacuum." [30]

It will be clear that when homosexuals are compelled by necessity to lead a double life and that when there are no possibilities to organize, that by implication, there are also hardly any possibilities for setting up friendship circles or relationships, or for living together, let alone for developing a homosexual lifestyle, something which has become so characteristic of the homosexual scene in the West, particularly during the last twenty years. As of this moment it is impossible to develop a homosexual subculture in Cuba. Because of the always present possibility of police raids and the hostile reactions of the population, meeting places for homosexuals change constantly and courage or indifference is required in order to run the risk of being spotted at those places. Apart from the impossibility for homosexuals to develop a homosexual lifestyle, fierce anti-homosexuality has an influence on the lives of all men and women. The pressure of heterosexuality and being forced to conform to roles, together with the fear and uncertainty of deviation, affect everybody.

When meeting Cuban homosexual men and women, it seems to us that most of them have adopted the prevailing sexual ideology of how men and woman ought to behave. To take a different stand is almost impossible when one is not acquainted with the developments and practice in other parts of the world or in other periods in history. Many homosexuals consider their homosexuality to be a personal fate, a coincidence, a strictly personal matter. It might be possible that a number of homosexuals go to a psychiatrist "of their own accord" for this reason. Cubans, homo- and heterosexuals, are hardly equipped to make an analysis of how both homosexuality and antihomosexuality are part of the social organization of sexuality. This might be explained as being an element of underdevelopment as well. Although this article makes explicit statements particularly pertaining to (homosexual) men, much of what has been written also applies to lesbian women.

Developments in the West have shown the way in which science played and plays a big part in frustrating and liberating homosexuality. With respect to the latter, especially the activities of homosexuals themselves have been of great importance. We would like to conclude this article by giving an indication of how perhaps by academic interference with homosexuality a dark chapter of Cuban history could close. In 1967 Fidel already stated, "I believe that people get acquainted with new conceptions and ideas as a result of more scientific development, cultural progress, and the rejection of certain prejudices."[31] In 1971 the congress pointed to the necessity of solving this "complex problem on the basis of a thorough study which should indicate measures to be taken" as well.[32]

With the National Committee on Sexual Education (GNTES)—set up in 1977 and led by Professor Lajonchere and Dr. Monika Krause—an important step seems to be taken. What are the reasons for starting sexual education just now? In the seventies it was noticed that with changes in the social-economic structure, changes in values, norms, and behavior concerning sexuality and relations had remained behind. Thus, the economic independence of women, their entrance into education, and the wide availability of contraceptives led to an enormous increase in the number of divorces; to pregnancies and abortions at a very young age, to generation conflicts, and to confusion about gender roles. The GNTES was instructed to examine the present situation, to develop new concepts; to compile and to distribute informative material; and to educate "cadres," physicians, psychologists, and pedagogues in the field of sexuality and relationships. The committee makes great use of the media, and the interest of the population in its activities is enormous. GNTES has a permanent status at the highest level of the state, is connected to the Cuban parliament (Poder Popular), and is assisted by the Ministry of Public Health (Minsap) and the women's organization (FMC). From outside Cuba it is supported by the United Nations, the International Planned Parenthood Federation, scientists from the GDR, and friendly persons and agencies from the West.

Although Lajonchere and Krause emphasize that homosexuality is not the most important part of the program, it definitely is a striking part if we consider that the view they advocate is diametrically opposed to what have been the prevailing views up till now.

The introduction of new ideas is a difficult thing to accomplish, as developments in Western countries have shown as well. All too often wrong views have been replaced by views no less wrong. Although at first they seemed to be a "redemption" for homosexuals, finally they turned out to be nothing more than a new form of control over homosexuality, even human sexuality. GNTES considers the difficult position of homosexuals to be a problem for the entire population. Lajonchere: "Thus, our work is not primarily aimed at homosexuals themselves, but especially at heterosexuals, that they understand that homosexuals exist and how they live. On a medium-range basis our aim is for a more rational attitude toward homosexuality to arise among the population. The first thing we did was to do away with myths around homosexuality. The myth which says that homosexuality is taught by bad education or instruction and that it thereby becomes the responsibility of the family to make sure that there are no homosexuals. Another myth, which existed and which very many psychologists shared, is that it is curable and that it thereby becomes the responsibility of physicians to make sure that there are no homosexuals. Yet another myth which has been done away with was that there was no reason to consider it an innate quality."[33] During conversations with a psychiatrist,[34] who incidentally stated that she classified homosexuals according to international norms as formulated by the World Health Organization (WHO), it became evident that indeed attempts are made to "cure" homosexuals. Monika Krause is of the opinion that this as well is a matter of ignorance. "Sometimes it can be successful to make homosexuals conform and by using coercion to make them live as heterosexuals, but this does not mean that they are cured."[35] In addition, she did not avoid stating that attempts to cure homosexuals are criminal acts. As of this moment the committee does not work together with homosexuals—and preeminent experts in their situation—because up till now homosexuals have not made or have not dared to make contact with them, and according to Krause, "Because of prejudice and homophobia it would work the wrong way." [36]

Since 1979 a number of handbooks—translated from GDR—on sexual education have been published in which mention is made of homosexuality. The first book, *Men and Women in Intimacy*, written by the GDR sexologist Schnabl, gave rise to much discussion, particularly in connection with Chapter 10, on homosexuality. Krause writes in her thesis about this: "Chapter 10 was criticized heavily by many readers. In this way the prevailing, disproportionate interference and concern with the problem of homosexuals became visible. The leadership of the committee had taken such a reaction into account and yet decided not to omit this chapter, but to bring about a revision of anachronistic, unscientific views, prejudices, and taboos and work gradually toward a tolerant, scientifically based, and objective attitude on the part of specialists and the whole population." [37] Lajonchere: "We realized that the moment had come when we would have to talk about these kinds of things." [38] Although several statements in Chapter 10 confirm prejudices or are dubious, Cubans can also read: "Scientists tried to discover physical characteristics and behavioral patterns, but they have been unable to bring them together systematically. Typical homosexuals do not exist." [39] For the first time since 1959, this new way of thinking was carried through in subsequent publications. In contrast with the first, the next edition was increased by hundreds of thousands of copies and was available to the whole population. "However, one thing is clear which must be understood by all and that is that it does not depend upon the will of the person to know to which sex he or she feels him or herself to be sexually attracted to. That is why it would be wrong to disqualify a homosexual solely on the grounds of sexual orientation and to interpret this orientation as a character weakness, something that many people still do, alas, on the basis of the presence of ignorance, miscomprehension, and prejudice." [40] About homosexual youth it is stated that: "It is necessary to avoid situations in which those youth become the target of mockery or persecution out of miscomprehension or ignorance."[41] For Cuba, where many parents say that they would rather have a dead child than a homosexual child, this is indeed a statement of great significance.

The authors of those books from the GDR do not unequivocally oppose research on the causes of homosexuality with a view to possibly curing or preventing homosexuality in the future, as is carried out by their countryman Dorner. According to Lajonchere and Krause, this kind of research is indeed necessary to convince the population of the inevitability of the existence of homosexuals and to prove that a person is not homosexual out of free will, but that he or she is "like that."

Cuba is a developing country, and for several reasons it is deprived of the more recent developments in the field of science. To become cognizant of recent developments in the field of homosexuality in the West, Krause and Lajonchere spent two weeks in the Netherlands in June 1984. Their visit was the result of already existing contacts with the Dutch Committee on Sexuality in Cuba of Venceremos.[42] During their stay, Krause and Lajonchere had conversations with scientists, social workers, members of gay caucuses within political parties, and with action groups such as the COC. More personal conversations were held with those who are directly involved with what it means to be homosexual, homosexuals and people married to or the parents of a homosexual child. In this way at least these two Cubans, authorities in this field in their country, have had an opportunity to hold conversations with homosexuals in an atmosphere of openness and frankness, which is apparently impossible in Cuba at this moment.

It seems that within the GNTES there is willingness to deny no longer that homosexuality is a part of human sexuality. About the outcome of its goals not much can be said. Certainly in the case of Cuba this depends on many national and international factors. It is clear that as in the Western countries the struggle will be tough. For Cuban homosexual men and women who carry the burden of homosexual discrimination the truth of Krause's words that much time is needed is all too sad. "We cannot jump over our own shadow." [43]

NOTES

1. Conversation at the head office of the Dutch Communist Party (CPN), Amsterdam (June 14, 1984).

2. See, among other things, Allen Young, *Gays Under the Cuban Revolution* (San Francisco: Grey Fox Press 1981); Boogaard, Henk van den. *Homoseksualiteit: ideologie en Politiek/Cuba* (Amsterdam: SUA, 1982), and the documentary made by Netor Almendros and Orlando Jiménez Leal, *Mauvaise Conduite* (Paris, 1983).

3. C. Franqui, *Retrato de familia con Fidel* (Barcelona: Seix Barral, 1981).

4. Ibid.

5. *The Advocate* (July 10, 1984).

6. Mentioned in K. S. Karol, *Guerillas [sic] in Power* (New York, 1970).

7. Lee Lockwood, *Castro's Cuba, Cuba's Fidel; an American Journalist's Inside Look at Today's Cuba in Text and Picture* (New York: Macmillan, 1967).

8. M. Looney, "Social Control in Cuba," in *Politics and Deviance* (London, 1973).

9. *Final Statement of the First National Congress on Education and Culture* (Havana, 1971).

10. Ibid.

11. Havana (October 20, 1980).

12. From *Unity*, magazine of the Universal Fellowship of Metropolitan Community Churches (September/October 1980).

13. *Granma* (April 7, 1980).

14. H. Thomas, *Cuba: The Pursuit of Freedom* (London: Eyre & Spottiswoode, 1971).

15. L. Salas, *Social Control and Deviance in Cuba.*

16. *Código de Familia* (Havana, 1975).

17. *Constitución de la República de Cuba* (Havana, 1982).

18. Samuel Feijóo in *El Mundo* (April 1965).

19. *Unión de Jóvenes Comunistas, Estatutos* (Havana, 1977).

20. *Cuban Women* (Havana, 1980).

21. *Bohemia* (August 22, 1980).

22. *Código Penal* (Havana, 1979).

23. J. J. de Jonge and A. v. d. Plas in *Recht en Kritiek* (Amsterdam, 1981).

24. Ibid.

25. Ibid.

26. *Gaceta oficial de la República de Cuba* (Havana, January 13, 1978).

27. L. Salas.

28. D. Cohen and R. Dyer, "The Politics of Gay Culture" in *Homosexuality: Power and Politics,* ed. Gay Left Collective (London: Allison and Busby, 1980).

29. *Granma—resumen semanal* (from June 11, 1984) and in the Nicaraguan newspaper *Nuevo Diario* (July 12, 1984).

30. *The San Francisco Bay Guardian* (June 27, 1984).

31. L. Lockwood.

32. *Final Statement of the First National Congress on Education and Culture* (Havana, 1971).

33. Havana (December 23, 1982).

34. Havana (February 23, 1984).

35. Amsterdam (June 15, 1984).

36. Ibid.

37. *Vorbereitung de junge Generation auf Liebe, Ehe und Familie in der Republik Kuba* (Rostick, GDR, 1983) (not published).

38. Havana (December 23, 1982).

39. Dr. S. Schnabl, *El Hómbre y la Mujer en la intimidad* (Havana, 1979).
40. Dr. S. Schnabl, "En defensa del amor" (Havana, 1981).
41. H. Bruckner, *¿Piensas ya en al amor?* (Havana, 1981).
42. Venceremos, Dutch Society of Friendship with Cuba.
43. Nijmegen, the Netherlands (June 12, 1984).

IRAN, THE MIDDLE EAST, AND NORTH AFRICA

The article that follows, written by Rex Wockner, constitutes what is certainly a pioneering effort in English-language journalism into the investigation of contemporary homosexual behavior and attitudes in the Arab and Moslem worlds. Mr. Wockner is a staff reporter at *Outlines,* a Chicago-based gay/lesbian newsmagazine, and founder of Outlines News Service, which feeds hard news to forty-five gay and lesbian newspapers across the United States and in ten other countries. This article originally appeared in *Outlines, BLK, The Weekly News* (Miami), and *Capital Gay* (London).

The article is to be commended in several ways. First, Mr. Wockner is highly informative, and he adds credibility to his material by soliciting input from such authoritative sources as ILGA (the International Lesbian and Gay Association); Amnesty International; and Dr. Jeanette Wakin, a lecturer in Islamic Studies at Columbia University. Second, the article utilizes the testimony of men and women from the Arab and Moslem worlds. Given the pervasive fear of being "found out" and the need for anonymity, seemingly characteristic of Arabic and Moslem gays and lesbians, even when living abroad, this is no small accomplishment. Third, Mr. Wockner remains respectful of the differences in cultural context not only between the West and the Arab and Moslem world, but among the latter countries as well.

However one may decide to interpret homosexual behavior in Iran, the Middle East, and North Africa after reading the article, it would be hard to disagree with Robert Bray's statement, cited by the author in concluding: ". . . I see the real question as one of sexual freedom, and sexual freedom transcends cultures. The movement for gay freedom is [about] affirmation and visibility and living your life in truth."

"Homosexuality in the Arab and Moslem World," by Rex Wockner, from *Outlines, BLK, The Weekly News* (Miami), and *Capital Gay* (London).

In the aftermath of the Persian Gulf War, gays and lesbians are wondering aloud about their brothers and sisters in the Arab and Moslem world.

The questions Western gays and lesbians have are difficult to answer, since there are no gay/lesbian organizations anywhere in the region save for Israel, which has a Western-style gay community and movement.

But a journalist can piece together a sketchy picture with help from immigrants, the international gay press, human rights activists, and the few organizations interested in international gay/lesbian issues.

And there is at least one thing we can apparently say with certainty: Male homosexuality is very widespread—perhaps even ubiquitous—in the Arab and Moslem world. But it is rarely, if ever, a topic of conversation.

Sources familiar with the region insist that virtually all men have sex with other men throughout their lives. They all also get married and father children.

Since men, unlike women, are free to set their own schedules, their rendezvous take place in the evenings, at night, or on weekend trips together, immigrants say. Neither the wives nor anyone else ask any questions, even though the sexual status quo is "common knowledge."

"The topic never comes up," said one immigrant.

"It is no one's concern," said another.

"Such questions are just not asked—by anyone," added a third immigrant.

Lesbianism is all but invisible in the region, probably because of the extreme institutionalized sexism, by Western standards, of the Arab and Islamic world.

Still, sources familiar with the region believe that at least some women do have sex with each other. They would never consider themselves lesbians, however.

This is the first of two major dichotomies. The Arab and Moslem world is apparently one of the most homosexualized areas of the globe—especially among men—but there are few if any gays and lesbians.

The second dichotomy is this: In this highly homosexualized region, one also finds the world's harshest penalties for homosexual sex acts, ranging from a few years in prison to being thrown off a mountain or burned alive.

Homosexuality is often illegal under both civil and Islamic law, the latter calling for execution by any number of grisly means in some countries.

This can be traced to the Islamic Sharia code, a Koran- and revelation-based legal system roughly comparable to the Talmudic tradition in Judaism. There are numerous schools of thought in Sharia law, and penalties for homosexual acts vary from country to country (and sometimes within the same country).

The Koran is the Islamic Bible, composed of writings accepted by Moslems as revelations made to the prophet Muhammad by Allah (God) through the angel Gabriel. The Koran itself doesn't say anything about homosexuality, according to Dr. Jeanette Wakin, a senior lecturer in Islamic studies at Columbia University.

But religious lawyers have created extensive and detailed laws based on their study and interpretation of the Koran—much as Catholic canon lawyers do with the Bible.

One of the harshest versions of Sharia law is apparently in force in Iran, where evidence exists, which will be detailed below, that the fundamentalist Islamic government has been executing gays and lesbians for more than a year—chopping off their heads and stoning them to death, two of the many options permitted under Iranian Sharia.

Although it is not the case in Iran, often only gay-male sex is illegal under *civil* law. This is not because lawmakers are prolesbian. Rather, they consider women so inconsequential that they forget to include them in antigay legislation.

IN THEIR OWN WORDS: OVERVIEW

"Most Islamic cultures don't take kindly to organized homosexuality, even though male homoeroticism is deep within their cultural roots," says Lisa Power, cosecretary general of the International Lesbian and Gay Association.

"ILGA receives individual communications from a number of Arab countries, although not from countries where there are death penalties. But most people are far too nervous to organize, even in countries with a high level of homosexuality.

"For lesbians, it varies by country, but female sexuality is generally very sublimated," Power said. "Women in many Islamic cultures spend much of their time with other women, but sexuality only seems to be part of a woman when it's referring to men."

Jehan Agrama, an Egyptian lesbian who is president of the Los Angeles chapter of the Gay and Lesbian Alliance Against Defamation, has other suspicions. She believes there is significant woman-woman sex in the Arab world—although it certainly is not considered "lesbian."

"Women can have sex with other women and feel friendship and not necessarily identify as a lesbian," Agrama said. "I know people in Egypt who have these relationships and wouldn't even consider themselves bisexual. It's not part of the consciousness. Maybe the women are just enjoying their anonymity and having a ball.

"But as in all countries [of the region]," Agrama continued, "nobody goes around saying that they are lesbian—or gay either. There is no freedom to do that. It's very hypocritical since there's so much same-sex going on, especially men."

Trig Tarazi, a Palestinian born in Kuwait who now lives in Boston, agrees. "The Arab world is very much into the family unit," Tarazi said, "and men must fulfill their family role. But as long as they do that, they are free to do whatever else they want and this is not questioned.

"And since nobody talks about homosexuality, they don't have to fear somebody is going to say this—or even think this—about them. It's very strange to have men come up to you in bars and show you pictures of their kids and then say, 'OK, let's go [have sex] now,' " Tarazi continued. "To them, being gay is a sexual thing. It's not emotional. And the tiny minority who do see themselves as gay in the Western sense—as loving men—are frustrated; they feel oppressed the most.

"The rest of the men," Tarazi said, "are very comfortable. They think it's the best of all possible worlds. Since nobody recognizes homosexuality as even existing, they can get away with things we cannot get away with here. But if you start actually talking about homosexuality, they get very uncomfortable."

"Arab men realize they are bisexual," echoed John Elkholy, president of the Los Angeles chapter of the U.S. Gay and Lesbian Arabic Society. "They get married because of societal pressure, but they have flings with men throughout their lives. It's a pretty open thing. It's a macho thing, actually, for a man to have another man and be dominant or whatever."

Elkholy says that until the formation of GLAS/LA a year ago, "I thought I was the only Arab who was out of the closet in L.A. I had no one to talk to except for Hispanic people who have similar cultural background."

GLAS/LA now has 30 names on its mailing list, six of which are women, while the original GLAS chapter in Washington, D.C., boasts a mailing list of 182 individuals from around the nation.

But a discrete mailing list is a long step from public activism.

GLAS organizers said there were no recent immigrants on their mailing lists who would talk to reporters.

THE REPORTED IRANIAN "GENOCIDE"

Perhaps the situation in Iran is a good place to begin to understand the social-psychological terror that leads most Arab and Moslem gays and lesbians to remain closeted, even when they are thousands of miles away from their oppressive—and in some cases murderous —homelands.

There is evidence that for the past year Iranian authorities have been executing men and women found guilty of engaging in homosexual sex. This was first reported in January 1990 by U.S. columnist Jack Anderson. He wrote that according to his sources and shortwave radio broadcasts, "The medieval government of Iran celebrated the New Year [of 1990] by beheading homosexuals."

Anderson continued: "On New Year's Eve, Iran's Chief Justice Morteza Moghtadai held private discussions with lower judges and court officials to outline a new policy toward homosexuals.

"The religious punishment for the despicable act of homosexuality is death for both parties," Anderson quoted Moghtadai as saying.

Under Sharia, "the judge presiding over the case had five options for execution of homosexuals," Anderson detailed: "beheaded by a sword; stoned to death; thrown down from a height such as a mountain or tall building; die under the rubble of a wall demolished on their head; or burned alive."

Anderson said that three gay men were beheaded in the city square of Nahavand and two lesbians stoned to death in the city of Langrood on New Year's Day 1990.

Attempts to confirm Anderson's report were thwarted for months. U.S. interests in Iran are handled by the Swiss embassy. Several calls to different offices at the embassy were met with alarm. Press attaché Jean Daniel Bieler's response was typical.

"If it is not an administrative or practical matter, it is not possible to discuss it by telephone," Bieler interrupted. "We cannot speak about anything political on the telephone. You *must* understand." Bieler's voice inflections hinted that he was familiar with the topic, however.

In the meantime, the U.S. State Department's public-affairs adviser for Near Eastern and South Asian Affairs, George Malleck, agreed to order several computer searches through the department's Foreign Broadcast Information Service. "Nothing turned up, at least nothing that had been translated."

But Malleck suggested: "If Iran is bragging about this [antigay campaign] on [shortwave] radio, then it's probably true. Those people have committed so many offenses against common decency, you shouldn't be surprised that this is just one more group of people who have been chosen for the regime's ire. They kill lots of people for lots of reasons, none of which makes lots of sense."

Months passed with no more news on the situation of Iranian gays and lesbians until the British Broadcasting Corporation Monitoring Service, the intelligence-gathering wing of England's state radio and TV, picked up another shortwave broadcast from the Voice of the Islamic Republic, on May 18, 1990.

According to a BBC transcript, evidence that Anderson's report may have been accurate came during a replay of "a second Friday prayers sermon delivered at Teheran University May 18 by Ayatollah Musavi-Ardebili," one of Iran's key political and spiritual leaders.

"For homosexuals, men or women, Islam has prescribed the most severe punishments," Musavi-Ardebili said. "After it has been proved on the basis of Sharia, they should seize him (or her), they should keep him standing, they should split him from the head.

"He will fall down," the Ayatollah continued. "After he is dead, they bring logs, make a fire, and place the corpse on the logs, set fire to it, and burn it. Or it should be taken to the top of a mountain and thrown down. Then the parts of the corpse should be gathered together and burned. Or they should dig a hole, make a fire in the hole, and throw him alive into the fire. We do not have such punishments for other offenses.

"There cannot be the slightest degree of mercy or compassion toward those who observe inadequate Islamic dress or toward prohibitions. There should not be the slightest degree of mercy toward these criminals."

Musavi-Ardebili stressed the importance of developing an "antivice culture. . . . The people should learn to see evil to a degree that even the perpetrator of a vice should tremble with a tormented conscience after having committed that vice under the compulsion of physical desire," he said.

Columbia's Dr. Wakin was aghast when read Musavi-Ardebili's remarks, saying: "This is the opinion of a crazy man who is probably sublimating something. This is not the Sharia."

But Wakin acknowledged that different schools of Sharia lawyers have created varied interpretations of the Koran and religious tradition.

According to Amnesty International, the Iranian press reported the New Year's Day executions mentioned by Jack Anderson but did not link them to homosexuality per se.

"We have reports from the official Farsi press of the beheadings in Nahavand and Langrood," said Alice Miller, a lesbian who directs Amnesty USA's Death Penalty Program. "But according to the Iranian government, the three men were convicted of raping two [male] youth while drunk and the two women were convicted of 'spreading corruption,' 'prohibited things,' and 'adultery.' "

Miller said "prohibited things" often means drunkenness, while "adultery" can only be committed "by a married woman who has sex with a man who is not her husband."

"However," Miller continued, "Iran is executing 1,500 people a year and they're not terribly careful on what they get the persons for. They sentence you to death and kill you the same day, so we're basically reduced to just tracking executions."

(The conflict within Amnesty International on whether to adopt people imprisoned solely because they are gay or lesbian continues to rage and will be addressed again in September at a general meeting in Japan. At present, homosexuals jailed simply for being gay do not fall under Amnesty's definition of "prisoner of conscience" and are not eligible for assistance from the organization.

On the other hand, gay activists who have been jailed because of their activism have occasionally been adopted by Amnesty because their persecution was seen as a free-speech issue. Miller says the delay in adding homosexuals per se to the "prisoner of conscience" list results from religious objections by Amnesty members in Asian, African, and Islamic nations.)*

The latest word on the general social situation of Iranian gays comes from a Teheran gay man who recently immigrated to Sweden. "Mansour" left his home "after realizing that the religious and political pressure left me with no future opportunities."

"Every [man] in Iran is involved in male-to-male sex," Mansour said, "because premarital sex and sex outside marriage are not only a sin, but also very difficult [to find]. But being gay and having a gay identity is a Western phenomenon. [Iranian men] act in a very cliché male/female role. One is either the active or the passive partner. But all men are involved in male sex."

Mansour joined delegates to ILGA's annual conference last summer in Stockholm for a rowdy demonstration against Iran's reported murder of homosexuals. In a letter to the Iranian government, ILGA protested, "It is shocking that such ignorant, sadistic, and blood-thirsty behavior can be associated with any religion or group of people."

There was no response from Iran.

Another Iranian immigrant living in Sweden, "Farid," recently told the newspaper *Kom Ut* the antigay sentiment in Iran has become so severe that "No one feeling an attraction for someone of the same sex dares act on such a feeling [now.]

---

* At their meeting in Yokohama in September 1991, Amnesty International finally voted to adopt as prisoners of conscience those imprisoned for their homosexuality, including those arrested for homosexual acts. (Ed.)

"The Iranian ayatollahs do not merely condemn homosexuality, they are doing their utmost to root it out of Iran totally," Farid said.

Farid told *Kom Ut* that in the early 1980s, 70 gays and lesbians were tossed off a mountain, in accordance with the Sharia code, after they tried to start a gay/lesbian organization.

Sharia began to be enforced after the 1979 ouster of Shah Mohammad Reza Pahlavi, Farid said, adding that "In certain circles, it was rumored that the Shah was bisexual—that he met a young man he liked in Switzerland who followed him back to Iran [where] they lived together."

It was not possible to confirm Farid's mountain-execution report or the Shah's alleged homosexuality. It is also impossible to determine whether Farid is correct in saying that everyone is afraid to have gay sex now or whether Mansour is correct in saying everyone still does so.

KUWAIT

According to the *Spartacus International Gay Guide,* Kuwaiti men in search of sex with each other have long met in the saunas of the Kuwait Hilton and the Kuwait SAS Hotel—two of the hotels where Iraqi forces held American hostages—and at the beaches behind the Carlton Hotel, in front of the Sheraton Hotel, and near Central Park.

"In accordance with the Islamic Sharia code, homosexuality between men is prohibited and is punishable by death," the book reported. "One occasionally hears of executions; however, all cases that have become known were also mixed up with political crimes, which leads us to suppose that political opponents are denounced as homosexuals."

The national GLAS chapter in Washington has no Kuwaitis among its members who are willing to talk to reporters.

"Most had a very hard time contacting us in the first place," said GLAS founder Ramzi Zakharia. "They are way into the closet and most have never [read the gay press] and wouldn't know what [it] is."

ILGA also has no contact with open Kuwaiti gays or lesbians. Phone calls to Kuwait itself did not go through during the preparation of this report.

IRAQ

Homosexuality is not illegal in Iraq, according to *Spartacus* and ILGA's *Pink Book*. "The attitude toward gayness of the average Iraqi citizen is about as ambivalent as it could get," *Spartacus* said. "On the one hand, gays who have been exposed are . . . damned while on the other hand, secret gay activity is going on throughout the male population. . . . There are no magazines, bars, etc., in Iraq."

Again, neither GLAS nor ILGA knew of any gay/lesbian Iraqis who would talk to a reporter.

Meanwhile, Amnesty in December published a report on human-rights violations allegedly committed by Iraqi soldiers occupying Kuwait, including widespread incidents of male rape, especially of young men.

The report also detailed such tortures as "inserting bottle necks, sometimes when broken, into the rectum; tying a string around the penis and pulling it tightly; [and] pumping air using a pipe through the anus, particularly of young boys."

"It's the same appalling shit," said Amnesty's Miller. "The horrific rape of men detailed in this report is consistent with what we see all over the world—South America, Southeast Asia, and it's quite common to document this in the Mideast."

THE REGION AT A GLANCE

The social situation for homosexual men throughout the Arab and Moslem world would appear to be consistent with the themes presented by immigrants in this report, but punishment for gay sex acts varies widely—from none (officially) to short jail terms to execution.

Gay and lesbian sex is illegal in Saudi Arabia but "secret gay activity" is the norm, according to the *Spartacus* guide, which directs tourists specifically to the markets and shopping areas in the city of Jeddah.

Gay sex in Syria is punishable by three years in prison. Yet men reportedly meet at a bar, a coffee shop, a hotel, two movie theaters, six saunas, a park, a public garden, and two streets.

The smaller nations of the area—Oman, Qatar, the United Arab Emirates, and the reunited Yemens—also have varied "gay" life and varying antigay laws.

Oman permits three months to three years' imprisonment for gay *or lesbian* sex but sources say homosexuality is tolerated as long as it is confined to private spheres. Gay sex is illegal in Qatar but is said to be widespread—albeit in utter secrecy.

In the UAE, men who engage in homosexual acts can be sentenced to 14 years in prison, and anyone who admits to being gay —whether he acts upon his sexual orientation or not—is deemed "at odds with public morality" and can be jailed for two years. Still, it is considered normal for married and unmarried men to have sex with each other. Dubai, the capital, has six mixed bars and two cruisy areas.

Yemen (as distinguished from the former People's Democratic Republic of Yemen) formerly had a death penalty for "haad" offenses, which, according to Amnesty, "are offenses against the divine will." Prior to reunification, the Penal Code required that Sharia executions be done "without drama or torture"; for example: "be-

heading or shooting . . . although stoning may be used in some instances." Men in San'a, the capital, meet at three hotels and on
three cruisy streets.

NORTH AFRICA

An immigrant from Egypt describes the situation there for gays and
lesbians as "life-threatening." Hamdy Adham says clandestine gay
organizing has begun in Cairo and activists may soon invite "informal and discreet" support from outside the country. But homosexuality is taboo, he said, and the word "gay" is considered "an
insult."

Homosexuality is not illegal in Egypt, according to Amnesty, but
it is not talked about, and social control is rigid except in Alexandria. *Spartacus* says it is normal for Egyptian men to have gay sex
both before and during marriage, and lists as pickup spots a coffee
shop, a restaurant, four hotels, and six cruisy areas in Alexandria;
and two bars, three restaurants, a hotel, six saunas, three beaches,
and seven cruisy spots in Cairo.

Boston's Tarazi, who has traveled extensively in Egypt, says he
found gay life there more open than anywhere in the Arab world.
"It's a huge country," Tarazi said, "so you don't have the nosy-
neighbor attitude. There are bars that cater to gays in most major
hotels. I would call the gay scene almost 'thriving and open' but
Arab gays would never press the situation."

L.A.'s Agrama agreed. "There is a climate of permissibility in
Cairo, although the religious people are getting more powerful,"
she said. "But you go out at night, there's liquor, it's a wonderful
place for nightlife. No one comes home until dawn."

For men, Agrama said, "there's a distinction . . . between active
and passive sex. If you're passive, that's looked down on. But the
aggressor can be straight and then this is okay. Well, it's not exactly

condoned, but if you're going to do it, it's much better to be the active party."

Libya, which reported its first AIDS case last October, has some clandestine meeting places in Tripoli, including bars, movie theaters, and cruisy areas. But the Sharia code punishes homosexual acts by throwing the performer of the acts down from the highest level. Alternately, the civil Penal Code calls for three to five years in prison.

With the exception of Israel, the story throughout the remaining nations of North Africa and the Middle East is repetitious. Country by country, the reports from immigrants, *Spartacus,* ILGA, and Amnesty blur into common themes. The Islamic concept of tossing homosexuals off mountains, etc., is particularly ubiquitous.

It's no wonder that Arab men and women who somehow realize they are "gay"—despite the virtual nonexistence of the concept in their cultures—may attempt to emigrate to or study in the West.

But with the fear of total ostracization and/or the death penalty behind them, most Arab and Moslem emigrants still apparently stay close to their closet doors. As with millions of Westerners in more enlightened societies, the homophobic cultural and religious baggage is apparently just too heavy.

"An Egyptian friend of mine who came here about a month ago won't talk to anyone [about being gay]," said L.A.'s Elkholy. "They go into a society that is more open but they are still afraid that somehow coming out will go back to their families at home."

For Arab and Moslem gays and lesbians who never left home, multiply the fear level by a factor of about 100, immigrants say. And that is the bottom line on gays and lesbians in the Arab and Moslem world.

. . . Along with the near-universal availability of "straight" men who are willing to engage in insertive anal intercourse.

Is this hypocritical? Or a different world? Are these "straight" men really "gays" who are overdue for liberation? Or are humans by nature bisexual, with Arab and Moslem men better tuned into reality than Westerners? Probably all of the above.

Robert Bray, public information director for the U.S. National Gay and Lesbian Task Force and an officer in ILGA, says: "Certainly cultural differences make the definition and the shading of homosexuality different among peoples.

"But I see the real question as one of sexual freedom, and sexual freedom transcends cultures. The movement for gay freedom is [about] affirmation and visibility and living your life in truth.

"My personal experience in Morocco and southern Spain is that gay men—I didn't meet any lesbians—were somewhat stunned at the concept of gay political organizing and societal visibility, but at the same time they were envious—that we could walk around and be visible and tell our parents we are gay," Bray said.

"At least one guy expressed a longing to just be gay and not have to live within the prescribed sexual behaviors, and he said there were others like him.

"I believe this longing is universal.

"I sense it in Moslem culture and elsewhere around the world when people see me expressing joy at being openly gay."

CHAPTER TWO

NEW UNDERSTANDINGS (MANIFESTOS AND ANALYSES)

Gay liberation, as it developed after Stonewall in 1969, was influenced by a number of other political and social movements. From elements of the U.S. civil rights and antiwar movements, the New Left, and the May 1968 uprisings in France came an emphasis on direct action, coalition politics, the need to empower the disenfranchised, and a realization that only a total social and political revolution could bring about long-lasting and meaningful change. From the women's movement came the formation of consciousness-raising groups, the idea that the personal is political, and the understanding that traditional sex roles were a primary instrument in perpetuating oppression. In the United States especially, there was also a healthy distrust of political ideologies, whether they reflected the American two-party system or Marxist alternatives.

In countries with strong left-wing traditions, gay activists oftentimes saw their goal as the melding together of socialist thought and sexual politics. Thus in Western Europe and various Latin American countries, the gay liberation manifestos that emerged reflected an awareness of class consciousness and more likely than not placed gay oppression within a framework of capitalist exploitation. This is not to imply that acceptance by traditional Marxist parties was automatic; indeed, more often than not, the gay socialist groups were branded as divisive, "decadent," or just not taken seriously by the party ideologues.

Few individuals had as much influence on the development of gay liberation ideology as did Herbert Marcuse. His book *Eros and Civilization,* first published in 1955, and his various essays and teachings at American universities helped to popularize the concept of "polymorphous perversity." The idea is that we are born with various potentials, many of which are repressed during our socialization process. Which tendencies are repressed and which are encouraged to be developed is oftentimes the result of cultural conditioning. According to such a theory, we are all, for example, potentially bisexual human beings. However, in our sex-negative Judeo-Christian culture we are expected to repress the homosexual component that lies within ourselves. This has various consequences, depending upon our interpretation, but at the very least it can be maintained that we are crippled as a result. Theorists such as Hocquenghem in France, Altman from Australia, or Mieli in Italy argue, then, that such notions as "homosexual" or "heterosexual" do not describe categories of persons but rather components of our general sexuality. To create a healthier society, what is needed is to release the homosexual component in all people.

This understanding of sexuality—the need to liberate the homosexual element in all persons—was a basic ingredient of most gay liberation movements in the early 1970s. Indeed, some activists even discouraged a separate gay cultural identity from developing, fearing it would only serve to stigmatize certain people, unnecessarily marginalize them, and encourage their exploitation. However, as the New Left began to dissipate and as revolutionary movements and ideas either were effectively repressed or became co-opted, such lines of thinking by the mid-1970s were replaced by more limited, if not conservative, views. Political goals became more local and less global in character. Along with a lesbian and gay identity, gay ghettos appeared and thrived throughout much of Europe and North America. The struggle refocused more on practical demands, such as changes in antigay legislation, the struggle for civil rights, protection against discrimination, and finally the battle against AIDS.

In the preface to *La Cuestion Homosexual* by Jean Nicolas, Spanish theorists R. de Gaimon and Lubara Guilver give us a key to understanding the various tendencies in gay liberation struggles. They see within the movement three ideological trends: the *reformist*, the radical, and the revolutionary. The reformist encompasses the battle against repressive laws, and the struggle by gays to be granted recognition as equal citizens. It is a struggle by gays to integrate into middle-class society, adjust, and be accepted. Reformists will often live as couples in family units that ape but don't challenge traditional masculine and feminine roles. Gay men or lesbians who are too "obvious" are an embarrassment to them. Those involved in the radical tendency, according to these authors, share with the reformists a strong tie to "gay identity." They, however, see something inherently special in their status as gays, as if by their very existence, in subverting the "norm," they are revolutionaries. They choose to isolate themselves in ghettos, see transvestism as the most politically correct way to live as gays, and (talking of gay males) are often misogynist. Those ideas reflective of the revolutionary tendency reject a gay identity and understand the core problem to be the repression of homosexuality in all of society. The true struggle for revolutionaries is, in conjunction with the women's movement, workers, and the socially marginalized (alcoholics, the disabled, the mentally ill, drug addicts), combating sexism, phallocracy, and heterosexism. Sex roles are criticized (active/passive, masculine/feminine, etc.), as are the nuclear family and marriage. In this revolutionary schema, the ghettoization of gays must end, whether it be the golden ghettos of commercial exploitation (baths and bars) or the furtive ghettos of public toilets, parks at night, and movie theaters. This analysis, written in 1978, still offers valuable insight, especially when examining gay life in Western Europe, the United States, Canada, Australia, and such Latin American countries as Argentina and Mexico, where distinct gay subcultures have evolved.

Another important approach to understanding the ideological framework of gay liberation brings us to feminism and lesbian-feminist politics. The split of gay women from the gay movement began as early as 1969, when it was found that gay men not only dominated most gay movements but also were uninterested in or unresponsive to lesbian concerns. In addition, as gay males were also socialized as men, many of their attitudes, some of their behavior, and certainly their privileged position as males in the society posed problems for gay women. Separatist lesbian organizations sprang up, while many gay women opted to work within the feminist movement. The root source of gay oppression, it was commonly argued, is misogyny. Gay men, after all, were being stigmatized chiefly for betraying their male privilege and taking on what were perceived as "feminine" and thus "inferior" traits and behaviors. To combat heterosexism, women had first to break away from male definitions of them, redefine what being a woman is, and stop cooperating in their own oppression.

A third approach to the meaning of the gay revolution is articulated by David Fernbach in his book *The Spiral Path*. Here the author argues that the contribution of gay liberation to history lies in the possibilities it has opened for sexual relations to occur between partners on an equal footing. In history, a gender system has always dictated that males act in a certain way regarding behavior and temperament, and females in another. Since females are placed in a subordinate position, human relationships have taken the form of a dominant person interacting with a subordinate one. This has been not only the standard male-female heterosexual model but also the one on which homosexuality between men has most often been fashioned. In traditional societies where man-boy relations are institutionalized, or where males and females play out the gender roles of their sexual opposites (as do the berdaches among Native Americans), we still find one partner dominant (the older male or the "insertee" in terms of the sex act), and the other subordinated into the lesser role of "woman." By challenging gender roles, the gay movement, along with the feminist, can, for the first time, equalize human relationships, and in doing so bring about the possibility of revolutionary social change.

AUSTRALIA

Dennis Altman's *Homosexual: Oppression and Liberation* was a pioneering work when it appeared in 1971. It was one of the first books in English to articulate the major ideas and aspirations of the gay liberation movement as it was developing after Stonewall. In the work, Altman, an Australian Fulbright scholar with degrees from the University of Tasmania and Cornell, examines the nature of homosexual oppression, calling into question the concepts of normalcy and deviance. In the excerpt that follows from his book, taken from Chapter Three, "Liberation: Toward the Polymorphous Whole," the author looks at the history and possible reasons for the repression of homosexuality in Western societies and discusses the concept of polymorphous perversity. He then projects what liberation would mean and its consequences on society as we now know it.

From "Liberation: Toward the Polymorphous Whole," in *Homosexual: Oppression and Liberation* by Dennis Altman (1971).

Liberation implies more than the mere absence of oppression. Obviously there is a need to end laws that discriminate against homosexuals, to proscribe police harassment, to break down the psychiatric ideologies that see us as sick and maladjusted. Yet to remove the obvious forms of oppression is only a necessary rather than a sufficient step toward liberation. To achieve liberation, as

Marcuse has pointed out in another context, will demand a new morality and a revised notion of "human nature."

Thus to talk of gay liberation demands a broader examination of sexual mores than merely the attitudes toward homosexuality, for the liberation of the homosexual can only be achieved within the context of a much broader sexual liberation. What is needed in fact is a theory of sexuality and of the place sexuality occupies within human life. Inevitably any such theory will rely heavily on Freud. Indeed, despite the hostility of many in the sexual liberation movements to elements of Freudian—and particularly of neo-Freudian —thought, these very movements are in fact part of a contemporary revival of Freudian thought, in particular its emphasis on the central and paramount role that sexuality plays in both social and individual life. (This revival, in which Herbert Marcuse and Norman O. Brown have played a leading role, belongs to a general contemporary attack on positivistic social science and a resurrection of metaphysical speculation.) In this discussion I am particularly indebted to Marcuse for his exploration of the concepts of repression and liberation.

PATTERNS OF SEXUAL REPRESSION

Western societies are remarkable for their strong repression of sexuality, a repression that has traditionally been expressed and legitimized in the Judeo-Christian religious tradition. This repression is expressed in three closely related ways.

Above all, sex is linked with guilt. Despite theological refinement, the Fall of Adam and Eve is popularly viewed as being caused by their discovery of sex. Sex becomes a sin, and this equation gives rise to strong feelings of guilt about enjoying sexual pleasure. Today this concept of sin has been modified, but it is by no means dead. Indeed, one may still find traces of an Elmer Gantry concept of sin, as in the decision of the Tennessee Baptist Convention in 1970 to ban dancing in its colleges. One preacher, it was reported, was cheered for his comment that: "Any man who says he can dance and keep his thoughts pure is less than a man or he is a liar." Women's thoughts were not mentioned.

America has a particularly strong fundamentalist tradition in which sex is viewed as sin, and probably the current boom in pornography and "permissiveness" feeds on the feelings of guilt so imbued into the American consciousness, reinforcing, as such permissiveness does, the whole feeling that sex is dirty and secretive. But guilt about sex is expressed in far broader terms. It may be profitable to regard the whole Western mystique about love as a means of resolving guilt feelings about sex (an argument that Germaine Greer hints at in her attacks on romantic love in *The Female Eunuch*). Nor is it only in the United States that politicians find it more profitable to talk about pornography than poverty, or tolerate unwanted births, bungled abortions, and syphilis epidemics rather than provide proper education about contraception and venereal disease. Attitudes toward sex in prisons and hospitals—where authorities prefer to deny sexual feelings exist rather than provide proper facilities and opportunities for sexual activity—underline just how far general repression of sexuality remains in the so-called permissive society.

Secondly, sex has been firmly linked, and nowhere more clearly than in Christian theology, with the institution of the family and with childbearing. Sex is thus legitimized for its utilitarian principles, rather than as an end in itself, and marriage becomes a "sacred partnership" entered into for the purpose of begetting children. Even where sexual pleasure is accepted as a complementary goal, the connection between marriage and sex still remains, and is reinforced by countless television advertisements and magazine articles. It is from this particular form of sexual repression—and the nature of the resulting family institution—Wilhelm Reich has argued, that stems the repressive nature of modern society.

How strongly this particular view of sex is held to be true is suggested by the fact, already mentioned, that many homosexuals mold their behavior essentially on that of heterosexual couples, even, in some cases, playing out socially prescribed roles of husband and wife. Indeed, Dotson Rader, a journalist and novelist with a strong interest in homosexuality, has claimed that many homosexuals have a desire for pregnancy. Comparably, those who have sought to explain *Who's Afraid of Virginia Woolf?* as a homosexual play manqué make much of the imaginary child that Martha and George have created. I think that Rader makes the point far too strongly, but inasmuch as he is correct, it suggests how strongly the view of sex-as-procreation has permeated.

Thirdly, and as a consequence of the utilitarian view of sex, there is an extremely strong negative attitude toward all sexual urges other than those that are genital and heterosexual. Counter to this is Freud's belief that the infant is polymorphous perverse at birth, that is, that the infant enjoys an undifferentiated ability to take sexual pleasure from all parts of the body. As part of this view Freud also believed in the essential bisexual nature of our original sex drive. (This is a view supported by considerable historical and anthropological evidence. "The Greeks," wrote the British anthropologist Rattray Taylor, "recognized that the sexual nature of every human being contains both homosexual and heterosexual elements.") Yet, while positing the bisexual character of sex drive, Freud also linked it to a linear concept of sexual development that made heterosexuality more mature than homosexuality. One of his more sophisticated followers, Sandor Ferenczi, whose paper "The Nosology of Male Homosexuality" introduces a subtle if unconvincing distinction between "subjective" and "objective" homosexuality, took another view: "The extension of object homoerotism is an abnormal reaction to the disproportionately exaggerated repression of the homoerotic instinct component by civilized man, that is, a failure of this repression." He goes on to argue: "It is thinkable that the sense of cleanliness, which has been so specially reinforced in the past few centuries, that is, the repression of anal eroticism, has provided the strongest motive in this direction, for homoeroticism, even the most sublimated, stands in a more or less unconscious associative connection with pederastia, that is, anal-erotic activity."

Which brings to mind Rattray Taylor's comment that "the Greeks distributed their sexuality and were as interested in bosom and buttocks as in genitals," a polymorphousness that declined with the development of guilt and the justification of sex-as-procreation.

Now, the traditional libertarian view of sexual repression has tended to stress and sought to change the first two attitudes that help generate it, while ignoring the last. The traditional position is most clearly expressed in Reich's concept of sexual liberation as demanding a perfect orgasm, which could be achieved only through genital heterosexual coupling by individuals within the same generation. It is from Reich's views that Norman Mailer has derived his cult of the orgasm, and hence his suspicion of homosexuality and of contraception, which are seen as preventing full sexual "freedom." The importance of Marcuse and Brown is that they have stressed the third of the major forms of repression, and have reminded us —correctly, I believe—that any real theory of sexual liberation must take into account the essentially polymorphous and bisexual needs of the human being.

There exist a number of explanations of how sexual repression of the sort I have discussed came into being. The simplest review will help clarify the issues involved. The simplest explanation is a theory that attributes sexual repression to a need, developed early in the history of humankind, to beget large numbers of children for both economic and defense purposes. This would explain why homosexuality and nongenital sexuality came to be subordinated to heterosexual coupling organized in the patriarchal family. Women for biological reasons were seen primarily as bearers of children, and by extension as their rearers as well. In this view both repression of our polymorphous instincts and the creation of the patriarchal family can be linked to the importance attributed to procreation.

Freud himself advanced a partly anthropological argument, in which repression stems from the assertion of domination of one individual over others, that individual being the father. Through such domination, the patriarchal form of society is established, based on the inferiority of women and on the strong repression of sexuality channeled into socially approved forms. Freud argued that even when the sons banded together to overthrow the father, thus ushering in a new period in which women played an increasingly important role, they were unable to escape fully from the domination of the father, and patriarchal authority came to reassert itself. Marcuse quotes Otto Rank's version of this argument: "The development of the paternal domination into an increasingly powerful state system administered by man is thus a continuance of the primal repression, which has [as] its purpose the ever wider exclusion of woman."

Freud linked his theory of patriarchal authority with the rise of religion, and in particular the triumph in the Western world of monotheism. Support for this connection is found in Rattray Taylor's argument that "a remarkable psychological change" emerged in the classical world after 500 B.C. This change, he claims, led to an increasing repression of sexuality and the development of a sense of guilt, both of which factors facilitated the triumph of the more repressive Jewish view of sex over that of the early Greek view.

A related explanation of sexual repression sees its causes in just this fact, the dominance of the Western Judeo-Christian tradition. Unlike Freud's view, this explanation stresses the particular as against the universal forms of sexual repression, seeing religion as not merely a rationalization and legitimization of sexual repression but as a major cause. Certainly there is considerable evidence that the Western religious tradition has placed great stress on sexual repression. At times indeed, especially during the Middle Ages, to repress sexual desire totally was considered a mark of virtue, and the resulting hysteria, masochism, and persecution set the tone of much of the underside of life in medieval Europe. Continence for all was hardly a practical policy for an entire society, leading as it does to its own self-annihilation, but the next best thing was the development of the view that sex exists merely as a means of procreation—hence continuing Catholic opposition to birth control and masturbation, and the institution of clerical celibacy. To the best of my knowledge the Church has advanced beyond its teachings that made sex illegal three days each week and eleven weeks each year; yet the rhythm method, when followed conscientiously, has a similar effect.

Religion may well have been a particularly important influence on the repression of bisexuality, for the Jewish view of sex came to supplant the Greek in the Western world, homosexuality was more and more frowned upon, and biblical evidence was produced to show its inherent sinfulness. Thus the story of Sodom and Gomorrah has long been used (probably inaccurately) as proof of the homosexual's sin; in Leviticus 20 we read that: "If a man also lie with mankind as he lieth with a woman, both of them have committed an abomination; they shall surely be put to death; their blood shall be upon them." To which Paul, never one to encourage sexuality, added his condemnation in the Epistle to the Romans.

To the Jewish heritage, so much bound up with the whole history of the patriarchal family, was added the Christian theology of "natural law," whence a long line of popes (denied, one assumes, a firsthand experience) have derived the Catholic views on sex. The linkage of sexuality exclusively with procreation made homosexuality (plus a considerable number of heterosexual acts) unnatural and hence sinful. The concept of "natural" sex has affected even those who are not practicing Christians, and indeed provides the argument most often advanced against homosexuality. But there is no necessity to link sex exclusively with procreation, and few societies have applied this ideology as rigidly as the Western Judeo-Christian. Even the most repressed admit the dual function of the (male) sex organ: sex and bodily evacuation. It is, theoretically, no more difficult to admit that the sexual act itself has more than one function, and that sensual gratification is as much its purpose as is procreation.

There has also been an attempt to link Marx to Freud and relate sexual repression to a theory of economic development. In this view Freud's theory of the origin of patriarchal authority is taken as having symbolic rather than anthropological reality, and is related to the organization of society around certain forms of productive relationships. Something of this approach is expressed—faultily, in my opinion—in an article by Roxanne Dunbar in a collection of women's liberation articles, *Notes from the Second Year:* "The patriarchal family is economically and historically tied to private property, and under Western capitalism with the development of the national state. The masculine ideology most strongly asserts home and country as primary values, with wealth and power an individual's greatest goal. The same upper class of men who created private property and founded nation-states also created the family." Yet the patriarchal family long preceded Western concepts of property and nation-states, and is indeed very much in evidence in societies that are in no real sense capitalist. Furthermore, most civilizations of which we have any knowledge have defined "male" and "female" as sharply differentiated categories, and one might in fact argue that the subordination of women under Western capitalism, while certainly real, has been less than in, say, precapitalist Chinese or Arab society. The eagerness to wed Marx to Freud has too often ignored the realities of both history and anthropology.

Nonetheless, it is undoubtedly true that sexual repression was highly functional for the rise of capitalism and later industrialization, which, at least in the early stages, demanded considerable repression in the interests of economic development. One can make connections between, for example, the rapid industrial growth of nineteenth-century England and the ideology of the Victorian era toward sex. Similarly, it is hardly surprising that countries seeking rapid industrialization, from Russia under Stalin to much of the Third World today, adopt rigid puritanical codes similar to those now being rejected in the West.

Marcuse has argued that the sexual repression that is brought about under the primal dictatorship is linked to economic subordination—through this dictatorship the sons come to channel their energies into unpleasant but necessary activity. However, as Paul Robinson has pointed out in his book *The Freudian Left,* Marcuse neither makes clear whether sexual repression causes economic subordination or vice versa, nor, most important for our purposes, does he connect his use of Freud's notion of the primal crime with his own ideas about the repression of nongenital and homosexual drives. This last point is important because one of the primary differences between Freud and Marcuse is the latter's belief in the desirability of overcoming the repression of polymorphous perversity.

For Marcuse the homosexual occupies a particular role—Robinson interprets some of his writings as suggesting that "in a certain sense, then, the social function of the homosexual was analogous to that of the critical philosopher"—and it is perhaps surprising that Marcuse's works, and in particular *Eros and Civilization,* to which Robinson is referring, are rarely if ever referred to in gay liberation literature. Marcuse seems to suggest that the homosexual represents a constant reminder of the repressed part of human sexuality, not only in his/her interest in the same sex, but also in the variety of nonconventional sexual behavior that homosexuality implies. Sodomy, of course, recalls repressed feeling of anal eroticism, as Ferenczi suggests—not that sodomy is restricted to homosexuals, as Rozjak in Mailer's *American Dream* should remind us. Even more do female homosexuals disturb the myth that sex need be phalluscentered, a belief that underlies what Mailer has called the "peculiar difficulty" of lesbianism. "Man we can do without it and keep it going longer too!" wrote Martha Shelley in the gay liberation newspaper *Come Out!*

Anatomy has forced the homosexual to explore the realities of polymorphous eroticism beyond the experiences of most heterosexuals, for we are denied the apparently "natural" navel-to-navel coupling of men/women. There is among most homosexuals, I suspect, an awareness of their body, a knowledge of human sensuality, that is one of their strengths, although this is easily distorted in the body-building cult among men or the disregard of physical appearance among women.

Because homosexuality cannot find its justification in procreation nor in religiously sanctioned marriage, it represents an assertion of sexuality as an expression of hedonism/love free of any utilitarian social ends, and it is this very fact that may help explain the horror with which homosexuality is regarded. Marcuse has observed in *Eros and Civilization* that: "Against a society which employs sexuality as a means for a useful end, the perversions uphold sexuality as an end in itself; they thus place themselves outside the domination of the performance principle [Marcuse's term for the particular variety of repression necessary for the organization of capitalism] and challenge its very foundations." This is spelled out by Marcuse in detail in the case of Orpheus, traditionally associated with the introduction of homosexuality, who "like Narcissus . . . protests against the repressive order of procreative sexuality. The Orphic and Narcissistic Eros is to the end the negation of this order—the Great Refusal." In the context of a society based on rigorous repression of polymorphous and bisexual urges, the homosexual thus comes to represent a challenge to the conventional norms. This challenge makes him/her a revolutionary.

Still, even in the Marcusian variation of Freudian thought, exclusive homosexuality represents a repression that is as great as exclusive heterosexuality, despite the fact that, because of the legitimization of sex-as-procreation, it places the homosexual outside society in a way that is not true for the heterosexual. Homosexuals who like to point out that "everyone is queer"—"either latent or blatant," as one girl put it—rarely concede that "everyone" is equally "straight" and that to repress the one is as damaging as to repress the other. It may be the historic function of the homosexual to overcome this particular form of repression—to accept his/her heterosexuality as well—and bring to its logical conclusion the Freudian belief in our inherent bisexuality.

SEX ROLES AND REPRESSION

The repression of polymorphous perversity in Western societies has two major components: the removal of the erotic from all areas of life other than the explicitly sexual, and the denial of our inherent bisexuality. The latter in particular is bound up with the development of very clear-cut concepts of "masculine" and "feminine" that dominate our consciousness—and help maintain male supremacy. It is awareness of the socially imposed masculine/feminine dichotomy that especially characterizes the analyses associated with women's liberation.

The deerotization of our lives is the primary concern of Norman O. Brown, who ascribes the grand neuroses that he associates with organized civilization to the subordination of the generally erotic to specifically genital urges. This view is argued, too, by Marcuse, though he is less willing to move to the ultimate conclusion extolled by Brown. Marcuse sees modern industrial society as being particularly repressive of our nonspecific erotic instincts; thus in *One Dimensional Man,* his major critique of modern society, he writes of the "reduction of erotic to sexual experience and satisfaction."

> For example, compare love-making in a meadow and in an automobile, on a lover's walk outside the town walls and on a Manhattan street. In the former cases, the environment partakes of and invites libidinal cathexis and tends to be eroticized. Libido transcends beyond the immediate erotogenic zones—a process of nonrepressive sublimation. In contrast, a mechanized environment seems to block such self-transcendence of libido. Impelled in the struggle to extend the field of erotic gratification, libido becomes less "polymorphous," less capable of eroticism beyond localized sexuality, and the latter is intensified.[1]

One might note that there is a strong romanticism to Marcuse's views, which is echoed in the moves to establish rural communes that have become so marked in the United States in recent years.

As the whole structure of socialization acts so as to channel our polymorphous perverse instincts into narrow but socially approved norms, there is not only a repression of general eroticism but also of bisexuality. There is a marked connection in our society between

the repression of bisexuality and the development of clearly demar-
cated sex roles. Now this is not a necessary connection. There are
few societies which have not held up models of masculine and
feminine into which recalcitrants were to be forced, but a sharp
distinction between the two roles does not of itself produce repression of homosexual urges. The ancient Greeks extolled both bisexuality and the supremacy of men, and homoeroticism thrives, in
fact, where men and women are kept apart and sharply differentiated (as, for example, in the Arab custom of addressing love songs
to boys because women are regarded as too inferior to be objects of
such praise). Unlike Greek society, however, ours is one that defines
masculinity and femininity very much in heterosexual terms, so that
the social stereotype—and often, indeed, the self-image—of the
homosexual is someone who rejects his/her masculinity/femininity.
Thus, as already suggested, one finds the two extremes of male
homosexual role playing: the drag queen who tends to accentuate
the image of the homosexual as a man-who-would-be-a-woman,
and the "leather" type who seeks to overcome it. To a lesser extent
comparable stereotypes exist among lesbians.

It is in fact probably true that individuals are often forced into
exclusive homosexuality because of both the way in which society
brands those who deny its roles and the penalties meted out to
those who are unwilling to accept them.

Whether it be the educational system—boys are naturally good
at math and science, girls at languages and arts—or the Tiffany's
notice—"We do not, nor will we in future, carry earrings for men"
—sex roles are a first, and central, distinction made by society.
Being male and female is, above all, defined in terms of the other:
Men learn that their masculinity depends on being able to make it
with women, women that fulfillment can only be obtained through
being bound to a man. In a society based on the assumption that
heterosexuality represents all that is sexually normal, children are
taught to view as natural and inevitable that they in turn will
become "mommies" and "daddies" and are encouraged to rehearse

for these roles in their games. In an article on the importance of feminism, Theodore Roszak observes: "The woman most desperately in need of liberation is the 'woman' every man has locked up in the dungeons of his own psyche. *That* is the basic act of oppression that still waits to be undone, though the undoing might well produce the most cataclysmic reinterpretation of the sexual roles and of sexual 'normalcy' in all human history." And equally there is need to unlock the "man" every woman has in the dungeons of *her* psyche.

The way in which our concepts of sex roles are bound up with making it with the opposite sex illustrates how far our definitions of these roles are influenced by the fears of homosexuality that most straights have repressed. Proving one's man/womanhood is in the popular imagination bound up with the rejection of any fag or dyke characteristics. If this seems more obvious in the case of men, it is because women have traditionally been defined as inferior, and whereas there is some grudging respect accorded women with masculine qualities, none is given to "womanly" men. Even among children "tomboys" are more acceptable than "sissies."

That lesbianism is stigmatized less than male homosexuality is one of the clichés about homosexuality, and to the extent that it is true it reflects the inferior position of women in our society. (Reports of group sex activities—see, for example, an article in *Newsweek*,[2] June 21, 1971—suggest that sex between women is far more easily accepted by "middle Americans" than that between men.) Nor, even apart from apocryphal stories about Queen Victoria's disbelief in lesbianism, thereby exempting lesbians from legal sanction, is this lesser condemnation of lesbians restricted to modern times. Derrick Bailey, in his book *Homosexuality and the Western Christian Tradition,* points out that this difference was equally true of early and medieval Christianity, and argues it is due to the inferior position of women, in particular to the fact that male homosexual acts, and particularly sodomy, "involves the degradation, not so much of human nature itself as of the male, since in it he stimulates or encourages or compels another to simulate the coital function of the female—a 'perversion' intolerable in its implications to any society organized in accordance with the theory that woman is essentially subordinate to man." Indeed, female homosexuality may well touch on that deep-hidden fear of men, the suspicion that women are in fact more capable of sexual enjoyment than they, an attitude that helps explain the male-created ideology that for a long time denied sexual feelings to women.

Gay women are, after all, doubly oppressed, and suffer particularly from the social norms that expect women to repress not only their homosexual but even, to a considerable extent, their heterosexual urges. In some ways the equivalent of the compulsively promiscuous male who never dares know his partners may well be the woman who cannot admit the sexual component of her love for other women; both are victims of the sexual expectations of a society that perceives masculinity as "making it," femininity as preserving one's virtue. It is often claimed, for example, that men react more to physical stimuli than women. Yet if the media bombarded us constantly with pictures of pretty boys and semiclad men, who knows whether [heterosexual] women might not in fact objectify beautiful men with all the single-mindedness of the *Playboy* male? And, by extension, whether lesbians might not behave more like men, both straight and gay, than like straight women?

The major way in which children are socialized into particular forms of sexual repression and concepts of sex roles is through the family, and, indeed, achieving this development may be the only major socialization task that the family retains in modern society (which may explain the strength of opposition to providing sex education in schools, thus usurping even this role of the family). The patriarchal family as we know it in our time is essentially a nuclear family; indeed, the transformation from the extended (or stem) to the nuclear family has been one of the major effects of industrialization, irrespective of whether industrialization is achieved through capitalist or noncapitalist means. As this change has occurred, most of the functions performed by the extended family necessarily have dropped away. Yet the family still retains one of them, albeit in a modified form—that is, teaching children to make clear-cut role distinctions between the sexes.

Equally, the institution of the family as we know it contributes very importantly to the development of the repression of homosexuality and the stigma attached to it. As all parents are either fully heterosexual in behavior—or, except in special cases, will appear so to their children—it follows that children are exposed to models of sexual role playing that are fully heterosexual, and denied virtually all contact with homosexuals, for even friends or relatives who are gay will by and large conceal this in front of children. A social system that provided instead an opportunity for children to grow up regarding both homo- and heterosexuality as part of the human condition, a system perhaps approximated—for men—in ancient Greece, would be a far better one for enabling children to come to terms with their own diverse sexual impulses. As long as homosexuals are denied any role in childrearing—in which numbers, of course, participate through their careers, but concealing in almost all cases their homosexuality—it is unlikely that children can grow up with other than a distorted view of what is natural. . . .

TOWARD LIBERATION

Any discussion of sexual liberation involves some concept of overcoming sexual repression, although there is considerable debate as to how far we can in fact dispense with any form of repression at all. Freud distinguished between repression and sublimation, and argued not only that the latter was a healthy variant of the former but that it was in fact essential for the maintenance of civilization. Norman O. Brown, on the other hand, appears to be arguing for a total end to repression and a return to the infantile state of "poly-morphous perversity," a position that is more utopian than pro-grammatic. If one accepts the centrality of the sexual urge, it is difficult to argue for a total relaxation of repression without an-swering the claim that this would mean an end to all forms of socially necessary activity. Marcuse seeks to overcome this objection with his concept of "surplus repression," that part of sexual repres-sion which acts so as to maintain the domination of the ruling class but which is not necessary for the maintenance of a genuinely cooperative human community. He also suggests the possibility of the eroticization of everyday life, including work. I would further argue that there are other basic human needs and urges apart from the erotic, and that because of these some forms of sexual repression would be freely accepted even by an individual totally untouched by social conditioning. At the very least I suspect one needs to accept the need for some form of postponed gratification.

Kate Millett in *Sexual Politics* defined a "sexual revolution" as follows:

[It] would require, perhaps first of all, an end of traditional sexual inhibitions and taboos, particularly those that most threaten patriarchal monogamous marriage: homosexuality, "il-legitimacy," adolescent, pre- and extramarital sexuality. The neg-ative aura with which sexual activity has generally been surrounded would necessarily be eliminated, together with the double standard and prostitution. The goal of revolution would be a permissive single standard of sexual freedom, and one un-corrupted by the crass and exploitative economic bases of tradi-tional sexual alliances.

Primarily, however, a sexual revolution would bring the insti-tution of patriarchy to an end, abolishing both the ideology of male supremacy and the traditional socialization by which it is upheld in matters of status, role, and temperament. This would produce an integration of the separate sexual subcultures, an assimilation by both sides of previously segregated human expe-rience. . . . [3]

Millett, like most women's liberationists, is primarily concerned here with sex roles, which she sees as underlying the nuclear family structure (which in turn, as Reich saw, "forms the mass psychological basis for a *certain* culture, namely the *patriarchal authoritarian one in all of its forms*"). I would not dispute Millett's aims. Yet it seems to me that liberation requires, as well, a general erotization of human life—by which I mean an acceptance of the sensuality that we all possess, and a willingness to let it imbue all personal contacts —and a move toward polymorphous perversity that includes more than reassessment of sex roles.

Let me make clear at once a point to which I shall have reason to return: Liberation as a concept embraces far more than sexual liberation. Moreover, the concepts of liberation with which we shall be concerned relate almost entirely to affluent Western societies; as Susan Sontag and others have pointed out, to change consciousness in an underdeveloped and once neocolonial state like Cuba must in some ways reverse the changes applicable to North American/Western Europe/Australasia. (Though I am less willing than she, writing in *Ramparts* in 1969, to excuse Cuban treatment of homosexuals.) Were I concerned with broader conceptions of liberation I should, of course, need to concern myself as much with the nature of Western capitalism/imperialism/consumerism, etc., as with sexual repression and freedom.

How far sexual freedom can be conceived without coming to grips with the basic features of our society is a key ideological concern of both the women's and the gay movements. Yet there is a sense in which we should be suspicious of attempts to deny the centrality of sexuality in any discussion of liberation. "I do not believe in a nonerotic philosophy. I do not trust any desexualized idea," wrote the Pole Witold Gombrowicz in his diary. It is the desexualization of the concept of liberation that accounts for much of the abstruse intellectualism of sections of the left—and the common tendency of revolutionaries to become vicious and puritanical on winning power. As the song goes in Peter Weiss's *Marat/ Sade:*

What's the point of a revolution
Without general copulation?

The more difficult question with which we have to come to grips is
what's the *possibility* of a revolution without . . .

Liberation, then, in the restricted context with which we are
primarily concerned implies freedom from the surplus repression
that prevents us recognizing our essential androgynous and erotic
natures. "Originally," wrote Marcuse in *Eros and Civilization,* "the sex
instinct had no extraneous temporal and spatial limitations on its
subject and object; sexuality is by nature 'polymorphous perverse.' "
And as examples of "surplus repression" Marcuse notes not only
our total concentration on genital coupling but phenomena such as
the repression of smell/taste in sexual life. For both him and Brown
liberation implies a return to original sexuality.

Yet this definition is perhaps too narrow. Liberation entails not
just freedom from sexual restraint, but also freedom for the fulfillment of human potential, a large part of which has been unnecessarily restricted by tradition, prejudice, and the requirements of
social organization. If it is true that social needs still demand a
certain degree of repression of sexuality, it is also true that affluent,
postindustrial societies, such as those of the developed Western
world, offer an unparalleled opportunity for freedom. Technology,
which too often becomes restrictive, in fact allows the individual far
greater liberty from toil and opens up the possibility that work
might truly become play, not just for a small minority as at present
but instead for the vast majority. Which in turn opens up the
possibility for breaking down the rigid lines our society draws between art and life, or in other words the possibility of the eroticization of everyday living. Underdeveloped countries are not in this
position, which is why they must define liberation differently; on
the other hand, the degree of affluence in America, if properly
distributed, is far greater than would be needed for an immediate
and considerable decrease in personal restrictions. Liberation demands a renunciation of the traditional puritan ethic, so successfully

imitated by Communist states, that sees hard work and expanding production as goods in themselves. Instead it requires a new examination of the basic erotic instincts that we have repressed in the name of morality and production:

> As human beings we are unique among animals in having a largely unspecified potential. Besides the basic biological needs for food, water, and rest, we have needs which are specifically human and subject to conscious development: the need for relationship, the need to create and build. We are all erotic beings. We experience our lives as a striving for realization and satisfaction. We experience our lives sexually, as enlivened by beauty and feeling. At base we have a need for active evolvement [sic] and creation, the need to give form and meaning to our environment and ourselves. [From *Gay Liberation,* a pamphlet of the Red Butterfly movement, a group of revolutionary Socialists that existed within gay liberation.]

One of the problems involved in discussing liberation is that we live in a time in which traditional sexual restraints are apparently collapsing, and the individual's freedom for sexual expression appears greater than ever before. As Abbie Hoffman put it, society is "simultaneously more repressive and more tolerant," a truth Marcuse attempts to explain through the concept of "repressive tolerance."

The present experience of the homosexual, in particular the liberal tolerance of which I have already written, seems to bear out all Marcuse's fears of "repressive desublimation," that is, greater apparent freedom but a freedom manipulated into acceptable channels. Thus most of the Western world has abolished legal restrictions against homosexuality while maintaining social prejudices. But to realize the falsity of the idea that existing bourgeois society has in fact permitted full personal liberation, it is instructive to examine the position of the homosexual in the Netherlands, a society often held up as a model of enlightenment.

In an article with the typical snideness of most that deal with homosexuality, *Newsweek* described Amsterdam in 1968 as the "mecca of homosexuals." What this means in practice, however, is that homosexuals are not bothered by the police and that they are allowed to meet freely in their own clubs and organizations. Men may dance with men and women with women—but only in certain specified places, and attempts to break this down have led to scuffles —for example, at a dance in The Hague in May 1970. Some extremely progressive social measures—for example, in regard to housing—have been achieved. Yet the entire bias of the media and of education remains heterosexual—Dutch schools, for example, do not teach the equal validity of homosexual and heterosexual love —and the prevailing social climate is one of tolerance rather than acceptance. Opinion polls have shown that dislike of homosexuality remains strong, and it is thus not surprising that other studies have revealed that Dutch homosexuals, particularly teenagers, are oppressed by the same feelings of guilt and social outcasteness as are American.

"Repressive tolerance" underlies contemporary permissiveness. Sex in our time has become increasingly used as a commodity, and the first principle of advertising appears to be to imply that your product enhances sex appeal. It takes little imagination to see how this helps maintain the capitalist need for continuing production. "If you work hard and earn lots of money then you, too, can have a beautiful man/woman" is the barely concealed message. Indeed, we are so programmed into accepting fashionable standards of beauty that the more "permissive" the society becomes—meaning the more that pleasant but standardized bodies are displayed—the more discontented we become with the inevitable flaws of our own, and our lovers' bodies, and the more unable to perceive the beauty that lies in those unlike the current stereotype.

But the gap between sexual freedom and repressed eroticism goes deeper. "In America," Kate Millett has said, "you can either fuck or shake hands," and this sums up the situation. The ability to feel, to hold, to embrace, to take comfort from the warmth of other human beings is sadly lacking; we look for it in the artificial situations of encounter groups rather than accepting it in our total lives. From the rock-musical *Salvation:*

> If you let me make love to you
> Then why can't I touch you . . .

Perhaps there lies the difference between sex and eroticism.

The cartoonist Jules Feiffer is reported to have said that "the love ethic went to Chicago, was polarized, and came out as the fuck ethic," and it is certainly true that the permissive society with its high component of voyeurism, sexual objectification, and "dildo journalism" is hardly a liberated one. Nonetheless, I am less sure than Marcuse that growing sexual freedom is all illusionary. Without it movements like women's and gay liberation could hardly have come into being. But it is necessary now to transform sexuality into eroticism. As Marcuse writes in *Eros and Civilization,* there must be "not simply a release but a transformation of the libido: from sexuality constrained under genital supremacy to erotization of the entire personality. It is a spread rather than an explosion of the libido—a spread over private and societal relations which bridges the gap maintained between them by a repressive reality principle."

Liberation would involve a resurrection of our original impulse to take enjoyment from the total body, and indeed to accept the seeking of sensual enjoyment as an end in itself, free from procreation or status enhancement. To quote Marcuse again: "The full force of civilized morality was mobilized against the use of the body as mere object, means, instrument of pleasure: such reification was tabooed and remained the ill-reputed privilege of whores, degenerates, and perverts." Which is why "whores, degenerates, and perverts" become the new antihero(in)es of books such as *Last Exit to Brooklyn.*

But there are, I think, some reservations to Marcuse's argument, which he partly avoids by the sheer abstractness of his writing. For one, if there were in fact an erotization of the entire personality, this would act *against* the use of the body "as mere object, means, instrument of pleasure." A concept of liberation that involves a transformation of the libido would not include, it would argue, sex based solely on the objectification of the body (the clearest example of which is necrophilia—though such objectification is evident in much of the depersonalized sex of the permissive society), for sex would be seen as a means of expanding contact and creating community with other persons, and would demand some reciprocity other than the purely physical. Sex as much as everyday life would be eroticized and would become a means of human communication rather than purely physical gratification or consummation of a sacred union. One of the implications of this, of course, is that sexual activity among children would be encouraged rather than, as is now the case, hindered.

Affirmation of the total body involves, as Brown puts it in *Life Against Death,* "a union with others and with the world around us based not on anxiety and aggression but on narcissism and erotic exuberance." It involves, too, an acceptance of the funkiness of the body, a rejection of the plastic, odorless, hairless, and blemishless creations of *Playboy* and its homosexual equivalents, and a new sense of play and spontaneity, a move toward what Brown, perhaps unfortunately, called "a science of enjoyment rather than a science of accumulation." "The Underground," claims Richard Neville in *Playpower,* "is turning sex back into play."

Paul Goodman has suggested that the homosexual has, in fact, already partly achieved this:

A happy property of sexual acts, and perhaps especially of homosexual acts, is that they are dirty, like life: as Augustine said, "Inter urinas et feces nascitur." In a society as middle-class, orderly, and technological as ours, it is essential to break down squeamishness, which is an important factor in what is called racism, as well as in cruelty to children and the sterile putting away of the sick and aged. Also, the illegal and catch-as-catch-can nature of many homosexual acts at present breaks down other conventional attitudes. Although I wish I could have had many a party with less apprehension and more unhurriedly—we would have enjoyed them more—yet it has been an advantage to learn that the ends of docks, the backs of trucks, back alleys, behind the stairs, abandoned bunkers on the beach, and the washrooms of trains are all adequate samples of all the space there is. For both good and bad, homosexual behavior retains some of the alarm and excitement of childish sexuality.[4]

With Goodman's formulation I would agree and disagree. Undoubtedly there is a positive side to the sordidness of traditional gay life, in that it represents an acceptance of sexuality in a way that perhaps fewer heterosexuals have experienced. *Some* one-night stands can be rewarding, just as *some* lasting relations can be disastrous. In arguing for the erotization of everyday life, I am certainly not extolling some new form of puritanism that would deny the possibility of transitory sexual encounters, nor would I want to uphold monogamy as either necessary or, indeed, desirable. Casual sex can be a good way of getting to know people.

But it is hardly sufficient. Goodman was attacked in *Come Out!* by the poet Milani for advocating "lust without the rhythms of Eros," and the accusation, though I think overdone, has its point. Promiscuity, even selective, hardly equals liberation, nor is the ability to appreciate the varieties of human eroticism—unlike Reich, I am a firm believer in nonorgasmic sex in certain situations, and the extension of sexual play to large areas of life appears to me as a necessary part of liberation—a substitute for the creation of real relationships.

Nonetheless, we need to move toward a full acceptance of the erotic qualities of humankind and of the many different kinds and levels of sexual encounters that are possible. As part of this there is required an acceptance of our basic androgyny. To turn again to Brown: "The 'magical' body which the poet seeks is the 'subtle' or 'spiritual' or 'translucent' body of occidental mysticism, and the 'diamond' body of oriental mysticism, and in psychoanalysis the polymorphous perverse body of childhood. Thus, for example, psychoanalysis declares the fundamentally bisexual nature of human nature; Boehme insists on the androgynous character of human perfection; Taoist mysticism invokes feminine passivity to counteract masculine aggressivity; and Rilke's poetic quest is a quest for a hermaphroditic body." There is a danger in Brown of the realities of the body dissolving into metaphysical flights, so that his concept of polymorphous perversity becomes ultimately an asexual one, and he seems to envision not a move to expand sexuality from its obsessive genitality but rather the total supplanting of that genitality. It is often, indeed, difficult to relate Brown's writings to the real world of sexuality in which bodies tend to impose on us in more than "spiritual" or "translucent" ways. Nor am I as concerned as he to break down all differences between the sexes, beyond, of course, ending the false dichotomies imposed by social roles.

With liberation, homosexuality and heterosexuality would cease to be viewed as separate conditions, the former being a perversion of the latter, but would be seen rather as components of us all. Liberation would also, as women's liberation theorists have pointed out, mean an end to the nuclear family as the central organizing principle of our society. It would not, emphatically, mean an end to the importance of human relationships, although it would suggest an end to legalizing them, to compulsory monogamy and possessiveness, to the assumption, often echoed by homosexuals, that it is "natural" to divide up into couples who live isolated by and large from other couples. Perhaps it is our cult of acquisitiveness that makes us feel that love need be rationed. I suspect, in contrast to such a view, that the more one gives the more one is replenished, and that humans are capable of many more love relationships, both sexual and nonsexual, than social norms prescribe. (It is this realization among young people that underlies the considerable experimentation with communal living that is already occurring.)

In a situation of liberation there would develop radical changes in the attitude toward bearing and rearing children, changes related —but only in part—to the fact that for the first time in human history it is technologically possible to control the rate of childbirth.

Brown, relying largely on Nietzsche, argues that the desire for children is often a product of suffering, of a need to reject oneself. "Joy," he quotes Nietzsche as saying, "does not want heirs or children—joy wants itself, wants eternity, wants recurrence, wants everything eternally the same." Free from a sense of guilt and of the social pressures toward procreation, with a decline, too, in the institution of the patriarchal and monogamous family structure, one might expect both a substantial number of women to consciously decide against having children and, conversely, an increase in communal childrearing which would involve nonparent adults, including homosexuals. Both for society—which faces the specter of overpopulation—and for individual children who hardly benefit from the smothering effect of the present family—"being sole focus of attention for an adult who has little to worry about but your psyche is too much burden for an adult, let alone a small child," Marge Piercy argued in the first issue of the radical quarterly *Defiance*—the changes would be an improvement. There are great advantages for children in communal living, representing as it does a compromise between the tyranny of overpossessive parents and the repression of the typical education system. It is also probably the only really effective way to break down the sex-role stereotypes into which the family structure tends to force us. The idea that a child "belongs" to his parents is a logical extension of the cult of property, only exceeded in horror by the concept that the child "belongs" to the state.

Ultimately, as Marcuse insists, liberation implies a new biological person, one "no longer capable of tolerating the aggressiveness, brutality, and ugliness of the established way of life." Speaking to the 1967 Congress of the Dialectics of Liberation, Marcuse argued that this new person would be "a man [one assumes also a woman] who rejects the performance principles governing the established societies; a type of man who has rid himself of the aggressiveness and brutality that are inherent in the organization of established society, and in their hypocritical, puritan morality; a type of man who is biologically incapable of fighting wars and creating suffering;

a type of man who has a good conscience of joy and pleasure, and who works collectively and individually for a social and natural environment in which such an existence becomes possible." And elaborating on this in *An Essay on Liberation* he argues that as such new men (women) appear, they will redefine the objectives and the strategy of the political structure.

Those who seek to relate sexual to total liberation tend often to argue that the two are interdependent in some chicken-and-egg manner. This has been put strongly by the gay revolutionary Social-ist group the Red Butterfly, who claim: "To break our chains and become free we are going to have to work for fundamental changes in the institutions which oppress us, such as the existing family system with its web of supports: male chauvinism, sex typing of personality traits and arbitrary labels such as 'gay' and 'straight.' But to change any one basic institution will require changes in related ones. Change in family patterns would mean changes in education, in the economy, in laws, etc. This will mean coming up against vested interests, those who gain at the expense of our oppression. It will mean a struggle to free ourselves." From the Red Butterfly perspective, the upshot would be some genuine form of socialism.

It seems to me that the connection between sexual liberation and total liberation should be made somewhat differently. Liberation is a process that individuals strive toward, and part of this striving involves a recognition of the way in which oppression is implanted in the very structures of our society. To overcome the stigma society places on homosexuality, for example, does mean radical alterations in the way in which we order the socialization process. More than this, as individuals come to a greater acceptance of their erotic/sexual being they tend spontaneously to reject the "performance principle" that underlies the dominant ethos of property, competi-tion, and aggression. Thus, between individual and social liberation there is a dialectic relationship, and as Marcuse puts it in his *Essay on Liberation*, "radical change in consciousness is the beginning, the first step in changing social existence: emergence of the new Sub-ject." (Brown's views on the other hand seem to me less acceptable, for he seems to posit a personal liberation within a social vacuum.) Only a socialism highly flavored by anarchism would seem to me consistent with sexual liberation, for conventional notions of socialism do not contain sufficient protection for the individual vis-à-vis the collective. One might note, however, that individual rights are not the same as property rights, and that those who most ardently extol the latter are often those most willing to impinge on the former.

One of the most important statements of the gay movement is Carl Wittman's "The Gay Manifesto," where he argues—a position with which I would basically agree—that a change in individual consciousness is a basic requirement for any qualitative social change. Until we have come to grips with the meaning of liberation for ourselves, to talk of liberation for others (that is, society) is meaningless. In terms of social actuality I find most persuasive the argument of the American antipsychiatrist Jo Berke in *Counter-Culture* that: "As more and more groups associate with each other we shall see the large-scale creation of 'liberated zones' within bourgeois society, who will have the same relationship to themselves and established institutions as 'liberated areas' of Mozambique and Vietnam have to each other and to the Portuguese or Americans." Such "liberated zones" will be defined, however, more by a shared consciousness than a geographic base, although the commune movement attempts to combine the two.

One last point, and here I may seem to be contradicting myself: Any theory of liberation needs to take into account the problem of aggression. I have already argued that much violence is the product of repression and that the disappearance of the latter would lead to a sharp decline in the former. Yet just as I would argue that there are instincts other than the sexual with which we need come to terms, so I would argue that an end to repression does not automatically mean an end to human aggression. Aggression is partly a product of sexual restraints and of socially imposed sex roles, but it most likely has an existence within the individual independent of these two factors. But I would argue that liberation from the sex-role stereotypes that force men to prove their masculinity through violence and liberation of the erotic impulses that both sexes are taught to restrain would make the management of human aggression far easier than it now is. Liberation does not imply some insipid state of languid flowerdom. Yet if we were less hung up sexually, aggression might be expressed not through guns, wars, and suicidal automobile driving—remember all those pop songs about "chicken" drivers—but through less violent means, perhaps through increased creativity, or, as Goodman seems to hope, through raucous play and athletics. (The play, one hopes, would be individual feats like Horatio's bike ride in *Empire City,* or communal activities, like the street softball match in *Making Do,* rather than the authoritarian and conformist qualities of competitive spectator sports.) It is impossible to know how far aggression is innate and how far a product of particular social forms and economic scarcity. It would be dishonest to dismiss this as a problem.

I argued at the beginning of this chapter that gay liberation as a concept makes sense only within a broader context. Yet my concern is basically with the homosexual, and the move from tolerance to acceptance. While one would expect a liberated society to regard bisexuality as the norm, this view would not mean that all persons would behave bisexually—or at least not in the symmetrical way suggested by Gore Vidal when he wrote "that it is possible to have a mature sexual relationship with a woman on Monday, and a mature sexual relationship with a man on Tuesday, and perhaps on Wednesday have both together. . . ." The nonrepressed person recognizes his bisexual potential; he is not some ideal person midway along the Kinsey behavioral scale. People would still fall in love and form relationships, and those relationships would be homosexual as well as heterosexual. What would be different is that the social difference between the two would vanish, and once this happened, we would lose the feeling of being limited, of having to choose between an exclusively straight or exclusively gay world. The lack of any available sense of identity for the bisexual in present society, and the pressures on him/her from both sides—for bisexuality threatens the exclusive homo- as much as heterosexual—probably explain why it is relatively uncommon. Given a change in social repression we would all be less uptight about the whole thing— and probably accept some experimentation with each sex as natural.

Liberation would mean the end of the gay world as we now know it, with its high premium on momentary and furtive contacts. It would involve a breakdown of the barriers between male and female homosexuals, and between gays and straights. Masculinity and femininity would cease to be sharply differentiated categories, and one would expect an end to the homosexual parodies of role playing in the cult of leather and of drag. The nuclear family would come to be seen as only one form of possible social organization, not as the norm from which everything seems a deviation. This would mean an end not only to the oppression of gays, but major changes in general consciousness. Sexuality, once it became fully accepted, would be joyful, spontaneous, and erotic, and with that one could hope for a withering away of both *Playboy* and the League of Decency. Above all, liberation implies a new diversity, an acceptance of the vast possibilities of human experience, and an end to the attempt to channel these possibilities into ends sanctioned by religious and economic guidelines.

If the homosexual cannot achieve full sexual liberation within society as it exists—for this can only be achieved through a revolutionary change in both social attitudes and structures—he/she can, however, achieve liberation from at least much of the internal oppression imposed by social stereotypes and roles. To overcome this is not sufficient for liberation, but it is an essential step toward it for those who have been deeply stigmatized. And by overcoming this part of her/his stigma, the homosexual is also able to move toward liberation from the restraints of sex roles and the repression of eroticism.

One cannot prescribe liberation, for it arises out of the individual consciousness and demands a greater sense both of autonomy and of community than at present exists. Above all, there is need for a new sense of sister/brotherhood, a willingness to fully accept one's own erotic and sexual being, and a search to construct new sorts of human relationships. It may indeed be profitable to regard liberation as a process rather than an attainable goal, to regard the writings of men like Marcuse and Brown as providing us with aims for which we strive. Liberation does not mean an end to struggle, but it does alter the ends for and the means by which we struggle.

NOTES

1. Boston: Beacon Press, 1955.
2. "Group Sex," *Newsweek,* 21 June 1971, pp. 98–99.
3. Kate Millett, *Sexual Politics* (Garden City: Doubleday, 1970), p. 62.
4. Paul Goodman, "Memoirs of an Ancient Activist," *Win Magazine,* Nov. 15, 1969.

ITALY

Mario Mieli (1953–83) was well known both as a theorist and as an activist in the gay movement. He was a founder in 1971–72 of FUORI (Fronte Unitario Omosessuale Rivoluzionario Italiano), the Italian gay liberation movement. He also published, in 1977, *Homosexuality and Liberation: Elements of a Gay Critique,* from which the following excerpts are taken. Mieli had tremendous personal flair, and in his attempt to live out his ideals, was the subject of frequent scandal. Sadism and masochism, transvestism, and coprophagy were among the elements he incorporated into his personal lifestyle. In *Homosexuality and Liberation,* Mieli merges psychoanalytic theory with Marxism and his own personal experiences to produce a work that is at once insightful, provocative, and even at times humorous. Eros, in Mieli's view, is an undifferentiated desire that our culture, through repression, forces into the straightjacket of compulsive heterosexuality. Only in giving expression to the various elements of our polymorphous potential, including homosexuality, will we attain the state Mieli calls "transsexuality." New levels of interpersonal and erotic communication will then help pave the way to true communism. Meanwhile, gays are a living symbol of the anti-Norm, of that which refuses to be repressed. As such, they are revolutionaries even in their daily acts. In the first three of the four following excerpts, Mieli discusses the pitfalls of social tolerance and the linkage in our society between aggression against gays and paternalism. We must reject being ghettoized and marginalized by our society, he writes. True liberation implies rejecting and subverting the Norm and working toward the liberation of the homosexual that lies repressed in all individuals. In the fourth selection, Mieli discusses the heterosexual fear of anal eroticism, the expression of which has been made taboo in our sex-negative culture.

From *Homosexuality and Liberation: Elements of a Gay Critique* by Mario Mieli, translated by David Fernbach (1980).

1.

The object of the revolutionary struggle of homosexuals is not that of winning social tolerance for gays, but rather the liberation of the homoerotic desire in every human being. If the only result were that so-called normal people should "accept" homosexuals, then the human race would not have recognized its own deep homosexual desire, it would not have come to terms with the universal presence of this, and would go on suffering without remedy from the consequences of this repression. We revolutionary homosexuals, today, do seek to lead other people to follow us, to come with us, so that together we can undertake the subversion of the Norm that represses (homo)eroticism.

Today, the persistence of the antigay taboo provides a sure and potent weapon in the capitalist arsenal. It serves to stupefy people, to maintain a neurotic and submissive "calm." The taboo transforms into a source of horror and guilt one of the basic erotic tendencies, denying every human being the possibility of erotic relations with half the population, dividing people and keeping them apart, preventing love between man and man and woman and woman, and making a fundamental contribution to perpetuating the opposition between the sexes. People "know very well" (even if they don't have a clear understanding) that they have homosexual impulses. The system can then play on their guilt, severely prohibiting homosexuality, on which it stamps the mark of infamy. "Normal" people feel guilty because, underneath it all, they know that they are a little queer themselves. But the sense of guilt is the umbilical cord that chains the human species to capital and half strangles it. If we want to live, we cannot but make a clean break with all such monstrous bonds.

Today, the great fear that surrounds homosexuality is not sustained just on thin air. Deep down inside, everyone can sense the blood that has been shed over the millennia to keep the taboo respected and feared (including castration, imprisonment, exile, torture, and death). Within him or herself, each individual knows he or she is potentially condemned to the flames.

2.

Repressive Desublimation and Reformism

It is impossible to avoid showing up this implicit or even explicit intention to recuperate homosexuals that lies behind the new "progressive" attitude of certain churches and state. It is necessary also to stress how the slow evolution of religious morality and of certain strata of public opinion toward more understanding and tolerant positions tends partially to replace the traditional form of aggression toward us gays by an attitude of protection. But if aggression is phallocratic and protection paternalist, phallocracy and paternalism are simply two sides of the same patriarchal coin. As Oscar Wilde said during his trial: "The one disgraceful, unpardonable, and to all time contemptible action of my life was my allowing myself to be forced into appealing to Society for help and protection. . . ."[1]

The protection of homosexuals, "permissive" morality, tolerance, and political emancipation all together, within certain limits, in the countries of capitalist domination, all these aspects proving in substance functional to the program of commercialization and exploitation of homosexuality on the part of capitalist enterprise. The commercialization of the ghetto pays well: Bars, clubs, hotels, discos, saunas, cinemas, and pornography provide important footholds for those seeking to exploit the "third sex." Capital is working for a repressive desublimation of homosexuality. "Sexuality is liberated (or rather liberalized) in socially constructive forms. The notion implies that there are repressive modes of desublimation. . . ."[2]

The system deploys the same maneuver with respect to other so-called perversions. Voyeurism, for example, is one of the most profitable "perversions" for capital (cinema, pornography, etc.), while remaining in reality repressive. People go to the cinema to see a commodity make love, and this involves a repressive desublimation of the voyeuristic component of our desire, instead of us watching one another make love, enjoying and understanding ourselves, and fusing voyeurism with other forms of pleasure. Repressive desublimation and commercial exploitation are inseparable; Eros remains geared to work and the production of alienating commodities, to the extent that its repressive desublimation provides a market for these.

Tolerance, on the other hand—"repressive tolerance," as Marcuse calls it—simply confirms our marginalization. Toleration of the homosexual minority, in fact, without the majority putting in question the repression of their own homoerotic desire, means recognizing the right of those who are "deviant" to live on the basis of their "deviance" and hence to be marginalized. And this favors the highly increased exploitation of homosexuals on the part of the system that marginalizes them.

In the Italian cities, in Spain, Greece, Portugal, and other countries noted for their generally backward customs, a semiclandestine industry of the "third sex" flourishes, based on ties of strict convenience between entrepreneurs, the police, and organized crime. In the United States, too, the great majority of bars where gay people meet are controlled by the Mafia. Paradoxically, the laws of the State of New York still consider homosexuality as such a crime, though New York City, along with Tokyo and San Francisco, contains what is undoubtedly one of the most extensive, most magnetic, and best organized of homosexual ghettos in the world (including its nearby outcrops of Fire Island and Provincetown). Further evidence of the "rational character of capitalist irrationality" (Marcuse) is given by the link that exists between economic organizations revolving around the exploitation of homoeroticism, and the judicial system. What is prohibited can be sold at a higher price.

What we need to bear in mind, above all, is the effective linkage in capitalist society between aggression and protection, as two sides of the same relationship to us gays. There is no middle zone between the two. In the last instance, the homosexual must be the object of aggression, so that he can then be protected and effectively exploited. On the other hand, protection and integration provide gays with palliative gratifications as well as inuring them to submission and weakening the force of their protest (and apparently, its very motivations). It is clear that neither aggressors nor protectors are aware of the mechanisms that exist between violence and protection, nor are they concerned to become aware of these. Protection provides the medium linking aggression to exploitation, a fact which only revolutionary gays have properly understood.

By far the greater part of homosexuals, even today, remain trapped in the illusions of political emancipation within the existing inhuman capitalist structures. Far from being surprising, this must be viewed as the product of thousands of years of habituation to the Norm (both "normal" and normative), which induces homosexuals, the transgressors, to feel guilty. In the hope of integration, many gays indulge the fantasy of having the father system forgive sins that they have not in fact committed. But the sense of guilt is essentially functional to perpetuating the rules of capital, and liberalization and tolerance themselves provide footholds for the guilt feeling of those who are content merely to be tolerated, the better to be exploited. A homosexual has to feel in a certain sense guilty in order to put up with the anguish and anxiety of the ghetto and to renounce any genuine freedom. Capital, on the other hand, cannot forgive any sin. Firstly, because there are no such things, and secondly, because capital is itself a monstrous industry of sin.

The ideal of political emancipation does not involve any qualitative leap vis-à-vis the conditions of marginalization and exploitation in which homosexuals are presently placed, nor a repudiation of the sense of guilt which would shed light on those really responsible for homosexual suffering. It is time for homosexuals to regain the energies that this guilt has confiscated, and channel them into a genuinely emancipatory struggle, both pleasurable and subversive.

3.

A critical theory, growing as a function of a gay revolutionary project, cannot but take into account everything that is eccentric to the narrow confines of what the dominant subculture considers "normal," permissible, rational. For us homosexuals, there is a clear alternative. Either to adapt to the established uni-verse, and hence to marginalization, the ghetto, and derision, adopting as our own values the hypocritical morality of heterosexual idiocy that is functional to the system (even if with that inevitable and visible variant that is difficult to renounce with a cock up one's arse), and hence to opt for a *hetero*nomy; or else to oppose ourselves to the Norm, and the society of which this is the reflection, and to overturn the entire imposed morality, to specify the particular character of our existential objectives from our own standpoint of marginalization, from our "different" being, as lesbian, bum-boy, gay, in open contrast to the one-dimensional rule of hetero monosexuality. In other words, to opt for our "homonomy." As Sartre wrote about Gide:

> In the fundamental conflict between sexual anomaly and accepted normality, he took sides with former against the latter, and has gradually eaten away the rigorous principles which impeded him like an acid. In spite of a thousand relapses, he has moved forward toward *his* morality; he has done his utmost to invent a new Table of the Law ... he wanted to free himself

from other peoples' Good; he refused from the first to allow himself to be treated like a black sheep.[3]

Gide's position is not essentially different from that of all of us other homosexuals. It is a question of opposing the "normal" morality and of choosing what is good and what is bad from our own marginalized point of view. If we aspire to liberation, we must reject the existing standards. It is a question of making a choice that rejects the Norm. But a gay moralization of life, which combats the misery, egoism, and hypocrisy, the repressive character and the immorality of customary morality, cannot take place unless we root out the sense of guilt, the false guilt which still ties so many of us to the status quo, to its ideology and its death-dealing principles, preventing us from moving with gay seriousness in the direction of a totalizing revolutionary project.

4.

Anal Eroticism

To those who want to give the proletariat the religion of a name, a (false) consciousness, a suit-and-tie and halo, a credibility for the respectable, it is legitimate to counterpose a proletariat that is violent and wild, unconscious, autonomous, and the trinity: SHIT, DEVIL, REVOLUTION.[4]

It is necessary at this point to stress the relationship that exists between the rejection of homosexuality and the repression of the anal component of Eros. In his *Essays on Sexuality,* Freud showed the temporary concentration of infantile libido on the anal erogenous zone: the anal phase that lies between oral eroticism and a fixation on the genital zone that is generally definitive. The stabilization of sexual impulses on the genitals almost always provokes a repression of anal desires, which may even be absolute—except, as a general rule, in "cases" of overt male homosexuality, and a few others.

As Geza Roheim ironically put it, "when . . . excretory functions have become 'not nice' we have reached a high stage of culture." [5] But even Queen Elizabeth goes to the toilet. The present repression of anal pleasure, coprophilia, and urophilia is the result of a historically specific suppression. The anal desire displayed by every child reveals a potential for pleasure that is latent in every adult, and reflects (in the development of the individual) an atavistic erotic expression of the species, which has been progressively more negated over the millennia, and particularly in the last few centuries of capitalism.

The demand for the restoration of anal pleasure is one of the basic elements in the critique made by the gay movement of the hypostatizing of the heterosexual-genital status quo by the dominant ideology. As the French gay liberationists expressed it:

> We have to ask the bourgeoisie: What is your relationship with your arsehole, apart from having to use it to shit with? Is it part of your body, your speech, your senses, in the same way as your mouth or ears? And if you've decided that the only purpose of the anus is to defecate, then why do you use your mouth for the other things besides eating? [6]

In his essay on oral eroticism, Freud shed light on the causal relationship between the unconscious fixation of repressed anal eroticism and certain expressions of character, such as obsessional and sometimes manic attachment to orderliness, parsimony, and obstinacy. In concluding his analysis, he added:

> If there is any basis in fact for the relation posited here between anal eroticism and this triad of character traits, one may expect to find no very marked degree of "anal character" in people who have retained the anal zone's erotogenic character in adult life, as happens, for instance, with certain homosexuals. Unless I am

much mistaken, the evidence of experience tallies well on the whole with this inference.[7]

In my own experience, it is indeed rare to meet gay men who enjoy being fucked and are at the same time obsessively orderly, stingy, and stubborn. But that is not the point.

The point is that if you get fucked, if you know what tremendous enjoyment is to be had from anal intercourse, then you necessarily become different from the "normal" run of people with a frigid arse. You know yourself more deeply. How right De Sade was in writing:

> Ah, did you but know how delicate is one's enjoyment when a heavy prick fills the behind, when, driven to the balls, it flutters there, palpitating, and, then, withdrawn to the foreskin, it hesitates, and returns, plunges in again, up to the hair! No, no, in the wide world there is no pleasure to rival this one: It is the delight of philosophers, that of heroes, it would be that of the gods were not the parts used in his [sic] divine conjugation the only gods we on earth should reverence![8]

Of all the aspects of homosexuality, I would say that the one heterosexual men fear above all is anal intercourse. This is undoubtedly due not just to the repression of their anal desire, but also to their fear of castration—in essence, the fear of falling off the masculine pedestal into the "female" role. The fear of castration, in every male, is the counterpart of his phallic conception of sexuality as erection. Any male heterosexual goes wild at the idea of "not being able to get it up." This is the very end of his virility, and he fears that above all else, as repression has made him identify with the virile model, making him into a wretched guardian of the heterosexual order. The man fears losing his virility because he fears more than anything losing his identity. And he knows very well that behind the boastful facade, this virile identity is fragile indeed, just as the equilibrium in which he balances between rigid phallicism and fear of castration is decidedly unstable.

The absolute male, as a mutilated being, is exclusively "active." And any heterosexual man, who prides himself on identifying absolutely with the male, considers the "passive role" as shameful, abject, and "effeminate." For people of this kind, to be fucked means to be ruined. But if we remove the negative connotation of being "taken from behind," so typically and neurotically masculine, then being fucked can be seen as the great pleasure that it is, a meeting and fusion of bodies, a gay entertainment, delicious both in the arse itself and in the mind. As a general rule, the more fear a man has of being fucked, the more he himself fucks badly, with scant consideration for the other person, who is reduced to a mere hole, a receptacle for his blind phallic egoism. Someone who likes being fucked, on the other hand, will himself know how to fuck well. He knows how to give pleasure, as he knows how to receive it, and he unblocks the restricted fixation of stereotyped roles. To fuck then truly does become a relation of reciprocity, an intersubjective art.

The psychoanalytic conception of the sexual "object" derives from the male heterosexual's sadly crippled view of sexual intercourse. And if Rank indicated the origin of neurosis in the condition of the foetus in the maternal womb, we would go even further and see in heterosexual coitus itself, from which life proceeds, i.e., in the male supremacist and neurotic manner in which this is generally conducted, one of the primary causes of the universal neurosis that afflicts our species.

NOTES

1. Philippe Julian, *Oscar Wilde* (London: Paladin, Grafton, 1971).
2. Herbert Marcuse, *One Dimensional Man* (London: Sphere, 1968).
3. Jean-Paul Sartre, *Baudelaire,* trans. Martin Turnell (London: Horizon, 1949), pp. 48–49.
4. Luciano Parinetto, "Analreligion e dintorni," *L'Ebra Voglio* 26 (June–July 1976), p. 24.
5. Geza Roheim, *The Riddle of the Sphinx* (London: 1934), p. 231.
6. FHAR, *Rapport contre la normalité* (Paris: Éditions Champ Libre 1971), p. 55.
7. S. Freud, "Character and Anal Eroticism," *Standard Edition* 9.
8. Donatien Alphonse François de Sade, *Justine* and other writings (New York: Putnam, 1966).

FRANCE

Guy Hocquenghem (1944–88) was a person of many talents. He earned his reputation as a filmmaker, essayist, novelist, and as one of the first activists in FHAR (Front Homosexual d'Action Revolutionnaire), the French gay liberation movement that was formed in March 1971. As a theorist, one of his major works was *Homosexual Desire* (1972), in which he examines society's fear of homosexuality and sees the movement for sexual revolution as key to any meaningful social change. As with Mieli in France and many of the European intellectuals writing on the gay revolution, Hocquenghem is heavily influenced by both Freud and Marx. Hocquenghem was a supporter, like Genet, of the Black Panther Party in the United States, and was concerned with the issue of racism against foreigners in France, especially the Arab minorities. Hocquenghem taught philosophy at the University of Paris. In the following essay, Hocquenghem, in a manifestolike format, spells out the ways our capitalist, Judeo-Christian, and heterosexist culture has crippled and alienated us from our very bodies, and calls form the liberation of our energies, desires, and passions in the context of a revolution against institutionalized systems of oppression.

**"To Destroy Sexuality" by Guy Hocquenghem,
translated by Tom Gora, from *Semiotext(e)* (1981).**

TO PUT

Although the capitalist order appears to be tolerant, it in fact has always controlled life through its expressive, sexual, emotional, and affective aspects, constraining it to the dictates of its totalitarian organization based on exploitation, private property, male dominance, profit, and profitability. It exercises this control under all of its various guises: the family, schools, the workplace, the army, rules, discourse. It unfailingly pursues its abject mission of castrating, oppressing, torturing, and mangling the body, all the better to inscribe its laws upon our flesh, to rivet into our unconscious its mechanisms for propagating slavery.

The capitalist state uses retention, stasis, scarification, and neurosis to impose its norms and models, imprint its characters, assign its roles, promulgate its programs. . . . It permeates our bodies, forcing its roots of death deep into our smallest crevices. It takes over our organs, robs us of our vital functions, mutilates our pleasures, harnesses all of our "life" productivity under its own paralyzing administration. It turns each of us into a cripple, cut off from his own body. A stranger to his own desires.

AN END

The forces of capitalist occupation continually refine their system of aggression, provocation, extortion so as to use it along with a massive reinforcement of social terror (individual guilt) to repress, exclude, and neutralize all those practices of our will that don't reproduce these forms of domination, and so this thousand-year-old reign of unhappy gratification, sacrifice, resignation, codified masochism, and death perpetuates itself. Here reigns castration, reducing the "subject" to a guilt-ridden, neurotic, industrious being, little more than a manual laborer. This old order, reeking of rotting bodies, is indeed horrifying, but it has forced us to direct the revolutionary struggle against capitalist oppression there where it is most deeply rooted—in the living flesh of our own body.

TO THE

We want to free the space—the context, the locus—of the body and its own specific desires from this "foreign" grip. It is along this "path" that we propose to "work" toward the liberation of social space. There is no separation between the two; I oppress myself because this "I" is the product of a system of oppression operating across all forms of experience.

A "revolutionary consciousness" is nothing but a chimera as long as it remains outside of a "revolutionary body." A body that generates its own freedom.

Here we find women, revolting against the male power that has been inseminated in their bodies for centuries; homosexuals, revolting against the terrorizing fascism of normality; adolescence, revolting against the pathological authority of adults. They have begun, collectively, to open up the body's space to subversion and to open up the space of subversion to the "immediate needs of the body."

Here we find people beginning to question and investigate the various modes by which desire is produced. The links between jouissance—the height of cognitive and sexual fulfillment—and power. Between the body and subject as consciousness, as they exist everywhere throughout capitalist society, even among radical groups.

SLAUGHTER OF

Here we find people who have short-circuited the hackneyed separation between "politics" and lived experience. A separation bringing generous returns to the managers of our bourgeois society as well as to those who pretend to represent the masses and to speak in their name.

Here we find people preparing a great uprising of life against all of the manifestations of death which continually insinuate themselves into our body, ever more subtly binding our energies, desires, reality to the imperatives of the established order. They form the contours of a new fissure. A more radical and definitive confrontation, according to which these revolutionary forces are "necessarily" arranging themselves.

THE BODY

We can no longer stand by idly while we are robbed of our mouths, our anuses, our sexual members, our guts, our veins . . . just so they can turn them into parts for their ignominious machine which produces capital, exploitation, and the family.

We can no longer stand by idly while they control, regulate, and occupy our mucous membranes, the pores of our skin, the entire sentient surface of our body.

We can no longer stand by idly while they use our nervous system as a relay in the system of capitalist, federal, patriarchal exploitation. Nor while they use our brain as a means of punishment programmed by ambient power.

We can no longer not "come" or hold back our shit, our saliva, our energy according to their laws with their minor, tolerated infractions. We want to explode the frigid, inhibited, mortified body that capitalism wants so desperately to make out of our living body.

TO ESCAPE FROM THE SEDENTARY

Wanting the fundamental freedom to enter into these revolutionary practices entails our escaping from the limits of our own "self." We must turn the "subject" within ourselves upside down; escape from the sedentary, from the "civilized state" and cross the spaces of a limitless body; live in the willful mobility beyond sexuality, beyond the territory and repertory of normality. This is how some of us have come to feel the vital need to free ourselves "together" from the grip of the forces that oppress and repress our desires.

We strive to take our personal, intimate life experiences and confront them, explore them, live them collectively. We strive to break down the concrete wall that serves the dominant social order by separating being from appearance, spoken from unspoken, private from social.

We strive to elucidate in common the mechanism behind attraction, repulsion, resistance, orgasm; to make clear the universe of our representations, fetishes, obsessions, phobias. The "unmentionable" has become our preoccupation, our message, our political time bomb since in the realm of social interaction politics exhibits a fundamental wish to be "alive."

We have decided to explode the unbearable secret that power uses against everyone whose lives include any sensual, sexual, or affective involvement whatsoever—the same kind of control it exercises over any real social action that produces or reproduces forms of oppression.

TO DESTROY SEXUALITY.

In order to explore mutually our individual histories, we undertook to determine how our lives as reflected through our desires were entirely controlled by the basic laws of our bureaucratic, bourgeois, and Judeo-Christian society, and how they were subsumed under its rules of maximum profitability, surplus value, and reproducibility. We confronted our individual "experiences" by recognizing that, however "free" they may have appeared to us, we continually conform to the stereotypes of an official sexuality that controls every sexual experience from the conjugal bed to the bordello to say nothing of public toilets, discos, factories, confessionals, sex shops, prisons, schools, subways, etc.

We're not concerned with simply breaking down this official sexuality as one would break down the condition of one's imprisonment within any structure; we want to destroy it, to get rid of it because in the final analysis it functions as an infinitely repeating castration machine designed to reproduce everywhere and in everyone the unquestioning obedience of a slave.

"Sexuality" is just as monstrous in what it "permits" as in what it restricts; clearly, "liberalized" sexual mores and the extension of "eroticism" through advertising to all social life structured and controlled by the managers of "advanced" capitalism do nothing more than increase the efficiency of the "reproductive" function of the "official" libido. Rather than reduce sexual discontent, these practices in fact extend the realm of frustration and "lack" that facilitates the transformation of desire into a compulsive consumerism and guarantees "the creation of demand," the driving power behind capitalism's apologies. There is no fundamental difference between the "immaculate conception" and the publicity-minded prostitute, between conjugal duty and the "enlightened" promiscuity of the bourgeoisie: The progression is unbroken. The same restrictions apply, the same fragmentation of the body as source of desire continues unabated. Only the strategy changes.

What we want, what we desire is to kick in the facade over sexuality and its representations so that we might discover just what our living body is.

TO GET RID OF PROGRAMMED TRAINING.

We want to free, release, unfetter, and relieve this living body so as to free all of its energies, desires, passions crushed by our conscriptive and programmed social system.

We want to be able to exercise each of our vital functions experiencing their full complement of pleasure.

We want to rediscover sensations as basic as the pleasure in breathing that has been smothered by the forces of oppression and pollution; or the pleasure in eating and digesting that has been interrupted by the rhythm of profitability and the ersatz food it produces; or the pleasure in shitting and pederasty that has been systematically assaulted by the capitalist establishment's opinion of the sphincter. It inscribes directly upon this flesh its fundamental principles: the power lines of exploitation. The neurosis of accumulation, the mystique of property and propriety, etc. We want to rediscover the pleasure in shaking ourselves joyously, without shame, not because of need or compensation, but just for the sheer pleasure of shaking ourselves. We want to rediscover the pleasures of vibrating, humming, speaking, walking, moving, expressing ourselves, raving, singing, finding pleasure in our body in all ways possible. We want to rediscover the pleasure in producing pleasure and in creating pleasure that has been ruthlessly straitjacketed by the educational system in charge of producing workers-command consumers.

TO LIBERATE ENERGIES

We seek to open our body to other bodies, to another body; to transmit vibrations, to circulate energies, to arrange desires so that each is free to play out its fantasies and ecstasies, so that we might live without guilt and without inhibiting all the sensual intra- and interpersonal practices we need so our day-to-day reality won't turn into the slow agony that capitalism and bureaucracy project as a model existence. We seek to rip out of ourselves the festering rumor of guilt that for thousands of years has been at the root of all oppression.

Of course, we realize how many obstacles we have to overcome to make our aspirations into something more than the dreams of a small and marginal minority. We are keenly aware that liberating the body for sensual, sexual, affective, and ecstatic relationships is inseparably linked to liberating women and destroying male dominance and role models—especially sexual role models. It is likewise linked to destroying all forms of oppression and "normality."

WE WANT TO BE RID OF ALL ROLES AND IDENTITIES BASED ON THE PHALLUS.

We want to be rid of sexual segregation. We want to be rid of the categories of man and woman, gay and straight, possessor and possessed, greater and lesser, master and slave. We want instead to be transsexual, autonomous, mobile, and multiple human beings with varying differences who can interchange desires, gratifications, ecstacies, and tender emotions without referring back to tables of surplus value or power structures that aren't already in the rules of the game.

We have begun and shall continue to produce a new societal

reality in which the greatest ecstasy combines with the greatest consciousness. We have begun with the body, with the revolutionary body, the productive space of "subversive" strength and the effective space of all oppression. Consequently, we have reunited "political" practice with the reality of the body and its functions by collectively investigating all the various modes of liberation. This is our only chance to fight against the oppressive capitalist state where it works directly. This is the only approach that can truly strengthen us against a system of domination that continually expands its powers of "weakening" and "molding" the individual to its axioms, affiliating him to its order of dogs.

UNITED STATES

Lesbian Nation (1973) is author and former *Village Voice* columnist Jill Johnston's odyssey of coming out as a lesbian and the evolvement of her commitment to lesbian-feminist politics. The book's style is highly engaging: It is witty, quickly paced, and filled with brilliant insights. Johnston mixes the personal with the political as she examines what it means to be both a gay woman and a feminist in the context of a male-dominated and patriarchal society. In the selection that follows, the author discusses the significance of the gay revolution in challenging institutionalized heterosexuality—the mainstay of male power. For her, the roots of gay oppression lie in the oppression of women. The feminist, however, to the extent her struggle remains within the confines of the present patriarchal social order, is limited. It is the lesbian, who is disenfranchised from both the gay movement, where she has experienced sexism, and the feminist movement, where she is treated with fear, who is the key figure in the struggle to end the sexual caste system. It is the gay movement, with its reassertion of the female principle, which can herald a revolution unlike all others in history, where economic and political change meant merely the substitution of one ruling class by another, and no challenge to heterosexual male dominance and the oppression of women.

"Woman Prime," by Jill Johnston, from
Lesbian Nation (1973).

WOMAN PRIME

The continuing emergence of the insurgent gay liberation literature
may soon make it apparent that the gay revolutionary movement
constitutes the first significant challenge to the existing social structures. The counter culture has produced its most important bastard.
The counter culture itself is being exposed as an integral part of the
system challenged by the gay revolution. The culture of hippie
gangbang or folk and hard rock groupie sex. The true counter
culture may now be defined as the gay revolution. The overthrow
of the system implicit in counter culture theory and activities clearly
belongs to the solutions of historical revolutionary change in which
the grounds for the necessities of change have remained unacknowl-
edged and unchallenged. Revolutionary social change in the past has
occurred within systems characterized by institutionalized heterosexuality and oppression of the female. Historically, revolution has
meant the overthrow of one class by another, leaving the oppressive
institution itself intact. Such revolutions result in new class systems
or a return to a previous social order in a new disguise. Gay revolution addresses itself to the total elimination of the sexual caste
system around which our oppressive society is organized and
through which distinctions of class and race are reinforced and
maintained. The target remains the same—the ruling class male,
and the ruling class aspirations of every other male, but not by the
old definition of that target as simply economically oppressive. It is
now recognized that any Marxist-Socialist analysis must acknowledge the sexist underpinnings of every political power base. Gay
liberation cannot be considered apart from women's liberation. Gay
liberation *is* in reality a feminist movement. The oppression of
women is pivotal in the strategy and goals of the gay sexual revolu-

tion. The more overt discrimination and persecution of the male homosexual makes this point clear. I mean that the hatred of the gay male is rooted in the fear of the loss of male power and prestige. Since society accords many special benefits to men it is considered worse for a man to "act like a woman" than the reverse. The upfront gay male surrenders his prestige in a sense by acknowledging he is not participating in the system by oppressing the woman where her oppression begins—in bed. Gay liberation emerged out of women's liberation and through the critically intermediate figure of the lesbian the two liberation fronts unite as a Gay/Feminist movement. The mere feminist is an incipient revolutionary. She is a woman in revolt against her prescribed and confined feminine role but she has not yet envisioned the solution to her dilemma for she persists in recognizing the brute sexual prerogative of the male while seeking reforms to alter her condition *within* the male defined structures *dictated* by that sexual prerogative. The rights of the father to the mother. She has forgotten her own rights to the mother as she once experienced the same erotic and nutritive dependency on the mother as did her son and brother. Her conditioning has been so complete that she has forgotten. The lesbian is the woman who somehow never lost the link or who remembered by some accident of love or contact in an environment that was conducive to remembrance (i.e., jail, boarding school, camp, the WACS, etc.). The lesbian is the key figure in the social revolution to end the sexual caste system, or heterosexual institution, for she is the clearly disenfranchised of the four sexes. She has abdicated her inherited right, or rather command, to participate in the male privilege by association, through bed and marriage and even friendship. From the consciousness of this remoteness from the sources of real power and her corresponding social ineffectuality or position without sanction the lesbian is the figure at this moment in history in the proper place to seize the initiative for change by affirming her own or woman's identity through tactics of mutual support right down at the very level of her social impotence—where she consciously abandons the male system to build her own. The lesbian has experienced male prejudice within gay liberation and heterosexual fear within women's liberation. Both fear/prejudice phenomena are blood kin to the oppressor: the straight ruling class male. The angry lesbian naturally at first joined forces with gay men in the camaraderie of the shared interest of loving one's own sex and the illusion of an "outside" oppressor common to both. That oppressor, of course, being the conventionally straight woman (as well as her male keeper), who also turned out to be many a fearful feminist. In the fast realization of the sexism of her gay brothers, who, after all, partake in the general male privilege, the lesbians made the correct and inevitable withdrawal from organizational and personal alliance with gay men to align themselves with the feminists, who were ill prepared to accept their most rebellious element. It's one thing for a man to be homosexual. Quite another for a woman. The issue keeps turning back over and over to the oppression of women. And then again to the lesbian, who is the most oppressed of women for being most like a woman. Here again is the key to revolution through the lesbian woman. The logic is by now devastatingly clear. The least oppressed woman is the woman most like a man; that is, the straight identified woman who has been called the "real woman" and has been fooled by this definition of herself into thinking her womanhood *depends* on her relation to the straight man who defines her and has called her this "real woman" according as how she suits his needs and remains at his service. This is the ultimate hype for all women. And from this superior cultural vantage point of participation in the male privilege the straight woman (and the straight feminist) see, ironically, the lesbian as the "male identified woman." It should not be so amazing that the most oppressed women will be those who are most womanly (the same principle by the way operating within distinctions of class and race). The woman whose *imitation* of the style of the man, if such it is—and this I resent from the point of view of comfort, men's clothes being far more comfortable and easier to get around in than women's wear—has given people the impression that she is somehow the most manly of women. It seems important right now to make the distinction between imitation and connection. The lesbian may affect a stylistic imitation, but her connection to the actual life and mystique of the male is minimal to nonexistent. The lesbian as practicing woman is now reversing the cultural appraisal of womanhood. The lesbian is woman prime. The woman who maintains or regains her integrity as a woman. By (re)uniting with her feminine principle. The reunion of the mother and the daughter into the true sister principle. The straight woman will discover how she has been colossally duped by being robbed of her womanhood. The irony of this reversal is the crux of the revolution. Its outrageousness is the measure of its truth. The test case of the oppressed woman is the woman who is the most woman. Since it is the nature of woman to be oppressed by societies organized around the heterosexual institution which is defined by the domination of one sex over another the woman who is most oppressed will be the one who refuses to be oppressed by acting independently of the oppressor. And thus not being recognized. And as such being severely oppressed through extreme identity confusion. The liberated political lesbian by this reasoning is of course no longer a woman. Woman being defined as an oppressed person. Defined, in other words, by man. The language is no longer adequate to signify the liberated sex. The woman identified woman was an excellent phrase to help define the lesbian in her prime womanhood in distinction to all women who still partake of male privilege through bed, marriage, and fraternization, but "woman" is too overwhelmingly the name of the sex so called and thus checked and retained by the man. My own use of the word here was convenient to expose the fraud of the "real woman" and establish the is-ness of the lesbian as the sex with the organs commonly referred to as woman. It is not so confusing if we remember that the author always creates her own definitions. Woman creates herself and she can refuse to call herself the name she is oppressed by. Or she can use the name by which she was the *most* oppressed before she recognized that her very oppression was the key to her liberation. The Lesbian. Being so most completely outside the straight system even as a secret lesbian pretending to be straight in certain aspects of her life being thus so being most ideally positioned to seize her own destiny as total woman long predating culturally defined woman once the gay revolution released her consciousness to recognize the institution of oppression and unite with her more truly oppressed "male identified" sisters. All but the most radical of feminists remain the oppressor of both themselves and the lesbian or the lesbian within them waiting to be liberated. As the lesbian sees it the feminist movement is still basically a "reform" movement directed toward bigger and better participation in the male privilege through equality in his system and thus a further denial of her own identity in the wages of power in the same sexual caste system which she claims to be the source of her deprivation. Even so, the lesbian is now dedicated to the true radicalization of feminism by weaning her straight sisters away from their efforts to reform the institution of oppression itself. The constant identification of the media of the lesbian with the male homosexual movement is a clever device to separate women from each other, as though women are not already separated enough, and to continue the negation of the sexuality of women by the subtle (if unconscious) co-option of the most upfront sexual woman (the political lesbian) by the already overwhelmingly recognized sexuality of the male, whether straight or gay, and perhaps especially the gay in his well-known pursuit of variety and quantity. The woman is again a token—this time in the context of the gay revolution. By media pronouncement at least. For in reality the lesbian feminists constitute the revolutionary core of the feminist movement. Gay/Feminism advocates an end to the oppressive heterosexual institution. The lesbian and the gay male by their very existence are a threat to the program of marriage/family/ home that every child is conditioned to believe is "the true way." For gay is roleless, or consists of relations of equality naturally obtaining between members of the same sex. Biological equals. The feminist rhetoric is steeped in a denial of biological destiny. For if they can deny the biological forces that created the cultural conditions of oppression, they can start with the culture and work from the top as it were to reform things where they appeared to go amiss,

and thus retain the man with whom they consider themselves originally (that is, biologically) parous. But biology is not simply ancient
or primeval history. Biology is right now. One can observe the
constant renewal of biological imperatives creating their novel if
always patriarchal forms of cultural oppression. It is impossible to
disentangle biology and culture. The cultural takeover of the male
is biologically motivated. All systems of inequity are rooted in some
biological imperative of the male. The female was originally the self-
sufficient self-re-creating creature. The male one of her offspring.
The male could re-create himself only through the female. Herein
lies the desperation of man and culture. Or: all systems of inequity.
Family, church, state, racism, despotism, feudalism, capitalism, nationalism, imperialism, communism, etc. The primary creature was
parthenogenetic, whether you call her a female or not. The cultural
repression of woman is rooted in womb envy. If you can do it and
I can't, that's *all* you can do. Man and culture are synonymous. The
theory Engels developed to account for the transition from matriarchy to patriarchy remains as good as any to describe the simultaneous evolution of culture and the captivity of woman. If the
woman had in some transient sense needed the male to re-create
herself by impregnation she nonetheless was never in any doubt as
to her self-re-creation or the identity of her offspring. The domination of the female by which the sexual caste system was effected
must have occurred in prolonged periods of great historical change
during which the male in his restless quest for identity somehow
invented the concrete means of imposing parental primacy through
the secondary phenomenon of culture—the institutions of control
and submission. The ownership of tools, property, etc. Then the law
to safeguard that ownership. Then the institutions of learning to
transmit the law. And so forth. The ultimate property always being
women and children. The female was gradually weakened in all her
powers, except for periodic outbursts of insanity, by her captivity
enforced around her "reproductive sexuality" and related role playing evolving over centuries into the rigid structures of correctness
by which she eagerly embraces her own coercion in the mores of

forgetfulness. The female has forgotten her freedom and her struggle to resist the moment of her coercion. Gay revolution is the first significant challenge to the existing social structures which are characterized by oppression of the female. The contemporary gay revolutionary male is the first homosexual male in history to relinquish some crucial aspect of his male privilege by not leading the double life by which he had it both ways in the sense of maintaining a straight pretense thus oppressing women and of participating in the gay underworld. This is not to underestimate the problems of identity for gay males in all societies rigidly defined as straight. Some of these revolutionary types remain straight identified males who oppress each other in the manner of role playing heterosexuality, rejecting the woman without consciousness of women's oppression. This is the gay male with a gay head in rebellion against the suppression of his gay identity, without a feminist consciousness or an active struggle with his own sexism. There are very few Gay/Feminist males. In some sense there can't be. A gay male might come closest to experiencing woman's oppression by appearing at large, not as a transvestite or passing for female, but as an obvious male who is surrendering privilege by overt female dress and behavior. A beard and a skirt and stockings, say. Even so, the gay revolutionary male has withdrawn support from the nuclear weapon of the sexual caste system by which he is damned and curtailed in his freedom to love his own sex: the family. Home, church, and state are the enemies of sexual revolution. The most virulent outspoken enemy of homosexuality before the advent of the psychiatric profession was the church. As the chief agent of the patriarchal judeo-christian tradition the church sustained the task of legitimizing oppression to safeguard the system of its own profit and continuation in collaboration with the state or man, or culture, however you have it. Gay liberation has moved so far in a decade beyond the conventional notions of deviancy and abnormalcy imposed by these agencies that it seems a commonplace now to remind anyone who may not know that the gay revolutionary is no longer interested in being tolerated or accepted by a society we consider to be sick in its straightness.

During the 1960s homosexuals were still seeking integration into society—agreeing that homosexuality was deviant while pleading to be given a chance to show society how square—if not straight—they could be. Gay militancy is defined by its refusal to conform to an oppressive culture by submitting to therapy or by pretending to be straight. Psychiatry favors individual solutions rather than social change. The emphasis is on conformity and adjustment rather than liberation. As Dennis Altman said, "No longer is the claim made that gay people can fit into american society, that they are as decent, as patriotic, as clean living as anyone else. Rather, it is argued, it is american society itself that needs to change." The axis of gay revolution is the shift from apology to affirmation and from affirmation to aggressive redefinition. The aim is an end to the organization of society around the sexual polarities of "male" and "female." An end, in other words, to sexual duality or the two-sex system and a gradual evolutionary movement through the massive liberation of homosexuality back to the true parthenogenetic species. All men start off as women and that's the way they'll end up if they don't destroy us all first. All forms of civilized culture are expressions of the profound conflict between man and woman. The congealed institutions of oppression at every level reflect the outcome of a struggle for parental primacy which the woman lost. Yet the woman is parent prime, and the man in his anxiety and desperation to become the master of himself has pitched himself against "nature" (woman) in his creation of culture as a kind of monstrous compensation for a real or at least felt inadequacy. The world in the 20th century is a spectacle of the gross amplification of the insecure man. Certain of his own immortality only through the subjugation of woman. Man is completely out of phase with nature. Nature is woman. Man is the intruder. The man who reattunes himself with nature is the man who de-mans himself or eliminates himself as man. The man correctly attempts to do this in his wars against himself but he carries too much of nature along with him as he does it. Gay revolution or the reassertion of the female principle is the peaceful means of de-manning society by reintegration with the polymorphous sexuality of perverse equalities. "Heterosexual men are driven to abuse women because they can't directly express the love they have for each other. They literally fuck their friends' women because they are unable to fuck their friends." (Steve Dansky, "Hey, Man," in *Gay Flames Collective*) Or Altman: "The argument that men fight each other because they are unable to love each other is a version of Marcuse's formulation that aggression results from a failure to give sexuality free reign." Revolutionary social change in the past has occurred within systems characterized by institutionalized heterosexuality and oppression of the female. Historically, revolution has meant the overthrow of one class by another, leaving the oppressive institution itself intact. Such revolutions result in new class systems or a return to a previous social order in a new disguise. Gay revolution means an end to the sexist underpinnings of every political-economic power base extant which have remained unchallenged in the successive waves of class and racial disorder leading to novel forms of oppression.

ARGENTINA

In 1973, the Frente de Liberación Homosexual (Homosexual Liberation Front) made its appearance in Argentina. It was a leftist-oriented movement with well-articulated goals and objectives. By 1976, however, military dictatorship returned once again to the country, and large numbers of individuals perceived of as threats to the new social order began to disappear—many, as it later turned out, having been tortured and murdered. As the gay movement was very politicized and antidictatorial, the Frente was disbanded and its members either were murdered by the state or forced underground. The following excerpts are taken from one of its documents, *Sex and Revolution*. It is a scientific analysis rooted in Marxist and neo-Freudian ideas. The arguments, however, are well articulated and are presented without the dogmatism sometimes associated with leftist analyses. After examining the family and its role in perpetuating male dominance and the inequalities of the status quo, the authors talk of the repression of pleasure and the need for revolution. As in writings by gay movements in other countries with strong Marxist traditions, answers are given to typical objections gay movements are confronted with by established leftist organizations, namely the charge that the gay movement is sectarian and thus divisive, and that homosexuality is the result of bourgeois decadence.

**From "Sex and Revolution," a document by the
Homosexual Liberation Front of Argentina (1974),
translated by Sam Larson.**

1.

The human being faces, beginning at birth, a primary group: the
family. What is meant by family? For a human being, whose period
of apprenticeship (infancy) is the most prolonged on a biological
scale, a specific social agency is needed that will provide orientation,
help, and maintenance during this process. This means that the
family is a factory of social human beings. Now, just as a social
group based on exploitation needs people who are preadapted to
enter into the process of alienated production, so the family, as a
sustainer, must become a de-forming agent.

The family is a microsociety that reproduces on a seedbed the
system that nourishes it. The worn-out affirmation that "the family
is the base of society" acquires validity. This is because it reproduces
all its characteristics and because it is the agent of production for
human beings who are conditioned to the system.

Within a standard family, there exists a deforcer of power, the
male. Not only does he control the economic power of the family
and the political power within society, but he also controls by self-
appointed right the system of familial relationships and its extension,
social relationships. His object of domination is, firstly, the woman;
and, secondly, the children, who are the commodity-product of the
familial fabric. The ultimate reason for the family is to produce
beings who can replace their progenitors in the world of work,
ingraining in them beforehand the mechanisms of domination so
that they will perform them without protest. In such a manner,
what is verified and assured at this level, and on other levels of
social life, is the dichotomy of oppressor/oppressed.

This domination is not only a question of abstract theory. Its essence is revealed in the sexual power of the male over the female during intercourse. Intercourse becomes an institution culturally structured for the satisfaction of the man, who retains all initiative and who alone possesses the legitimate right to pleasure. This domination in intercourse is the ultimate example of, in an ideological field, the objective manifestation of the domination of the woman by the man in daily life. This is how the woman becomes an object of pleasure and reproduction. It is necessary to emphasize that the system imposes on her the obligation to carry out housework without giving her any right to remuneration, which unmasks her true situation, domestic slavery.

This schema of the couple corresponded more or less with the laws of our civilization (the males govern, the females obey), until the moment in which the capitalist process started to incorporate women into the productive apparatus by virtue of its growing needs of production. This insertion undermined male authority to some extent and instilled new requirements onto women. Nevertheless, the male did not renounce his power: He was obligated to make concessions; and at the same time, a large part of his authority over the family was transferred to the state, which exercises it, directly or not, through other ideological apparatuses, such as schools and mass media. The collective achievements of women have not managed to change—even now—the essence of the system of male domination. The men, in fact, continue controlling the basic means of production and continue playing the principal role in sex. The nucleus for the oppression of women thus remains intact.

This unit of domination, in which the new equality is a "bluff," reproduces itself and has children, thus playing out the role for which it is formed. The children are the objects of paternal domination. The father, who controls the income, possesses concomitantly the power to give unappealable orders, supported by the deceitful ideology that the child is a chronically disabled individual without any power of right to choose. The child is sanctified by the judicial concept of the home. It is deprived of rights to the point that, in the area of sexuality, infantile sexuality is considered "a recent discovery."

The first main sexual object for a child in current literature—the mother—is prohibited to him by an immemorial taboo: the taboo of incest, which is one of the multiple ends that consist to reinforce the authority of the father and his exclusive right to sexual access to the mother. In general all sexual activity is prohibited to the child: touching, masturbation, etc. Infantile sexuality, however, shows a variety of impulses, coprophilic, homosexual, fetishistic, heterosexual, bestial, autoerotic, etc., that by manifesting themselves prior to the process of socialization, proves that they are inalienable parts of a libidinal human "polymorphic pervert" (in the language of families, "that little degenerate"). Infantile sexuality shows the variety of impulses of all types that form the human libido, and in this sense is the truest face of life.

The truth is that, in sexuality, in the multiplicity and richness of its potentialities, there is inscribed the first hint of freedom that we find in nature, and it is this enormous river of potential energy of the libido that must be diverted toward the social goal of alienated work.

The castration of sexuality has as an objective introducing the characteristic domination of the system into the mind itself, into its innermost recesses, to "soften" the human being in fertile ground for the ideology of the system and alienated labor. A human being who transfers his sexual impulses to an object of domination would not be surprised to find repressed and dominated individuals in the social world; a human being who transfers his sexual impulses to an object of domination is prepared to adopt without questioning the role of dominator and/or dominated. In the system of castes, males are educated in domination and females in submission. The individual internalizes the same roles found in the family; the father will be an oppressor if he is male, and the mother submissive if she is female. The authoritarian father figure is reproduced later in the form of the police, the landlord, the State, and, above all, sustainers of the system that individuals will bow down to as before the father. In this way the schema of domination is faithfully transferred to the individual through the family. In the class system, each person receives the training according to the place that is predestined for him. The son of the bourgeoisie is taught to command the proletarian and at the same time obey his hierarchical superiors. The son of the proletarian is taught to be a worker, or in other words to obey the boss—or to eventually try to be a boss also.

The domination of the libido (sexuality) culminates with its reduction to specific parts of the body, the genitals. In reality, the *whole* body is capable of contributing to sexual pleasure, but the society of domination needs the maximum areas of the body possible to assign them to work. Genitalization is designed to deprive the body of its function as a producer of pleasure and to convert it into an instrument of alienated production, leaving to sexuality only that which is deemed indispensable for reproduction. This is why the system condemns with special severity all forms of sexual activity that is not the penetration of the penis into the vagina, calling them "perversions," pathological deviations, etc. To chain the human being to alienated work it is necessary to mutilate him, reducing his sexuality to the genitals.

2.

But this is not the entire picture of male oppression. Those individuals who do not comply with the established sexual roles, the homosexuals, are seen as a maximum danger by this system, for not only do they defy it, but they belie its pretensions of identifying itself with the natural order. Nothing in the biological sciences authorizes us to overvalue one form of sexual relation to the detriment of others. The desexualization of the human body is the work of the culture. In the case of the man, passive anal intercourse, the use of the anus as a sexual zone, is punished—despite the fact that it is surrounded by erotic nerve endings. A strict taboo is also constructed concerning male nipples, despite their being an erogenous zone, by the simple similarity to female anatomy.

The sexual ideology of the system does not get its validity from a correct biological theory, as it sometimes pretends through its scientific spokesperson, but instead it structures its standards according to its interest in domination. These interests militate against pleasure that would debilitate the reserve of alienated work, and instead places reproduction as the sole objective of sex. Everything else is sin. . . .

This is why male culture needs to classify homosexuals as "degenerates," "sick," "abnormal," and "delinquents." In reality, the homosexuals revindicate the inherent plastic possibilities of the human libido that the sexist system of domination is compelled to mutilate. As we saw before, the libido encompasses in itself, without conflict, the total gamut of possibilities of human relations: The homo- and heterosexual tendencies live together within it in perfect harmony. It is the process of alienated socialization that introduces the separation between good and evil, guilt and bad conscience.

This unequal repartition of sexual power in favor of heterosexual men is reflected in a powerful ideology (internalized compulsively by members of our society). Those who violate its laws—some of which are written and some not, although both types are effectively enforced—not only receive a moral sanction (i.e., guilt), but are imprisoned through the same repressive apparatus of the State. For example, the exercising of sexuality by minors—those for whom the system denies the rights of pleasure—brings about punishment for the partner and qualifies the judge to confine the minor in a reformatory, as if a crime had been committed. But it is the homosexuals that are the scapegoats of sexual repression, upon whom the most severe and immediate punishments fall. Take, for example, a police edict being enforced in the capital that prohibits, without discrimination, any public incitement of sex. In practice, this law is never applied to male heterosexuals who publicly make passes at women, even when they are made in a brutal fashion; but a woman who makes a pass at a man, or a homosexual who looks at another man in the street, automatically suffers the full weight of oppression. Other antihomosexual edicts penalize private gatherings of homosexuals, or if an alleged homosexual walks along the street with a minor. These examples reveal the existence of a discriminatory persecution, which is exercised by the State through the police against the unconventional forms of sexuality, and reflect the overt enforcement of the male system, and likewise the purpose of those who exercise the power to perpetuate it.

3.

The Homosexual Liberation Front considers that the historic moment has arrived for a revolution that simultaneously, along with the economic and political bases of the system, liquidates its sexist ideological bases, taking into account that the system of oppression would otherwise automatically reproduce itself after a revolutionary process that would only have altered the political and economic spheres. Our movement arises as a homosexual organization of both sexes that refuses to continue supporting a situation of marginalization and persecution, due to the exercising of one of the forms of sexuality. As we have tried showing through this document, this persecution has a purely political root. Sex itself is a political question. In this manner, the liberation we postulate cannot have a place within an economic system of domination, such as the dependent capitalism of Argentina. But starting from the point of our own marginalization, questioning a sexist society, we reach a global questioning of society. We homosexuals are a segment of society that suffers from a form of discriminate and specific repression, one that originates in the interests of the system itself and is being internalized by the majority of the population, including some segments that pretend to be revolutionary.

In this sense, many of the forms of antihomosexual prejudice remain intact, disguised as political criticisms. As an example, it is put forth as an objection that homosexuality is a product of decadent capitalism. But societies that were not capitalist or decadent, like the Incas, practiced and praised it. We have already seen that the original human libido does not disdain *any* of its possibilities. Behind that criticism hides the incapacity to formulate a new order, one that can truly revolutionize everyday life. Faced with the moral crises of the bourgeoisie, there exists the pretense of returning to the Hispanic morality of the nineteenth century, putting aside the repeated cases of indigenous Americans that our conquerors burned alive for having practiced in light of day "the unnameable offense."

Another objection is that the Homosexual Liberation Front is a sectarian movement in that it does not integrate itself into the other movements of liberation politics. The answer is very simple: We, like almost all marginalized people, are not going to be defended by anyone except ourselves. In reality, the argument is false, for it is they who marginalize us. What is important is the nucleation and politicization of a sector traditionally denied and marginalized that has remained, as such, separated from all power of decision, including the right to make use of one's own body.

Some consider as contradictory the fact that while we postulate sexual liberation, we organize ourselves as homosexuals. To do it otherwise would mean dissolving our specific oppression, forgetting that on us weighs a specific condemnation. Those who are oppressed specifically by the sexism in the heart of this capitalist society are us, the homosexual men and women, while the heterosexual males objectively acquire, socially speaking, the characteristic of being the oppressive group. Of course, this characteristic of oppressor is not chosen freely by them, but it is culturally imposed by a society of domination—which is not an obstacle for them to freely enjoy the advantages that their position offers them over women and homosexuals. . . .

Machismo is eminently counterrevolutionary and antihuman in that it represents the exacerbation of the standards of economic and sexual domination. We characterize it as in-house fascism. The bourgeoisie use it to dominate more effectively; for the oppressed, machismo represents the only level in which they can equal themselves to their master, and as such works as a compensation mechanism, as inefficient as it is illusionary from a critical perspective, because it props the foundations of oppression on which the system is built. In this way, the machista attitudes are a "boomerang" in the hands of the working class. It is a method by which the worker oppresses his wife or a homosexual to seek vengeance from his master who "fucks him" (who exploits and dominates him) and his companions on a daily basis. This is why, as long as our thinking does not elaborate a new formulation of what daily life needs to be, people will continue being revolutionary in the streets and counter-revolutionary in the home, where they, furthermore, will reproduce in their children the schema of domination.

GREAT BRITAIN

David Fernbach is a cofounder of Gay Men's Press in London, the author of several articles, and the translator of both *The Men with the Pink Triangle* and Mario Mieli's *Homosexuality and Liberation*. In his monograph *The Spiral Path* (1981), the author examines the contribution of gay liberation to human survival. He attributes much of the world's most serious problems (the threat of ecological disaster and nuclear holocaust) not only to exploitative economic systems but also to the propensity for violence endemic to masculine culture. Gay liberation and the feminist movement, in his estimation, offer a challenge to the gender system and thus an important link in the advancement to a Communist and egalitarian society. In the selections that follow, Fernbach clarifies how traditional patterns of homosexuality, unlike the present gay movement, differed little from the male-female model. There can be no true liberation until the gender system and the masculinization of culture are overturned.

From *The Spiral Path: A Gay Contribution to Human Survival*, by David Fernbach (1981).

1.

Sexuality and the Gender System

Homosexuality, like heterosexuality, can take a whole range of possible forms. It can be separated from the emotion of love, or it can combine with this in the way that forms the specifically human pair-bond—whether temporary or permanent, exclusive or nonexclusive. It can display the various "perversions" in which a particular partial drive, such as fixation to a certain fetish, comes to dominate sexual release. And as with heterosexuality, too, its object need by no means be simply the same sex in general, but can be restricted to a particular type of individual. Given the plasticity and adaptability of human sexuality, it would be completely within the spectrum of possibility, therefore, that the great majority of children should grow up to be preferentially homosexual, rather than preferentially heterosexual. If there is so far no single human society that has not allotted heterosexuality pride of place, this is certainly not a function of the biological need to procreate. For only a very small amount of heterosexual activity is required, relative to the general human need for sexual satisfaction, to bring about an average of one pregnancy per adult woman every few years. The real reason is the sexual division of labor which is common in some form or another to all human societies to date, and requires the heterosexual pair-bond as its cement. This in no way rules out homosexuality, but it ascribes it always a secondary role—even when exalted as the "highest form of love," as, for example, by the slaveowners of ancient Greece. The position that homosexuality assumes in a society is circumscribed, in the first place, by the parameters of institutionalized heterosexuality.

For the present purpose I am not concerned with those human societies in which male domination is as yet virtually undeveloped, but rather with the forms that homosexuality takes in the context of the fully developed gender system. If the sexual division of labor imposes a first set of parameters on homosexuality, then male domination very definitely imposes a further set. This is the situation in which we find ourselves today, the combination in the gender system of the sexual division of labor and male domination. And it is not hard to see what this means for the expression of male homosexuality.

In the gender system, male dominance over women is expressed in the sexual sphere by a relative suppression of female sexuality. The man alone is brought up to be an active subject; the woman is relegated to a passive object, whose primary task in sex is to meet the needs of the man. Within this context, the space left for female sexual satisfaction can vary. In certain societies—Japan, for example—clitoral sexuality is recognized, and the successful satisfaction of female desire is incumbent on the man, if he is to be deemed a good lover. But so long as women are subservient to men politically and economically, this is simply a bonus.

A more typical case is that of our own Western society, where female sexuality has been reduced to a "vaginal" pleasure at best, if not annulled altogether. And there are many societies, especially in Africa, that practice the cruelest and most extreme forms of clitoridectomy and infibulation.

The normal man, then, is the man who fucks, the man for whom pleasing his partner is at best secondary, at worst simply unnecessary, even incomprehensible. It is no coincidence that the word for the "male role" in sex, heterosex in particular, has come to be associated with violence and oppression.

If heterosexuality has always been institutionalized in the family, homosexuality has no such universal necessity. It is perfectly possible to do without it, i.e., to bring up children so that in the normal case they are exclusively heterosexual, and to use the system of social control to clamp down on any obstinate minority who persist in a homosexual preference. This is the pattern that our own society has favored for thousands of years. As part of the campaign by the gay movement to gain social acceptance, it was understandable that we should turn to other societies where homosexuality is allowed a legitimate existence, and present these as a counterexample. But if the forms this takes are examined, they invariably turn out to be quite other than gay. For where homosexuality is permitted, and even institutionalized, this is always in forms that are consonant with the gender system, whereas our gayness is irredeemably contrary to the gender system and comes into being in objective opposition to it.

The Ford and Beach survey of homosexuality, in their book *Patterns of Sexual Behavior,*[1] is still the most comprehensive of its kind. They found some form of homosexuality to be socially acceptable in 47 of the 76 societies in their sample. This study, which followed hard on the heels of the first Kinsey reports and was directly inspired by Kinsey's own work, is often cited as evidence that homosexuality is quite normal to human society and that our Western society is untypical in repressing it. Careful study of the Ford and Beach findings, however, gives little encouragement to gay liberationists. Right for a start, the 29 societies where homosexuality is "not to be found," and even sometimes fiercely repressed, included many that are still firmly in the gathering/hunting stage, such as the Sanpoil Indians and the Trukese of Oceania, so that it is quite impossible to look back, as John Lauritsen, for example, does in his *Religious Roots of the Taboo on Homosexuality,*[2] to some assumed "golden age" before the development of monotheism.

Among the 47 societies where some form of homosexuality is acceptable, the most common form, according to Ford and Beach, is that of the berdache. Though most commonly associated with the indigenous peoples of North America, this phenomenon is to be found in every continent. A certain proportion of young men here either decide, or it is decided for them, to reject the masculine role and live instead as "women." The extent to which they are subsequently differentiated from biological women may vary. In some societies a berdache can be married to a man in a very similar way as a regular woman; in others the berdache plays a religious role outside the family system, or may serve as a [very respected] prostitute.

It might seem strange that gay men should look back to the berdache as an ancestor, since his role is far more akin to the contemporary male-to-"female" transsexual, who refuses to define himself as gay and clings to the quite false belief that he is really a woman. If we are justified in so doing, it is only to the extent that the berdache, like gay men today, is characterized by an effeminacy that brings him into conflict with the masculine role. Yet in societies where the berdache appears there is no real space for an intermediate category between "proper" men and "proper" women. If you can't be a "proper" man, then you must at least try to be a "proper" woman, inasmuch as this is at all possible for a biological male.

Far less common than the berdache, but still found in 13 of the 76 societies in this survey, is a form of homosexuality in which adult men have sexual relations with young boys, as yet uninitiated into manhood. Here the homosexual relationship may often be harnessed to an educational role, but this is not necessarily so. In the Egyptian desert, for example, "prominent Siwans lend their sons to each other, and they talk about their masculine love affairs as openly as they discuss their love of women."[3] In this form, male homosexuality is evidently constructed quite differently to the berdache. If the berdache phenomenon involves a small minority of males who are pressed back into normalcy through transfer to the feminine role, man-boy relations of this kind are completely normal for both parties involved, as part and parcel of standard masculine behavior. Yet there is still a basic affinity between these two forms. In both, normal adult men relate to their partners, whether berdache or boy, in a way modeled on penis-vagina intercourse. Anal intercourse, with the adult man in the "active" role, is the universal form. What pleasure the "passive" partner receives is at best secondary, just as it is for women in a male-dominant society. For the berdache, this fact needs no justification, since the berdache is defined as a woman.

For boys who are to grow up into normal men, however, the situation is more complicated. Their need to be fucked may be justified in the name of education, as in ancient Greece. Among the Kiwai of New Guinea, "sodomy is practiced in connection with initiation to make young men strong,"[4] and similar myths are retailed by the neighboring Keraki. Ultimately, young boys are smaller and weaker than their elders and betters, and have to do what they are told. They can always console themselves by knowing that the time will come when they in turn will assume the adult role. But it is even less possible here than in the case of the berdache to see anything corresponding to our contemporary conception of gayness.

Far more rare than anal intercourse, according to Ford and Beach, is mutual masturbation between males, with only three societies out of the 76 where this was practiced among adults. Here again, this is a standard part of adult male behavior. But for men already used to coitus with women this can only be a secondary outlet, possibly associated with the long periods in which women are considered unclean, following childbirth or menstruation. And finally, "oral-genital contact," found only in one case, the native American Crow, turns out to involve a kind of berdache, known as the *bate*. Any sexual relationship between adult men on an equal basis is thus virtually nonexistent.[5]

Given not only the institutionalization of heterosexuality, but in most cases male domination into the bargain, these data are in no way surprising. The gender system offers men sexual satisfaction based on an unequal ascription to them of the role of active subject. Sex is thus their own pleasure above all, a mutual pleasure only secondarily at best. And the general form in which this unequal relationship is practiced is that of the active man fucking his partner-object, whether this is a woman, a young boy, a berdache, or even an animal. The masculine sexuality constructed in this way is certainly one-sided, but this does not mean that other components are repressed (e.g., homosexuality, in those societies where this is not to be found). There may well be a balanced "sex economy" in the Reichian concept, which might actually have something to be said for it once it is freed from the false assumption that female sexuality is vaginal and follows the same rhythms as male. Men do not necessarily have anything to gain, in this situation, from exploring forms of sexuality that are socially defined as deviant. And even in a situation of generalized sexual repression, such as our own society is just emerging out of, this repression, as far as most men are concerned, means the suppression of their heterosexual outlets —that, is of the sexuality that society has brought them up to develop, but then not allowed them sufficiently to practice.

The gender system is a system of domination of women by men, generally associated with a hierarchical order among men themselves. Both male and female sexuality, in this context, cannot but assume forms that the system impresses on them. As far as male homosexuality goes, there are only a very few possibilities. The berdache phenomenon and sexual relations between men and boys are two of these, each very different in content but each equally consonant with the norms of the gender system. Within this system there is very little room indeed for sexual relations between males on an equal basis.

Even in Western society, forms of homosexuality that are constant with the gender system are not entirely absent. One of these is that characteristic of institutions such as prisons, where both male and female homosexuality have always carried on a furtive existence. Among men, here, the general rule is for the older or stronger to fuck the younger or weaker, reducing him not just in status, but in a very material sense, to the subordinate position of a woman. (Which is not to say that the dominant male does not generally offer certain tidbits, in the form of protection or even presents, in return for sexual services.) This is a form of homosexuality among normal men. As an emergency outlet when women are unavailable, it is largely free of the taboo and stigma that would otherwise attach to male homosexuality. Yet in the absence of the kind of institutionalization found in certain other societies, it is inherently unstable. It is maintained in the prison situation only by brute force.

A second quasi-acceptable form of male homosexuality is the

mutual masturbation of adolescent boys, which again is considered perfectly normal. But this is similarly unstable. It breaks down precisely because the peculiar conditions of the prison situation do not obtain; the older boys generally do not have any means of forcing the younger boys to accept being fucked, and are free to seek a "cavity" elsewhere, as Freud so inimitably puts it.[6] Homosexuality between normal men, in our society, exists only in these unstable interstices where heterosexuality is uncharacteristically excluded. But just as with the forms of berdache and man-boy sexual relations in certain other societies, our own forms of normal homosexuality also have nothing gay about them. However much it might provide material for gay fantasies, normal homosexuality is the diametrical opposite of gayness. Homosexuality between normal men is structured by the gender system and can take a stable form only as a relationship between dominant and subordinate modeled on that between man and woman. Gayness, on the other hand, comes into being in objective opposition to the gender system, as a deviant form, and the more it escapes the vicious influences of the gendered society around it, the more it takes a form that is inherently egalitarian.

2.

There are three things in the concept of "sexual liberation" that are perfectly valid. First, the insistence that mere liberalization is not enough; the complex of sex-negative attitudes must be completely overthrown, and sex must be seen clearly for what it is, a source of tremendous pleasure and satisfaction that can validly be pursued for its own sake. Second, the insight that sexual repression leads to repressive and authoritarian attitudes in other fields as well, and generally makes it far more difficult for people to formulate their interests and needs in a rational way. And thirdly, that with the separation of heterosex from procreation, there is no reason whatsoever why homosexuality should not be as universal and acceptable as heterosexuality. (A conclusion not generally drawn by theorists of "sexual liberation" before the rise of the gay liberation movement, Wilhelm Reich being the most notoriously antihomosexual of these.)

Yet the preconditions of gay liberation go far beyond this. Not in the false sense of making sex the be-all and end-all of human existence; but in the sense that there can be no true solution to the problem of the subordinate status of homosexuality and the oppressed position of the gay minority until the gender system is completely done away with. For as I have argued, it is not simply sexual activity with other men that the gender system suppresses, but more fundamentally our characteristic effeminacy. As long as masculinization is the rule, then the ideology of the gender system will torture gay men with our failure to live up to its norm, as will the queer-bashers who are straining every nerve in their determination to be "proper" men. (It is important to note that queer-bashing has not undergone any significant decline in the last three decades of the "sex wave." Nor do more enlightened policies of containment on the part of the legal and moral order seem to have had much effort on this gut-level hostility toward the effeminate.)

The greatest achievement of gay liberation, therefore, has been its recognition that our oppression can only be brought to an end by the abolition of the gender system, in convergence with the women's liberation movement. This goal is not only possible today, because child care no longer need be ascribed solely to women; it is also essential, as the masculine specialization in violence must be eliminated if we are not going to use the high-technology weapons that our science has developed in a cataclysmic spiral of destruction. This crucial link with the feminist movement, and through it with the movement for communism in general, was first made in the early days of GLF, and marks a qualitative transformation in the significance of the gay movement.

Of course, it is only a minority, even among those actively engaged in the gay movement, who have a clear understanding of this goal. This is a problem encountered by all movements against oppression, and indeed a radical formulation of the requirements of liberation can rarely obtain a mass audience, except at those times of crisis when political consciousness is heightened and momentous decisions have to be made. The same problem is certainly shared by the women's movement, by the movement of the working class, and others. But the crisis is already looming, and the time is rapidly coming when the illusion of the eternal character of the present social order will be most rudely shattered. If even a minority have some notion in advance of the direction to take for survival, this may prove a great asset for our society as a whole.

NOTES

1. C. S. Ford and F. A. Beach, *Patterns of Sexual Behavior* (London: Methuen, 1970).

2. John Lauritsen, *Religious Roots of the Taboo on Homosexuality: A Materialist View* (New York: the author, 1974).

3. Ford and Beach, op. cit., p. 139.

4. Ibid., p. 140.

5. It is useful to compare the data on female homosexuality. There is only information for this among 17 of the societies in the Ford and Beach survey, and in many of these a penis substitute is employed, no matter how redundant this is in terms of clitoral stimulation. Even among the Australian Aranda, when women stimulate one another's clitoris, "one of them will say to the other 'a man will come with a big penis and cohabit with you.' " (p. 141). The space for female homosexuality, in other words, seems to be as strictly confined to that compatible with the heterosexual role as is the case with male homosexuality.

6. S. Freud, "Three Essays on the Theory of Sexuality," *Standard Edition,* vol. 7 (London: Hogarth, 1975), p. 222.

MEXICO

The Mexican Gay Liberation Movement has consisted of several movements, centered chiefly around the country's two largest cities, Mexico City and Guadalajara. In Mexico City itself, in 1971, the Frente de Liberación Homosexual came into existence, largely in response to the firing by Sears of several gay employees. The organization was short-lived, however. Then, in 1978, after a period of increasing assaults and incidents of police harassment against gays, the Frente Homosexual de Acción Revolucionaria (FHAR) was formed. In its Declaration of Principles, the Frente called for an end to social, political, economic, and cultural discrimination against gays and lesbians, a stop to police harassment, and more media responsibility in its portrayals of homosexuals. The struggle, it claimed, must be carried out by gays and lesbians in solidarity with the feminist movement, the marginalized groupings in society, and workers. The ultimate goal, and the only one that could put an end to systematic oppression, was a radical transformation of society. This would require the clarification through analysis and discussion of the interrelationship that exists between class struggle and sexuality.

The following excerpt, taken from the FHAR journal *Política Sexual* (Vol. I, No. 1, 1979), reports on an important encounter between lesbians (members of FHAR) and feminists in Cuernavaca, Mexico, at the end of 1978. It lists four important conclusions that were discussed and agreed upon. As with leftist-orientated gay groups in Western Europe, reference is made to the class nature of society and the need for all working people to unite in common struggle. There is a rejection of the bourgeois concept separating political life from personal life, and an understanding that sexual repression is a means the dominant class uses to manipulate and control those dispossessed of power.

From "First Encounter of Lesbians and Feminists," in *Política Sexual, Cuadernos del Frente Homosexual de Acción Revolucionaria* (1979), translated by Stephan Likosky.

The following conclusions were among the most important to come from this meeting:

FIRST: That the repression of homosexuality and the imposition of heterosexuality are responses to specific economic and political objectives that are part of the system of domination. And that the imposition of the sexual roles of masculine and feminine cover over a social relation of power, of the submission of the woman and the deformation of the man. . . .

SECOND: That the dominant class, through the apparatus of production and ideology, produces and reproduces the myths of *the eternal feminine* and *the eternal masculine;* that is to say, an imposed heterosexuality. And the means for affirming these myths can be found in consumer production. An example is the consumer aspect of the massive means of communication that is directed at women, manipulating repressed sexuality, and offering as substitutes to authentic self-realization the fetishism of consumer products.

THIRD: That the repression and manipulation of sexuality is the psychological basis for economic exploitation and political repression. In the case of the woman, her sexual nature is the justification for her political and economic marginalization, and for considering her domestic labor (read: the physical, biological, and ideological reproduction of the work force) as natural to her sex and as unproductive from the standpoint of capital.

FOURTH: That the questioning of ideological elements that are introduced psychically, such as sexuality, the forms of human relations and culture, etc., must not remain at the margin of the proletariat's revolutionary perspective. Otherwise, there is the risk of our giving birth to and ending up with only an economic transformation, rather than a more integral one. This means that subversive revolutionary strategy needs to break with bourgeois conceptions that divide political life from private life, confining to the social microuniverse (the family) those economic, social, psychological, and sexual problems that are generated by the system as a whole and that respond to a politics set forth by the dominant class.

These conclusions are critical in the long road ahead and will assuredly provoke much discussion in the future. For our part, we hope that this meeting will be the beginning of a large movement in support of the organization and revolutionary consciousness of all Mexican workers (heterosexuals, homosexuals, feminists, lesbians, and men) with the aim of destroying the myths that oppress us, and thus allowing us to enter true history: *communism without sexism*. At least this is the cherished desire of the lesbians and homosexuals of FHAR.

SPAIN

In the late 1970s, the various gay liberation movements in Spain united their struggles after agreeing on some common objectives and a common platform. Their manifesto, which follows, is quite ingenious. It succeeds in articulating a number of very concrete demands upon the society and government, yet never loses sight of an overall perspective of liberation. Rights for gays, such as freedom from discrimination at the workplace, are to be struggled for, yet homosexual desire, it is made clear, is a vital component in all persons that must no longer be allowed to be repressed. The gay struggle, also, is not an isolated one; recognition is given to other marginalized and disenfranchised groups, including women, and the working class movement, without whom a true social transformation cannot take place. This platform, in my estimation, is one of the most articulate and politically sound to have emerged since Stonewall. It could well serve as a model for other movements that need to define goals and strategies within their own social and political context.

Common Platform authored by the organizations which constitute the Coordinated Homosexual Liberation Fronts of the Spanish State (COFLHEE), translated by Stephan Likosky.

A. Complete sexual liberation and, specifically, access to all rights on the part of all homosexuals.

B. We consider homosexual desire as one more variant of desire in general, a variant that is found as a component in every individual from birth.

C. We don't accept as valid the ideological categories of "homosexual and heterosexual," since its maintenance goes hand in hand with the repression of homosexuality. In this sense, we propose the abolition of "roles"—whether they be man/woman, masculine/feminine, or active/passive, as they prevent an individual's becoming aware of his/her sexual identity, adding instead to feelings of shame, guilt, and self-hatred.

D. An end to the homosexual ghetto, so that we no longer allow ourselves to be relegated in a way that prevents us from normal participation in civic life.

E. The moving forward to the creation of free human relations, which can substitute for the patriarchal family and institutionalized marriage.

We consider these five objectives as strategic. The Platform of the COFLHEE consists of the following 18 points:

1. Amnesty for all those imprisoned, confined, and subject to measures of security and rehabilitation through application of legislation which is repressive of sexuality or for reasons of sexual behavior.

2. Immediate repeal of the Law of Danger and Social Rehabilitation (4-8-70), cancellation of its antecedents, and dissolution of the special courts that apply it and all those articles of the Penal and Military codes that punish homosexuality, public scandal, the corruption of minors, prostitution, cohabitation, acts against morality, chastity, and so-called public decency and all sexual relations in general, when there is no force, deceit, violence, or abuse of any type involved.

3. An equalizing of minimum age for civil and work status. Noting the fact that the Civil Code permits the marriage of males at 14 and females at 12, we demand that 14 years of age be set as the minimum age for consensual sexual relations without any type of intervention or coercion, whether by family or religion.

4. Equalization of the woman to the man at all levels and an end to all discrimination which has its origins in the sexual practice of persons.

5. Obligation to impart an adequate sexual education at all levels of teaching, treating sexuality not only as a means of reproduction but also and fundamentally as a source of pleasure and of interpersonal communication, as necessary for the psychological well-being of an individual, and making no discrimination between "heteros," homosexuals, or any other type of sexual manifestation. Likewise, a public recognition that infant sexuality is not to be directed, limited, or repressed.

6. Homosexuality is no longer to be considered as a sickness in education or in medical and psychological practice, and consequently, an explicit prohibition that neither aversion therapies nor any other type of treatment be applied that tries to change sexual behavior.

7. Recognition and guarantee of the right of homosexuals to demonstrate their affection in public and of all persons to dress and adorn themselves as they wish.

8. Recognition and guarantee of the right to personal privacy.

9. Total separation of church and state and no interference of the moral doctrine of the Catholic Church or of any other institution, religious or not, in the regulation of the sexual norm.

10. An end to any type of censorship in the media of social communications that is enforced for reasons of sexual morality.

11. Obligation on the part of Social Security to act in a preventive manner in respect to the venereal diseases, using timely infor-

mational and research campaigns, and the creation of appropriate centers and organizations that can facilitate periodic and free check-ups of interested persons.

12. An end to discrimination in the workplace for reasons of ideology or sexuality. Reduction of the working day so as to be able to dedicate free time to one's own cultural and human development and to permit for a satisfactory sexual life.

13. Introduction of divorce laws that can provide free and timely help for all those citizens wanting it.

14. Decriminalization of abortion. Authorization of free use of contraceptives, which can be given to all persons—men or women—who desire it, whatever their civil status.

15. Obligation for institutions in power to take on the issue of prostitution, providing it with legal channels for its realization (unions, social security, hygiene, etc.). Still, we declare ourselves in disagreement with any type of prostitution, female as well as male, because we consider it a result of an unjust system that leads some of its members to the exploitation of their own bodies for suste-nance.

16. No social, legal, or workplace discrimination against those who have undergone or are undergoing sex change operations.

17. Freedom of expression, meeting, demonstrating, and associ-ating, and the immediate cancellation of all those articles in the Penal and Civil codes or other legal norms that prohibit the estab-lishment of associations that oppose the [traditional] morality and so-called public decency.

18. Social recognition of the inalienable right of every human being over use of his/her own body, and not to be discriminated against for reason of his/her sexual orientation.

Our struggle will only attain its objectives when closely united with those movements being developed by feminists, young persons, prisoners, and the marginalized, which together with the working-class movement can make possible a society without classes and with full democratic freedoms for all, including the national minorities.

CHAPTER THREE

FORMS OF STRUGGLE

Lesbians and gay men, both as individuals and in organized fashion, have been waging struggles over the past decades in many countries around the globe. There are, of course, some common denominators as regards the forms, content, and goals of such struggles, but there are vast differences as well. Ultimately each struggle needs to be seen within the context of the social and political arena in which it is waged.

To illustrate some key issues, let us consider the following. In Europe and countries of Anglo-Saxon legal heritage (Great Britain, Australia, the United States, and Ireland, for example), there have generally been harsh penal codes against homosexual behavior, especially male. In addition, there has been a long history of religious intolerance toward homosexuality. In response, the struggles of lesbians and gays in these countries have more often than not centered on abolishing oppressive laws and countering the effects of religious prejudice. Organized struggles began in Europe as early as the 1890s, and continued into the decades preceding World War II. In Germany, for example, a well-organized and highly publicized campaign was waged to abolish Paragraph 175, legislation criminalizing homosexual behavior. These early movements were largely educational in nature, and pleaded for a more humanitarian understanding of sexual minorities. With the rise of fascism, the gay Holocaust in World War II, and the adoption by Communist nations of puritanical moral codes, such as happened in China and the USSR, gay politics largely disappeared from visibility. In the postwar era, gays reorganized, mainly in Europe and countries of Anglo-Saxon heritage, and struggles continued for recognition and an end to legal repression. It was no easy task. When the Mattachine Society was founded in the United States in 1951, even casual socialization by gays could prove dangerous and result in blackmail, loss of job, or arrest. (A favorite ploy of Senator McCarthy, it should be remembered, was to associate homosexual behavior with suspicion of Communist subversion.) In Germany, many of the gay survivors of concentration camps were subsequently rearrested in accordance with German penal codes after the war.

The movements that formed in Europe, the Americas, and Australia after Stonewall were less apologetic in tone and far more aggressive in putting forth their demands. Some activists joined their goals of gay liberation with those of socialist struggle. Many activists committed themselves to gaining recognition for gays as a minority within the society and deserving of equal rights. Some lesbians joined their struggle to that of feminists and targeted patriarchal institutions and sexist values. Means of struggle have been as varied as the human imagination allows: direct action "zaps," electoral campaigning, guerrilla theater, passive resistance, street battles, and day-to-day encounters in the workplace, school, or at home. In the current battle against AIDS, interestingly enough, lesbians and gay men are again beginning to work together and in coalition with nongays, and direct action, a tactic popular with the gay liberation movements of the 1970s, has now reappeared.

In many Islamic countries, despite long traditions of man-boy love, repressive legislation was enacted severely penalizing homosexual behavior. In Iran, for example, recent reports tell of summary executions of homosexuals by beheading and stoning. Paradoxically, male-male sex seems to be ubiquitous throughout the Arab world, yet is rarely mentioned, while a distinct lesbian or gay identity is yet to emerge. Where movements are forming, as in Egypt, participants feel the need to be highly secretive.

In countries of Southeast Asia, Japan, and Thailand, for example, homosexuality has never been regarded as sinful and rarely has it been criminalized. Instead, social pressure on single persons to marry and have families is extremely strong and has helped prevent self-identified lesbian and gay communities from developing. Oppression does exist in that homosexual desires are not publicly recognized or are met with disapproval, and persons with gay identities often feel the need to marry and lead double lives. Yet struggles by organized gays are only now beginning, and what direction they will take is largely undetermined.

In Africa, gay movements have formed in Egypt, Liberia, Ghana, Zimbabwe, and South Africa. In South Africa itself, Africa's first Gay Pride parade was held in October 1990. Simon Nkoli, a well-known anti-apartheid gay activist who had been arrested for treason in 1984, addressed the crowd of over eight hundred lesbians and gay men of all colors. Not long afterward, the African National Congress (ANC) included a gay-rights law in its draft bill of rights for the new South African Constitution.

On a personal level, it should be noted, it can often be seen as a political act for lesbians and gays even to socialize openly. Job and housing discrimination, rejection by families, self-hatred, imprisonment—many are the consequences of gay oppression. And many are the stories of individual struggles to accept oneself, affirm one's feelings, and integrate one's sexuality into one's life void of secrecy or shame.

There are no prototypes for the struggles that lesbians and gay men can or will follow throughout the world. Many movements in the Third World, for example, wish to avoid the commercialization and ghettoization they see dominating the lifestyles of gays under advanced capitalism. Yet if there is any common denominator in the struggles of lesbians and gays throughout the world, it is certainly the desire for freedom to express one's homosexual desires without fear of recrimination. To the degree that this goal, as the goals of feminists, are viewed as subversive to patriarchal power and privilege, the struggles by gays will remain political in scope and continue to embody the seeds for radical social change.

EUSKADI

In the following selection, a Canadian visitor to Spain's Basque region is introduced to the dynamic interrelationship of the Basque nationalist movement, socialist politics, and the emerging gay liberation movement. Traditionally, the Basque country, though waging a leftist-type struggle for independence from Madrid, has been rather repressive regarding sexual morality. The senseless murder of a transvestite by a national policeman in a Basque town in 1979 acted to bring the community together and served as a catalyst for drawing public attention to the issue of gay oppression. Because openly identified lesbians and gays have chosen to integrate their struggle with that of their fellow Basque nationalists, their movement has not been marginalized nor their lives ghettoized. Lesbians in the region, whether choosing to work with the male-dominated gay movement, the feminists' and women's associations, or in separate lesbian organizations, continue to cooperate on a friendly basis with the gay males. All of this, the author notes, is in contrast to Canada and, one might add, many Western nations, where the acceptance of gay issues by leftist and working-class political groups has not been easy, if indeed it has happened at all.

"Out in the Basque Country" by Tim McCaskell, from *The Body Politic: A Magazine for Gay Liberation* (August 1980).

Sunday, June 10, 1979, 3:30 A.M. The Apolo Bar was almost empty. Stale cigarette smoke hung in the air as a few clients nursed their drinks.

Vincente Vadillo sat alone at his table. No one remembers when Vadillo, an immigrant from Spain's rural south, had first arrived in Renteria, one of the towns making up the industrial belt that surrounds the Basque city of San Sebastian, a few miles from the French border.

In Renteria, Vincente Vadillo was better known as Francis the Queer. Francis was one of the thirty-two-year-old transvestite's stage names, and after a few years in the town, all Renteria had become his stage. He was a local character, treated with bemused tolerance, mixed perhaps with contempt. Everyone knew him.

The Apolo often featured transvestite shows, but Francis had not been working that night. He was dressed "normally" as a man.

Another man entered the bar. Witnesses said he had a wild look in his eyes, as if he were drunk or stoned. He asked for a drink. The bartender replied that it was too late. The bar was closed. The man was loud, aggressive. He said he was a member of the National Police. He demanded service. The bartender refused.

The policeman pulled out his pistol and began waving it around. "You Basques all hate us just because we belong to the Spanish Police," he shouted. "I've never killed anybody, but you look at me as if I were an invader or a murderer. I'm so sick of it tonight I *am* ready to kill one of you bastards."

"Well, if you need to kill someone so bad, here I am," said the sarcastic voice of the transvestite. The cop, his face distorted with rage, turned and fired his pistol at close range. The bullet entered Vadillo's left eye. Francis the Queer was dead before he hit the floor.

Renteria is a town of more than fifty thousand people. But perhaps because they are squeezed so closely together in lumbering old apartments, or perhaps because the residents' common working-class background generates such a feeling of community, the place has a grapevine that functions better than that of most small villages. By Sunday afternoon there were few who did not know that a Spanish cop had killed somebody in the Apolo the night before. A crowd of two hundred people gathered spontaneously in the town square. They decided to hold a public meeting the next day and fanned out to the bar and other public gathering places to pass the word.

There is a latent fury that runs through the people of the Basque country, a nationalistic fury against the Madrid government and its police force that trampled on Basque national rights, language, and culture during the forty years of Franco's dictatorship. To the people of Renteria, this was simply one more victim, one more atrocity committed by an occupying army.

The morning paper, controlled by sympathizers of Franco's heirs and their police forces, reported the incident the following Monday. The headline read, "Man dressed as woman killed in bar." Obviously this was not something to get upset about—after all, it was just a faggot. But in spite of this attempt to defuse the issue, and despite the danger of police attack, more than four thousand people gathered in the town square Monday afternoon. They were angry and ready to hear and to shout back the familiar demands for regional autonomy, withdrawal of the National Police, and an end to the vestiges of Spain's years of Fascist dictatorship.

But then something happened that was not at all familiar in Basque nationalist or working-class politics. "Our next speaker is a representative of EHGAM, the Basque Gay Liberation Front." Interest gave way to astonishment as a familiar face took the stage. The young man was a lifelong resident of the town, a union militant, and a well-known political activist. Mikel Conde, who had secretly joined EHGAM less than a year before, was coming out in style.

Conde read the communiqué prepared by his organization. He denounced the press for trying to manipulate public opinion and for using fag-baiting to divert public attention from the crimes of the National Police. He pointed out how sexual repression in general and the oppression of homosexuals in particular were part and parcel of the system that oppressed the Basque country and exploited its working-class citizens. He demanded that people have the freedom to dress however they wished without fear of ridicule or police harassment. He called on workers to organize a general strike and to discuss sexual liberation and oppression in their assemblies.

A few minutes later, police dispersed the crowd with tear gas, rubber bullets, and clubs. The battled raged for hours. But the word was out. On Tuesday, the industrial suburb closed down in a general strike protesting the killing. Sexual liberation was a focus of discussion in dozens of workplaces. Two thousand people marched through San Sebastian under the banners of EHGAM in the group's first public demonstration in the city. In Renteria, the working people took up a collection to send the body of Francis back to his father in southern Spain.

The light of the late afternoon sun illuminated two massive faces of rock cleft by a canyon with almost perpendicular stone walls. "If this isn't the gateway to the Basque country, it should be," I thought. The road wound its way through the pass, solid rock on the right and a churning river on the left. The arid rolling country of Spain was transformed into a thousand shades of green. Euskadi, as the Basque country is called, appeared to be a cross between Ireland and the Swiss Alps—green forests studded with pastures and picturesque stone villages, and, when one least expected it, rocky crags that leapt into the sky.

The terrain helps explain why the Basques were able to maintain their independence and culture for so many years. Never conquered by the invading Moors, Euskadi was not even fully Christianized until the eleventh century. Euskera, the national language, is not related to Spanish or French. In fact, it is in a language group all its own, and its origins are shrouded in mystery and scientific dispute.

The Autonomous Basque Republic was a major center of resistance to Franco's armies during the civil war. Gernika, the spiritual capital of the Basque people, was only subdued after massive Fascist bombing, which left most of the town in ruins, an event immortalized in paint by Picasso. But neither military defeat nor the subsequent years of repression was able to extinguish Basque aspirations for national autonomy and social justice.

We descended from the pass toward San Sebastian, through quaint rural towns dominated by heavy old apartment buildings. In the late nineteenth century, the rich iron deposits here were the basis of Spain's first industrial revolution. The three Basque provinces of Araba, Bizkaia, and Gipuzkoa are still among the most industrialized and urbanized in Spain. San Sebastian, a slightly faded but still elegant seaside resort, is the capital of Gipuzkoa. An aristocratic promenade, ideal for cruising, overlooks the sweeping beach that once attracted the better families of Europe on their summer vacations. The water is still clean, since the city's industries are located in a belt of smaller, less "sophisticated" towns on the periphery—towns such as Renteria.

While the flavor of elegant leisure still lingers on in San Sebastian, Renteria has a different kind of class. It is dominated by chunky apartment buildings—workers' flats—and a sense of community that makes it impossible to walk two blocks without bumping into a neighbor or a workmate or a friend.

Mikel is unemployed. He was fired from his job over a year ago for union agitation. Like most unmarried young men in Renteria, he lives with his family. His mother is Basque, his father an immigrant laborer from the south who came looking for work after the civil war. Theirs is a tightly knit, fiercely protective family—republican, anti-Fascist, and anticlerical. It is also a family that has learned to accept a faggot son and is learning to talk gay politics around the dinner table.

"It gave us a bit of a scare at first," said Mikel's mother as she dished another helping of food on my plate. "We didn't understand much about it. Now it's all right. We realize that everybody is different, that everybody has the right to live as they want to, as they need to."

"I'd never really hid the fact, but I hadn't actually come out to them either," Mikel explained later as we sipped soft drinks and ate olives in the community association bar. "But after I read the EHGAM communiqué to the demonstration, I knew I was going to have to talk to them, because they were going to read it in the papers anyway. So I explained that the cop had killed Francis and I had spoken as a member of EGHAM in the town square. I told them it wasn't just a matter of being able to love men, but that it was a political struggle. We had to struggle for our freedom the same way that the workers had to struggle against the capitalists— that helped them understand. My mother has always been pretty traditional in her beliefs. She began to cry. She said I should be really careful not to get beaten up by machos. My father was a bit uptight. He didn't want anyone to say he had a faggot son.

"Since then, they've understood a lot more. My relationship with them is more equal. I've met other people from the organization. But I want to teach them more than tolerance. I want them to take a part in the struggle against the repressive morality of this society." To go beyond tolerance was no personal ideal of Mikel's. As I was to find out later, it was of central importance to the organization to which he belonged.

Mikel's relationship to his community was even more remarkable. During my visit we never left the house without sporting pink triangles. Nor was it possible to walk two blocks without saying hello or stopping to chat with someone. It seemed as if he knew everyone in town and was on a first-name basis with all of them. And everyone knew that Mikel was a fag.

I was astonished at Mikel's integration into his community. I found myself asking him, "Was he gay? Is she lesbian?" The answer was usually no. I began to realize how accustomed I was to neat categories, to a world cleanly divided into gay and straight continents. Not knowing people's sexual orientation was a little disturbing.

The Basques, in spite of their streak of political radicalism, have always been reputed to be one of the most conservative and traditional of the Spanish minorities. Yet Mikel had managed to come out and link his personal struggle with the broader struggle of his community, and therefore found himself neither isolated nor exiled to the ghetto.

Almost as surprising for me as his integration into a straight, working-class world was Mikel's deep relationship with lesbian friends. A lesbian couple who lived a few blocks away were just breaking up after a seven-year relationship. It was a painful time for a wide circle of friends, straight and gay, which included Mikel's family. The problem worried everybody. The chasms between lesbians and gay men, or between gay people and straight, that I knew in North America seemed insignificant here. Advice, support, and sympathy were offered from all sides.

This personal integration was not, however, reflected in EHGAM's organization. The San Sebastian group has been all-male from the beginning. When I asked him, Mikel felt it was obvious that lesbians were oppressed both for their sex and their sexuality. When they were ready, they would organize themselves independently within the women's movement. As I traveled on, I found there was little consensus on the best political relationship between gay men and lesbians in Euskadi. But whether lesbians remained unorganized, as in San Sebastian, or organized separately, as in Bilbao, or belonged to EHGAM, as in Vitoria, the pattern of personal interaction and warm friendships between gay women and men was the same.

· · ·

It was a cool, wet afternoon as I hitchhiked to Bilbao. The peaks of the mountains lost themselves in a heavy sky. "Typical Basque weather," I was told.

While I waited to meet my contact from EHGAM, I walked through the winding stone streets of the old city center, alive with bars, cafés, and restaurants. I was surprised to find walls and hoardings papered with purple and white posters. "Lesbian," they said, "reconquer your identity." In a central square, I found a large poster advertising an educational forum organized by EHGAM.

Bilbao, the capital of Bizkaia, is the industrial heart of Euskadi. With its surrounding towns, the metropolitan area reaches a population of two million. It was here that EHGAM was first organized in 1976.

José Mari Gil has been working with EHGAM in Bilbao for the last two and a half years and does much of the artwork for their magazine *Gay Hosta*. He is one of the lucky few who do not live at home. His father is a custodian in a local school and has also built up a small business as a traveling salesman. José supports himself selling woolen goods in the markets of the small towns surrounding Bilbao. His apartment is half full of boxes of sweaters and socks.

"I came out to my parents a couple of years ago," he told me. "I think our relationship has been much more honest since." The two friends who share his apartment weren't so lucky. They were both thrown out of their homes when they came out. "That's pretty much the norm here," says Jon, who has been working with EHGAM for only two months. "If my parents found out, I'm sure I'd be out on the street."

Unlike Mikel, who decided he was gay after reading an EHGAM manifesto in a left-wing magazine, neither José Mari nor Jon had experience working with the parties of the political left.

José Mari had been suspicious of politics, but came to his first EHGAM meeting after he was fed up with the "superficial" life he had found in Bilbao's rather closety ghetto. Jon decided he had to get involved when he returned from military service. Both found the organization offered them satisfaction and personal relationships which they were unable to find elsewhere, and were swept up in its ongoing work. "When I started to help out months ago, I said I couldn't do any public work," Jon told me. "But after a few days, I sort of got carried away. I was out on the street putting up posters and going to political meetings. We were really involved in this last election campaign. We put up literature tables at the meetings of the left-wing parties and often would read a communiqué. Although we are nonpartisan, we supported the left. Our slogan was, 'Gays, don't vote for those who oppress you.' "

April 14—the anniversary of the founding of the Spanish republic —a subversive anniversary. Spain is officially a monarchy—part of the Franco heritage. In Renteria, a grotesque dummy of His Royal Highness Juan Carlos I was hanged by the neck from a pavilion in the central square. Groups of townspeople stood around and clapped with delight.

I attended a semiclandestine meeting organized by the EMK, the Basque Communist Movement, to celebrate the founding of Republican Spain in the 1930s. From the faces and hands and clothes of the people around me, I could see I was in a room of working people; there was also a small number of students. The EMK is part of the Spanish Communist Movement—the largest Marxist-Leninist group to the left of the officially Eurocommunist Spanish Communist Party.

Marxist-Leninists in Canada do not have a very inspiring record when it comes to supporting gay people. Yet here, when it was announced that I and a Dutch lesbian also visiting Mikel had been delegates to the International Gay Association Conference in Barcelona, there was thunderous applause.

Mikel has been a member of the EMK since he was sixteen. He is obviously out, well known, and well liked. When I told him about the attitude of some Marxist-Leninists in Canada, he frowned. "The party never discouraged me from speaking for EHGAM. The attitude at first was that we didn't know much about gay liberation, but that didn't mean we should be against it. So lesbian and gay party militants were encouraged to work to educate the party in this respect. The party had become conscious that machismo is a problem even for its own members.

"My comrades really helped me a lot. Since there is such sexual repression in Spain, people who aren't married have a hard time finding a place to sleep together—for two men it's even worse. So anybody in the party who has a private place makes it available. I've often been lent places to be with a friend to have sex."

Josetxu, another acquaintance, told me he is a militant in the PTE—the Spanish Workers' Party. I am quite surprised. The PTE is the pro-Chinese party in Spain. Militants of its sister party in Canada, the Workers' Communist Party, have explained to me on various occasions that homosexuality is a symptom of bourgeois decadence. With a naïveté that would make Anita Bryant blush, they have described how former homosexuals inspired by Marxism-Leninism-Mao Zedong thought have, upon joining the party, left their wanton ways and now lead perfectly happy heterosexual lives. Yet in Spain Josetxu works openly for EHGAM and is preparing papers for an internal party discussion to develop a position on the gay question. Ana, organizing lesbians in Bilbao, tells me that the Spanish Communist Party has been very helpful in lending her rooms at their headquarters for meetings.

The men who make up the vast majority of EHGAM find their personal and political lives far more intertwined with lesbians and with straight people of both sexes than gay men are apt to in North America. The common understanding of the goals of sexual liberation helps bridge the gaps even when familiar kinds of divisions do assert themselves.

I met with Ana Urkijo and Fabiola Alberdi in Lamiak, a coffeeshop-*cum*-bar in the old part of Bilbao. In Basque mythology, the Lamiak were the good witches. The place, owned by four women who belong to the Bilbao Women's Assembly, is referred to as a "feminist" bar. It is a huge old building with heavy stone walls and

massive black beams in the ceiling. Flowered tablecloths, warm
lighting, and gentle Basque folk music produce a friendly, relaxed
atmosphere. People play dice games, and one is pushed to consume.
It is a favorite haunt of Bilbao's young progressives. As I talk to the
two women, a group of ten men from EHGAM is having a committee meeting at the next table.

"It has been a year since the four of us left EHGAM," says Ana
as she begins to describe the formation of the Basque country's first
lesbian organization, ESAM. "Personally I never felt any trauma
about loving women, but I learned early that I had to keep quiet
about it. It's really difficult for a lesbian to come out. There isn't
any ghetto here for us. When a friend told me about EHGAM
several years ago, I went to a meeting. It was an incredible liberation
for me."

"It was really good to meet other women," says Fabiola, who
had stumbled across EHGAM's address and written the group.
"Two other women had joined, so there were four of us. But after
a while we all began to feel that work around lesbian issues was not
being carried out in EHGAM. The men just weren't interested
enough. We found ourselves absorbed by the work of the organization—work around male homosexuality. We weren't attracting
more women. They just weren't interested in an organization which
they saw was mostly concerned with men.

"The same kind of thing was happening in the Women's Assembly, the coalition of women's groups and feminists here. Only there,
lesbian issues weren't being taken up because there was fear that
the organization would be labeled as lesbian. So the four of us began
to meet separately. We decided that we need an autonomous group.
I guess it was the right decision: In less than a year, we now have
twenty-two new members.

"We don't automatically reject men. In fact, we're working with
EHGAM right now on the June gay pride festival. Last year, for the
first time, we had a pretty strong lesbian contingent in the gay pride
march. Our banner read: 'Women's Sexuality Is Also Sexuality

Between Women.' The reaction of a lot of the bystanders was really funny. They were saying, 'Look at those women. What are they doing here? They must be sympathizers marching with the queers to show their solidarity.' It never occurred to them that we might be dykes. They don't know such a thing existed. There's really a huge ignorance about women's sexuality. Sexuality is so bound up with the idea of penetration that many people think where there's no penetration there's no sexuality."

"We've made a lot of headway in the Women's Assembly, too," added Ana. "We've been working there as an independent lesbian group and we've participated in all the campaigns for divorce and abortion reform and the rest. We got them to take up lesbian issues last International Women's Day. Now we're working to open up a real debate on the question of lesbian sexuality. But there are still a lot of lesbians in the assembly who don't work with ESAM because they feel the feminist movement can only advance through the general women's movement."

In a year's steady growth and exploration, ESAM has begun to map out the topography of a lesbian world which few suspected existed. "Before we began, we really idealized lesbians," says Ana. "The only ones we knew were younger progressive people like ourselves. But we've stumbled across a whole new world. There are women who have been living in couples for years with all the traditional roles, possessiveness, jealousy, and domination of straight relationships. We found other groups of ten to fifteen women who know each other but are completely isolated from the women's movement. Many of these people are quite antifeminist. Others are living with their parents or are married and don't know anyone. We are realizing that we were missing a lot of the reality of lesbian life. One of our struggles is going to be to contact these groups and learn how we can work with them."

The women who make up ESAM are mostly in their twenties. Only three are university graduates. The rest are office workers or are unemployed. Most have little political experience. About ten have left their parents' home, but the economic problems that most Spanish young people must face make it difficult for most to set up an independent life. Many of the weekly meetings of ESAM's first year have been spent in the reading and discussion of feminist literature to raise the group's political level. A dossier has been prepared based on this work and the personal experiences of the women involved, which is now ready to go to press.

But ESAM's work has been far from completely internal. The posters that plaster downtown Bilbao testify to that. Three pamphlets have been issued—one directed at lesbians for distribution at women's meetings and the other two aimed at educating a more general audience.

Work was under way to prepare for the first meeting of lesbians from across Spain to take place in Madrid in June. "It will be our first contact on a national level," says Fabiola. "We may even be able to set up a coordinating committee."

One can sense the growing confidence the group has produced. "In the beginning, we didn't want to call ourselves a group of lesbians. That's why we chose the name ESAM, which means Women's Sexual Liberation Movement. Now we understand it is necessary to identify ourselves as lesbians. But we don't just want rights for lesbians—we want a total sexual liberation that will allow everyone to realize the plurality of her sexuality. We want to be recognized as lesbians and women. Our group is a feminist group, and we have a sense of feminist struggle as valid as anyone's. The ideal would be for all the sexual liberation groups—lesbians, straight women, and gay men—to be together, but that's still a long way off."

It was still raining when I arrived in Vitoria at 3:00 A.M. and was deposited at the apartment that an EHGAM member shares with a straight couple. I had been given a lift by several members of the group who had come down to Bilbao to enjoy the ghetto. Vitoria's magnificent cathedral and ancient architecture may attract tourists like pigeons, but gay life is subdued in this, the smallest and poorest of the Basque capitals. I was given a guided tour of the city the next day, beginning with the principal monuments and going on to the principal cruising grounds, the La Florida park and the railway station. The station was the most interesting: One simply waits for a train, and in the early evening there are lots of commuter trains to choose from. A middle-aged man walking two dogs approached us. He turned out to be the friend of one of the young EHGAM militants showing me the town. We chatted as we watched the men watching the men getting on and off the train.

The economic situation and more conservative family life make it more difficult for people to come out in Vitoria. Many young gays leave the city to go to Bilbao or Barcelona, where work and the ghetto provide greater possibilities. EHGAM is relatively new here. Its members are working hard just to keep the organization alive. But the emergence of the Vitoria group meant that EHGAM's claim to represent all Basque gays was becoming a reality.

I was invited to go to a disco with Josetxu and several other friends. "A gay disco?" I asked.

"No, there aren't any gay spots here in Vitoria," I was told. Once again, I found it hardly mattered. We arrived early, and I danced with my friends from EHGAM on a nearly empty dance floor. No one seemed to notice. As the place filled up, most of the couples did seem to be heterosexual, but there was no pressure to be closeted. Our group left in the small hours of the morning without incident. I can't imagine such a place in Toronto.

We pulled out into the freeway in the little pickup José Mari uses to carry his woolen goods to the different markets. The previous day, the newspapers had reported that a member of the National Police had raped a young Basque girl in the fishing town of Bermeo. The Women's Assembly in the town and the left and nationalist parties had called a demonstration in protest. I decided to see firsthand how sexual, social, and nationalist politics mix.

We stop in Gernika to pick up more members of EHGAM. I'm given a quick tour of the most revered sites of the Basque nation—

the National Assembly and the Great Tree, under which Basque elders have held their traditional councils for centuries.

We are packed like sardines in the pickup as we bounce along the winding road to Bermeo. "If you see a police block, pull over quick. They'll use the fact that we're overloaded to arrest us if they think we're going to the demonstration." Luckily there is no road-block. We park in the main square, which overlooks a picturesque harbor. The square is already filled with people, the majority women —housewives or workers. My friends are hastily preparing signs identifying themselves as members of EHGAM. We all wear pink triangles.

I've been warned to leave my camera at home in case the police attack. "They really go after cameras," says José Mari. As we march off through the drizzle, five thousand strong, there is no sign of police.

We wind through the narrow streets, calling for justice for rapists and the disbanding of the repressive forces of the National Police. The marchers are militant but peaceful. We loop through the town and are almost back to the square again, where the crowd will disperse. All of sudden, I notice men with rifles to my right. "That's the barracks of the National Police," says Bittor, as we walk hand in hand. Bittor is a sailor on shore leave who is just coming out. "It doesn't look like we'll get any action today," I say. "I should have brought my camera. There's nothing to provoke them."

"They don't need any provocation," he replies.

The crowd roars out its condemnation as it passes the building in the narrow street. I can see two parade marshals in a heated conversation with the head of the police. Other marshals are trying to hurry us on. I overhear the cop say, "You've got two minutes to disperse. This is an illegal demonstration."

"Two minutes, that's impossible," says the marshal. "Look, peo-ple are still coming down the street. There's no place for them to go."

"Two minutes," says the cop.

I am swept onward by the crowd. We reach the square and stop to watch what will happen as the people continue to spill out of the narrow street. Suddenly we hear the explosions—rifles firing.

"It's crazy," I say to Bittor. "People were dispersing. There's no need for them to do anything now."

"Run," he says.

Tear gas canisters are arcing through the air and bouncing along the pavement. Brave souls pick them up and hurl them into the harbor. People are dashing in all directions. "Are they using rubber bullets?"

There is a brief pause in the firing. Now it's the turn of the enraged townspeople. They run back toward the barracks and start to throw anything they can get their hands on. The police charge the crowd again. More gas, and sirens.

Sirens, I learn, are a bad sign. They mean the police are coming out to get us. We retreat into a bar. Outside, a police car swoops down on a hapless demonstrator. He is dragged kicking and punching into the car, and it roars off. "They'll come in here next," says Bittor. The bar empties, and we run to the far end of the square. A volley of tear gas can be heard exploding in the town above us. "They must be circling around through the back streets." A knot of us stand at a corner, not sure which way to go. "If they get too close, come up here," shouts someone from a window above us. "The fourth floor."

We hear a siren coming down the street. "Let's go."

We scramble up four flights of stairs. The apartment seems to be owned by some elderly women, but soon it is full of demonstrators. We crowd the window to watch the action on the square. The police car screams past below us, its blue flashing light reflecting off the buildings. Small groups of demonstrators are still running around in a serious game of cat and mouse with the forces of order. It begins to get dark. A half hour later, we are ready to venture downstairs. We scurry into a bar. Whenever a police siren gets too close, the bartender locks the door and pulls down the blind. The regulars continue watching the soccer game on television. An hour later, it seems safe to cross the square to the car.

I understand a little better the coalition of sexual, leftist, and nationalist politics that has marked the development of Basque gay liberation. The common enemy is obvious.

We rumble back to Gernika and spend the night in the apartment of some women friends of José Mari's. The place soon fills up with people eager to discuss the demonstration. The politics is contagious. I forget to ask who's gay and who's straight.

It doesn't seem to make much difference when we're all running in the same direction.

UNITED STATES AND HOLLAND

The Netherlands has long enjoyed the reputation of being a mecca for gays. Progressive legislation regarding lesbians and gay males and a tradition of tolerance have added strength to the notion that it is easier to be "out" here than perhaps anywhere else in the world. In the following article, two lesbians, one from the United States and one from the Netherlands, discuss their experiences living in the other's respective country. The notion of tolerance is examined in Dutch society, where despite the mainstream nature of the gay movement, there is still strong pressure to conform outwardly. Lesbian life in America, on the other hand, though subject to more repressive societal norms, is credited as generating a stronger lesbian identity and making more lucid the issues for struggle. Ultimately, the women seem to agree, the enemy is the same: the heterosexist bias that permeates both societies.

"Lesbian Struggle Against a Pillow or a Wall: A Dutch-American Dialogue," by Gail Pheterson and Leny Jansen, from *Gay Life in Dutch Society* (1987).

This shall be a dialogue between a Dutch lesbian living in Chicago and an American lesbian living in Amsterdam. When first invited to write a comparison of lesbian lives in our two countries, we felt cautious about the dangers of overgeneralizing culture and lesbian life as well as of biasing our analysis with personal impressions. In order to avoid such dangers and still initiate some examination of Dutch and American lesbian contexts, we decided to abandon any attempt at scientific objectivity at this stage, and rather to speculate on cultural nuances in the interest of guiding further study. At the risk of egocentrism, we have chosen to grasp those nuances from our own cross-cultural experience.

Given the Dutch focus of this issue of the *Journal of Homosexuality,* strongest emphasis will be put on the Netherlands, with the United States as a counterpoint for cultural contrast. Both American and Dutch societies are dominated by male prerogatives and heterosexual presumptions, and in that way they are not unrepresentative of the world at large. An examination of lesbian life is therefore necessarily an examination of the specific pressures and permissions which determine the quality and quantity of struggle within each society. Such struggle is rarely unilateral, however. No one is *just* a lesbian. Every lesbian is a *woman* of a certain color, class, religion, age, language, history, culture, city or village, and so on. It is that constellation of identities within the dominant cultural setting which depicts each lesbian's experience.

The perspective of this article will reflect our personal identities and histories: Leny is 44 years old, white middle class, and is of a Dutch Calvinist, rural working-class background. Gail is 39 years old, white, middle class, and is of an urban American Jewish, second-generation immigrant background.

GAIL: Leny, tell something about your situation in the United States and about your experience as a lesbian.

LENY: I came to the United States to study community organizing and then history at the graduate school of the University of Chicago. My studies and a lover (I came out as a lesbian in the United States) were the reasons I stayed at the university and lived in the city's Hyde Park neighborhood for 10 years. One of the things that I found particularly attractive was the combination of "high power" academia and a homey neighborhood. It was an intellectually challenging environment, something I had missed in the Netherlands. Dutch society, even the university world, is far less intellectually oriented. And the racially and culturally integrated neighborhood (blacks, whites, Asians, and many foreigners) had an easygoing atmosphere in which I felt very much at home. For American standards, the neighborhood was protected and quite tolerant of differences; any behavior which could be put under the heading "eccentric" was acceptable. So, as a lesbian, I didn't have to cramp my style.

GAIL: What is your impression of lesbian life beyond Hyde Park?

LENY: The minute I contemplated moving to other cities in the United States, except where there were large lesbian communities, I got scared. My impression of lesbian life beyond my neighborhood was one of strong discrimination. I couldn't be myself out there. As a lesbian I would have had to make a fist for myself in preparation either for the "barricades" or for hiding. That's the case in most American communities. The big American hero is still the tough pioneer or the rough freedom-loving cowboy who shoots everybody standing in his way, or the jock with muscles. Those characters are the ones American men identify with and many heterosexual women cheer on. I find the images rather frightening. They set the tone of American society in general and of the relationship between men and women in particular. The struggle of lesbian women is intense and very clear. If you gain a small piece of territory in this society, it is a major achievement.

GAIL: Did you have any direct experience in that realm of society or did you manage to avoid it?

LENY: I had firsthand experience. I worked for several years as a community organizer in a suburban Chicago school setting where I was definitely in the closet. Under no circumstances would I have been able to maintain my position if I had come out to my colleagues, the school board, or my community. Homophobia was rampant. And now, in my new profession in the downtown business world of Chicago, I again cannot come out without jeopardizing my job or, in any case, my opportunities for promotion.

GAIL: Did you have a different experience in the Netherlands?

LENY: Yes, when I went back there for three years in between my studies, I was out as a lesbian at work. I never felt any threat, danger, or discomfort. I experienced tremendous toleration and openness. Not disclosing my lesbianism there would have felt like a personally neurotic choice instead of a sensible reaction to a discriminating society.

GAIL: Unfortunately, discrimination in the Netherlands seems to be on the increase, if not obviously, then subtly. For example, a man was rejected for a personnel position at the Dutch Royal Palace after it was discovered that he was homosexual. The stated reason for rejection was not his homosexuality but his self-concealment. Why hadn't he told that he was a homosexual? Some members of Parliament claimed that such intentional concealment might indicate that the applicant was untrustworthy and posed a security risk —that is, he would be vulnerable to blackmail. Homosexuality seems to be a threat whether revealed or concealed. Still, I'm certain that different cultures have different styles of oppression. From your exposure to both societies, Leny, how do you view the difference?

LENY: That's a broad question. I can start by telling you my view of Dutch men, which admittedly will be stereotyped and overgeneralized. Rather than tough, rough, and muscled, the Dutch male hero is a mild-mannered fellow. Although the society is male and heterosexually dominated, the men are less likely than American men to come across as domineering figures. Dutch male domination is very subtle; the men are soft and pleasant. They are more family oriented than American men, and they downplay aggressive assertion.

GAIL: Are you saying that the relationship of men toward women is less offensive in the Netherlands than in the United States?

LENY: In a way, yes. There are a few hard edges, but generally the exchanges seem pleasant. Nevertheless, women are dominated. Male heterosexual bias is ever-present. But it is difficult against someone who is sweet and caring; as a lesbian and feminist, you come across as a harsh bitch. When you make a fist you punch against a pillow instead of a wall. Compared to that almost unrecognizable absorbing domination, the situation in the United States is crystal clear.

GAIL: In other words, lesbian oppression in the Netherlands is more subtle than in the States, but nevertheless it is present.

LENY: Yes, definitely. However, the situation is a lot more mystified. The oppression is less obvious; you can't put your finger on it. This mystification process is a quality of Dutch life in general. The Dutch tend to absorb variations from the norm instead of them coughing them out. They at first accept diverse behavior instead of isolating it. Isolation encourages dissent; the Dutch apply subtle group pressure to discourage dissent and nonconformity.

GAIL: If lesbians are not oppressed by being tucked in the closet, nor by losing their jobs, in what ways are they oppressed?

LENY: They are still THE LESBIANS; they are freaks. Lesbians enjoy civil rights and protection as human beings within a society which prides itself on its human decency. You are *allowed* to be a lesbian, but you have to behave like the rest of the population. If you live a life according to a lesbian-identified worldview, you are a freak. *That* is unacceptable. If you give a lesbian interpretation to political events, to psychological mechanisms in human exchange, to social dynamics, you will be made to look ridiculous.

GAIL: As a Dutch person, what else have you noticed about lesbian life in the United States?

LENY: As a lesbian you experience little freedom in the male heterosexual world, but you do experience great freedom of expression with other lesbians. That division may be the reason for the strong identity of lesbians. Lesbian women in the United States. For instance, when I go to a women-identified or lesbian culture activity and see all those women, I rediscover by identification: "This is my world, Dyke City." The clear sense of "we women together" is extremely exhilarating. I never had such a distinct experience in the Netherlands, although I know all-women's cultural events are becoming bigger and more frequent happenings there as well. Still, my impression is that the situation there is much more diffuse. For example, my discussions with lesbian friends in the Netherlands are more about life in general than about our position as lesbians. When I meet lesbian friends in Chicago, we might talk about our personal lives, but sooner or later we will discuss the lesbian stance, lesbian experience, lesbian horrors, and so forth. Being lesbian is always on our minds. I am not sure whether that's the case in the Netherlands. But then perhaps I am not qualified to make that kind of observation because I lived there as a lesbian for only three years, and that was some time ago.

GAIL: If you experience life in the Netherlands to be so much easier, why do you choose to live in the United States?

LENY: I like the clarity of the struggle, and I like identifying with an adamant, courageous lesbian stance. What about you? What has your experience been within the two societies?

GAIL: I identify with your feelings about the clarity and intensity of the lesbian struggle in the United States. Before moving to the Netherlands, I lived openly as a lesbian for four years in Southern California, first as a graduate student and then as a university lecturer. My lesbian world was an activist feminist one, my work world a male-dominated heterosexual one with enclaves of academic feminists, both heterosexual and closeted lesbians. When I came out at the university by expressing indignation about the male heterosexual bias in the psychology textbooks, my department chairman warned me that I was seriously jeopardizing my professional career. At the same time, I experienced enormous pressure from my heterosexual friends and family. Associating with a lesbian was stigmatized behavior for any heterosexual, and surely for heterosexuals whose family included a lesbian. Of course, some people were more titillated than offended, but all reacted intensely. I soon realized that as an openly lesbian woman, the rest of my identity faded into the background; I had become "the lesbian," or, as you said, "the freak."

Basically, the struggle demanded a great deal of courage and was frightening for me. Yet it was also energizing and self-affirming. I wouldn't wish it on anyone, but perhaps such blatant oppression does foster the development of a strong identity. If so, that development usually occurs in isolation from the heterosexual world. When I lived in California, I considered such isolation to be a disability, and in fact, my move to the Netherlands was in part an attempt to extricate myself from that constriction.

LENY: I would like to hear more about your experience as an American lesbian in the Netherlands.

GAIL: I first went to the Netherlands in 1975 to facilitate a series of feminist therapy workshops. During the introductions on the first day, I was immediately confronted with a difference between the United States and the Netherlands, or so it seemed. Of the 30 women present, the majority of whom were heterosexual feminists, many introduced themselves as married women who lived with a husband and children, but whose most intimate relationship was with a woman lover. "Wow," I thought, "it is easy to be a lesbian in the Netherlands. Lots of women, even married women, have a woman lover." I felt free and immediately concluded that the Netherlands was nearly a paradise for lesbians. I continued to glorify Dutch lesbian life there during the workshops and for about a year after I returned to live in the Netherlands. In fact, my awe of Dutch decency and naturalness grew as I learned more. I was particularly impressed with the civil liberties that lesbians and gay men had under Dutch law, and with the integration of lesbians in the women's movement, the gay movement, and heterosexual society. For example, when I first arrived in the Netherlands and needed to establish legal residency, I was amazed to learn that a stable (meaning three-year) homosexual relationship between a foreigner and a Dutch citizen served as a legal justification for the foreigner to remain in the Netherlands. The existence of such a legal ruling is indicative of Dutch ethics. And the Dutch do apply their ethics. For example, they went so far as to write letters, signed by members of Parliament, to Florida newspapers and President Carter in the 1970s protesting the discrimination of homosexuals which was incited by Anita Bryant, and urging the government of the United States to protect human rights.

LENY: So as a lesbian you felt integrated.

GAIL: Yes, more or less. And at the beginning of my residency in the Netherlands, I experienced the integration as a great relief. I suppose I was partially recovering from the painful isolation I had experienced in the United States. But after a while I began to see the dangers and freedoms of both integration and isolation.

LENY: What dangers and freedoms did you discover in the integration of Dutch lesbians?

GAIL: Well, my first example is a continuation of the story of those heterosexual feminists with a husband, child(ren), ¹and a woman lover. One certainly gets the picture of "perfect" integration, one big happy family. However, such an arrangement can be politically mystifying and personally insulting. The married woman ends up benefiting from heterosexual privilege and colluding with lesbian oppression by keeping a lesbian of her own in the closet. As a lesbian myself, I became less and less excited about the liberalism of Dutch liberty. What a mistake for me to think that if women were to be free to make love with other women, then they must be *free* of heterosexual bias. I had known theoretically all along, although much less so on a personal level, that sexuality is only a small part of lesbian life and of lesbian oppression. In fact, sexual license can become an excuse to discount the oppression that lesbians suffer. I would hear, "What's the big deal about being a lesbian? I sleep with women, too." For a long time I questioned myself and blamed myself for making a big deal of nothing because, after all, it was easy to be a lesbian in the Netherlands. It took me years to uncover the mystification, and I still struggle with it. It doesn't feel good for the married woman either after a while because basically, in trying to get everything and fit in everywhere, she misses herself. And in any case, she gets very tired trying to keep everyone happy.

LENY: I think the situation in the United States is comparable, but one is less proud of it because the cultural pressure for harmony is less in American than Dutch society. Granted, the pressure on women *as women* in both societies is to maintain harmony, and to feel guilty and personally responsible for all disharmony. In that way, Dutch values as a whole reinforce sexist pressures on women.

GAIL: Yes, a harmony model of integration can be a mixed blessing. By the way, Dutch integration is not complete. Separatist lesbian voices do arise in the Netherlands, and they are increasing in number on a grass roots social/cultural level. But the most significant action-oriented feminism grows out of a unison of lesbians and heterosexual women. Most of those women are white, however, because Dutch society seems to claim its lesbians more than its (ex-) colonized people of color. Nonetheless, more and more lesbians of color are coming out and finding one another and they, more than their heterosexual counterparts, are active in both the white women's movement and the black women's movement(s). Heterosexual and lesbian feminists of color share the tension experienced in the United States between the struggle against racism and the struggle against sexism. So when I talk about the integration of lesbians of *color,* or of *Jewish* lesbians, *older* lesbians, *disabled* lesbians, or so forth, I am merely referring to lesbians as *lesbians.* Many of us experience other interrelated struggles as well.

LENY: I don't know much about the activities of the Dutch political lesbians. Can you elaborate on that subject?

GAIL: Just as in the United States, the political vanguard of lesbians in the Netherlands is split into the feminist movement and the homosexual movement. In the feminist one, lesbians make their primary alliance with heterosexual women; in the homosexual one, women make their primary alliance with homosexual men. In the Netherlands, the homosexual movement has a longer history than in the United States, and has a very solid integrated place in Dutch society. In fact, it has become an institutionalized organization which has a voice within the media, social services, educational institutions, and government policy. The homosexual movement in the Netherlands, therefore, is not a radical departure from mainstream Dutch society. Although the issues raised by the movement are progressive and challenging to the society, the existence of such an organization is quite Dutch. Financial support and political accountability are benefits of integration. Unfortunately, in the context of the gay movement, the word "lesbian" often disappears. We all become homosexuals, which means that women often vanish, that male homosexual assumptions are applied to women, and that, on the "positive" side, lesbian women get to slide in under the rights that gay men manage to secure for themselves. And, to note the danger as well as the freedom of integration, those *rights,* for men as well as women, are sometimes used to deny the continued presence of homophobic *attitudes.* For example, some homosexual Dutch policymakers, satisfied with government spending on AIDS research and medical care, argue that they can best keep a low profile on AIDS in order to avoid panic and prejudice among heterosexuals. In the United States, a shortage of funds forces homosexuals to confront prejudices in their struggle to gain financial support. I don't want to discount Dutch rights or plea for American struggle, but rather to stress that government rights do not necessarily imply public acceptance.

LENY: I agree. The integration of homosexuals in Dutch society has achieved a great deal in terms of civil liberties, but not necessarily in terms of changing values. The Dutch are proud to say that homosexuals have the same rights as heterosexuals, but that doesn't mean that the Dutch are ready to give them the same validation.

GAIL: Indeed, lesbians and gay men are still an offense to the fabric of Dutch society; namely, the heterosexual nuclear family.

LENY: Exactly. The Dutch are very family oriented. In the Netherlands, the family is not just a nurturing base, but also a primary source of male identity. Men in the Netherlands have homes as well as work sources of self-expression and accomplishment, such as their gardens, their cooking, their social graces, and the like. And women are far more bound to the home than in the United States. About 50 percent of U.S. women work, whereas the Netherlands has one of the lowest percentages of working women in the West.

GAIL: On the one hand, if men do not need to monopolize the workplace because they also have another avenue of expression, the home, then lesbians—or any working women—might experience less discrimination, feel less excluded, and be less fearful of their male colleagues. On the other hand, if the taboo on working for women is greater in the Netherlands, then women might experience even more discrimination. In any case, tolerance of homosexuals dose not necessarily change the basic Dutch value system, in particular around the prescribed role for women. Still, I don't want to deny the enormous importance of basic civil liberties. I'll take tolerance above abuse any day, and I am deeply impressed with Dutch society in that it has gone further than perhaps any country in the world to assure those liberties.

LENY: What have you observed about the relationship between the women's movement and the gay movement?

GAIL: In the Netherlands, I can see very clearly how feminism has infiltrated and changed the gay movement, and how the Dutch gay liberation tradition has been responsible for much of the consciousness and mystification within the women's movement. Still, the gay movement is male-dominated, and the women's movement is heterosexual-dominated. In the last few years the main cooperation I've seen between the two movements has been at demonstrations, an example being the yearly homosexual demonstration that has a strong feminist presence; and in taking common stances on certain political issues, such as an antidiscrimination law that includes women, heterosexual couples living together "out of wedlock," and homosexuals. Also, an international conference called "Among Women, Among Men: Forms of Recognition of Female and Male Relationships" was organized jointly by gay and women's studies at the university, which I considered a significant step toward augmenting lesbian visibility in both movements. The university has not been a sphere of lesbian activism, neither in gay nor women's studies. In fact, despite the growing attention at the university to homosexuality (Homostudies) and to feminism (Women's Studies), the Dutch university has been only a limited source of lesbian political energy or insight. More influential have been the social services and social work educational institutions. In the Netherlands, social workers have not only been more likely than academics to be visible as lesbians, but also to champion the ideals and strategies of feminism within their work. As my cousin, Martha Becker, reminded me, social work has been strongly influenced by lesbians in the United States as well. Women such as Lillian Wald and Jane Addams were in the forefront of social work development and reform in the nineteenth century, and lesbians have continued to play a major role in American social work since then. But unlike social workers in the Netherlands, those women did not fight for *lesbians*. They were leaders in their field, but closeted as lesbians. Still, the lesbian presence within social work, closeted or activist, is probably of significance.

LENY: The strength of Dutch initiative within social work, as opposed to academia, is rooted in the pragmatic tradition of the country, for in all areas there is greater concern with application than with theory. People are likely to be well versed in ideas imported from abroad, often from the United States, but are themselves more prone to organize than to analyze. Americans certainly have a pragmatic tradition as well, but the tradition nestles alongside a fervent intellectual one.

CONCLUSION

Our observations suggest that the benefits of Dutch culture for lesbians include civil liberties, toleration, liberal social services, and integrated access to mainstream opportunities. The benefits of American culture include a context for the development of identity, an exhilarating lesbian culture, intellectual fervor, and clarity of struggle. As for the oppression, generally Dutch oppression could be characterized as mystification, and American oppression as isolation. It would be misleading, however, to posture the two societies in an even balance. It is less life-threatening to be a lesbian in the Netherlands than in the United States, and the pressure to protect the rights of lesbians along the way will come from the Netherlands.

BRAZIL

The emergence of a gay liberation movement in Brazil in the 1970s was the result of a long and arduous struggle by its members. João S. Trevisan, a founder of the gay movement and editor of its paper, *Lampião,* documents that movement's history as part of his study on homosexuals in Brazil, *Perverts in Paradise,* from which the following excerpt is taken. One aspect of the struggle revolves around overcoming the personal guilt and denial endemic to gays living in a macho culture, where "passive" sexual behavior on the part of males is scorned and denigrated; a second concerns the identification and promotion of issues of concern to the gay and lesbian communities, and the struggle to have them legitimized in the eyes of the mainstream leftist movements. (As with the left in many countries, gay issues, as is true of feminist, racial, and ecological, are often seen as being of secondary importance to the class struggle—or even divisive.) Avoiding the pitfalls of bureaucracy and authoritarianism, resisting physical harassment from both the police and left-wing goons, redefining politics to incorporate the personal with the public —all these are issues with which the new movement is confronted. Foreign models are helpful to an extent, but ultimately the Brazilian gay movement realizes it has to formulate its own path of struggle. Much of the excitement of the early gay struggle and its experimentation with new forms of relating person-to-person is captured in the narrative. All the sadder to learn that the movement subsequently, in the early 1980s, became manipulated and then dominated by a traditional left-wing organization, while many of its radical ideas and lifestyles gave way to the consumerist ethic and growing ghettoization.

From "Gay Politics and the Manipulation of Homosexuality," from *Perverts In Paradise* by João S. Trevisan, translated by Martin Foreman (1986).

> I go out in secret,
> I look for you
> but they find me.
> Dad hits me.
> The headmaster punishes me.
> The left tries to kill me.
> —*Glauco Mattoso (1982)*

One of the most serious problems in countries rigidly controlled by a dominant elite is that history passes them by like water over an impermeable riverbed. At least that is the impression in Brazil, where history twists along a course that seems to return to the same spot until explosively exhausting a cycle and leaping violently onto the next stage. Partly because it lives on the periphery of the West and partly because few of its inhabitants are consumers of culture, Brazil appears to have great difficulty in absorbing contemporary themes, preferring to modernize itself only when confronted by *faits accomplis.* Accustomed to grand spectacles, its cultural elite copies the latest fashions from Paris or New York but is seldom inclined toward real change. As a result, modernity in Brazil is easily reduced to a phenomenon that simply follows the latest fashion. Gay liberation has developed along the same lines. If it arrived in Brazil at least a decade late and then entered a cul-de-sac, this is largely due to the basic conservatism, insensitivity, and self-indulgence of a cultural elite which feeds on fashions in order to recycle itself. Thus the present profusion of homosexual characters on Brazilian radio, television, and cinema is a source of excitement for this modernized elite, which prides itself on being able to accept queers and dykes—"Except in my family, of course! . . ." Let's be up-to-date, yes, but there's no need to go too far.

A DELAYED START

Living on the periphery, we Brazilians feel distanced from the rest of the world. It could be said that the emerging gay movement is part of the same vain attempt to open up, seek a dialogue with our contemporaries and modernize ourselves. Since 1985, the relaxation of the most recent in the cycle of Brazilian dictatorships has been accompanied by the outline of a new movement toward cosmopolitanism. It was hardly a secret that the 1964 military coup was marked by an element of nationalism and xenophobia which the left shared—despite the serious differences between the two ideological poles. Paradoxically, by causing the exile of a large number of intellectuals and placing them in brutal contact with the outside world, the military caused a compulsory modernization, culturally speaking, in this period of Brazilian life. Years later, when the amnesty allowed them to return, they brought back experiences which they had absorbed in the time they had been forced to stay away from home. Eurocommunism came to us in this way, as did ecological concerns, feminism, and antiracism, which at that time were all flourishing in advanced capitalist countries. At the very least this is an aspect of the "Anthropophagy" very common in Brazilian life—the phenomenon of absorbing the foreign in order to secure the perilous identity. Modernization, therefore, can also be seen as a Brazilian means of survival.

I, too, went into exile (for three years, voluntarily), and, on coming back to Brazil in 1976, brought back novelties from the outside world. Being totally involved in the facts narrated below, I have absolutely no intention of being scientific in writing about them. On the contrary, I intend to make a kind of statement as the protagonist I often was. The truth is that, returning from a fruitful stay in the United States, Mexico, and various other Latin American countries, I felt I had become a very hybrid being whose characteristics could not be restricted to one cultural identity. Outside Brazil

I had had innumerable experiences, from which I had retained the aspects that seemed to me most important and most pleasant. Having lived with militant American gays, foreign feminists, and exiled Brazilian revolutionaries, I felt doubly alone when I returned "home." I could not exchange ideas with my old comrades, I was shocked by the lack of punctuality and the irresponsibility of drivers, and I was irritated by the consumer mentality of the enlarged gay ghetto which I found in Brazil at the end of the seventies.

This feeling of inadequacy led me to try to bring together some gay university students in São Paulo in 1976, to form a discussion group on homosexuality. There were never more than a dozen at the meetings, all young men. Some came with vague liberal and assertive propositions, while the thoughts and feelings of others were hampered by the ideology of the old left. We tried to study some texts. However, the participants, who were very reticent about the experiment, were paralyzed by feelings of guilt—even when they had been humiliated by their party comrades for being homosexual. The big question they asked themselves, frequently heard in gay groups in the movement's first phase, was: Is it politically valid for us to meet to discuss sexuality, something generally considered secondary given the serious situation in Brazil? All movements ran up against this question, without reaching a clear answer. As if that was not enough, 70 percent of the group frankly admitted that they considered themselves abnormal because of their homosexuality. In such circumstances it is not surprising that the project fell apart after a few painful meetings.

Two years later the political scene had appreciably evolved. There was a certain insolence in the air, as much toward the official left as toward the police state. In 1978 groups of women—who were still very stifled by the party line—began to explore, timidly and from an increasingly feminist perspective, such sacrilegious topics as sexuality and abortion. They also tried to impose a principle of autonomy on their discussions, which broadened as newspapers were founded and women returned home from exile. Blacks, too, began their first attempts at discussing racism, culture, and organization outside the iron circle of the old left's parties and centralism. At the same time several serious ecological disasters—poisoned rivers, excess pollution that caused the birth of acephalous children, oppressive devastation of the Amazon forest, and the babylonian nuclear program secretly begun by the military dictatorship—had led to the setting up of various ecological action groups. All this presented new problems for the orthodox left. While the topics of sexuality and racism were discussed outside the parameters of the class struggle (or "greater struggle," in their jargon), abortion created disagreeable friction with the left's ally, the progressive wing of the Catholic Church. Furthermore, the question of nuclear technology emerged as fundamental to the continental geopolitical situation insofar as nuclear development in Brazil and Argentina signified a crack in American imperialist hegemony, by making possible the proliferation of atomic weapons which the United States so feared.

It was in this context of agitation that some gay intellectuals and artists from São Paulo and Rio de Janeiro met at the end of 1977 to discuss an anthology of gay Latin American literature to be edited by Winston Leyland of Gay Sunshine Press. From there came the idea of forming a collective to found a newspaper for homosexuals which would discuss a wide range of matters and be sold monthly at newsstands throughout the country. The group (of which I was one) met frequently and the project flourished, although with an uncertain financial infrastructure. Number 0 of Lampião appeared in April 1978—an almost scandalous event for the prurient left and right, who were accustomed, above all, to reticence. For good or bad, Lampião signified a break: Eleven mature men, some well known and intellectually respected, were involved in a project where the topics dealt with were those considered "secondary"—sexuality, racial discrimination, the arts, ecology, machismo—and all this in the generally camp and insolent language of the homosexual ghetto. As well as publishing guides to gay cruising in towns all over the country, it used words forbidden in respectable vocabulary (such as viado and bicha [both = "queer"]), allowing its articles to enjoy a healthy independence and a difficult equidistance from the various groups of the institutionalized left. It was in many ways a disobedient paper.

At the same time as *Lampião* was born in Rio de Janeiro, in São Paulo a group of homosexuals interested in organizing discussions and liberationist activity began to meet; I was very happy to join it. Predominantly made up of young actors, members of the liberal professions, and students, the group was small and remained so for almost a year, going on to serve as a model for those which came afterward. From then on the gay movement in Brazil had a backbone of groups which brought activists together rather in the manner of private clubs for gay men and lesbians. Of course, each group tried to have its individual style, accentuating differences in order to find its identity—principles which might be considered as defense systems against a hostile environment. Something similar seems to have occurred in the early days of the American and European gay liberation movements, with the Mattachine Society in the United States and Arcadie in France.

From our very first gatherings, styles and concerns emerged which were rare in the meetings of young leftists of the time. We tried to focus topics on the individuals present and their daily experiences, doubts, problems, and plans, the aim being to act on reality, starting not with *another* but with ourselves. Up to a point the model was the American gay consciousness-raising group, through which we sought a social identity. In any case this attitude came from a firm decision to take responsibility for ourselves, to become aware of our own bodies and sexuality, and to reactivate forgotten aspects of our personalities in the group relationship. The experience or contact which many of us had had with political parties of the left also preoccupied us with disaligning ourselves, in the sense that we wanted to undertake political actions whose roots were deep within our lives and far from any central committee. We deliberately intended to put aside the hysterical and sterile political discussions which organized the revolution of *others*. From the beginning we were concerned with bringing our public and private lives together to allow our individual consciousness to levels, and to transform society. We knew that many militants of the left plunged blindly into political activism as the result of a subtle sexual repression. In an article collectively signed by the group, we considered the sexual act as a political act because political activity should "be full of the tenderness which we have learned both in the bedroom and elsewhere."[1] We began, at first timidly, to consider pleasure as every citizen's legitimate right. We wanted to believe that joy was not ruled out by poverty, particularly in such a poor country as Brazil. We encouraged demonstrations of tenderness and fraternity among ourselves and opposed parliamentary-style representation and all forms of leadership. In addition, the topics that were emerging centered on the tearing down of the sex roles, the breaking of the heterosexist model of relationships, and polygamy as a proposal of potential transformation. In short, we saw the time offered by weekly meetings as a fundamental opportunity for solidarity and transformation where frequent cruising and sexual activity also took place—and were considered legitimate components of these meetings.

Meanwhile, one problem that we were constantly aware of in this initial period was that the number of women was small and fluctuating. Those who happened to come—generally brought by gay male friends—did so once and did not return. The situation was considered serious by those members of the group who were interested in a feminist analysis of sexual repression and in an alliance with the groups of liberationist women then emerging. It was not, however, only the number of women that fluctuated. Many men came to look and did not come back, disappointed by our "lack of objectivity and organization" and by the fact that, compared to political groups of the time, we had not "ideological consistency." Before leaving, many asked us to tell them when the group was ready to take a definite line. People who still had links with the student movement found it difficult to understand that the group was formless and restless precisely because its aim was to ferment new ideas of political practice. There was therefore a growing concern with opposing activism as a form of seeking and exercising power. Even if it was at random, our small group wanted to challenge the very question of power, aware that our sexuality (our no-man's-land) suffered under the social control inherent in any form of disputed and conquered power. It was a very bold suggestion at a time when the echoes of Guevara-style revolution were still heard and obeyed, for it also challenged the legitimacy of self-appointed vanguards of the left taking power "in the name of the people."

New Ideas to the Fore

In February 1979 the group found itself at an impasse when it made its public debut in debate at the Social Sciences Faculty of the University of São Paulo, one of the centers of official Brazilian progressivism. The auditorium was full. Onstage were the group's representatives (myself included), who had stuffed themselves with tranquilizers and were suffering from diarrhea. Positions hardened. On one side students and teachers of the university left proclaimed their faith in the dogma of class struggle and in the divine grace of the proletariat. On the other side we stood by the originality of our argument and the independence of our analysis, which was not necessarily part of the class struggle but was no less concerned with social change. The first position represented the "greater struggle," according to which there were revolutionary priorities—the greatest priority, of course, being the struggle of the proletariat, which would ignite and lead the revolution, in the widest meaning of the term, while anything else, in terms of social revolution, was irrelevant and even divisive. In comparison, we were the "lesser struggle" for the very reason that we questioned the sanctification of the working class. Blacks, who had begun to organize against racial discrimination and to assert their culture, had already been accused of initiating worthless "existential discussion" of their problems.

Nevertheless, since those of us on the platform that night knew that the auditorium was full of gay men and lesbians, we had agreed to throw questions back to the public whenever possible. They could then take over the debate and there would be no need for spokespeople. When, at the end of heated discussion, a member of the orthodox left commented that the homosexual struggle greatly devalued the issue of class struggle, I could not contain my anger. I stood on a chair and asked people in the audience to give concrete evidence about how *we* homosexuals were devalued in the very name of class struggle. The reaction was devastating. Men and women, emotionally moved and unafraid to appear in public as gay, stood to describe how they had personally experienced discrimination by progressives for being homosexual. One example given was that of a teacher of that same university who had asked students for an essay analyzing the reasons for the absence of homosexuals among the working class.[2] That was, furthermore, the same opinion held by Lula, a messianic union leader who at the time considered feminism "something for those who have nothing to do."[3] Insults were exchanged between representatives of the student movement and homosexuals—a sign that we were no longer apologizing for our actions.

At the end, our sweat-soaked shirts gave the impression that the Brazilian gay movement had just taken its rightful place in society. We were thrilled and kissed each other in public, no longer shy. We did not know that this first public confrontation with the student left would be neither the last nor the most violent. Later we learned that in the same faculty where the debate had taken place, a gay activist (who provocatively liked to introduce himself as Taís—a woman's name—and to walk through the streets of São Paulo at night in drag) had been pulled into some bushes in the neighborhood and given a beating which cost him a broken tooth. As they hit him, the four militant leftists (whom he knew) accused him of trying to divide the proletarian struggle and advised him to stop "this impudence of a homosexual movement."

The most concrete result of the debate was a surprising increase in the number of participants in the group, which from then on called itself *Somos* (We Are)—a name that was "expressive, assertive, palindromic, rich in meaning, and with no negative connotations," as stated in a document we published at the time.[4] From just ten we soon became an average of a hundred people. Since various smaller groups had formed to talk and exchange ideas, such affluence forced us to reorganize our structure into a more systematic form. Meetings were held in rotation in the houses of different members; we had nowhere like a headquarters and, to avoid being centralized and bureaucratic, did not want one. We also wanted to maintain an air of semisecrecy, then still necessary in Brazil, and because there were signs that the police were watching us. After a time no new member joined *Somos* without first attending informal meetings where people talked and exchanged experiences in what came to be called the "admission or identification" group, the molecular base of our activism in its initial phase.

Most surprising of all was the fact that the number of women suddenly grew until it almost equaled the number of men. Gradually the majority of them felt they had to meet in an exclusively women's group, the arguments for which were related to the discriminatory and chauvinist way in which gay men in general treated them. It was true that men could often be heard referring to the women in pejorative terms. The situation was a hot potato for all of us. When the men tried to be unprejudiced the result was almost fatally paternalistic. It was then that we began general discussions on chauvinism and feminism, but these did not always end well, the women becoming very impatient and the men stubborn. In any case the lesbians' intention to form an autonomous and exclusively feminine subgroup started a heated debate which lasted several weeks and made it very clear that being a homosexual man did not automatically mean a closeness to women—sometimes even the opposite.

In Rio de Janeiro, meanwhile, things were not going well for *Lampião*. Since August 1978 we had been the subject of a police inquiry in both Rio and São Paulo, accused of offending public morality. The letter from the federal police requesting the inquiry referred to the editors as "individuals suffering from serious behavioral problems," so much so, they claimed, that we were cases on the boundary of pathological medicine. The letter asked that we be tried and sentenced under the so-called Press Law, under which we could receive up to a year in prison. Even before any trial began we were threatened and interrogated by the police, photographed, and identified as criminals; in short, they had prejudged and found us guilty. One of the first questions put to various of the editors under interrogation was to confirm that they were homosexual. Luckily, the Journalists' Union in Rio and São Paulo offered the free services of a lawyer and gave *Lampião* every help. I remember that I was photographed with a kind of yoke around my neck. On it, coincidentally or not, was the number 0240. In Brazil the number 24 is pejorative, being equivalent to "queer."

Soon afterward, in a subtle change of tactics, the police demanded the paper's account books in the hope of finding irregularities and closing it for tax reasons. In the second half of 1979 bombs exploded at kiosks in various parts of the country while anonymous leaflets demanded that they stop selling alternative papers (almost always left-wing) or periodicals they considered pornographic (*Lampião* appeared on one of the lists). The government vaguely blamed the bombs on paramilitary groups. However, no enquiry was set up to find out where the members of such groups—New Fatherland Phalange, Moral Brigades, and Anti-Communist Commandos— came from or who they were. This dark cloud hovered over *Lampião* until the middle of 1979, when the police inquiry was shelved for lack of evidence. In any case, it was amusing to discover that the primary accusation against us was the cover story of issue 0 on Celso Curi, a journalist who had been on trial since 1977 for the same crime of offending public morality. This had allegedly been by a gay column in a São Paulo daily in which, according to the Public Prosecutor, he had encouraged "meetings between abnormals." [5] Luckily Celso Curi was acquitted shortly afterward, the judge stating that he did not consider it a crime for homosexuals to try "to place themselves as a structured segment within society."

By that time there were other gay activist groups in São Paulo, Rio de Janeiro, Niterói, Belo Horizonte, Salvador, Brasília, Recife, João Pessoa, and the interior of the state of São Paulo. *Somos,* meanwhile, had matured and the group tried to tackle more complex issues. As it grew, so did its bureaucracy, although it still tried to keep to the principles of autonomy. From each work group—which ranged from research to writing letters of protest, organizing public debates, parties, and contact with other countries—a coordinator was elected to sit on the general coordination committee for one or two months. In this way we tried to be better organized without being less flexible, since the large turnover of people within the group very often brought work in progress to a halt. As part of our intention to claim our place, we tried to undertake actions in coordination with two other gay groups in São Paulo. A Committee for the Defense of Homosexual Rights was set up, but it was not really effective and did not last long. One of the few joint activities was participation in public debates, seminars, and university symposia. However, this was not the only diet for liberationist gay men and lesbians. Much attention was paid to leisure—after all, one of the demands we all agreed on was the right to pleasure. Parties were often held in private houses or gay clubs, and members went on excursions to the country. These were also ways of trying to increase the possibilities of meeting others outside the consumerist limitations of the ghetto.

I believe that in the golden era of *Somos* there was a series of interesting attempts at different styles of political experience on the day-to-day level. One of the key ideas, present since the group's beginnings, was that homosexuality should be determined by homosexuals themselves. We viewed with antipathy the assaults of psychiatrists, judges, and priests and their theories and dogmas on the subject. We did not like being objects of research. I remember the violent discussion which exploded when one of the group, an anthropology student who had decided to write his thesis on *Somos* and gay activism in Brazil, started taking exhaustive notes at meetings. He was only allowed to continue under a series of conditions, the most important being that he write a paper about himself.

Another topic frequently discussed was the rejection of leadership in order to avoid once again becoming the victims of spokespeople and interpreters. I do not know how viable this might be. In any case informal proposals of self-propagation and direct action developed gradually and unanimously in *Somos,* perhaps a result of the disagreeable experiences which many of us had had with the centralism of the orthodox left. The preoccupation with challenging the messianism of leaders, however, came from the concern that each of us should control our own destiny. That was also the source of our principle of independence, autonomy, and nonalignment with party politics—*Somos'* most consistent political attitude until the confrontation with Trotskyists who shortly afterward took over the group and imposed their own party line. What we wanted, in short, was that organized homosexuals should discover their own way of taking action, which would be an indication of their originality as a new movement in Brazilian life. We wanted to offer our own contribution to restructuring society and demanded our own place within it where we might grow. I fear that this has been denied us by the institutionalized opposition as much as by the system itself. We will soon see how.

Other important themes—either discussion topics or permanent aspects of the group's activities—centered on change at the day-to-day level. It was thought that the revolution should start at home and concern itself with major taboos—such as monogamy and possessiveness in love. Group sexual activity was therefore not uncommon. There was also the common practice of changing partners, which sometimes led to more stable relationships. We often discussed our relationship with our own bodies, thinking of a more gentle and less genitalized sexuality. In this respect I had a singular experience in *Somos'* studies subgroup. We no longer knew what to study, since, ill at ease as zoological specimens, we could not take any overtheoretical debate on homosexuality seriously. So we said: If we are to study ourselves, why don't we begin by looking at our own bodies, the first and most confusing evidence that we are different from each other? We decided to meet with the sole aim of undressing in order to touch each other indiscriminately and so reveal the flesh which our campaigning activities insisted on camouflaging. The intention was perhaps very naive, but it made sense at the time, for we were eager to throw daily life into the whirlwind of change that we dreamed about.

The truth is that it was more difficult than we expected. Some members of the subgroup opposed the idea from the beginning and withdrew, horrified. Almost two months went by as we discussed whether or not to meet in the dark, with or without music, what type of music, where, etc., etc. Prolonging the discussion to such an extent was proof of the panic which undressing (unmasking) provoked. At last, one night one of the queens dressed up as a harem woman and danced for us, then the collective striptease took place. Our glances became adolescent and we measured each other up in astonishment as if we had just got to know each other properly. So that was what his chest looked like? and his backside? and his cock? I didn't know he had spots on his back and so many hairs on his thighs! Everyone was fascinated. We resolved to repeat the dose another time. On that occasion we touched each other in the dark, indiscriminately, for more than an hour. I remember the fascination of feeling with one hand the swollen texture of an Afro haircut and with the other the swelling of a generous prick, both giving themselves to my caress. We were so enchanted by the experience that we thought sarcastically of proposing general nudity at left-wing party meetings in order to subvert discussions on the different paths to revolution. That was at the end of 1979 and seems to have been the swan song of our attempts at political activity and autonomy.

NOTES

1. "Grupo *Somos*, uma experiência," *Lampião* 12 (May 1979).
2. João Silvério Trevisan, "Quem tem medo das 'minorias'?" *Lampião* 10 (March 1979).
3. "ABC de Lula," *Lampião* 14 (July 1979).
4. "Grupo *Somos*, uma experiência," op. cit.
5. João Silvério Trevisan, "Mas qual é o crime de Celso Curi?" *Lampião* 0 (April 1978).

AOTEAROA/NEW ZEALAND

Alison J. Laurie's story "From Kamp Girls to Political Dykes" is a tribute to the author's personal courage and her determination to survive. It is also an odyssey that takes us from the dark ages of the 1950s, when lesbian life throughout the West was hidden and most references to it linked only to notions of criminal behavior, abnormal psychology, or sin, to the exciting days of gay liberation and the subsequent right-wing backlash of the early 1980s. Having lived and experienced gay life not only in her native Aotearoa/New Zealand but also in England and Denmark, Ms. Laurie also makes us aware of the tremendous impact ideas of sexual liberation have had across national borders. *The Well of Loneliness,* a classic lesbian novel from England, brought to her attention the fact that not all persons with feelings like she had toward members of her own sex were in prisons and mental institutions; a copy of American writer Donald Cory's *The Homosexual in America,* smuggled in to Aotearoa/New Zealand, allowed her to establish contacts with lesbian groups in the United States; and the exhilarating news of the Stonewall Rebellion meant for her that lesbians need no longer beg for acceptance but could come out of the closets at last. The author's experiences, both personal and political, have helped her to link up with other lesbians in common struggle and prompted her as well into an exploration of the lives of other gay women of Aotearoa/New Zealand hidden from history. Ms. Laurie is a lecturer in Women's Studies at Victoria University of Wellington, Aotearoa/New Zealand. She has been active in lesbian and feminist politics since the 1960's and has written and broadcast extensively on lesbian and feminist topics.

She is of working class background and is of mixed Pakeha and Maori ancestry.

"From Kamp Girls to Political Dykes" by Alison J. Laurie, from *Finding the Lesbians: Personal Accounts From Around the World,* eds. Julia Penelope and Sarah Valentine (1990).

I began my unrelenting search for the "others" when I was fifteen. It was 1956, and I had heard the word *lesbian* and identified with it. I had been having kisses, cuddles, and crushes on other girls since I was ten.

The first word I had found was *homosexual.* In the typical ignorance about sex of the fifties, I had been trying to get a sex education at the Wellington Public Library. I discovered Freud in the Reference Section, and learned that the "others" who were attracted to their own sex were all either in prisons or in mental institutions. This was not hopeful.

There were, of course, "others" at my all-girls' school, among both the teachers and students. But we were all afraid, and there was no way to discuss this subject.

Coffee bars began in Wellington. They were daring and new, bohemian. The first one was the Man Friday, followed by the Sorrento, the Picasso, and the Casa Fontana. Writers, artists, unusual people went to them. I went every night. But there were no "others" there. At every opportunity I asked if anyone had ever met someone "like that." I did not say that I thought I was one.

It was now 1957 and I was a sixth-former. I played hockey every Saturday. In the morning I played for school and in the afternoon for Old Girls. I was sure that some of the Old Girls were "like that," but I was only sixteen and they were cool, distant, guarded.

One day someone at the coffee bar talked about a "dreadful woman" who had made a pass at her. I found out the woman's name and where she worked.

She worked on the pattern counter of the D.I.C. store in Wellington. I went to see her and wore a tie so that she would realize that I was "one." She invited me home. We made love. She lent me a copy of *The Well of Loneliness*. I thought it was a wonderful book. It meant that there were indeed "others" and that they were not in prisons or mental institutions. They wore tweed suits and lived in London. Since they lived in London, perhaps some might live in Auckland? It was a much bigger city than Wellington. . . .

My new friend didn't know. She wasn't much use at all really. She didn't know any "others" and said that she wasn't "like that." She said she only made love to women sometimes.

School finished. I went to Auckland. I stayed with writers and artists—friends of the bohemian coffee bar crowd in Wellington. I asked them about lesbians and grew bolder. I now said that "I thought I might be one."

At last I met a man who took me to the Ca d'Oro. It was early 1958. The Ca d'Oro was full of fluffy young men in chiffon scarves and makeup. I felt that I had come home. The young men and I went everywhere together. I wore a tie. The streets were dark and dangerous. People often chased us and tried to beat us up. "Queers!" they would shout. I was a fast runner. I had gone in full drag to a Trades Hall dance, passed as a boy, and danced with girls. Afterward I had to run ten blocks to safety pursued by a gang of milk-bar cowboys.

The young men did not know any other lesbians—except for two who had gone to Sydney. "That's where all the kamp girls are," they said. I liked being a kamp girl. I learned a new vocabulary that was called "the palare."

palare—*used by kamp boys and girls until the late sixties*
homi—man
polone—woman
homi-polone—homosexual
kamp—homosexual (possibly derived from police records, an

abbreviation for "known as male prostitute"; used in the scene for
both sexes)
bona—good
naff—bad
on jon wa—over there
square—heterosexual
trade—sex
rough trade—sex with squares (used by men)
butch—sexually "active"
bitch—sexually "passive"

British queens off the Home Boats had brought the palare to
Aotearoa/New Zealand. Port cities like Auckland and Wellington
had regular influxes of foreign queens who brought news of "others" in every port in the world. They influenced the Aotearoa/New
Zealand scene profoundly in those days before general air travel.

But they brought no news of other kamp girls in Aotearoa/New
Zealand. Still, I was able to return to Wellington with contacts for
the kamp scene and to mix with kamp boys and go to parties. This
was a great relief.

I looked everywhere for kamp girls. Anyone I thought might be,
I put on my tie and went to visit. I went to Christchurch, made an
appointment to see Ngaio Marsh. She was polite and we discussed
theater—my stated reason for seeking her out. I was too nervous
to bring up my hidden agenda directly.

At last I heard about another kamp girl. We were introduced at
a party. She was from Christchurch, newly arrived in Wellington.
She knew no one else either. We became lovers. One afternoon we
were making love at my parents' home while they were out at work.
They returned unexpectedly and my lover hid in the wardrobe. My
father moved forward, exclaiming, "I know you've got a man in
here." He flung open the wardrobe door and out stepped a naked
woman. He retreated and my mother advanced. I immediately left
home and we began to live together as lovers in a small flat in the
inner city. I was seventeen.

One day we were out driving by Central Park. We saw two young women walking. They looked "different." We stopped the car and asked them for the time. We all had dinner together. We moved into a flat in Watson Street together. This flat became a center for the "funny" parties. Kamp boys came, and bohemians. Some women came sometimes who said they "might be like that." The police raided our parties. We kept on having them.

We heard about two others in Auckland. We immediately jumped in the car and drove there to meet them. Now we were six.

It was November 1958. We Wellington four decided to go to Sydney, where all those others were. We sailed on the *Monowai,* our friends holding streamers as the boat hooted away with the entire known Wellington lesbian community. We went straight to Kings Cross. The beer garden behind the Rex Hotel was full of lesbians. Some wore ties and suits and others frilly dresses.

"Are you butch or bitch?" asked Young Jerry, tall and tough. It seemed more prestigious to be butch, so I opted for this role socially and remained largely bitch in bed with my older lovers. I kept this a secret. It was frowned upon—called "turning." There were a lot of rules in the subculture. Breaking any of them meant you got beaten up. I learned to fight—the instruction was very similar to a modern women's self-defense course, except that it was free, informal, and for real.

As squares were always trying to bash up kamps, it was vitally necessary, too. Some of the Sydney butches were amazingly good fighters. Dutch Kerry, Motorbike Bobby, Young Jerry were especially good. Tramtracks, Big Jan, Kiwi Jean, French Jackie, and Flake were useful but not as outstanding. Everyone had butch names, just as the kamp boys had their kamp names. The kamp boys were called things like The Countess, Gigi, Scotch Annie. My butch name was New Zealand Bobby.

The police raided the Rex often. I became an expert at eluding them—leave through the front bars before they locked the glass doors at quarter to ten (closing time at ten), or climb the iron fence, run like hell. They charged lesbians usually with consorting—which meant "habitually consorting with *known* [not convicted] criminals." Nine "consorting bookings" and you could go up for two years. I only ever got four (in South Australia). Otherwise there was always vagrancy (few out kamps could get or hold regular jobs); drunkenness, obscene language, resisting arrest, or even "being in possession of a stolen hotel glass"—after they'd pushed you out the gate with it. They were the Sydney Vice Squad, and they ruled the Cross, hunting homosexuals and prostitutes. Lesbians were seen as prostitutes—some were—and as *sexual outlaws* who had broken all the rules and should be able to be arrested for *something*. They treated us like hunted animals; our visibility angered them, and they wanted us to disappear.

As for us, we saw the police as a natural catastrophe—like floods, fires, earthquakes. There was nothing you could do about these things except to try and escape them. We had no analysis, no understanding that society could be changed. We simply tried to survive, as ourselves, as kamp girls, natural rebels. We did not feel that the police might not be entitled to hunt us, but accepted them as inevitable.

I was beaten up for suggesting that a woman ask for a lawyer. It was seen as a stupid—even dangerous—suggestion. Fighting back with threats of lawyers would only make the police even angrier at us. But part of me felt that what was happening was unfair and unjust, though I had no idea how things could ever be different.

Melbourne and Adelaide were exactly the same. The public lesbian scene was dangerous and difficult. There were many other New Zealand lesbians around, too. In spite of everything, I loved it. The "mateship" was amazing and close, important enough for any risk. And the freedom to be ourselves, to be real, to be queer, affirmed us.

There were private, closeted scenes, too, but they were hard to find and cliquey. They were fearful of being "sprung" by kamps who were too obvious. They were mainly older, middle-class women. I knew some of them, learned many things from them— like how to behave in a nice restaurant if you are taken to dinner.

But they, too, had no sense of anything being able to change—except for the one strange woman who danced naked to Beethoven and lent me de Beauvoir's *The Second Sex*. She sowed some wild ideas, more than a decade too early for them to make any sense.

I returned to Aotearoa/New Zealand. There were a few more lesbians around. I had an affair with Anna Hoffman. Anna was a woman constantly harassed by the police. She had hit New Zealand headlines as early as 1956 when, as a sixteen-year-old, she had been deported home from Australia as a social menace. She'd had a lesbian affair with artist Rosaleen Norton, billed as "the witch of Kings Cross," sensationalized in the Sydney press. After this both the New Zealand police and press hounded her—including the police actually holding up the Lyttelton train when we were on it, in order to take us off and find out what the notorious Anna was doing in their Lyttelton.

As for me, I broke up with Anna and went to work for broadcasting, trying to be more closety by now. The police still raided our parties, so we tried to establish a pub for lesbians. Very important, because drinking was vital—women weren't supposed to, so it was a rebellion and an affirmation of our denial of conventional femininity. We did not identify with square women. There were us kamps—both boys and girls—and them, all those heterosexuals. If anything, we had more contact with heterosexual men, some of whom were quite friendly to lesbians. Most heterosexual women were uptight and nasty to us—especially the "fruit flies," the square girls who hung around the kamp boys.

Women couldn't drink in public bars in those days of six-o'clock closing—in fact, some hotels did not admit women at all. This meant we couldn't drink at the Royal Oak Hotel, where the kamp boys went, unless we managed to sneak in wearing drag. Finally we found the Western Park, a scungy, unpopular pub then, which agreed to allow kamp girls to drink there.

It was 1961 and the kamp girls' scene had grown larger. Many Maori had begun moving to the cities, and among them were not only many more Maori drag queens but also Maori kamp girls. They formed the basis of our first lesbian communities, some of them ex-services with additional knowledge of closet networks there. By now there were about fifteen of us in Wellington who were prepared to "mix" in the kamp life. There were maybe a few more in Auckland, which we visited frequently, driving all Friday night in ancient Fords or Morrises at 40 mph top speed, to socialize together for a Saturday. We also knew kamp girls in Christchurch—about five of them—and we would take the overnight boat to Lyttelton on Friday night, returning Saturday night, as it didn't sail on Sundays. Intercity relationships were the rage, given our small numbers in each place, and most of our weekly wages were spent on travel.

Some Australian kamp girls visited here, too, inspired by the large numbers of kamps from Aotearoa/New Zealand living over there. Motorbike Bobby and Little Hank made a great impression as they toured in full drag down Queen Street, Lambton Quay, and in Cathedral Square. These were great events in our lives.

There were by now quite a lot of rules in our Aotearoa/New Zealand subculture:

- Don't spring your mates at work or with their families and square friends.

- Always be loyal to all other kamps.

- Tell the police nothing.

- Be butch or bitch, and if you do turn, don't admit it.

- Maintain that you were "born this way" if you want to be accepted as a real kamp.

- Never have sex with men unless you do it for money.

- Know how to fight, and don't ever be a coward.

- Drink lots, take your shout at the bar, and be drunk often.

- Dress with kamp style, always press your pants and iron your shirt, never be sloppy.

- Be very clean, shower a lot, and keep your fingernails very short or you'll hurt someone—and wear short hair.

- Learn to dance the latest. (It was the twist.)

- Don't get off with your mates' girlfriends.

- Don't break up couples.

- Most importantly, learn to lead a double life if you want to hold down a job. Dresses at work—pants were totally unacceptable in any job then—and high heels. Learn to tell lies, to monitor yourself constantly, to always hold back. Kamp girls get fired, kicked out of flats—always, if "they" find out.

And so we lived. But I was also a socialist and involved with the Campaign for Nuclear Disarmament (CND). The socialists kicked me out, afraid that I was a "security risk"—queers can be pressured, you know. CND didn't seem to mind as much—but they were mostly fringe people themselves then. I read a lot, and began to believe in social change.

I read a book, *The Homosexual in America,* by Donald Webster Cory. A kamp boy had smuggled it in—no such books were available on open sale in Aotearoa/New Zealand then. This book spoke of social acceptance. It also listed the addresses of some American homosexual organizations—One Incorporated and Mattachine. I was very excited. I wrote away immediately for their magazines. Through these I discovered the Daughters of Bilitis—the American lesbian organization started in 1958.

It was hard to get foreign exchange in 1963 but I was able to change some pounds on the street with a U.S. sailor for American dollars and to get a few issues of DOB's publication, *The Ladder.* (One and Mattachine had luckily sent their sample magazines free.)

Through *The Ladder* I found out about the Minorities Research Group (MRG), Britain's first lesbian organization, started in 1962. I wrote to them, and subscribed to *Arena Three,* their magazine. I passed it around the crowd, but very few others were interested.

They thought subscribing to such a magazine was really risky, and what was the point anyway?

By now the crowd was much larger. The Royal Oak had opened the Bristro Bar, and women could drink there. With the increasing urban shift more Maori kamps had come to Wellington. I had an important relationship with a Maori kamp girl from Nelson, whose Mormon family, though initially welcoming, finally tried to break the relationship up. But Wellington seemed safer than it had been just three years earlier—there were more of us, and now we had a better place to meet.

But I thought it was important that we organize, as they were doing overseas. I put ads in *The Evening Post* for the "Radclyffe Hall Memorial Society." I did get replies and met a few more lesbians— but no one wanted to start a branch of the MRG in Aotearoa/New Zealand.

The kamp boys were quite numerous by now. They started the Dorian Society. We held a meeting with them but they refused to let kamp girls join. We were very disappointed.

I decided that I must go away, to where there was an organization that I could join, and be part of something that might work for some kind of change. So in late 1964 I left for London—and the MRG.

I sailed from Auckland on the *Castel Felice,* and the entire known Auckland lesbian community came to farewell me—all 25 of them by this time—holding the streamers and singing the songs in what was once an important leave-taking ritual for all those kamps from Aotearoa/New Zealand who went permanently into exile "overseas." I was sure, then, that I would never return.

I was pleased to find six other kamps on board the *Castel Felice,* and the five-week trip was interesting. We tried to find the "others" at Naples, but ended up in a brothel full of drag queens.

On arriving in London I went straight to the Gateways, already an herstoric place in 1964, and also found the Robin Hood. To me it seemed like a multitude of lesbians, but the best was yet to come. Within a week I was able to go to an MRG meeting—the first

known lesbian organization in Britain, which I had left Aotearoa/
New Zealand to find.

MRG had members all over Britain, ran advertisements in newspapers, and held monthly meetings in London as well as special-
interest group meetings. Many of the women who had started it
were "colonials," as we were called at that time, from Australia,
"South Africa," "Rhodesia," and Aotearoa/New Zealand. Some of
the "South African" women—whites—had tried in small ways to
oppose apartheid and felt that they had more than one reason to
reject their country and live in London.

My first political work as a homosexual girl—for in London we
were not kamp, and we were not yet women—was to help mail
out *Arena Three,* the monthly magazine, and to start getting up and
talking at meetings. There were often a hundred or so homosexual
girls at meetings, so this was quite intimidating at first. Then I
volunteered to run a group. The weekly Literary Group met at my
flat and a dozen of us read Dylan Thomas and other male authors
very seriously.

It did not occur to us to read many women authors. We knew
of few lesbian books except *The Well of Loneliness,* which we'd all
read and reread, and with no women's bookshops, or movement, or
politics, why should it have? We were lesbians, not women, so why
read women authors particularly?

Bryan Magee from the BBC wanted to make a TV program about
female homosexuals—he had just made one about male homosexuals. We were all very pleased at his interest. I was assigned the
task of showing him around the clubs. I took him to the Robin
Hood and the Gateways and introduced him to the girls. Everyone
was thrilled that the BBC would do a documentary on sex variants
like us, pleased that people like him were "sympathetic."

Other people came and wanted to do research; MRG cooperated
enthusiastically. We went along and filled out questionnaires, did
inkblot tests. It was so nice that the experts were willing to study
us, perhaps prove that we were mentally normal. This would help
us to win acceptance. We looked forward to a time when we might

be tolerated, might be allowed to live in peace, might be granted a few crumbs from the table.

This was a very radical view. Most London lesbians, who did not belong to MRG, thought that nothing could change and that the less the outside world knew about us the better. Then no one would suspect that we existed. That was much safer.

Then, in Easter 1965, I went as part of the MRG delegation to a lesbian conference in Holland. We became aware of this conference when an American lesbian living in Amsterdam visited London. Otherwise there had been few international links that we knew about.

That conference changed my life. There were 300 lesbians there, mainly from the Dutch mixed homophile organization, the COC. Holland had no laws against homosexuality; their society was quite tolerant of variants, apparently. At the conference many lesbians talked about social change—although no one except the British delegation was wearing slacks—and they all looked very serious and conservative. I was very impressed. My expectations began to expand. If not quite equal to heterosexuals, perhaps almost so . . . ?

I left London, and with lesbian friends explored Europe on the thumb. My decision to live in Copenhagen was based on a tall, Danish lesbian that I met in the piano bar *Lille Rosenberg* one romantic night, so it was hardly political at first. But I soon became involved with the Forbund of 1948, which was another of the European mixed homophile postwar organizations. I helped with mailings, until one day I found that I could speak Danish well enough to say a few things at meetings. As time went by I could say more and more, and I began to think and feel like a Dane.

I visited the United States, but returned to Denmark. The States seemed so apolitical, so disorganized apart from the Daughters of Bilitis, which I thought wasn't as effective as the Danish F48.

The Americans might be more free-wheeling and have lots more bars, but the Danes were getting articles into the newspapers about homophiles. And anyway, the bars in New York were all mafia-controlled, with thugs wearing guns guarding the doors, and everywhere in the States it seemed you could be arrested for wearing more than three items of male clothing. I had put away my tie and butch identity when I left Aotearoa/New Zealand, and was now trying out that new word "femme" as an identity, but I still wore pants and shirts.

And I liked being a homophile. *Homophile* was such a wonderful word, so much less sexual somehow, than being plain old *homosexual*. More dignified, too, very Greek and everything. I liked the Danish beer, and the piano bars where you danced waltzes, and the discos, which were just beginning with wilder, louder music, and the Danish lesbians who made jokes in bed and laughed a lot.

My new lover was Norwegian, though, and as we moved in together on New Year's Eve in 1969 neither of us knew that within a year our whole world would have changed.

When we read about New York's Stonewall riots (the first large-scale lesbian and gay rebellion against police harassment) that June, we were amazed. Homophile men and women rioting in the streets! We held weekend seminars to discuss it. Something called gay liberation had happened. What was it all about?

The new ideas were mind-blowing. You could be lesbian, gay, or however you wanted to be. You didn't have to integrate into society, or beg for tolerance and acceptance. You could do your own thing. You could be free to be yourself. You could—and should—come out of the closet.

We held our first public demonstration in the Faelled Park in the middle of Copenhagen. There were hippies all around, with long hair and beads, smoking hashish. People talked about civil rights, made comparisons with the Black civil rights movement in the States. People talked about the anti-Vietnam war movement. The sun was shining. At that moment everything seemed possible. We were going to be free at last, we were gay people, liberating ourselves and the world.

Then more things happened. A small group of heterosexual women calling themselves Redstockings who said they were feminist, whatever that was (something to do with that old suffrage movement, perhaps), invited the gay women from F48 to meet with them at a weekend seminar. We went, dubiously, and they talked about something called women's liberation. They said that they thought that we were oppressed by the gay men in F48, and that we should do something about it. And they said that we were oppressed by society in general as women!

We went away and started our own consciousness-raising groups to talk about all this. It was an amazing discovery, that we shared an oppression with 51 percent of the population, instead of our gay 10 percent. And what was even more amazing was that these women said that we were their sisters. They said they felt solidarity with us.

Soon we started a group called the Q-Activists—Q for queer and for *qvinde,* an old Danish word for women. We met at the newly seized women's house, an empty building we had helped our sisters liberate from the Copenhagen municipality. The top floor was lesbian space, and we began to refer to ourselves as lesbians, that frightening word we had always avoided.

We used the Q-Activists as a pressure group within the F48, to get more women onto the committee, and to get a women-only night at the Pan Club, owned by the organization. We held a Scandinavian lesbian conference at the women's house in 1972, and though not many came, it was a start.

I went to the States again that year, too, because that was where it was all happening now. I worked on an issue of *The Lesbian Tide,* met lesbians who were starting groups and magazines everywhere. I started to call myself a lesbian-feminist.

"All women are lesbian except those who don't know it yet," and "feminism the theory, lesbianism the practice," and "in a society where men oppress women, to be lesbian is a sign of mental health" were the slogans. Butch and femme were laid to rest. We were roleless, liberated—and any woman could choose to be lesbian —should choose to be lesbian. Few did, as yet.

We read Elizabeth Gould Davis's *The First Sex* and became excited about the matriarchy. Men were mutants, we said, women were actually superior to them!

The ideas were all developing. They were new, stimulating. I felt I was part of a movement which was forming them, finding them, exploring them. There were no limits anymore. I felt a strong urge to return to Aotearoa/New Zealand. Letters from friends implied that the revolution might actually reach there, too.

I packed a VW combi van with supplies and American lesbian magazines like *The Lesbian Tide* and *The Furies* and with my Norwegian lover and an escaped American headmistress set off from Denmark to drive overland to Aotearoa/New Zealand, shipping the vehicle across intervening oceans. We arrived in early 1973, to a blazing January. Gay liberation and women's liberation had already started in Auckland and in Wellington.

We were mainly in Wellington at first, where I was asked to speak at some early abortion meetings, and here and there about gay liberation overseas. About six of us went to a gay liberation party in Auckland, following a meeting where men had said they really wanted more lesbian involvement. We were all bashed up at the party by drunken gay misogynists and everyone ended up feeling that it was quite impossible to work with any of the men. As for me, I went back to Wellington and worked in the mixed gay liberation group until we split after a dance with half the takings and announced that we were going to organize separately as lesbians.

We met with Christchurch lesbians, and Sisters for Homophile Equality (SHE) was formed in both Christchurch and in Wellington. We might call ourselves lesbians but you couldn't have an organization with that in the title. . . . SHE was New Zealand's first and only national lesbian organization. We started *Circle* magazine in December 1973, and reprinted articles from my American lesbian magazines, which I was busily distributing around the country. Lesbian feminism hit Aotearoa/New Zealand as a fully formed blast from abroad, but fell on fertile ground, among many of the lesbians from gay liberation for starters.

Lesbians wrote to *Circle* from all over Aotearoa/New Zealand, and issues were put out from Christchurch and Auckland as well as Wellington. We held a national lesbian conference at Victoria University in Wellington at Easter 1974, and got media coverage although we held out for women journalists only. We were on radio talk-backs, were mentioned in the news. And we held a lesbian demo outside Parliament. We often sang "I Am Woman" and did ring dances. We believed in the sisterhood and the matriarchy-to-come.

I returned to Denmark in 1975 and was part of a group trying to set up an international lesbian front. To my surprise all kinds of new lesbians were "coming out" of the women's movement. Although we had wanted this to happen it was surprising when it did, and difficult to adjust to. I had known some of the women as heterosexual feminists and it was hard to accept them as the new experts on lesbian political theory. They seemed in some way to lack what I felt was a lesbian identity, though I was unable to analyze quite why.

I went to a lesbian conference in Amsterdam, with women who didn't know and couldn't have cared that there had been one there ten years before, and how important it had been. I sought out some of those 1965 lesbians and found them now quite antipolitical. "We can't stand all these new lesbians," they said, "they're so negative." I disagreed, of course, on principle, but somehow there was less joy in the air. Unemployment was starting to happen in Europe, political discussions seemed different, we talked more about rape and violence, about men and what they were doing to the world. We talked less and less about sisterhood until finally we didn't talk about it at all, because none of us could really believe in it quite the way we had when the sun shone and it was always summer, and the whole world was poised on the brink of change.

I asked one of the new lesbians to dance at a social after a meeting. Then I tried to kiss her, gently, as we had been doing for the previous five years. She pushed me away roughly and said I was behaving like a man. I felt hurt and didn't understand. I got drunk in a corner with some twenty-year-olds, crying into the schnapps bottle and trying to explain to them that there was something happening now that wasn't what I thought I'd fought to achieve. Something uptight, critical, rejecting. Something not quite—lesbian.

I was only 35, but I was beginning to feel like an old woman of the movement. Most of the lesbians my age were not to be found in the lesbian movement. Many were back working in the mixed homophile organizations, now changing their names to associations of gay men and women. Or they were branching out to start women's refuges, getting involved in the peace movement, active in the political women's movement.

I had moved to Norway and found that the only lesbian group I wanted to work in was one called The Panthers, involved in social and cultural activities of lesbian poetry, discussions, and sing-alongs.

I got involved with the Norwegian F48 and a huge split over Marxist-Leninist politics, which resulted in the formation of the Workers' Homophile Association (AHF)—which turned out to be not at all Marxist anyway. It all made for interesting political intrigues, but I grew tired and began working very hard so that I could spend part of each year back in Aotearoa/New Zealand.

My work as a tour guide made saving money easy, especially doing lots of trips through the USSR, where there were few consumer temptations. I did, of course, and dangerously, search for Soviet lesbians whenever I could.

Back in Aotearoa/New Zealand, by 1977 SHE was dying, though *Circle* still continued. Many lesbians had come out through the women's movement here, too, and certain conflicts were beginning to emerge. The sisterhood had turned out to be far more complicated than we had imagined.

We were becoming conscious of other oppression, like race and class, which created differences between lesbians. As yet we had little analysis of any of this and few lesbians attempted to really do anything about it. In 1978 a lesbian center started in Wellington and political work included forays into the Human Rights Commission, where chief commissioner Downey had concluded that "some kinds of discrimination cannot be outlawed." Newsletters were published, women's bookshops began providing regular access to the flood of books coming off the international women's presses, and women's music was strumming and beating its discs into every lesbian home. There were crafts, too, and poetry, and women's art in the Women's Gallery.

Overseas again, there was not the International Lesbian Information Service (ILIS) and the International Association of Lesbians, Gay Women, and Gay Men (IGA), providing regular international networking and holding annual conferences for delegates from as many as 30 countries.

Many lesbians were beginning to work with gay men again, though tentatively, and only on specific issues. Others continued to develop a strong separatist politics, and some women were moving to the land. Pornography became an important issue, though as yet no lesbian analysis had been made.

As for me, I returned to Aotearoa/New Zealand permanently. It was 1982, and I worked on a couple of issues of *Circle* for old times' sake, and then got into lesbian broadcasting on our first lesbian radio program, which still runs weekly here in Wellington. We performed some lesbian plays, saw the first lesbian center die and another begin, to vanish in its turn. We saw several lesbian clubs come and go in Wellington and other places, too, and lesbian phone-in services develop around the country. There were regular but informal links with lesbians everywhere.

But when the homosexual law reform campaign came, we had no lesbian political organization to tackle it and had to develop strategies on the run. We battled against a U.S.-inspired moral majority (so-called), which petitioned against us door-to-door and whose hatred thundered at us from public platforms throughout the country. They gathered a claimed 800,000 signatures from our population of three million, from children, old people in nursing homes, frightened lesbians, and gay men, and with many multiple signatures. They presented their petition to Parliament in a Nuremburg-style rally with God, the family, and our colonial flags waving while anthems were sung. We fought them and some of us were arrested; we disrupted their meetings and we ripped up their petitions when we could. We won some and lost some; male homosexuality was decriminalized, but human rights were ruled out for the time being. It was 1986 and many of us were exhausted by that campaign but we have survived it.

What do the political dykes of the eighties have in common with the kamp girls of the fifties? Our ability to survive is the single most important thing.

Not all of the kamp girls did survive. Some are dead, lost to suicide, or the slow deaths of stress diseases. Others married, to live a daily lie, a double life made tolerable by tranquilizers or booze, and perhaps an affair with the woman down the road. Some married gay men to provide a double disguise for two frightened people. Others lost their minds into alcoholism, living half lives in the shadows, while other good women were attacked by the shock treatments and drugs of psychiatric institutions. And every single one of us carries scars.

And I know how easy it would be to put us all right back into the fifties, with the no-communication and the no-visibility and a relentless search that finds you only four others.

Close the bookshops and ban or burn the magazines and the books; prohibit the phone lines and the public advertising; close the clubs and the centers. Only now do I know that there was world-wide movement once before—the first wave of lesbian and gay liberation smashed at its German center by the Nazis in 1938 and throughout the rest of occupied Europe from 1938 onward. It vanished with few traces; the first great Nazi book-burning in Berlin was of the lesbian and gay books, manuscripts, and records from an institute founded in the 1890s. I have heard lesbian and gay historians say that what was remarkable about the surviving copies of the last issues of the lesbian and gay magazines of the time is that they were so unsuspecting. Their last issues wrote of next month's dance, next issue's feature. They were all closed down without warning. I look at Clause 28 in Britain and I wonder what new state treachery is in store for us.

My own search for the others began in the fifties, long after the Homocaust of Europe. As yet we know very little about the lives of earlier lesbians in Aotearoa/New Zealand, either in the prewar period or during the past thousand years since the migrations or after the white invasion of the nineteenth century.

My search for others continues—back into our lesbian past, in our present, and on into our future. Sometimes I find them, and when I do I am convinced more and more of our ability to survive against all odds, and to reemerge from our hiding places in even the worst of societies. To find.the others we may need to redefine what we mean by lesbian, what we mean by sex, and how we understand love. But the others are always there somewhere if you keep on looking.

GREAT BRITAIN

Soon after gay liberation organizations began forming in 1969, one of the issues that emerged was that of male privilege. Though gay men and women certainly shared a wide range of common experience and shared certain goals, it became evident that critical differences still existed. Gay males often dominated political meetings; furthermore, they were less apt to put feminist issues such as employment discrimination, violence against women, and abortion rights high on the agenda. One result was the decision of many gay women to form movements of their own, or to join the feminist movement as a more appropriate arena for political activism. The reaction among gay males to the departure of gay women from among the ranks ranged from noncomprehension, to hostility, to a serious examination of their own sexism. Among those males willing to look critically at male privilege and their ingrained sexist behaviors and attitudes was a group in England called the Radical Feminists, or Rad Fems. They were a loosely defined group of gay males, not all initially politicized, who came to use drag as a political tool. Going out onto the streets outrageously dressed in women's clothing, they thought of themselves as the vanguard of political liberation. No only were they giving up their male privilege, they were also ridiculing society's objectification of women and beauty, and showing solidarity with women at the same time. There was a sense of joy in what they were doing, and much irony. In the United States, the term "gender-fucking" was coined to describe a similar form of radical street theater—an attempt by mixing masculine and feminine imagery to shock people into realizing the absurdity of rigid sex roles. Everybody, after all, was in drag; the women who wore skirts and nylons as a uniform to work, and the males who clung compulsively to their Levi's and work shirts as emblems of masculinity. Unfortunately, the Rad Fems, even though soon considered the most politically correct within the larger gay group to which they belonged, fell into the same aggressive stances and self-righteousness as the men they were trying not to be. However, their attempt to live out their politics is highly admirable and might even have something to say to today's younger generation, where, though men can now comfortably sport an earring openly in public, wearing two is still strictly taboo.

"The Rad Drag Queens," from *Men in Frocks* by Kris Kirk and Ed Heath (1984).

Gay Liberation Front was due to do the lunchtime "U.S. Troops Out of Vietnam" picket outside of the U.S. Embassy in Grosvenor Square, and we all turned up in our drag to find we were sharing the picket with the dockers. After a while we heard music in the park opposite and drifted over. It was a Philadelphia High School Band, and a couple of us soon started waltzing to *String of Pearls*. In no time, two dozen sparkling queens were whirling around, dancing with the typists and secretaries. The conductor, who was a queen himself, was totally fazed and curtailed the concert, so then we decided to go to the Dilly to talk to the rent boys. It was a bit patronizing, but we were rather crusading in those days! The afternoon ended in an impromptu march of 200 drag queens and rent boys from Piccadilly to Hyde Park. . . . They were crazy, amazing, joyful days. No wonder some of us began living and breathing GLF seven days a week. [Michael James]

However instinctively subversive they may have been, our drag queens have not until now appeared the most political of creatures. But with the advent of the seventies and GLF, a new strain of drag queen was to appear—the Radical Feminist. Frocks and politics made a heady mixture. What began in a spirit of pure playfulness ended in tears.

For most of its first year of existence—from October 1970 on —London GLF was pluralistic, idealistic, gloriously free. There was no mainstream GLF—as long as you were glad to be gay, you were part of this people's movement. At first there was only the most rudimentary theorizing—gay was good, and it was vitally important to come out to yourself and to others. The realization that there were many other people around who were open about their homosexuality gave you strength to openly do things which you had always wanted to do, so you went out and did them. GLF was a collection of autonomous groupings—some had an interest in left-wing politics, some were developing an interest in feminism, some were into dropping acid, some spent most of their time in clubs. At first this plurality was welcomed. Ideas and philosophies and attitudes cross-fertilized; each individual was too busy learning from everybody else to start drawing lines. If GLF was first of all a vehicle for personal liberation, there was also a commonly held belief that one could add something to the world, that gay people could help free human sexuality. Though there were few card-carrying Freudians in the movement, there was a general belief that repressed sexuality was responsible for many of the world's ills and that prejudice against homosexuality was the result of people's fear of the homosexuality within themselves; individuals oppressed each other and oppressed themselves by conforming to "norms" which were fictitious.

Unlike gay movements before it, GLF was not interested in equality with heterosexuals. On the contrary, one's duty—if one had a duty at all—was to liberate other people from their fears and prejudices and singles vision. Not everyone in GLF intellectualized to this degree, and not everyone who intellectualized agreed, but there was a fairly widespread assumption that the gender divisions of male and female, once held to be so watertight, were primarily the result of social conditioning rather than biology, and the "masculinity" and "femininity" were manufactured, artificial constructs.

Gender and sexuality were a spectrum—there was a "male" and "female" in everyone. An early popular slogan read: "There are as many sexes as there are people."

So where did drag fit into all this? Strangely, it was barely evident in the early days, though hippie wear was ubiquitous—and where does one draw the line?

It started with jellabas and kaftans and long hair and flowers . . . then we discovered glitter . . . and then nail varnish. Later, some of us—a quarter of the men, I'd say, at some time or other— would get a nice new frock for the next Gay Lib dance. Then a few people began wearing it to meetings. It just evolved. [Michael James]

As did drag in street theater. From wearing outrageous costumes on the tube it was a short step to the Miss Trial demo, the first real manifestation of drag as a political tool. While Women's Liberationists were being tried inside Bow Street Magistrates Court for disrupting the Miss World contest, men from GLF demonstrated outside as joke bathing beauties with punning titles on their sashes like "Miss Trial" and "Miss Used." If there was any political thinking here, it was that because the women were on trial for attacking sexual objectification of women by men, the best way of showing solidarity with them was to ridicule the idea of beauty objects with drag. Like beauty, irony is in the eye of the beholder; today they would probably be criticized for ridiculing women, a double bind which has dogged political drag ever since. But at the time the only objectors were Covent Garden street porters, who pelted them with tomatoes.

From then on, drag was an integral part of all the important zaps and demonstrations, including Operation Rupert, which totally disrupted the much heralded rally of the Festival of Light. Less well remembered is Doris Aversham, a fictitious, amorphous character created as a joke by two camp boys fresh from the gay scene. Doris's character changed each time she appeared: sometimes she was a symbolic heterosexual, a Mary Whitehouse type; at other times an auntie figure with gay connections and a dubious chauffeur called Gervaise. She was an agony auntie for the GLF paper *Come Together,* she wrote shocked letters to the newspapers, appeared at GLF meetings, and—still a caricature, but this time played by a woman —she appeared in Nottingham in 1975 to open a gay jumble sale.

Among all the ideas which had surfaced during GLF's first year of existence, there was one concept in particular which rang a bell with those people who were to become the Radical Drag queens, or Radical Feminists as they came to be known. This was sexism. There was a growing consensus in GLF, at least among regular attendees, male and female, that the American feminist writers were correct in diagnosing that many of society's ills were due to a system of oppression which was gender-based; the fiction that men were "superior" to women had been fashioned by men in order to gain power and privilege. More than anyone, the queens knew that "hypermasculinity" was a sham. At first it was presumed that gay men did not oppress women because they did not sleep with them, but it soon became obvious at the 500-strong weekly GLF meetings that many gay men, although prepared to pay lip service to anti-sexism, were as dominating and aggressive as the archetypal hetero-sexual men. The first people to feel this were the women, who comprised about one quarter of GLF. Many of the queens, who were as intimidated as the women by the men who tended to hold the floor, and who felt they were being treated as though they didn't have minds, aligned themselves with the women from the start. They began referring to those people whom, they felt, would not surrender the privileges that their masculinity brought them, as "the men"—1970 "hommes."

Whether a GLF queen started wearing drag because he enjoyed doing it or for political reasons—it was usually a combination of the two—it soon became a symbol of separation, a political act of defiance against the stereotype male image. It was a badge saying you disagreed with "male" value and wanted nothing more to do with them:

The dangerous thing with me for drag was that I put it off and put it off and put it off. And then I put it on. I totally agreed with what the people who were beginning to wear drag were saying, and in the end I decided, "Put your money where your mouth is." I went to the GLF meeting in a genuine Victorian velvet cape with a huge collar, an incredible scarlet lace dress cut on the cross, high-heel shoes, and lots of makeup. I felt nervous, but I felt great. I'm quite a masculine man, or at least I was brought up very butch, and when I got into drag I felt totally transformed. When I think about it, it brings tears to my eyes. I felt sensuous and relaxed in an extraordinary way. I sat down at the meeting. I don't know much about politics—I hadn't read many books and I hadn't been to college—but there was one particular college boy stomping around and giving it all out, not letting anyone else get a word in. This time, I started talking— and he listened. I sat with a cigarette, just sending him up. What I was wearing so overwhelmed him that it was then that I realized the power of a man wearing drag, as opposed to imper- sonating a woman—which is something I've never done. [Bette Bourne]

It was never the intention of the Rad Fems to pass as women. Michael James, who had previously worn drag on the gay scene, soon came to realize that:

The women were right about sexist drag. They never put down drag per se, but they put down men who got into low-cut dresses, false boobs, the fantasy Hollywood stereotype. But we began to realize that there were ways of using drag . . . it's a way of giving up the power of the male role. We were holding the mirror up to the men, showing that we rejected what maleness stood for. I was never, ever put down by a woman for wearing radical drag.

When the women finally split from GLF in February 1972, there was a crisis among the men. The Rad Fems—now in the intellectual vanguard, with all the criticisms of "the men's" chauvinism seemingly proven correct—began to dominate the meetings. It is extraordinary that a group which numbered no more than 30 or 40 at any one time should become so powerful. But they were respected —if not admired—because they appeared to practice what they preached. Eschewing privilege, they lived like monks: communally (in Notting Hill, Muswell Hill, Brixton); in poverty (no male-privilege jobs); and wearing skirts 24 hours a day. And like priests, they were the keepers of the conscience of GLF. No meeting was complete without the drag queens sitting at the front of All Saints Hall in Powis Square with their knitting putting down "the men"—they were nicknamed the Tricoteuses. Undoubtedly many of the men whom they accused of being sexist were, but it was not a good introduction to GLF for the ignorant newcomer:

> Some demanded that every man wear a frock, though of course you should only do it when you're ready to try. We wanted them to do it *now*. [Michael James]

The Rad Fems changed their self-image but hung on to that most masculine and undignified of characteristics—aggression—compounded by a measure of self-righteousness. Inevitably there was a lot of bad blood by the time the all-London meetings were discontinued in April 1972.

If nothing else, the drag queens' gumption was admirable:

> Being in drag all the time on the streets, we were putting ourselves right on the line, and we got all sorts of reactions. I remember wheeling a baby down Portobello Road once. I was wearing a nice summer print, and these yobs were going "Grrr, I'd really like to have you darling," and I just said, "You couldn't afford it, dears" and walked straight on. The women on the stalls died laughing, they thought it was wonderful. Everybody had different reactions. I'm an actor, and I was delighted that everybody was looking at me all the time. It was a stage every time I went out there, but of course you can't keep that up for long. [Bette Bourne]

And that was the trouble: Living on the front line 24 hours a day induces paranoia; outright and constant hostility wears out the defense mechanisms. And the Rad Fems, like some of the Pub Queens before them, discovered that frocks can lose their charm when you feel obliged to wear them:

> I felt I couldn't slip out of the commune in a pair of jeans to sunbathe. I didn't necessarily want to live like that for 24 hours a day, seven days a week. Drag was *de rigueur,* and I found that my freedom of choice had been taken away. [Michael James]

Rad Drag just petered away, though street drag and some of the images that the Rad Fems used are still with us today. Toward the end of 1973 some of the few surviving Rad Fems decided that the East End of London was ready for a bookshop owned and staffed by Rad Queens, but Bethnal Green was not ready for Bethnal Rouge, and in the end the communards went their separate ways. The dream, enunciated by someone who was once tempted to throw in his lot with the drag queens, had faded:

> Radical drag was constant street theater, to make ordinary people think about sex roles. Only by constant confrontation could the edifice of male domination start to crumble—in the face of the drag queens!

Radical drag was a tragicomedy. The queens began by thinking they could be a walking embodiment of a mix of the best of the "feminine" and the "masculine" sensibility, but their strong feelings against misogyny often seemed to have turned into the converse— man-hate. And because they were men, one might wonder how much self-hate this engendered. Frock wearing, then, is no easy way to perfection—the queens saw through the men's game, but started playing the same games themselves. The Rad Fems, like many others from GLF, have come out of the experience older and wiser. Many are prepared to admit, like Bette Bourne, that "a lot of things happened of which I'm not particularly proud." And, like Michael James, some see the positive side of the ending of the dream:

> It was necessary. If it hadn't come to that, I wouldn't have got to the stage of looking back on it. There was so much creative energy coming in, we were inundated with data. All those people went their own ways, to explore themselves in a new way, in their own way. Now they can come together and cross-refer, look at those ideas which were relevant and those which were transitory and begin looking at those that we have not yet got together.

But very few of the ex-Rad Fems still continue to wear frocks.

While all this was going on, something significant was happening in a totally different world. In 1971 a man who had been working with Lindsey Kemp put out an album called *The Man Who Sold the World*. The front cover showed David Bowie lying with shoulder-length hair on a chaise longue, wearing a full-length satin dress. When asked by a perplexed reporter why he was wearing a woman's dress, Bowie replied: "It's a man's dress." And so began that peculiarly modern phenomenon, the marriage of music and youth and drag.

KENYA

The struggle for lesbian and gay rights has been fought on the international level as well as the local. The results have been encouraging. Two organizations, the International Lesbian and Gay Association (ILGA) and the International Lesbian Information Service (ILIS), include representation from tens of countries around the globe. The European Parliament, part of the European Community (EC) and consisting of twelve nations, passed legislation in 1984 prohibiting discrimination based on sexual preference in the workplace. Then, in another ruling, the European Court for Human Rights declared that Ireland's law that mandated life imprisonment for male homosexual acts was a violation of the European Convention on Human Rights. (Not long afterward, Ireland overturned its sodomy law in response.) Efforts to encourage Amnesty International into placing imprisonment for reasons of sexual orientation on equal par with political imprisonment proved successful in September 1991, while the United Nations will soon consider whether to grant the ILGA official status as a nongovernmental organization (NGO).

In 1985, Nairobi, Kenya, was chosen as the site of the United Nations Women's Decade Conference. In the following article, Sylvia Borren, a founding member of ILIS, discusses lesbian visibility and presence in Nairobi and the struggles that preceded this important event. It was the first time that the word "lesbianism" was mentioned at a United Nations conference.

"United Nations Women's Decade Conference: The Decade Has Been Good for Us," from *Connexions* (summer/fall 1985).

The following resulted from an interview conducted by *Connexions* with Sylvia Borren, a founding member of ILIS. Borren currently lives in Holland and works with the COC, a Dutch gay rights organization. ILIS is a lesbian-feminist coordinating body working for the liberation of lesbians from political, legal, social, cultural, and economic oppression. Their work includes organizing international conferences, preparing reports on these conferences, and the publication of a bimonthly newsletter.

The first time we talked about doing something for Nairobi was at the April 1984 ILIS conference. Our aims were twofold: We wanted ILIS to become better known in order to network; and we wanted to further our discussions on a number of issues which we already deal with, such as education and health. We decided to set up national lesbian networks to try to get some idea of what the situation of lesbians is in our own countries. We met again a year later and found that only two or three countries had done some work on this.

In Holland we formed a political lesbian network through which we presented a report with our demands to the Dutch government. We also managed to get some of our material included in a government publication on the situation of women in Holland. At the ILIS conference [to prepare for Nairobi], we drafted five basic demands [see below], which we had printed up in a pamphlet. We're not sure yet, but we think we might actually get money for the printing from the Dutch government. This is important to us because it implies recognition.

We also wanted to get our demands and materials officially recognized and have the Dutch delegation present something about the position of lesbian women at the United Nations conference. We decided that Holland would probably be the only country we could get to talk about lesbian issues. We were surprisingly success-ful. A lot has happened in the last few years. I guess the decade has been good for us. This will be the first time that the word "lesbi-anism" will be mentioned at a United Nations conference.

We had quite a lot of fun getting our material here. Since we had about 4,000 pamphlets and 500 magazines, it was too heavy for us to carry by ourselves. So we made lots of little parcels of two kilos each and asked other Dutch women to take a few to Nairobi. Some women were wonderful about it; some were afraid and didn't want to.

The day we arrived was the first day of registration. We expected that we would be able to network with Western women. We also hoped we would be able to network with Latin American, Asian, and African women as well. We had no idea how many women would be here. A few of us started to hand out our pamphlets and we found that women were really very supportive. It was quite strange for me in comparison to the Netherlands where, when you hand out pamphlets, you usually get some negative reactions. Here people said, "Yeah, women loving women, good, wonderful." Or sometimes women would giggle or laugh. By the end of the day there weren't any pamphlets lying around.

On the second day of registration, we borrowed a table from the library, set up a stand, and hung up posters announcing when the lesbian workshops would take place. We hadn't been there for more than a quarter of an hour when Dame Nita Barrow, convener of the NGO Forum, came. She was very angry and said we had to go. It was terrible. She told us that absolutely no one was to hand out material on the lawn and that material had to be handed out at the controls. At that point there weren't any other people giving out material. We argued with her for a while, but she kept on saying, "I must protect you from the authorities. We have made arrange-ments with the Kenyan government." I think it was a homophobic reaction, or at least she panicked, I reckon.

So we got rid of the table and put our posters on the ground, as we have been doing every day since. That afternoon we were watched by about three different groups of Kenyan police. We felt quite strange about it, but women still came to us and asked us things. That was when we first started having conversations with women on the lawn.

The incident with Dame Nita Barrow was reported in the newspapers the next day. They said that we'd been kicked out of the Forum or something like that. At least that's how many people interpreted it. In effect, it made us very visible. And though I don't particularly like it being the first way people heard about us, in fact it worked extremely well. Two days later Dame Nita Barrow told both the mainstream and the NGO press that all women were welcome here. Her only concern was that we were handing things out on the grass. I think she felt embarrassed or worried about it. And, of course, after the Forum got started, everyone was handing out materials on the lawn, so the issue became totally irrelevant.

Because of all this coverage, whenever we sit on the lawn there are always between five and ten, and at times up to 100 people, mostly Kenyans, around us asking questions. They just don't know what lesbians are. They ask lots of questions. How do you find out? Do you want to have children? How do you have a relationship? Do you have sexual relationships? What do you do? How do you organize a dowry? Who looks after your parents? Who has the property? Who is the boss?

At first we were mainly talking to the men, because women were not asking many questions. After about the second day, there were so many men around that the authorities began to get worried. At one point they told the meeting to break up. They said it was an illegal meeting. The next day, they asked a few men for their identification but they left the women alone. Then we ourselves decided to focus more on the women. When men and women were around, we answered the women's questions. The first day lots of women couldn't find us because they didn't think that that great big group of men was us. Since then things have been going fine. There have been men around but not such large groups. So basically this has been going on all day, every day.

Apart from that, we caucus every day at five behind the Peace Tent so that lesbians can connect. They're just short little meetings which usually last about 20 minutes, and we sit around and chat with each other. It's been a good way to get to know one another.

We decided to have a special extra lesbian workshop on Sunday while the Forum wasn't meeting. I think altogether 120 women came. We split up into six workshops. Then we had a plenary to compare notes. That session was dominated by Western women, but there were women from Latin America, Asia, and Africa. There were also a few Kenyan women who were, as far as I'm concerned, identifying themselves as lesbians. One or two were quite clear about it; the others were not.

Yesterday we had our first officially scheduled workshop on lesbians and employment. When we walked in half an hour before the workshop started, it was already packed with Kenyans, mostly women. I think there were only about five men there. We talked about the importance of economic self-sufficiency, employment, the situation in different countries, the discrimination of lesbians on the job, the prices you pay for being in or out of the closet, compulsory heterosexuality and the constant pressure it puts on us. Then we discussed our basic demands and that we see ourselves as a liberation struggle. We talked about being in antiracist groups or in the peace or feminist movements and being able to identify yourself as a lesbian.

The workshop was so crowded. At the start there were 150 women and they were still coming in. The corridor was also crammed. It was amazing. There was a lot of pressure coming from the corridor, as well as anger, because women wanted to get inside. In the end there were about 170 women in the room. I guess we can't complain about lack of popularity.

One of the things which was yelled from the corridor was, "Observers out. Lesbians in." I got pissed off about that because I feel we shouldn't make judgments. A number of times during the workshop a Kenyan woman would get up and say, "In our country it does not exist." Then a whole group of Kenyan women would yell out, "Yes it does! Yes it does!"

We talked about equality in relationships and how we think heterosexual women should also have control over their bodies and stand up to their husbands if they boss them around. More and more recognition came from this. In some ways it isn't just the issue of lesbianism; it's the issue of having the freedom to control your own body. There is a kind of hunger for this information. I guess this is why they are coming to us. We are saying, "Well, you don't have to put up with it." I have no idea what the result of this will be, but lots of women have been taking the material.

In the workshop, some Western women talked about coming out. I had the feeling that some of these very concrete personal stories made the situation of lesbians much more real for Kenyan women. They realized it wasn't just a private matter of what you do in bed, but has to do with every aspect of your life. If you have to be in the closet, you become very schizophrenic about it.

At the end of the workshop, I told them what the symbol of the pink triangle is. I made it very clear that we use the pink triangle because there had been homosexuals killed during World War II, and most people don't even know about it. It's all sort of a lost chapter in history. We wear the pink triangle to identify ourselves and to stand up and say we will not be murdered again.

Five basic ILIS demands:

1. **Girls and women have the unconditional right to control their own bodies.** This means the freedom to develop and live their own sexual preference, the freedom from sexual use and abuse, the freedom to reproduce or not to, the freedom from poverty, hunger, and ill-health.

2. **Girls and women have the right to education which is not heterosexist.** This means that it includes positive information and identification about lesbians and lesbian lifestyles.

3. **Lesbians have the right to self-organization.** This means they can meet, publicize, and that they can advertise.

4. **All governments must get rid of legislation which criminalizes or which discriminates against homosexual women or men.** A start in this direction has been made with the Council of Europe in 1981 and should be also decided upon by the United Nations.

5. **All governments must pass human rights legislation to protect individuals against discrimination on the grounds of color, class, creed, sex, and sexual preference.**

Excerpt from ILIS flyer distributed at Forum '85.

BRAZIL

Herbert Daniel, a Brazilian PWA (Person with Aids) and AIDS activist, is no newcomer to political struggle. During the 1960s and 1970s he was involved with left-wing opposition to Brazil's dictatorship and forced into exile. Daniel returned to his country with an increased awareness of the need to incorporate the ideas of the feminist and gay movements into the political struggle. He had experienced firsthand the prejudice aimed at gays even within the leftist movements. His conclusion: Freedom must be all-inclusive. One cannot fight for class justice and ignore the oppression of women, racial minorities, or gays. Today, armed with the self-awareness and wisdom his personal experience as a PWA has given him, Daniel continues his involvement as an AIDS activist. In many ways he exemplifies the slogan "Think Globally, Act Locally." Daniel sees AIDS as a world epidemic in which countries must develop their own unique models for political activism while continuing to share and cooperate with one another. His astute understanding of the nature of oppression and the interlocking needs of Brazil's disenfranchised have won him the nomination for president of the Green Party, the political vehicle by which Brazilians of African descent, women, gays, workers, and the ecologically aware work together in common bond. The following interview with Herbert Daniel was conducted by gay activist and writer Jared Braiterman for Boston's gay paper *GCN* (Gay Community News) in April 1990.

"Fighting AIDS in Brazil," Jared Braiterman interviews Herbert Daniel, from *Gay Community News* (April 1990).

"We must illuminate the person with AIDS"
—Herbert Daniel, Brazilian PWA,
writer, and AIDS activist

The AIDS crisis, including the spread of HIV and the spread of prejudice and discrimination, has respected none of the traditional boundaries of sex, age, sexual preference, or national frontiers. A new consciousness is emerging that AIDS cannot be contained in any single community. With the epidemic now present in 177 countries and territories, people in the United States need to understand the policies as well as the epidemiology of AIDS beyond their own country's borders.

Brazil is second only to the United States in numbers of reported AIDS cases, according to official statistics by the World Health Organization. In the city of Santos, per capita AIDS infection surpasses New York City. Brazilian AIDS activists charge that the most recent official statistics, 7,787 cases, is the product of massive underreporting.

In the following interview, Herbert Daniel, 42—Brazilian PWA, prominent writer, and AIDS activist—discusses the AIDS crisis in Brazil, the work of a recently formed political group of seropositive people, and opportunities for international solidarity.

During the late 1960s and the 1970s, Daniel participated in the armed revolution sweeping Latin America, and was forced into exile for nearly a decade. As he describes in the interview, by the 1980s he shifted his political energies from class to sexual politics. He remains involved in broader political issues as a leader in the Green Party (which in Brazil addresses the rights of women, Black people, lesbians and gay men, and workers as well as ecology).

While Brazilian media and government policy frame the issue of AIDS by following a Western model, Daniel argues that underdevelopment, and incompetent government and a different sexual culture have produced a distinctly Brazilian version of the pandemic. Imported models, despite their seductive appeal to those who view themselves as like Americans (and unlike Africans), neither adequately predict the population affected by AIDS nor indicate appropriate strategies for education and treatment. What Daniel terms "chic" models serve to silence local interpretations and strategies.

Shortly after discovering that he had AIDS, Daniel helped found a political group of seropositive people called Pela Vidda ("For Life"), begun in Rio last May and now forming in other major cities. Pela Vidda combines cultural activism with political action to challenge meanings assigned to AIDS and those people it affects. In a country with little democratic tradition, Daniel speaks out for "citizenship," a rallying call uniting other disenfranchised groups fighting for their civil rights.

Pela Vidda produces printed materials for seropositive people and PWAs, and protests stigmatization and discrimination against those affected by the pandemic. The group's first street demonstration caused VARIG, the national airline, to halt its mandatory HIV testing for all job applicants. Above all, the group demands the creation of a national program for the prevention and treatment of AIDS.

In his latest book, Life Before Death *(Rio: Jaboti, 1989), Daniel writes that merely to affirm he is alive is a political act. Fighting back against the premature death that government policy and the media assign to HIV-positive people and PWAs, Daniel is an eloquent advocate for those who have chosen to live life positively. The courage to affirm life against all obstacles is a challenge faced by people with AIDS across the world.*

The rapid spread of the AIDS pandemic has demonstrated a collapsing of distance. Daniel argues that this phenomenon has created a space and an urgency for international solidarity to end AIDS.

I interviewed Daniel in August 1989 while in Brazil.

(Herbert Daniel died on March 29, 1992.)

JARED BRAITERMAN: *What can account for the speed with which the group Pela Vidda has grown so quickly?*

HERBERT DANIEL: This group, which means "For the Valorization, Integration and Dignity of Those with AIDS" [the acronym means "For Life"], has grown in such a surprising way because it corresponded to a pressing social need. Our idea from the beginning was to create a group that fights for citizenship and against prejudice and discrimination, a group that would produce specific materials directed at the population most directly affected by the virus. Our group is one of political pressure that will fight for the revindication of the rights of these people. We must demand that the government take measures to assist them. For this, we have marched in the street, and the group has lost the sense of shame characteristic of those who are going to die, in order to take on the boldness of those who are totally convinced that they are going to live, and live fully.

Our motto is "Viva a Vida" ("Long Live Life"), and when we shout "Viva a Vida" we are also transmitting an energy for a country that is confronting a grave situation of economic, social, political, and ethical crisis. Our group is within that crisis, it is the result of that crisis, and at the same time, it also express a global interest, in that AIDS is a world problem. The Brazilian crisis forms part of a much larger crisis, which is the crisis of contemporary civilization. We have a political consciousness that leads us to search for solutions not only for people with AIDS and for Brazil, but for a solution for humanity at the end of the second millennium.

It's impressive that your group has so quickly launched public demonstrations in a society where having AIDS and even being gay are usually hidden.

We are managing to come out from this clandestineness. Demonstrations are a surer way to respond to prejudice. We managed to bring to the first public demonstration we organized around 40 people who are HIV-positive and/or with AIDS, people who usually remain hidden. We believe that it is very important to fight against this clandestineness. This is not merely a Brazilian phenomenon. Everywhere in the world it is difficult to live as a homosexual.

Here there are no homosexual demonstrations. Only a few have revealed themselves publicly to defend their rights. This is an extremely serious problem, which makes AIDS even graver than in other parts of the world. The struggle against machismo and a retrograde society—one which stimulates the whole hypocrisy of living homosexuality clandestinely—has been a very important political necessity in Brazil. The best way to wage this battle is to break all the veils of hypocrisy and to show oneself. We must illuminate the person with AIDS who appears speaking on television [in government AIDS prevention campaigns] with his face darkened in shadows, as if this was being without a name or a history. The objective of Pela Vidda is to say, "We have names and these are our stories."

In your most recent book you warn against the seductiveness of foreign AIDS models imported to Brazil. What is the AIDS situation in Brazil, and how does it differ from other countries?

When I say that AIDS reflects the culture in which it is inscribed, I mean to say that it participates in interpersonal relations that are defining of a culture. Evidently, in accordance with the culture where it arises, [AIDS] will follow a path consonant with the material and symbolic resources with which people will react in relation to [it]. A society like the American, for example, which has a determinate relation to medicine—more privatist and efficient—will react in a different way than a culture like the French, where there is a social health system that is far more advanced.

From how the epidemic develops to the responses that are given to the epidemic, each culture defines AIDS, which is not only the epidemic of the virus, but also the epidemic of the ideological virus, the "Third Epidemic" [of panic and prejudice], as the WHO has called it.

In Brazil there are several distinguishing characteristics, like the matter of blood. This issue has a greater weight here than in other parts of the world, due to the immoral commerce of blood, which has produced a genocide against hemophiliacs and people in general who have received blood transfusions. [Blood products and transfusion are responsible for over half the AIDS cases in Rio de Janeiro, where the government has yet to safeguard the blood supply.]

From the point of view of the Brazilian sexual culture, its very diversity makes the issue of relations between men far more complex. The epidemic has reached many men who are not part of the homosexual group, which leads to transmission through sexual contacts to many women.

What does it mean to be homosexual in Brazil?

Every time people ask me if I am homosexual, I say "yes," but with a series of doubts because I believe that the word "homosexual," in the way it is used, seems like a clinical diagnosis. In Brazil there are many words that refer to behaviors and relations between men, many loaded with prejudice and discrimination. There is no word that has the value of "gay" in Brazil—that is a word produced by a political movement which took consciousness of its own needs.

In Brazil there is an intense need to struggle for citizenship, for the recognition of the right to difference. Our society is extremely antidemocratic and authoritarian in its workings and does not allow the exercise of difference. Violence explodes with great ease, many homosexuals are victims of violence—a permanent situation in Brazil, which is regarded almost with pleasure by the police—almost with delight by the most reactionary sectors of society.

The great difficulty in Brazil of living a masculine desire for another man is the fact that it is not recognized as a right by Brazilian citizens. There is a very easy relationship between men sexually, as long as one of them is sexually active and the other sexually passive. This is a relationship perfectly incorporated in our daily lives, but it is a relationship of oppression. And this active-passive dualism is what constitutes the source of all oppression with respect to sexuality in Brazil. Consequently, any movement for sexual freedom that arises in Brazil must address the question of women, that is, recognize that there exists neither active nor passive in a relationship, to break these labels. In this way we can end [sexual] oppression, including that against homosexuals.

Your life has always been very public and political. In the late 1960s and 1970s, you took up arms against the military dictatorship and faced many years in exile. In the 1980s, you became a well-known author on sexuality and now you struggle as an AIDS activist. How do you relate your class and sexual struggles?

I have always been a political militant focused on the struggle for democracy and freedom. Today I am a pacifist. At that time [of insurrection] I set out on the armed struggle because of a lack of political maturity and because of the historical situation of the time, which was different. In the 1970s I began to participate politically in the struggle for homosexual rights, because when I fought as a guerrilla I realized that the prejudice of the Left was as strong as that of the Right in relation to homosexuality. From there I began to see I had been fighting for political freedom forgetting that freedom is not divisible. Either you struggle for freedom as a whole —and sexual freedom is included within that freedom—or you are not struggling for freedom at all.

I thought it was very important to begin to discuss politically what the struggle for sexuality means and to put an end to the idea that politics is only based on certain predetermined structures, like vanguards, parties, and institutions. Politics must be made in our daily lives; and there is an extremely strong cultural component in all political action which has to be valorized.

When AIDS emerged, it turned into a great vehicle to expose the conflicts of society. I believe that to preserve oneself against AIDS, to carry out prevention campaigns, signifies a political activity that leads to a recognition of these fractures. Today there exists a political dimension to the fight against AIDS, which is precisely the reconstruction of a series of schemes of our Western society.

As an example I can cite our relation as white and Western men to the culture of the Indians. The Indians' relationship with the jungle and the forest is done with intense wisdom. Our attitude toward the jungle is one of ignorance or depredation, a posture we also adopt when we face death. With death, we behave as we would with the tree, which is life itself. This demonstrates our ignorance in our ecological relationships with the planet.

When I discovered that I had the HIV virus, the strongest thing that happened to me was the feeling that I had established a relationship of wisdom with my death. I felt like an Indian facing a tree. Upon establishing this wise relationship with death, I observed that this wisdom had transferred into my relationship with life. From then on, I began to appreciate much more my life and I began to insist on saying only one thing: "I am alive and I have AIDS." This paradox means that I guarantee life above all the threats that could be placed upon it. My sign of existence is to shout "Viva a Vida," and that is my Indian relationship with death or the jungle, which is to say, a relationship of wisdom that Western society must recover.

As a guerrilla you strongly condemned the United States for contributing to dictatorship in Brazil. How do you now view the United States?

I have believed in solidarity, even when I fought against the American government. The struggle was never against the American people. It was not the masses of the American people who supported the Brazilian dictatorship, but rather a large part of them guarantee a system of oppression and domination which makes the United States an unfortunate example of global degradation. I do not believe that only the United States represents this unfortunate example. The USSR can also be included in this picture.

Today when I see solidarity, I feel that many of my brothers and sisters are in the United States dying of this epidemic, and I feel absolutely like a brother to them. I am certain that all of us together can confront the sordid economic interests that still exist on earth, interests which suddenly make the [pharmaceutical] laboratories not want to cure the disease, but only invent medications, which is very different.

These interests establish extremely deteriorated North-South relations, something that the American movement that fights against AIDS should perceive. Many times, the fact that the epidemic started in the United States and from there spread to the rest of the world has created elements of dependency in other countries with respect to the United States. We depend, in order to treat our ill, on all the technology produced in the United States, which should be democratized in a more humane form, not to produce more profits for the United States, but to produce solutions for the health problems of the whole planet.

Perhaps AIDS is contributing to this more humane vision, because by appearing in such a developed country, one which thought that viruses were a thing of the Third World, [AIDS] has shown how a developed country like the United States can be vulnerable to the ecological disequilibriums of the whole world. And if AIDS is a huge problem in the United States, imagine the Chagas' disease, tuberculosis, leishmaniasis, and other plagues that devastate the Third World. Like the appeal for solidarity in relation to AIDS, it would be possible to appeal for solidarity in terms of understanding for all human beings and their right to life. This is a fact that should lead Americans to reflect a great deal because right now they are confronting a problem that millions of people around the world permanently confront. The question of solidarity should be much more complex, evaluated, in order to prevent newly discovered technologies from being yet another cause for domination, driving the poorest countries to an ever more wretched position.

What impact has AIDS had on the lives of Brazilian homosexuals?

The numbers we have with respect to the illness among Brazilian homosexuals are truly frightening. Recently I saw a study of São Paulo that estimates that roughly 300,000 homosexuals are already contaminated by the HIV virus. I do not think that the consciousness corresponds to the gravity of the problem. I think there exists the beginning of a consciousness and a certain panic, which does not translate into concrete actions for prevention. This worries me because panic confuses a great deal, but it never helps. People are not totally conscious, they are fearful, [a reaction] that does not solve anything because AIDS is only defeated when we do not fear it.

For the homosexuals of Brazil, it is important to get along with prevention, with the understanding of what AIDS is, with a great deal of clarity.

Do you see changes in behavior because of AIDS?

Some changes have occurred, people are using condoms, [engaging in] fewer risky sexual practices, but behavior has not changed so much. With AIDS it is not possible to employ such a mathematical reasoning. You do not prevent [AIDS] 50 percent by using condoms in 50 percent of [sexual] relations.

Changes have been more profound in the sense of incorporating AIDS as one more great problem in the difficulty of existing as homosexuals. It is already very difficult [for us] to live with family, with coworkers, with other homosexual people. The homosexual group does not have a very strong sense of solidarity; sex and class differences are significant in the homosexual milieu. This does not only occur between Brazilian homosexuals. Others, in various parts of the world—particularly older homosexuals—suffer very much from solitude and oppressions. Together with old age, you add the fact of physical deterioration which is AIDS. This has become one more element that compounds the existential difficulty of homosexuals.

What is important, and which has an element to be fought, is called "clandestineness" and, on the other hand—an element that needs to be stimulated—which is called "solidarity," which must operate in the homosexual world in order for us to be able to defeat AIDS.

With the defeat of AIDS, existence will be easier for homosexuals, who should understand that it is not enough to have sexual relationships with one another, but to have more profound relations, not only of love or sex, but relationships of work, friendship, care, and close companionship.

Brazil projects an image abroad as a place of tremendous sexual freedom, particularly through images of Carnival, transvestites, and the "Mulatto Woman." And yet the AIDS crisis has revealed the great silence and censure surrounding homosexuality in Brazil. Could you comment on this apparent contradiction?

There is not so much a contradiction. Carnival is a moment of exhibition, of freeing that which is most prohibited. People during Carnival do not exactly engage in sex, but rather engage in some activities which are most repressed during the rest of the year. The Brazilian man often dresses up [during Carnival] like a woman in order to scandalize that which he most criticizes and detests in women, which is the "scandalous, weak" side of women. Generally, it is the most machistic, arrogant, and authoritarian men who go dress up as women, with makeup and dresses from their wives and daughters. That act of masquerading [as women] does not represent an acceptance of women or homosexuals, but rather a refusal, an insult to those groups.

There is no greater freedom—what happens is that in the large Brazilian cities, principally Rio, which is a very sensual city, there is an easiness for the foreigner to enter the circuit of sexual commerce. That image of Brazil as ingenuous, sensual, and sexual is an image created to sell to the foreign tourist and not what operates in our daily lives. That side of sexual freedom does not exist, it is only an exterior side, of show, and in this side is also inscribed repression. There is no paradox in that; the fact is that there is a violent pressure and a reaction, a different image than what really exists.

You received [last summer] a letter from Dr. Jonathan Mann, director of World Health Organization's Global Program on AIDS, praising your work and extolling the importance of a global network of nongovernmental organizations, especially those composed of seropositive people and people with AIDS. Could you expand on this?

We have had contact with international groups, and it is important that they write to us so we can work together. Dr. Mann opened up the way for me to participate in the global AIDS program in Geneva. He spoke with me a great deal about the necessity of grass-roots groups working with AIDS to be not only *for* people with AIDS, but *by* people with AIDS. He sees people with AIDS not only as part of the problem, but a part of the solution to the problem, a politic which is fundamental. We also committed to elaborate here in Brazil the new logo for the global AIDS program, which will be based on our principle "Viva a Vida," [and] which will be translated into all languages, becoming a type of invitation for people to reflect on AIDS across the world.

Have you borrowed tactics from AIDS groups in other countries?

Different cultures produce very different political activities. At times it is very dangerous to have models. AIDS activism in the United States has a capacity for mobilization and a type of activity that does not always fit our country. U.S. activism focuses on certain revindications that are distant from ours—we have more things to demand than they. I do not believe that there exist models of group formation nor of activities. I believe that we can learn from experiences and understand differences.

There are very fine examples of heroism and human grandeur provided by nongovernmental [AIDS] organizations in the entire world. All those organizations are moving, in the sense that they possess a new understanding in the relation [of humanity] with epidemics, which is a permanent world risk. It looks like in the end of the 1980s we are changing toward a situation in which we are no longer dividing the world between sick and healthy people, between risk groups and nonrisk groups, and between those who inform and those who receive information. We are uniting, giving one another help. We are discovering the meaning of something fundamental, which is solidarity.

What experiences of yours could people in the United States learn from?

I do not believe that we have things to teach but rather [things] to participate [in] together, experiences to share. There ought to be politicization of the AIDS perspective in the United States, breaking with the idea that AIDS is an American problem. Americans seem to be very preoccupied with the questions of AIDS in the United

States. It is important that they become concerned about the questions of AIDS globally.

You were named the presidential candidate by the Green Party. [Daniel's resignation was accepted one month later.] You are also the first HIV-positive presidential candidate in the world. What are your plans for this campaign?

The campaign has a strongly symbolic character, which seeks to express that life is that which we construct, that it is possible to live in spite of all the contradictions and circumstances. We aim to give a great blow in the stomach of prejudice and discrimination, saying that it is possible that a homosexual be a candidate for the presidency of the republic, that a person with a publicly revealed and recognized illness can be a candidate for public office. We must construct a presidency in this country (after decades of military rule and authoritarianism), and we believe that we can only construct it based on certain elements of utopia, which has been discredited.

You are a person who radiates passion and hope. What is your vision of the future?

I have a great faith in the future because I believe it is now. Those who believe so much in the future and wait for it do not obtain anything. I am impassioned for the present, not for something that will happen. That is utopia—utopia is not something you realize in the future. You realize utopia now, here, in the immediate relations you have with people, in the smiles you give, in the hugs you make. To hug someone is to hug life. You must hug and grab the present, because there is no alternative, no other form.

I have many hopes, but it is not an expectation of what will come or what will occur. It is the possibility that I have now to construct what is already occurring. I project my utopia in my time, in my present, in my now. For this reason I am very impassioned.

Claudia and Marcelo Secron Bessa provided assistance in transcribing the interview. Karin Van Den Dool kindly offered improvements to the translation. Note: Daniel recently joined the global boycott of the Sixth International

AIDS Conference in San Francisco this June. Daniel decided not to come because the U.S. Immigration and Naturalization Service restricts the travel of HIV-positive people and denies them confidentiality. By holding this conference and scheduling the next three in countries with restrictive travel policies, the conference organizations and the World Health Organization have made a grave error; like the U.S. government, they fail to recognize PWAs as crucial members of the struggle against AIDS. Daniel's absence will be our loss. (Additionally, the INS has conducted the largest mandatory testing program in the world. Over four million people have been tested, and the United States deports even those infected here who have lived, worked, and paid taxes for more than eight years, immigrants who would otherwise qualify for citizenship under the amnesty program.)

QUEBEC

Reminiscent of Walt Whitman and his celebration of self as starting point in *Leaves of Grass,* Nicole Brossard, in her essay "Turning Platform," takes us also on a journey beginning with self. Hers, like Whitman's, is an exploration at once philosophical in its scope and sensuous in its style and imagery. Brossard, a leading writer and thinker in her native Quebec, shares with us her evolving awareness of being a woman raised in a patriarchal culture and inculcated with definitions of womanhood and concepts about her very body that are now foreign to her. It is only by critically exploring her own self, beginning with her body, her senses, that she can hope to reclaim what is rightfully hers. She writes primarily for herself—as a necessity for survival; yet she is aware of the important link to other women her use of words can have. The reader is enticed by the author's exquisite prose style, yet is left with no doubt as to the enormous power and originality of her thinking. It is no less than that of a woman colonized by accident of birth in a heterosexist and patriarchal culture, now in the act of self-redefinition, which is rebellion.

"Turning Platform" by Nicole Brossard, translated by Marlene Wildeman, from *The Aerial Letter* (1988).

For once I want to speak neither of nor for other people. I want to take a tour of myself on the turning platform. Mine: visceral, cerebral, chemical. Forgetting nothing of a history that is beginning to teeter in the postsurvival era, that is, outside its own reach.

For the rest of my days I'll be a spinning top, a relentless spiral, stuck fast in the spew of those last words the phallocracy will address to the new values settling in. I am thus in history until the end of my days; and whatever the unformulated certitudes or affirmed theoretics I manage to maintain about the procedures for transformation and mutation of the species, I'll have to be in the fray. Rudely accosted, I must protest. I cry out, I dream, I want things to change. I write, therefore. I know the content of the text I will write to the very end of my days: the quest of my orgasmic body, the knowledge of my body's ecstasy. This body—covered by laws, interdictions, words—wants to speak (to condemn the law that enforces its repression . . . what is obstructed here is desiring, and desire writes, empowered by the very law it transgresses); it wants to know the ecstasy of its own energy.

My woman's being uses men's knowledge to better resist and annihilate the violence and oppression on which this knowledge of men (of humanity) is built. All bodies know their fragility before the beast. The beast is in power. I write so that I won't be his dozing beast of burden. On these last days of my internment, the beast consumes itself.

In the days when I thought like a man, I had simple ideas. Now I have two sets. My form is encumbered by the I/me who didn't gaze upon my navel enough before it disappeared completely in the ninth month of the birth of the other girl, her's an obvious umbilicus, like a wound.

My form is encumbered by the refound feminine. I am pregnant with a form I'm not able to make my own and that marks me in my difference and in my other subject. I am made of man's knowledge and of a feminine condition: a hybrid. Patient, due to the luxury of a strength acquired with the help of *ideology's* institutions, not to mention of groups for *ideological struggle* (the circle quickly closed on the little academic who contested for her brothers an inheritance to which she herself would never be entitled); aggravated, for if I long pretended not to remember the little girl, the adolescent, the young bride, today it is I who crop up face to face with an opaque image, I who still do not acquiesce totally to the intimate memory of empty Sundays in white; and if I crop up at all it is by virtue of my alliance with other women, all in the same troubled waters, stretching out our fingers on the turning platform, history's island, on whose shores from now on we have taken hold. History picks up speed around an empty center—a white center— before plunging into its destructive depths. I am part of what accelerates, what points to the last bridges between a reproductive sexuality (our mythic or idealistic modalities are there only as de- layed self-realizations, programmed to retard us in long-term sado- masochism) and a bisexuality of a new order of consumption.

Difficult to clearly express reason and knowledge in a language for which the *raison d'être* is to be maternal. Who serves me when I dine, who pulls the covers up over my fantasy during the night, who is there for me when I cry or rage against powerlessness? Dad, Mom, you haunt me **like two strangers.**[1] As I eat up my living; as I earn my living. *I sit to the table. My mother is sweet and understands me. One aunt (there's always one in the family who knows absolutely every- thing) says things I don't understand yet. My father has nothing to say. Other men speak in his place.* Here the fathers keep quiet and the mothers whisper. You have to make an effort to hear what it's all about. Make an effort in order to live and speak normally. Making an effort to be normal, that's what it is to be colonized.

I exert myself elsewhere, of course, to write. To help the body get by. To cut a path through the trickery, the obvious, the effects of conditioning. To know the explorian female body, so knowledge- able from myriad cells, memory, and fiction in the cortex.

I'm tired of having a body of compartmentalized parts, a "corps- capital," a body whose stories are told by intermediaries. The trou- bling text is no doubt composed of the history of this fatigue, spread out live in the ghetto of the arts, where the powers that be— lacking imagination—go looking to scare something up (as they would in a brothel, a harem, a "hole"), something with which to revive their potency.

I have a score to settle with Knowledge* because it terrorizes
me from the moment it forces me to school, that is, forces me to
learn more about the master's fantasies than about knowledge itself.
And all this takes a very long time to sort out. Now I select within
knowledge, as though I were in a supermarket. I know the things I
want. Unconsciously, and for all time, the knowing body opposes
itself to the learned letter. But, everybody knows, what counts is
the letter. I write in self-defense. If I can find the lost stream,
writing interests me. And, of course, it will appear to me like
something no one's ever seen before, though it will simply be the
continuation of one and the same process: surviving, in spite of my
sex, my species, with my reptilian brain, my "thinking cap," and
my new cortex.

Typical or different, it amounts to the same thing because, in the
end, difference distinguishes between a power and a nonpower.
Power of words, political power. Power which encompasses differences, appropriates them like an organism which transforms the
dimensions of its stomach according to its appetite. The mouth
keeping always the same opening.

My own body is my difference and my sole standard for measur-
ing pleasure and pain. I cannot speak us without first knowing how
to reply in I. "If I know ecstasy," I am transposed. I have at my
disposal a domain of writing, and this domain can summon together
the us of the *retort* each one of us is; we all have the build for it. It
sows doubt. It breaks away, and brings up the question of liberation.
It makes imperative a time of historic solidarity. Resolute, ecstatic
women.

I me it: I can't deprive myself of it. The equilibrium needed in
order to survive this nonrenunciation is found in the solitary inti-

---

* As a woman and a Québecoise. I have a score to settle also with what's easy (with what would be
typical). And I refuse to be typical (symbolic or exemplary) in a scene of alienation under the eye of
the master (he alone defines what is typical and what is not), amused by folklore and vitality, fascinated
by the gaze he fixes on such beautiful beasts and more beautiful still because so passionate, disheveled,
or arrogant, but most certainly resplendent with interesting symptoms. *(Author's note in original French
edition.)*

mate act of writing—the personal of our political ("social" would be too nice) condition—an endless wanting to understand, which spreads out, seeking for itself, for its reading vision, the voluptuous practice of seeing further and further away forever.

(crossing the field of sirens, would this involve pleading or conventional entreaty? But how from writing would she make of herself this verdant within, flowing with foreknowledge, its images immolated one by one on the page?

you infringe upon me in my skin. I must speak then, squeezed like an enigmatic orange. Queerly dressed in my interests, I watch over them with a carnal and historic necessity. I've had it up to here. The humidity. History beseeches us. For the final heartbreak. The final assault.

the erasure inscribed on my eyeball. Ready to leap. No fixed address, undomesticated. What's your name? Nicole Brossard. What does your father do? He's an accountant. Surname, first name, profession. Brossard, Nicole, writer. How's your mother?)

I write fragment because passing or instantaneous in the continuum.

We women have been made to reproduce (and been had) more than loved whereas we have loved unconditionally and that makes for us a pretty condition indeed. Fine kettle: unspeakable, this circuit, where it is frustrated and exiled from within, where in pure waste of energy it turns in circles; and languishes in madness, disgust, death, which serve the handsome writer to compose, outlawed, his masterpiece and his major works. I do not accept that there are losers and yet, to sense the other or oneself almost fail, that's where the pleasure lies, in the falling away, in the cultural undoing or slip. "If I know ecstasy," there is a sexual loss, an area of abolished reproduction that certainly leaves no trace, nothing, no writing. "If I know ecstasy," this is the fragment, writing the conditional have, inscribing greed, the me who searches in the pantry (not the medicine cabinet) for the ecstatic totality of all these desiring fragments. Euphoriture.

I want us in a single movement that would be this or of the instant, all at once. Am I in the process of writing to the loving one or of signing myself with a force that extends me further and gets lost in words?

My relationship to writing is of the same order as I want you and keep the distance for me between what languishes on our skin, pearls in sweat, and what gets lost elsewhere when later I rise. Gravitate.

I wrote in a common-law relationship with and while men were reading me. But, deep down, I write only under a woman's gaze, feverishly received. Between us, the descent. Restless before the void, which is full to the bottom with sonorous, rhythmic breathing. It instructs me, replenishes me, gives me order, and undoes me. This is my most plausible continuity, demanding and ecstatic, my time full when it jumbles the cultural tracks for me, writing to survive someone else's madness, the same and other place of that which is not text but its surface. The ice slide. Snow and scarf and she who hangs onto my neck, who warms me. The blue mist of courtly winter and inside, silk, endlessly surprised. On this occasion, branching out like a translator's version, her slant justifiably oblique.

I see that when I write, I do it in struggle and for my survival. See very well what in my gaze sends me alarmed toward other women and solidarity. No hidden reef: I don't want to have to possess anything or anyone, text or persons, unless it's by mutual pleasure. This is the deduction one makes, and it goes all the way back to that first number in which he decided to inscribe his cash memory. Money ringing in. Grandfather clock, he calculates the hours and imposes his time and his times on me. He grazes on my new shoots. He shuts up: It doesn't blossom: I write. And choose the direction of my gaze when we read together.

How do I write? with a woman's gaze resting on me. Or with the body inclined toward her. Does this mean that I learn from my fatigue? From my exhaustion with another woman? I am not untouched by these feminine spheres where it trembles everywhere, the guts tremble, and the teeth, muscles swell, and the lips, anger, the unutterable. Expelling from oneself all superficiality, where it is required to smile, be nice, to soothe, keep the other warm for the sake of nothing but the other, the other's pleasure and pain. A woman's gaze, which is to say: she who knows how to read. Illiterates of desire that we are, when women know how to read on the body of the other who is similar, it means they know the rigors, the jarrings, the hysterical border inside which works them over for want of an exit. This spurs me on. If I desire a woman, if a woman desires me, then there is the beginning of writing. The word sets about to well up, to gush forth; it breaks us out of our isolation. We do more than keep each other company. We direct our common project. We exist in another difference, but without the foreignness, without the morbid fascination, in a sort of questioning which would go back over the course of exhaustion resistance has made us familiar with, in order not to give in to the existing order. Faced with a slap, a fondling, or a fuck. I do not submit to a woman's gaze, I reroute it to where it must go in, where it makes me cover all distances, reread at breakneck speed all the fragments of me silenced, pieced together or torn apart. Buried. To bury oneself in someone's skirt is the metaphor for understanding that is with clitoral ecstasy we touch, a capsizing of the species' historical body. "If I know ecstasy," it's because something in my equilibrium is shaken, something of the role that enrolls me. I invert word order. I pass Adam on his left. I split in two with my smooth navel. And there is my certain page.

"If I" allows for all ramification. For remembering forward into the open and for sequencing. It reminds us that everything is possible in the ardent vagueness. But, at the same time, always intercepted. It is lost and connects up with no reality (I know the depths when it is a question of inscribing on paper a discourse that reads by itself). "If I" is fictive, because I know that to tell of myself such as I am in a given environment, this is fragment: dry ink, wet ink, glistening with expanded meaning. Real I would be the other, the draining out, where I would make myself dizzy in the telling, where there would be no end of saying—I am a woman—I confuse foreignness with difference—I have a scar that cuts my belly in two. Noon, when it wearies of being vertical and the sun turns the eye's pupil clear.

I write because I cannot put aside the urgency of myself being mine known by me and interviewing in that which hurts me day after day. So that I won't succumb to madness or delirium. Silenced words/absent words. I write; I weigh my words. I figure into the balance. I sink deep into myself in order to understand. In order to exact the "certain body,"[2] to exact autonomy, the chemical or electric voyage. For this body is cornered in its *fin de siècle* and finished future. Forced into invention for each of its words, its embracing, its desires. To speed up all its processes of mastery and ecstasy. Fantasy.

My relationship to desire is undoubtedly less great since the child who has split all landscapes in two and has me take them with condensation on the lens; the eye myopic. And so my gaze is less inclined to take possession of itself than to restore continuity to color and form in space and from this, my fiction. From one detail seeing the whole and in the whole catching sight of myself, rather than rushing *straight on* to detail and taking it over for myself: taking it.

Around and with women, words, discourse, take form differently. Because we have nothing to prove to ourselves. Our life belt is that we first understand the energy within, then the power relationship. It follows from what's called taking pleasure in knowledge, when we have to trace words for and before ourselves to clear the stage of all its characters before eventually disappearing in turn as spectator. No more heroes, no more victims to immolate, no more plot. An immense calm. Meanwhile, inside, it is initiated to what was earlier given up.

And out of this my fiction. My connection. I venture to know better (other than in opposition; in process, rather) the different layers in me. I make discoveries through language. Through language I open myself unprotected. A space for breathing, the other for looking. And it crosses over, converges; makes itself fully sufficient for the exploration.

I commit myself to this which is my ruin and which transfers me from horizon to uterus. No pretense of the complex. I content myself with me the stranger who is consequential and not other. I step out of line with a carnal consequence only. According to fear in my belly: It's time now. What's the weather like? How old is your child?

I cannot write if in each of my internal networks and circulating blood there is not this surface on which we swim in the hope of waking to the simultaneous silence of self and tumult. I go all the way to the end of me. To be here and now a conscious woman and without solidarity, that makes no sense. What then is this space that is at once struggle, quest, and work which would be a revelation? Which forces me to grind along in the personal, the disarray and compassion when she opens her mouth and screams—without a nerve in her body—the inadmissible.

Her relationship to writing draws breath in blood rising to the brain (if this sex had not served so much to reproduce in the pink and the sweat, this sex, this serf): This sex surpasses its competence —it is ecstatic. And by this fact, contradicts history at the same moment it takes its place within it. For me, this is the risk taken in writing. Signature and initials on history's turning platform. We burn in vain around its belt, taking risks like circus bets; while it wears holes in itself, or endures, a live white center, the woman question around which I write myself. Obstructed question, we relieve it of debris left there by other interpretations.

My relationship to writing and to knowledge, which is also its support, seems to be cauterized. Burned as they are, the few (famil-ial and revolutionary) cells inside me are reproduced through a tradition, and by a bourgeoisie, that, although in Europe might have

produced new values for its own use, here has been content with
dumping, without batting an eye (and will never keep an eye open),
for it's the multinationals already here, and that puts the question
of bourgeois values and, correspondingly, of the revolutionary struggle, differently. Form serf to consumer. From the revenge of the
cradle to feminism. From marriage to homosexuality. It strikes one
that somewhere must be written the fantasy that flitted between
the sea and fresh water. The break, or what brought it about:
science and fiction of intervention.

Now, this has nothing to do with sex but with the condition $\boxed{f}$
or $\boxed{m}$. When we no longer make babies together, the future will be
the human condition. I take my fulcrum from that point. I'm in no
hurry for them to find themselves in me, to take up residence here.
Look elsewhere, within yourselves, in your own chest. And I'll look
in mine. The only exile I've known came from my condition and
not my body. That's the difference.

What is it with the persistent use of I in this text? How does it
differ from the *I* used in the diary, the intimate journal? *I* censors
itself as soon as it writes itself. *I* has meaning only in reality, that is,
in the written work. On this side, and beyond, *I* dissolves; it decomposes in an anarchy of forms. Me, that's an/other thing entirely. It
already brings me closer to myself than what I am. But it's an
esoteric approach I am afraid to use, the *I* cannot use because then
I would be extreme and vulnerable. "Myself" then is used in fiction
in a place that works away at reality, that leads reality to its downfall
and explodes all the inexpressible fragments. It is at work here, too,
but it opens on the inside of elsewhere.

I cannot be sorry for myself alone in this reality. I cannot write
entirely alone, but in this reality me in solidarity as in a single body
open yes.

In order to rise up. To end this, my scattered-woman cycle, and
to take up again at its source what left itself there at the very first
spray of white.[3]

But no lost origin. Repressed. Swallowed and defecated. Originally, it multiplies itself in the course of things. Conditions itself.

What was lost before I wrote; what is lost when I write? What it reproduces, what I infer from me or my condition?

I speak, by way of the written, to another subject. What is obvious is repressed from speech. To write, that will never be clear for me. I am overwhelmed, fraught with upheaval. Woman's speech/woman's writing, this is another set of links altogether. The likelihood of which worries me.

Writing it wipes out everything that opposes ecstasy and personal harmony. It wipes out someone, something, somewhere. White writing (?). Another writing, red, damned, condemns forever the part of self burning with rage, the part of the other that burns us slowly, little by little. I pledge myself to going against the grain. I wonder this over and understand its violence. To rise up.

Further exists when I say I want to go further. But I want to stay me because I prefer to learn from myself rather than at others' expense or against myself. Further exists when I write because through it I accomplish desire that is never quite fulfilled; I appropriate myself more by extension than by intention. Shifted forward or back by each fragment written. Up ahead of me. Set back from the essential that wordlessly explores itself, all of a body, all of an all.

Taking risks within, a finger down the throat to make the sleeping muse vomit. To see everything rise up all at the same time; myths burgeon forth, fauna oscillates in the hollows of the chest. She digs. She opens and restores to the glistening walls forgotten images; others are being engraved. The belly is heavy. The waters have begun to spread. Buried even deeper, an elated mother suddenly coincides and begins to get worked up about something. Echo. The crossing over.

"What is learned at the expense of one's body is never forgotten." By the orifices and the surface. By the root. By what circulates in the blood and is later transformed into words. Symbols clinging to the self. A rite of passage toward the exterior where *I* proves itself, submits to the test. And takes up the struggle in order to survive. Bewildered before the mirror, sees condense in its gaze the brimming drop that makes the self run over. Imprints itself on the page. Traces of what loves, gazes, touches.

The approach of text like a scenario of perfect consequences leading to what in itself exceeds. The approach of text, age-old attempt to undo the power that is organized around me, that clasps me firmly in a rape, holds on morbidly until the *o* in open disappears and until its city is built with so much quick-change artistry that you don't know whether it is looking for a woman or seeking in itself its woman, the malady that has hold of it, and decomposes it. Me, the tender one. Him, obsolete. I don't measure up. I'm too big. I can only exert this power if I shrink, and too much, from fear.

Sketched out in her fantasy, woman does not draw sustenance from herself except in parallel; when she writes, she discovers that one half cannot possibly satisfy her and she looks for a way to pass from the shadow into the clear light of morning—it would be so good for me to rest, me, too, after so many nights of bad dreams—it would feel good to stretch myself out on the double bed where I would be sponge and sea without being aware of it, swallowing my words in fantasies where no man, no woman, would come to decree that it's time for me to go to work.

Fury in my eye. I shift. I am displaced by several lines, and this recomposes all around me the episode thus begun, thus begun, lets loose, spreads out, enlarging my field of vision, my orbits. What do I risk of exile, if by an ardent breakthrough I make the axon circulate? An excitement. An accomplishment where you, my hysterical one, are surprised to find yourself mobile, traversing the Milky Way, intense, arched by a thousand liaisons, the only woman, page by page, to turn in your cycle. I spend from my gender, from a subject that seeks all subjects, so that a sentence happens, clings onto the hem of a dress, onto the verge of tears. Hangs in the balance.

It may consist of simply filling in all the white squares that made the chess and the check possible. Of crossing spaces no one's crossed before. Abolish conquest. But to write it: play black on white. Cards on the table: I and the ultimate personal of my condition. I within the ice, to make it melt. To feel the leaves starting up. Arouse oneself. Take one's time.

It always brings to light the question of within. Outside, what is obvious is. Within, so that it can speak itself in the fullness of day, become intoxicated with light, the white sun. By day, women chat, by night, they circulate in all the hollow parts of the body, their own, and those that snuggle up against them in sleep. One day, during the day, some women write and at night they sleep so profoundly that they know then how to go deeper without danger. In the morning, they surface and make text of their voyage.

An/other woman alone. The difference with her and me is that we know the way upstream, from object to subject. Resemblance, which makes us come together over touch and the idea of us we conceive for ourselves. Us as a function of: formal operation on which we concentrate our energy. Us as a function of, women, can this make sense; can it at least engender movement. Transfixed alive as though we had slipped into the breach we ourselves have created. Immobilized and ardent, at one and the same time. This book, will it be the end product of a fever or is it a major exercise of survival? A pelvic thrust and I am quit of the void. Hands red with ink scratching at the soil above me where patri-girls circulate on dry ground, stretch and put on their face, the one that will match the man's smooth cheek freshly shaved in the clear morning. Maternal clowns, the king's madwomen. Obliging. I see only their ankles, chained.

The difference is that I cannot live deferred. A stay of transformation, the synthesis of a same singular woman. And it's this same difference I ask of your body, the difference of other woman with my regard. Identical to yours. The same like a differential equation. Derived from our functions. Point-blank in the luminous spectrum. Projected against one another like a polysomic dream.

L'Amèr ou Le Chapitre effrité

NOTES

1. The phrase "like two strangers" appears in English in the original. English words in the source text appear in boldface print in translation.

2. Cf. Roland Barthes, *The Pleasure of the Text,* trans. Richard Miller (New York: Hill and Wang, 1975), pp. 29, 30.

3. Cf. Sartre's *écriture blanche* and Barthe's degree zero, or colorless, writing, means writing that is free of any obligation to a preordained state of language.

CHAPTER FOUR

ISSUES

Since Stonewall in 1969, there have been a large number of issues with which lesbians and gay men have been involved. Such concerns include, but are not limited to, the following:

- Lesbian separatism

- Gay parenting

- The "sexual minorities" or proclivities (sadomasochism, transvestism, transsexualism, man-boy love, male prostitution)

- Age of consent

- Rights of gay adolescents

- AIDS

- Pornography

- Changing discriminatory laws against gays

- Challenging the medical/psychiatric establishment's view of homosexuality as deviant or diseased

- Challenging the religious establishment's view of homosexuality as sin

- Ethnic and racial minorities within the gay community

- Homophobic violence and police harassment

- Exclusion of gays from the military

- Homophobia within political movements

* Ageism

* The gay disabled

* Defining gay identity

* Marginalization and ghettoization of gays

* Recognition of gay rights as a human rights issue for inclusion into
  the agendas of international organizations such as the United
  Nations, Amnesty International, and the European Parliament

Each of these issues arises out of a set of specific circumstances
within a particular political/economic/social context and definable
time frame and should, of course, be examined as such. The following selections provide a sampling of the materials available addressing these issues. My hope is that the reader will find each article to
be stimulating in and of itself, while realizing it is only the "tip of
an iceberg" regarding the subject matter discussed and its complex-
ities.

Articles represent a variety of countries, including Brazil, Italy,
the Soviet Union, Mexico, and Germany. The commonality of concern is perhaps as impressive as the diversity of views. The decision
by many lesbians, for example, to break away from the gay movement and identify for themselves the issues around which to organize has been made, independently, by groups in the United States,
England, Spain, France, and Yugoslavia (among others). The issue of
AIDS, likewise, is prominent on the agendas of gay organizations in
scores of countries throughout the world. And the need to end
discriminatory practices against transvestites is a commonly recognized one in Spain, the United States, Turkey and much of Latin
America. Yet these same issues almost always require different approaches, depending on the local circumstances. Confronting the
AIDS epidemic in Thailand, India, or Brazil, for example, where
sufficient supplies of clean needles and condoms are unavailable or
unaffordable, requires very different types of strategy than in Canada
or New Zealand. The struggle for rights of gay couples to adopt

children will vary from state to state within the United States, depending on local law, but cannot be expected to be a focus of attention in much of the Middle East, where gays lead double lives and can risk harsh punishment for openly loving a member of the same sex.

Furthermore, as movements emerge in the Third World, we can expect to have an even far greater range of issues to consider. The impact of European colonialism, with the particular legal and religious prohibitions against homosexuality it imposed on traditional societies, will no doubt need to be reexamined. Already Native American groups in the United States are attempting to reclaim the berdache tradition, erased largely due to Christianization, and gay African Americans are reexamining homosexuality in traditional African cultures as they establish ties with new gay groups forming throughout that continent. Meanwhile, important studies of Japanese and Chinese homosexual traditions have recently been published, again bringing to light a history hidden in large part as a result of Westernization and its homophobic legacy. And gay movements in many Third World nations, especially in Latin America, are now questioning the advisability of using European and North American gay communities as models for their own development. Here, fear of the commercialization and depoliticization of gay culture and its confinement to ghettolike communities have become important issues of discussion.

SEPARATISM

In the early 1970s, soon after the advent of the Gay Liberation Movement, many lesbians chose to dissociate themselves from the gay organizations and either work within the feminist movement or found their own organizations. Among the reasons given were that men too often continued to dominate political meetings and otherwise exhibit chauvinist behavior toward their gay sisters, and that many issues of concern to lesbians as feminists (e.g., violence against women and reproductive rights) were of little interest or low priority to gay men.

Some gay women then continued their struggle to challenge gender roles and institutionalized sexism in coalition with gay males and feminists. Others, including some who had experienced sexism in the gay movement and homophobia in the feminist movement, came to see men as the enemy. In their view, which was in juxtaposition to that of many feminists, there *were* important differences between the sexes: Men were inherently aggressive, hierarchical, and violent, whereas women were by nature more socially sensitive and nurturing. Since all men in one way or another oppressed all women, it was important to withdraw personally from men, and all manifestations of male values and influence in society. An exclusively women's culture could then be constructed, which could rid the world of most of its male-induced evils. Groups of women with a desire to implement this philosophy formed in various countries, including the United States, Great Britain, and Germany. Their ideas were to influence lesbian and feminist groups way beyond their numbers and throughout the world. In the following essay, Janet Dixon discusses her passage into separatism, her break with it, and gives us an appreciation of the lessons it can teach.

GREAT BRITAIN

"Separatism: A Look Back at Anger" by Janet Dixon, from _Radical Records: Thirty Years of Lesbian and Gay History, 1957–1987_, eds. Bob Cant and Susan Hemmings (1988).

Separatism is to feminism what fundamentalism is to Christianity. It is the center, the beating heart, the essence. The dogma is of absolutes, the lifestyle is of attempted purity, and the zealot is subject to continuous derision. My involvement with separatism lasted five years, but in a very real sense it will never leave me.

Separatism is not acquired politics. Clearly, you cannot inherit a taste for it by coming from a separatist family, nor by living in a separatist neighborhood. Equally, you cannot read about its history and be moved to sympathy by those revelations. Separatism is an exhausting act of faith, and because of insistent pressure on you to repent, it requires almost daily reaffirmation. The faith is in the belief that women, left to themselves, would make the world a beautiful place to live. It claims for all women a far greater potential in terms of powers and skills than any woman has ever demonstrated. Women are seen as the source of compassion, love, and harmony. It was ironic that as we deified womanhood, we unleashed more anger, suspicion, and even, I think, hatred—woman for woman—than any issue had aroused since feminism began.

So what caused this anger and mistrust? Why were heterosexual feminists outraged and repelled by us and all we stood for? Why did socialist feminists accuse us, at best, of being hedonistic female chauvinists, and at worst, Fascists? Why were lesbians angered when we questioned the sense of working with gay men in order to counter gay oppression?

It had, in part, to do with the nature of separatism being highly offensive to those who held traditional, broad, left views. Prior to the time, the early seventies, there was no real precedent for autonomous women's groups organizing around a woman-only issue. The definition of socialism that I can grasp most readily, because it is so simple, is the one given by George Bernard Shaw in 1928: "Socialism is an opinion as to how the income of the country should be distributed." I include it here because at no point was it ever put to me in such bald and comprehensible terms. We saw the goal of feminist socialists as raising the status of women and to include them in the share-out. In any case, however crude my understanding of it, socialism, to its everlasting credit, is about including everyone. Separatism is anathema to this. We saw socialism as yet another squabbling position in male politics. We thought that the women in socialism would never be seen by their men as anything except an "uppity" lump stuck on their side. Not only were we not interested in how socialism was realized, we didn't believe it would make the slightest difference to the position of women even if it were. We didn't want an equal slice of a male cake, we wanted the men and their cake out of our lives.

Gay oppression is class oppression: The people can't be free until the women are free. We saw this as a lot of sloganizing nonsense. This class dumping on that class, this class more oppressed than that class. As far as we were concerned, if you removed the architects and managers of the system, then the whole thing would collapse, and who, we asked, in the massive majority of cases were they, if not men?

Separatism is shamelessly exclusive. The rules are simple: Whatever your race or class, provided you are a woman, you are a potential separatist. Whatever your race or class, if you are a man you are irredeemably the enemy. The separatist position was clear. It was not that men held the power, but that men were the power. Something inherit in maleness necessitates its expression in systems of oppressive hierarchies. Competitiveness, aggression, brutality, and maleness are all one in the same. That Y chromosome, that mutated afterthought, was the cause of it all.

In the winter of 1970 I attended the second national conference of the Women's Liberation Movement, held in a grim out-of-season holiday camp at Skegness. I was, to put it mildly, wet behind the ears politically. In my first year in a London art school my two preoccupations were whether you really could see William Turner's late canvasses as a precursor to French Impressionism, and how the hell I could afford to clothe myself in the right gear to make a stunning impact on my friends at the Gateways. I went to the conference armed only with a general feeling of being pissed off that men seemed to have it all their own way. Along with taking LSD and deciding after some very unpleasant attempts never to fuck again, attending Skegness was one of the most powerful and formative experiences of that part of my life.

On the Saturday morning we shuffled into the camp's concert hall for a "plenary session." As I took my seat, it dawned on me. Among the couple of hundred or so there, were some twenty or thirty men. Not only that, on the stage was a long table, and yes, you've guessed it, among the dignitaries were several men. We sat through some very boring speeches which attempted to make the thoughts of Mao, Marx, and Lenin exciting and accessible to a bunch of dumb women, and then broke for coffee. In the camp canteen I looked for the woman who had encouraged me to come to what, by the minute, I was beginning to feel was a godforsaken hole. I wanted to know why she thought I would be the least bit interested in all that drivel I had just had to sit through. It turned out she was just as fed up as me, and we were not the only ones. A group of us hastily slung together a plan and went back into the concert hall in an effort to oust the ruling junta.

The bravest of us raised her hand and asked by what authority the Maoist Women's Liberation Front had commandeered the stage, and seen fit to hand out reams of papers as proposed discussion documents. The famous stuff hit the fan. After trading what were to become stereotypical insults about bourgeois middle-class women and hard left male domination, a very large number of us walked out and from then on abandoned the formal conference altogether. I spent the rest of the weekend in small discussion groups with women from all over the country with a wide variety of ideas and opinions. I was excited and happy and enthused with the thought of becoming more involved in both the WLM and GLF. As a codicil to this I should tell you that at the same time in another part of the camp, the National Union of Miners were holding some sort of conference themselves. On the Saturday evening they were having a social and were to watch a striptease. Some of us decided to get into the social and talk to the men. As it turned out, productive discussion proved impossible. Abuse followed insult, and eventually the police were called. The gutter press version went something like, "Libbers storm miners' social." If only we had.

In the early seventies I was active in both the Women's Movement and in Gay Liberation Front; more of GLF later. Of those very early times in the Women's Movement, I am left with a memory of two distinct feelings. The first is one of a self-conscious confusion, the second of discomfort at being a lesbian.

The first arose because even though I myself and the women I was involved with called ourselves feminists, I wasn't really clear what we were doing about it. I went to national and regional conferences and attended all sorts of local workshops. I went to Grosvenor Square and abused "American Imperialists," I got thumped about a bit on Troops Out demos, and I dutifully handed out time and money in support of "the miners' wives." Although I was convinced of the correctness of all these issues, I harbored unspoken doubts about their relevance to me, and I couldn't help wondering if the sight of our banners on the demos was always welcome.

As for my discomfort at being a lesbian, now, that was much more painful. The public reaction to the reawakening of feminism was to dismiss us all as bra-burning lesbians. The reaction of WLM was strenuously to deny this "insult." Heterosexual feminists argued that we had to be taken seriously as women, and if the media got

away with the label of lesbians, then "the women out there" would
be alienated. But wait a minute, I thought, hadn't I been a woman
out there? In any case, if the business of women's liberation was
what we were about, then shouldn't that mean all women, even
those of us with embarrassing sexual habits? I was told that what I
did in my bedroom was a private matter. I was made to feel that
wanting to have it openly discussed was just exhibitionist boat-
rocking.

As the seventies wore on, the numbers of lesbians in the WLM
increased dramatically, the rumbles of discontent turned into roars.
Lesbians put their weight behind issues such as child care, abortion,
race, battered wives, and rape. In return we wanted the skeleton of
sexuality wrenched from the closet and flesh put on its bones. The
WLM had begun to come of age. We had stopped trailing around
after the men in the left, contorting ourselves in the hope of receiving some grudging crumbs of approval. We had our own campaigns
and set of demands, and what's more, among them was a woman's
right to define her own sexuality.

The inclusion of this command, in the context of feminism, may
seem now to be obvious, but the struggle to make sexuality a
respectable platform was an acrimonious one. At national conferences such as Acton and Edinburgh, the lesbians in general, and the
separatists in particular, were accused of being elitist, divisive, of
tearing the women's movement apart, and taking energy away from
"the real struggle." Even at lesbian conferences such as Canterbury,
Nottingham, and Bristol, separatists were castigated for being smug
extremists. In both these settings, women who had been toiling in
their communities came to conference to exchange ideas and information, and to gain strength by being together. Because of the in-
house nature of separatism, we saw the conferences as opportunities
to disseminate our beliefs to huge numbers of women.

As you can see, I am once making great claims on behalf of
separatism. Were separatists really responsible for making lesbianism, eventually, respectable inside the WLM? Wouldn't it have
happened anyway? (Some might even say sooner!) Did separatists

really lift feminism from under the coattails of the male left and establish autonomous women's political activity? Wouldn't heterosexual women have tired in the end, of explaining why Marx ignored women and how rape was the result of capitalist oppression, and found less contrived answers? I don't think so. You only have to read what women in emerging feminist groups and movements are writing, to see that these patterns repeat themselves time and again. But, of course, the question of just how much in terms of autonomy can be attributed to separatism can never be definitely answered. Nevertheless, it is my belief that without us, feminism would never have been more than a caucus of the broad left. Separatism was right there in the middle, influencing all women, and, despite themselves, even those who were the most vociferous in their resistance to our ideas. What separatists did was to reduce the very complex set of circumstances which combine to oppress women, to a single uncluttered issue. That is the stark injustice of the total humiliation of women on all levels, by men. Separatism was the source of this theme and the means by which it spilled into every area of feminist activity.

To make the language of separatism less cumbersome, I want to call this central theme, pure separatism and the effects that pure separatism has caused, graduated separatism. Let me return to my own experiences to illustrate the relationship between pure and graduated separatism.

At the same time I was being bundled in and out of police vans for telling the troops in Northern Ireland exactly where they should go, I was also attending GLF meetings. I just can't remember when I found the time to wash my hair and iron creases into my flares. The weekly meetings, held on Thursdays, were megalithic in proportion. Upward of four and even five hundred people attended. We hired halls at the London School of Economics, the Middle Earth Club in Covent Garden, and the church hall of All Saints in Notting Hill. Of the hundreds who went, we were lucky if twenty-five of those were women. With the best will in the world, and there was initially a lot of it, lesbians found it hard to make their voices heard. Inevitably the inequality in numbers was reflected in the priority given to issues. Against the backdrop of queer bashing and police harassment, the more disguised problems associated with lesbianism fared badly. Even in the smaller specific groups, women often felt that they were struggling against thinly disguised misogyny.

Gay men who had been shown a stiff cock in a public lavatory by a policeman, and were then promptly arrested for showing an interest, weren't slow to remind us that, thanks to Queen Victoria, lesbianism was not illegal. The fact that none of the lesbians I knew wanted to pick up a woman in a public toilet underpinned those very basic differences in the sexuality of gay women and men, at that time, which eventually led to the split.

There were those men, lots of them, who quite simply ignored us, viewing our presence, I'm sure, as an intrusion. There were those men who made strained efforts to submerge their mistrust, dislike, and fear of us. And there were those men who encouraged us to reprimand them for sexist thoughts and deeds. In the end, once again, women were servicing men, women were raising the consciousness of men, women were giving their energy to men.

We, the lesbians, began to abandon the GLF dream. We gave up expecting the GLF to solve our problems because we could see that it was essentially a movement built around the freedom to choose and practice your own sexuality. Further, in terms of heterosexism, whatever your sexuality, if you are a woman you are always second best. Gay men, under pressure, could return to the closet and regain all the privileges of being male. Where could lesbians go?

We became increasingly angry and frustrated, feeling more and more that to work politically with men, whatever their sexuality, was simply a debilitating exercise. In 1972, a group of us, finally exhausted by our tokenist existence, announced at one of the mega meetings our intention to leave GLF and work politically only with women.

This decision, inspired by pure separatism, was graduated separatism. Not all of the women who took that decision were separatist by all means, but the fact that we had rejected men was not a gesture of feminism alone. After all, feminism alone does not exclude men. Some of the men in GLF had called themselves feminist, as had the Maoist men at Skegness. Graduated separatism, on the other hand, draws a line beyond which men cannot go.

Pure separatism involves a woman taking steps to remove men from her life. She must live with women, be a mother only to girl children. Male culture in all its manifestations is shunned. She must abandon all relationships with men, lovers, fathers, and brothers. Sexually she is either celibate or lesbian. Politically and socially, her contact is confined to women. The music she listens to must be composed and played by women, the books she reads must have a woman author. Her morality is not dictated by patriarchal norms, but rather guided by the belief that women's needs are her sole concern. To steal from men is not theft, it is reclamation.

Graduated separatism, the acceptable face of separatism, can be seen as the ripples which pass outward from this. Graduated separatist spaces, women-only spaces, can be moved into by all women. You do not have to be a separatist or even a lesbian to enjoy the benefits of graduated separatism. It has meant that women's groups of all kinds, even those outside mainstream feminism, can now quite legitimately organize around women-only issues. Having said this though, it is what goes on in the woman-only space which defines it as graduated separatism or not. Groups of women working or socializing together are not automatically separatist. Of course, there are many precedents for women-only societies. The Women's Institute is devoted to the service of husband and family, a convent of nuns to the service of a male god: Their very existence depends on this element of male service. Can you imagine how long a convent of sisters devoted to the worship of Hecate would have survived?

Women-only groups are active in local and national politics, at work, in job-training and skills courses, in youth work, in sports. The existence of Greenham Common, women's refuges, rape crisis centers, health care projects, women-only workshops at mixed events, and lesbian-only bars at gay gatherings: All these and more are examples of how the energy of pure separatism has filtered through to affect the lives of many women, including those who have no interest in politics of any kind, let alone separatism. Graduated separatism creates a space where women and girls can be free from the burden of men and their persistent sexism long enough to gain confidence and a skill, which would otherwise have been impossible.

Had separatism confined itself to a political context, then however violent the discussion, its impact and effects would not have been a fraction of what they are. Those of us who "became" separatist in the early seventies carried our politics into our lifestyle in a way that, to us, obviated our beliefs and put teeth into our thrashing gums. To our zealous eyes, hypocrisy was everywhere. A white antiracist was only a guilt-ridden ex-colonial WASP. A car-driving, homeowning, polytechnic lecturer with a fake northern accent was a bleating guilty liberal, not a socialist. Equally, a feminist who left the meeting, went home, and jumped into bed with hubbie or boyfriend was no better than a member of the fifth column. It was easy enough to demand racial equality, fair distribution of the wealth of the world, or equal rights for women: None of those would happen tomorrow, and none of them involved more than the most superficial cosmetic surgery to make yourself credible. Dialect, however moving and seductive, was just words. To us, lesbianism and feminism were synonymous, either one without the other was untenable. A nonfeminist lesbian was just a failed heterosexual. A nonlesbian feminist was just a male apologist. We demanded proof of intent, and that could only be achieved through living a separatist lifestyle. That was the revolution here and now.

On leaving GLF in 1972 I didn't realize that I was now a separatist; those of us who were didn't use the word. We called ourselves proudly the extremists, the vanguard, but it wasn't until we read the American CLIT papers in 1973 that we knew we had a name other than men-haters. In her SCUM (Society for Cutting Up Men) manifesto, Valerie Solanus outlined a matriarchal utopia with men as slave class. This was not what I wanted. For me, men had to disappear altogether. I didn't want a geographical solution—a women's farm or island or country. I didn't want, either, a sexual apartheid or to use violence or magic. All these solutions were current and much discussed. But I accepted what G. K. Chesterton had put so well in 1911: "A woman putting up her fists at a man is a woman putting herself in the one position which does not frighten him."

The first stage in the process of making men disappear was to ignore them totally. One by one the men in our mixed household left or were thrown out. We stopped going to GLF, and to mixed gay discos and on mixed demos. We sold all our male records, stopped reading the newspaper and watching the telly. When I wrote letters home I addressed them to my mother only. I sat alone in the canteen at college, I stopped drinking in pubs, and chatty male bus conductors and shop assistants were met with blank stares. To ignore men was to cut the umbilical cord once and for all, to deny them their very lifeforce. Men could only wield power if we, the women, let them. Without our minds and bodies to leech from, men would eventually shrivel and die. William Golding's book *Lord of the Flies* was to me an apt exercise in male self-disclosure, chronicling as it does what happens when the civilizing female influence is removed from the life of the male. Without women, men revert to animals, without men women could heal and restore to harmony a world raped and ravaged. We further argued that this mass withdrawal of support from men had to happen quickly if the world were not to be destroyed by pollution or holocaust. We couldn't wait around for the magic day when the men turned to us and said, "OK, girls, now it's your turn." Anyway, we didn't have to wait, we didn't have to persuade, we had simply to stop conspiring in our oppression. In *A Room of One's Own,* Virginia Woolf describes how

Women have served all these centuries as looking glasses possessing the magic and delicious power of reflecting the figure of man at twice its natural size . . . if she begins to tell the truth,

the figure in the looking glass shrinks; his fitness for life is
diminished. . . . The looking glass vision is of supreme importance
because it charges the vitality; it stimulates the nervous system.
Take it away and the man may die.

Without the telly, the pub, and most gay social life, I had time to
read and study. I experienced a personal Renaissance. Layer after
layer of male confusion cleared away from my eyes. I had almost
daily visions of a cathartic kind, with the total and even religious
intensity of those experienced by Paul on the road to Damascus—
an unfortunate comparison! You could not properly take account of
my experience of separatism without acknowledging my feelings of
being swept away by this sort of fervor. It had all been lies, everything men had ever told us. I reconstructed my life and all other
women's in the light of male distortion and women's stolen potential. Nothing men had said or written was to be trusted. I read
women authors voraciously, and when you consider this was in pre-
Women's Press and Virago days, it meant I read a strange variety of
subjects: history, travel, witchcraft, politics, poetry, theology, philosophy, even Victorian novelettes on the evils of alcohol inspired
by the Temperance League. When, in 1974, an American friend
brought me over from the States a copy of Elizabeth Gould-Davis's
The First Sex, I had a scholar's confirmation of my conclusions.

The squat we lived in was falling down, but like Patience and
Sara, we tackled our problems with a pioneering spirit. We saw it
as an opportunity to demystify the male world of plumbing, elec-
tricity, and carpentry. We read and experimented until we could
stride into builder's suppliers and ask for one-way cistern inlet
valves, 1.5 mm triplecore insulated or three-inch steel angle brackets, just as though we had been born knowing all about it, like men!
I stopped wearing Tampax (cotton wool pricks), and I stopped
eating meat in case the chunk of sizzling corpse I was about to sit
down to had come from a male animal.

At first it was men who were not allowed in the house, and
although this position resulted in a lot of criticism and ridicule,

most feminists had some sympathy so long as we didn't seriously advocate separatism for all women. But, of course, this was inevitably what we did do. It happened initially because at that time separatists were few in number, and across the country we all knew each other more or less. As a result of the huge curiosity our stance aroused, we had to continuously explain and defend our politics. We had literally hundreds of almost identical conversations. These were often emotional and traumatizing, and left us exhausted. We would often find out later that these conversations had been reported in a distorted way. All sorts of rumors spread about what went on in our house. We had "shaved our heads so as not to be sex objects, and boarded up our windows so that men in the street couldn't see in." We also "drowned male kittens, beat up the man who came to read the meter, and held covens where we stuck pins in male voodoo dollies." We were easy targets for ridicule, and because we were angered and hurt by all of this, we withdrew further into ourselves, and stopped having contact with heterosexual women almost entirely. At one point a group of us decided that the best way to stop being hassled about separatism was to publish installments of the CLIT papers in the weekly newsletter, which was mailed to women all over London and beyond. We thought that if women wanted to know about separatism they could read this, and then leave us in peace. It didn't work, and by about the third installment the outcry was such that we abandoned it.

Over the next few years the number of separatists grew. Women began to leave the cities and to establish women's houses in the countryside and in Scotland and Wales. We had contact with women from America, France, and Scandinavia. I began to read pieces about separatism written by women who I didn't know. All this meant that I no longer felt personally responsible for separatism. Sometimes many weeks went by without me having to defend my politics. I had time to think about where I was going and what I had become. I look back on 1975 as a year of the most painful self-scrutiny. I had made so many enemies. Had the means justified the end? In the winter of 1975 the council evicted us from our squat, and those of us who formed the nucleus of that original women's house were dispersed around the country. I felt very stuck. I was trapped by a set of dictates I had imposed on myself and others, and my aggressive public image doggedly intruded itself into my personal relationships. I was frustrated by my ghetto, sickened by my reputation. I needed a fresh start. I had to let go of separatism.

In the spring of 1976 I decided to act on a need I had felt for a very long time. I wanted a child. By June, after one attempt at conception, I was pregnant. (This, in the days before widespread artificial insemination, meant a public climb down from separatism.) My separatist friends said I was selling out, and taking on the role of mother was just doing what the patriarchy had trained me for. In any case, they would never sanction sex with a man for whatever reason, not to mention taking the risk of giving birth to a male child. Women who I had attacked for bringing up boy children wanted to know if it had been an immaculate conception or simply parthenogenesis, and what was I going to do with it if it were a boy? Although I did what I could to try to conceive a girl, I couldn't be sure that I had. In any event both sets of protagonists were right. My aggressive five-year ego trip along the path of separatism was over. I had to face the music, I had to face myself.

By the autumn of 1976, halfway through my pregnancy, I fell asleep one afternoon and had a very powerful dream. In it I saw my child's body inside my own, but it wasn't curled up like a fetus. It wasn't a baby, either, it was a child of about three, and what's more, it was a boy with a shock of fair hair. When I woke up I was almost as amazed by the fair hair as I was by the sex, because both his "father" and I are very dark. In the spring of 1977 I did indeed give birth to a boy, who later grew that shock of fair hair.

So what do I feel about separatism now, ten years on, and the mother of sons? How can I claim any loyalty to separatism after what has happened to me? Well, most obviously I have learned that what is good for me cannot necessarily be applied to everyone, although I still tend to dish out unsolicited advice. But, more importantly, I have learned not to see any stage of my life as the final one. Politics, sexuality, or whatever must be a framework to build on, not a rigid cage which restricts change.

All women who come to separatism do so as a reaction to the brutality and institutionalized sexism of men. The rage and sense of injustice, for a separatist, is not powerfully enough voiced anywhere else. But let me make the point here that separatism and man-hating are different things. A man-hater is someone (and it can be another man) inspired by revenge. A separatist, by definition, lives separately from men, although hatred of men does occur. The man-hater is locked into the initial stage of separation, where repressed hurt and previously unarticulated anger are explored. Many man-haters, in my experience, come fresh from a traumatic relationship with a man, or a recent realization about men. The overwhelming need to return the hurt, although this seems to be a necessary stage, can become the overriding passion. It can lead a woman into almost daily aggressive confrontations with men in order to sustain high levels of hatred. In some separatist spaces time and energy were spent in endless discussion on the evils of men. Here is the first uncomfortable contradiction of separatism. Whereas separatism should result in women devoting all their time and energy to women, in fact, and probably inevitably, men manage to exhaust us even in their absence.

If my withdrawal from separation had in part to do with feeling unhappy with a surfeit of hatred, which is mentally and spiritually very depleting, it also had to do with how you go about communicating feelings of being cleansed and enlightened. In contact with other women the separatist becomes more and more impatient with women who to them seem stubbornly bogged down in male values. As I have already said, it can reach the point where you have virtually no contact except with other separatists. This is an unreal place to be, because if you can't talk to other women, yet you believe all women must in the end come to separatism, then either those women have to be born separatist or they have to come to it through isolation, pain, and struggle. The process of separatism growing into a global force would thus take a very long time. In this sense, separatism doesn't address itself to the business of making life better for all women, and is then restricted in large part to acting as a channel for the energy of women once they have become embittered by heterosexism.

Finally, I think the issue which more than any other led me to break with pure separatism was women's compassion. In defining the source of women's oppression being promale sexism rather than capitalism, separatism shifted the emphasis of the whole of feminism. But, having done this, separatism went on to offer only one solution, an all-women world. Here separatism dissolves, at best, into romantic/cosmic/evolutionary answers, or at worst into violence and male genocide. Separatism, despite any protestation to the contrary, came up against the age-old problem of how to transpose the idea onto the material world.

However men "are gotten rid of," many women would be immeasurably hurt in the process. For separatists to impose their solution on all women, even if it was viewed as being "for her own good," you cannot escape the fact that you are simply replacing male domination with female. Women have massive amounts of love invested in fathers, lovers, and sons, and many of these women despise the systems their own men may be helping to sustain. Haven't women always so been torn? But to insist that women somehow amputate their love and compassion is to ask them to destroy the very thing which in my view favorably distinguishes us from men. Patriarchy has shown women that there is no such thing as peace, there are just gaps in the wars. To me, we were not offering anything different. If we were to solve our problem by disposing of our enemy, we would set a very disgusting precedent in terms of separatist problem-solving.

Graduated separatism accepts pure separatism's definition of the problem, but not the solution. Apart from anything else it is self-defeating to nurture girl children, to teach them self-respect and self-defense, and then have to watch them go to war with men and boys whose ideas are left unchallenged. Having said this, I don't mean that it is the job of women to reeducate men. Once a woman has decided what and who she wants to be, it is for the men in her life, if there are any, to reeducate themselves to take account of her.

Because I lived away from men for so long, part of me is now permanently closed to them. I can honestly say that I feel at least equal to them, often above them; and I don't enter any relations with them that aren't on my terms. I don't need men to make me feel secure, to be a mother, to frame my morals, to pay my bills, to organize my life, to give me self-esteem. I do not want matriarchy to replace patriarchy as an interim measure because I retain unshakable faith in women's ability to organize, to be caring, and to be, just in so many ways, superior to men. Eventually men could probably be readmitted to positions of influence, provided they had somehow overcome their taste for violence, greed, rape, and power for its own sake.

Although this may sound harsh and unreasonable, experience has made it hard for me to trust women who have never been through some form of separatist reaction. If, as a woman, you can see clearly what men have done to us, how can you stay calm? If you don't explore your anger, how can you stop internalizing it and shed the costume of the victim? So long as heterosexism continues, it will continue to spawn separatism. My hope is that we could develop the kind of separatism which doesn't make women, both on the inside and the outside of it, feel attacked, vilified, stuck, and lonely. To feel compassion for men without having been a separatist is dangerous. It is a love which has been kept in ignorance: Haven't women been kept uninformed for long enough?

TRANSVESTISM AND TRANSSEXUALISM

Transvestism, or cross-dressing, is a phenomenon found both cross-culturally and throughout history. It was common practice in ancient Greece, for example, during special festivals, and it has formed an integral part of Polynesian, eastern Siberian, Native American, and Southeast African cultures. Among Native Americans, cross-dressers, known as berdache, were often held in high esteem and relegated to positions of power in their societies. Cross-dressing is practiced today in Western cultures by both men and women, heterosexual and homosexual. Gay transvestites comprise a minority grouping within the larger homosexual community. In most countries under the influence of Judeo-Christian values, they suffer the consequences of being different. Heterosexual society generally, but also many "straight-identified" gay men continue to shun them or hold them in scorn. Ironically, transvestites were among the most militant participants in the Stonewall Rebellion of 1969, which heralded the beginnings of the current Gay Movement. Widespread prejudice has motivated many to found their own political organizations, such as STAR (Street Transvestite Action Revolutionaries) in the United States and the Transvestite-Transsexual Collective in Spain.

Transsexuals are persons who choose to undergo, surgically and/or hormonally, a change into the gender opposite of that to which they were born. As with transvestites, they, too, have been the object of discrimination and ridicule.

In the first two of the three excerpts that follow, Italian writer Mario Mieli examines the underlying reasons for society's rejection of transvestites. Beneath the laughter and hostility, he explains, is a feeling of anxiety, for transvestites challenge the rigid and sacred male/female dichotomy instilled in us from birth by family and society. They remind us, if unconsciously, of our repressed trans-sexuality and expose in us the unrecognized transvestism of our daily lives.

In the third selection, taken from *La Pluma,* a gay liberation magazine from Catalunya, Spain, the authors discuss the specific oppression of transvestites and transsexuals. Not only, for example, are they harassed, jailed, and subject to employment discrimination, but they are economically exploited as well. Transvestites are often forced into prostitution or into taking demeaning jobs as "exotic" entertainers in order to survive. Transsexuals, also, are ripe for exploitation by medical practitioners. Only by a collective struggle against repressive laws and for the rights of control over one's own body, the authors conclude, will marginalization and exploitation come to an end. There follows an interesting interview with members of the Transvestite-Transsexual collective of CCAG, a coordinating organization for gay liberation among Catalans.

ITALY

From *Homosexuality and Liberation: Elements of a Gay Critique* by Mario Mieli, translated by David Fernbach (1980).

1.

Society is especially harsh in its attack upon transsexuals or those who might appear as such: The butch lesbian, the queen or "effeminate" male homosexual bear a greater brunt of public execration and contempt, and are frequently criticized even by those reactionary homosexuals who are better adapted to the system, the "straight gays" who have managed to pass as "normal" or heterosexual. These reactionary homosexuals (homo-cops) make out that outrageous queens and transvestites ruin the gay scene and spoil the image of homosexuality. For our part, we outrageous queens see them as queens dressed up as straight men, unfortunate people who are forced to disguise themselves and act a role imposed by the system, and who find ideological arguments to justify their position as contented slaves. They wonder what it is the gay movement wants, what it is fighting for, because nowadays our society accepts diversity. True, even today we can't make love freely wherever we feel like it, on the buses or in the streets, but then not even straights are allowed to do that. So things aren't that bad. Some consolation!

Many feminists criticize us queens because we often tend in our dress and behavior to copy the stereotyped "feminine" fetish that women have to fight. But if a woman dressed like a starlet or cover girl is normal for the system today, a man dressed in a similar way is quite abnormal as far as "normal" people are concerned, and so our transvestism has a clear revolutionary character. There is no harm in us queens having our bit of fantasy. We demand the freedom to dress as we like, to choose a definite style one day and an ambiguous one the day after, to wear both feathers and ties, leopard skin and rompers, the leather queen's chains, black leather and whip, the greasy rags of the street porter, or a tulle maternity dress. We enjoy the bizarre, digging into (pre)history, the dustbins and uniforms of yesterday, today, and tomorrow, the trumpery, costumes, and symbols that best express the mood of the moment. As Antonio Donato puts it, we want to communicate by our clothing, too, the "schizophrenia" that underlies social life, hidden behind the censorious screen of the unrecognized transvestism of every day. From our vantage point, in fact, it is "normal" people who are the true transvestites. Just as the absolute heterosexuality that is so proudly flaunted masks the polymorphous but sadly inhibited disposition of their desire, so their standard outfits hide and debase the marvelous human being that lies suppressed within. Our transvestism is condemned because it shows up for all to see the funereal reality of the general transvestism, which has to remain silent and is simply taken for granted.

Far from being particularly odd, the transvestite exposes how tragically ridiculous the great majority of people are in their monstrous uniforms of man and "woman." You need only take a ride on the underground. If the transvestite seems ridiculous to the "normal" person who encounters him, far more ridiculous and sad, for the transvestite, is the nudity of the person who laughs, so properly dressed, in his face.

For a man, to dress as a "woman" does not necessarily mean projecting the "woman-object"; above all, because he is not a woman, and the male fetishism imposed by capital decrees that he should be dressed quite differently, reified in a quite different guise, dressed as a man or at least in unisex. Besides, a frock can be very comfortable, fresh and light when it's hot, and warm and cozy when it's cold. We can't just assume that women who normally go around dressed as men, swathed tightly in jeans, feel more comfortable than a queen dressed up as a witch, with full-bodied cloak and wide-brimmed hat.

But a man can also get pleasure from wearing a very uncomfortable "feminine" garb. It can be exciting, and quite trippy, for a gay man to wear high heels, elaborate makeup, suspender belt, and satin panties. Once again, those feminists who attack us gays, and in particular transvestites, for dressing as the "woman-object" are putting down gay humor, the transsexual aesthetic, and craziness of crazy queens. Their new morality is in fact the very old antigay morality, simply given a new gloss by modern categories stuffed with an ideological feminism, ideological because it provides a cover for the antihomosexual taboo, for the fear of homosexuality, for the intention to reform the Norm without eliminating it.

2.

So-called normal people are so adapted to the male heterosexual code that they are in no position to understand, as a general rule, the relativity, contingency, and limitation of the concept of "normality." They refuse to understand, the better to confirm themselves in their own prejudices. There is no shortage of "scientists" prepared to bend to the prevailing ideology. Thus if heterosexuals have always seen homoeroticism as a vice, some psychologist will come along and maintain that homosexuals are "immature and confused." "Perversions" have to be stigmatized, today by a scientific" veil made up of the most insolent lies: "as if they exerted a seductive influence; as if at bottom a secret envy of those who enjoy them had to be strangled."[1]

"Normal" people do not tolerate gays, and not just because, by our very presence, we display a dimension of pleasure that is covered by a taboo, but because we also confront anyone who meets us with the confusion of his monosexual existence, mutilated and beset by repression, induced to renunciation and adaptation to a "reality" imposed by the system as the most normal of destinies.

We can observe, for example, the attitude of "normal" people toward transvestites. Their general reaction is one of disgust, irritation, scandal. And laughter: We can well say that anyone who laughs at a transvestite is simply laughing at a distorted image of himself, like a reflection in a fairground mirror. In this absurd reflection he recognizes, without admitting it, the absurdity of his own image, and responds to this absurdity with laughter. Transvestism, in fact, translates the tragedy contained in the polarity of the sexes onto the level of comedy.

It is not hard to grasp the common denominator that links, in a relationship of affinity, all the various attitudes people assume toward queens, and toward transvestites in particular. These reactions, whether of laughter or something far more dangerous, only express, in different degree and in differing qualitative forms, a desire extraverted under the negative sign of aggression and fear— or more precisely, anxiety. It is not really the queen or transvestite who is an object of fear for "normal" people. We only represent the image that provides a medium between the orbit of their conscious observations and an obscure object of radical fear in their unconscious. This anxiety is converted into laughter, often accompanied by forms of verbal and even physical abuse.

The person who laughs at a transvestite is reacting to the faint intuition of this absurdity that he already has—as has every human being—and which the man dressed as a woman, who suddenly appears before him, externalizes in the "absurdity" of his external appearance. The encounter with the transvestite reawakens anxiety because it shakes to their foundations the rigidly dichotomous categories of the sexual duality, categories instilled into all of us by the male heterosexual culture, particularly by way of the family, which right from the start offers the child the opposition of father and mother, the "sacred" personifications of the sexes in their relationship of master and slave. We all form and establish our conceptions of "man" and "woman" on the models of our parents, the one as virility, privilege, and power, the other as femininity and subjection. To these models, which bind us to them thanks to the hallowed web of family ties that determines our personality, we adapt our conception of anyone who, in the course of life, we encounter or even merely think of. We think only in terms of "man" and "woman" to the point that we cannot even imagine anything but "men" or "women." In ourselves, too, we can recognize only the "man" or the "woman," despite our underlying transsexual nature and despite our formation in the family, where our existential misery is determined by our relationship to mother or father. The child of the master-slave relationship between the sexes sees in him or herself only one single sex. The singleness does not seem contradicted by the evident fact that we are born from a fusion of the sexes. And yet we need only look in the mirror (during a trip) to see clearly in our features both our mother and our father. Monosexuality springs from the repression of transsexuality, and transsexuality is already denied before birth. Conception itself, in fact, proceeds from the totalitarian negation of the female sex by the proclaimed uniqueness of the phallus as sexual organ in coitus and its "power" in the parental couple.

But the phallus does not just coincide with the penis, even if it is superimposed on it. While the penis is what distinguishes the male anatomically, the phallus represents the patriarchal absolutizing of the idea (of male power) which the penis embodies, an idea that characterizes all history to date as his-story. In a world of symbols, the idea of symbology of power assumes a phallic form.

Concretely, this "power" is based on the repression of Eros, which is a repression of the mind, the body, and the penis itself, and above all the negation of femininity. In the present prehistory, it is first and foremost a function of the oppression of women.

From the negation of the female sex in the heterosexual relationship, individuals are born either male or female, the former sexual (as bearers of the penis, the bodily vehicle of the unique sexual organ in the patriarchal phallic conception), the latter "female eunuchs." Either, or. The tragedy is that "normal" people cannot tolerate the transvestite showing up the grotesque aspects of this process, committing an act of sacrilege in confusing the sacred opposition between the sexes, given that he combines in himself both sexes, daring to impose a femininity which has been reduced to mere appearance onto the reality of a male self. The transvestite sins very gravely, demanding vengeance from the guardians of the Phallus.

NOTES

1. Sigmund Freud, "A General Introduction to Psychoanalysis," quoted by H. Marcuse in *Eros and Civilization: A Philosophical Inquiry into Freud* (New York: Vintage, 1962).

SPAIN

From "Transvestites and Transsexuals: Introduction to a Specific Type of Oppression," translated by Sam Larson, from *La Pluma* (July/August and October 1978).

> Queens and princesses
> of the night.
> Little dolls of pleasure
> come out into the light of day
> and exercise your power!
> Sleeping beauties
> disenchanted Snow Whites
> all of you grind your teeth
> because this fairy tale has come to an end.
> —Samantha

To try to find an explanation why some people feel the need to dress as transvestites or change their sex is, for the moment, a useless pursuit that does not resolve any problems. The reality is that transvestites and transsexuals exist, with their own brand of oppression. Their problems are marginalized by a system that only reluctantly will tolerate them, but does not accept them, that is, if it doesn't openly exploit their bodies through prostitution and exhibitionism in the cabarets for the enjoyment of others.

It is necessary, first, to clarify who is considered a transvestite and who a transsexual, because of the present confusion concerning this issue. To begin with, a person who dresses up occasionally in clothes that are used by the opposite sex is called a *transformist*. A *transvestite* is a person who habitually uses the clothing of the oppo-

site sex, disguising his or her true condition, and constantly imitating the attitudes and attributes that characterize the opposite sex in
that society. And finally, a person who not only habitually dresses
up as the opposite sex, but also has introduced physiological changes
into his or her body that would make them physically identical to
the opposite sex is called a *transsexual*. These changes are brought
about by hormones until a final operation, which consists of a sex
change. The transvestite who has had an operation is identical to
the opposite sex in all external aspects. Usually a transvestite is a
man who transforms himself into imitating a woman; however,
there are cases of the opposite as well, a woman who imitates and
cross-dresses as a man. As of now, there are still no known cases of
female transsexualism, that is, a sex change from a woman to a man
[*sic*]. The talk of transvestites and transsexuals today and their
oppression is to talk of men who have externally become women.
We will leave it for another time to discuss the opposite.

HOW THEIR SPECIFIC OPPRESSION IS MANIFESTED

The situation of transvestites and transsexuals seems at first glance
to be a bit ambiguous. On the one hand, the system rejects them
and marginalizes them, applying all the repressive means at its
disposal: the laws (specifically, the Law of Social Danger) detention,
preventing them from being able to find work like anyone else,
collective scorn, and insults. On the other hand, the system accepts
them, always, however, regarding them as strange and annoying
creatures whom it uses for the pleasure of those seeking the exotic
as an outlet for their own frustrations and self-oppression. This
ambiguity is completely illusionary in that we are talking about
manifestations of the same oppression.

The oppression that transvestites and transsexuals suffer has the
same characteristics that are suffered by homosexuals and lesbians.

If there are transvestites, who before changing their external aspect, were in their sexual choice practicing homosexuals, their experience of oppression does not always correspond to the same degree with those transvestites who behave heterosexually. Added to their oppression as homosexuals is the marginalization that the system generates toward all who transgress the norms of the system, that is, the domination of women by men, beginning with the physical, external differentiations. Thus the system will always oppose a man imitating a woman, because this breaks with the imposed norm of domination. Affected, then, will be the faggot who acts like a woman, without looking like her externally, but simply by virtue of his being a "queen."

To this oppression there is added the economic exploitation—prostitution and the world of the spectacle, the buying and selling of the human body as a product for sexual pleasure, or for the enjoyment of cabaretgoers and the profit of businessmen. And we can also add the exploitation of pornographic magazines, always in search of the spectacular and exciting in order to reap larger profits. This is no longer the exploitation of people's labor potential, but an exploitation of the human body itself, pure and simple, reducing it to a piece of merchandise that can be thrown out when no longer useful and replaced by another one in better condition.

But the oppression of transvestites and transsexuals does not end here. From the moment the sex change process is initiated with hormones through the final operation, a new form of exploitation opens up: exploitation on the part of the medical field and business. There are the expensive drugs and operations, sources of profit for the pharmaceutical companies and for doctors without scruples. There are the doctors who use their skills with little consideration of the person who comes for help, and are preoccupied only with performing the operation with no regard for preserving the sexual potential of the patient. How many postoperative transvestites find in this way their genital sexuality reduced!

Transvestites and transsexuals are also rejected and marginalized by homosexuals who are not transvestites but who are concerned with the image of being macho and maintaining a masculine image that does not break with the norm, a marginalization that introduces one more element into the oppression of transvestites and transsexuals.

IMITATION OF THE WOMAN-OBJECT?

The transvestite disturbs the system, the imposed norm of machismo, with its separation into categories of the differences between male and female. It breaks the norms of an imposed sexual domination. The hair disguised with makeup and the phallus that is hinted at underneath the skirts introduce into everyday life the destabilizing elements regarding the dominant/submissive relationship between people. The image of the macho man as well as the submissive female are parodied and shaken. Though transsexuals willingly reintroduce the differentiating physical elements of man and woman, thus accepting in a way the imposed norm, a new element is nonetheless introduced: the possibility of overcoming, even physically, these components that characteristically differentiate men and women. We have here a third sex, or simply people who are free to decide not only their sexual orientation but also the characteristics of their sex.

With the imitation of the woman by the cross-dressed or transsexed man, the imposed system is broken, opening up innumerable possibilities with respect to relationships between people, as well as control over one's body. But this imitation is faced with some barriers placed there by the system, for the imitation of women is tolerated, if minimally, only if it follows the image of the woman-object that society imposes. The opposite would be to suppose that the feminist battle has already achieved its objectives.

The system also tries to assimilate transvestites and transsexuals by commercializing their reality through the spectacle and prostitution. The intent is to exploit the role of woman-object using machismo ideology. To the extent that transvestites and transsexuals are willing to assume these roles without protest, bourgeois society will tolerate them, even though continuing to marginalize them.

TRANSVESTITES AND TRANSSEXUALS CONFRONTING THE SYSTEM

Confronting this situation, transvestites and transsexuals have only one escape: joining collectively and converting their struggle into a political confrontation with the system that oppresses them. A confrontation with the norms and the rules of conduct that have been imposed, and transforming cross-dressing and transsexualism into a radical critique of the system, its categorizations, and its structures [that perpetuate] domination and oppression.

The struggle entails putting an end to the myth of the natural conditioning of the man to be a man and the woman to be a woman. The advances of science and of medicine now make sex change possible. We should be able to make use of this possibility with complete liberty and confidence, and fight for the right over our own bodies. The struggle of transvestites and transsexuals also entails a complete rejection of the role of woman-object, which is the basis for the integration trap that the system extends to them. Any critique of imposed categories by transvestites and transsexuals supposes the rejection of this woman-object role.

And, finally, [the task entails] uniting the struggle of transvestites and transsexuals with that of gays and lesbians, and with those of women and all other oppressed and exploited people, to put an end to this system, which is truly the root cause of all of our problems.

TRANSVESTITES AND TRANSSEXUALS
SPEAK OUT

L: Isn't there a contradiction in your looking to find work which is not spectacle or prostitution? To find a job, what you have to do is hide the very fact of your transsexualism. You have to pretend, you have to pass as a woman and fool them. I think that it ends up being the same. They are not accepting you as a transsexual, they are accepting you as a person who is hiding his situation and appearing as just another woman, when it should be to the contrary.

O: But I think that society should accept us in the workplace.

B: From my point of view, I see that society, this society, finds it very difficult to accept you. I see it as being so difficult, that I myself would be willing to start a protest movement, if only to prove how much society marginalizes us.

S: I think that even if we work on just this type of protest movement to see if the city would accept someone in a job as a transvestite or transsexual, and not just another woman, it doesn't change the fact that, even if accepted as a third sex or transsexual, we can work at that level. We have completed a report and interviewed a lot of people on this issue, and the conclusion was that transvestites or transsexuals are marginalized much less than one thinks. Instead, it seems, at least to me, that things haven't progressed up till now because the transsexual has marginalized himself voluntarily before even trying. Let's say, well, that I know how to use a typewriter, I speak a little French, I would like to work—I think that as a transsexual, I can do it. Discrimination is there, too, for the young women who work in a bank where the men are older than 50 and they'd prefer a woman of 35 or 40 to a young woman in blue jeans. It all depends on the company. The problem is not so much whether one can or can't work, but whether the company is predisposed to accept you. In a firm with older men, the problem would exist as much for a young woman who has just graduated from Secretary School as for a transvestite. On the other hand, in a company with younger people and a more contemporary outlook, this problem would not exist. . . .

But it's not so much society's problem as that of the transvestite or transsexual and his interest in integrating himself. It's not as simple as saying—look, society does not accept us, therefore we cannot integrate ourselves—because there are schools and places where you can be trained for whatever profession you want, even though maybe only two schools out of the 20 or 30 will admit you. If there is the desire, I don't know why you can't do it. But if there is no aptitude in that direction, then it's easy to say "society does not accept us." I think that the professional training of transvestites today can be the same as for young people. In the same way that a young woman who is unattractive will not be hired as a stewardess or model, so it is with transvestites.

L: I don't think that it's so easy for a transsexual to find work. It's the exceptions that come to mind, because they don't paint themselves up and they behave normally. Just like in our everyday life as homosexuals, there are problems. As an example, a homosexual is not permitted to come to work in drag, even if they know he is a homosexual. They only permit him to be there if he conducts himself according to the rules. For transsexuals, even more problems exist. For that reason, I do not think that it is because the transsexual has not tried, but rather because there are many obstacles which have to be overcome. Even if there are exceptions. Besides, I see something else. A firm can accept a transvestite as long as he behaves along the lines of the desired image, or in other words, like a woman, as the image of a very friendly woman, attentive, delicate, and, of course, he must have the necessary skills. Isn't that right? What they will not tolerate is a transvestite that comes from a working-class family, had little schooling due to his background, and presents himself as a no-frills transvestite. . . .

With all the problems associated with being a transvestite, one that wants to be known as such at work will not enter the workplace. He will enter only when his condition is disguised, and when he can behave like a woman-object.

F: What about the majority of transvestites?

L: Well, I think that the problem of transvestites is what Samantha has said: The majority of transvestites do not have the skills necessary to work, for example, at an administrative position, not because they are stupid, but because of their social origin. The problem is global, it is social. When young people, homosexuals, and old people are marginalized, and society doesn't offer the necessary job training, the transvestite is also affected. At the same time, he has the additional problem of being oppressed as a transvestite.

L: Exactly. Well, we're speaking about finding work or a company's accepting you. But I also think that it is important that your coworkers accept you. We can never be sure how they will react toward you. If I know how to perform a specific job and the company has accepted me, but later my coworkers are hostile toward me, I think I would not be able to continue with the job.

S: I think I have a reference point that is useful. I have seen the problems of immigrant workers from other countries or of other races, such as a people of color, or members of a religious minority —and the issues are similar. The truth is, if I am Jewish and I have come from Germany and I am a transsexual, then I am an alien in reference to the country in which I now live, I belong to a different race—and I have a little of everything going against me. And for that I shoot myself, right? Then they say to me: The problem is that you are an alien. The issue of denying work to someone from Spain is more important than the issue of integrating you as a transvestite into society. It seems to me that there are different ways of regarding the problem. There are current social problems vis-à-vis professional training that affect everyone. There is the problem of minorities being accepted. There is the marginalization at all levels —for adolescents and for seniors. Still, I know that in other countries there are transsexuals who have had access to whatever careers they have desired and who have been able to work with no further obstacles.

B: Well, I think that if you do not come across as a boy and you get a job meant for a girl, and you act the role with naturalness and confidence, they will accept you as a normal girl. But if you say that you are a transsexual, the ground quickly gives out and they will not accept you. . . .

S: But it's a reciprocal thing, the rejection. It seems to me that the issue is not only demanding that society understand the homosexual, but also the transsexual understanding the reason why society does not understand transsexuals. It is reciprocal. If I go to an office, I go understanding that I am not going to enter the office, saying, "O.K., girls! I'm a transsexual." . . . No, because no doubt there is going to be some 50-year-old lady who is not prepared to understand what this means. Here I have the responsibility of understanding that I can cause a heart attack for that woman. . . . But then, I want to say, and it's very easy to do so, that society does not understand me and marginalizes me. . . . No, it is not that, we have to understand society and have respect for the ignorance or lack of understanding that the people we come in contact with may have. There are some people for whom this is not an issue, because they are informed. But because others are not, I have the responsibility of being respectful toward them so they will not be spooked.

L: Regarding this, there is also the obvious fact that society does not do anything to try to accept or understand transsexuals, except in isolated instances. So the problem is one of education. What society and the government are not doing is educating people into knowing that we all have the opportunity to change our sex if we so desire, to have sexual relations with whomever we want, etc. Instead, the opposite happens, creating more oppression for all those who deviate from the norm.

AIDS

As early as 1981, when AIDS first came to public attention as a mysterious new disease, it has been an issue of vital concern for the gay community. Gay men, at least in the United States and Western Europe, were seen initially as the chief carriers of the disease, then called GRID, Gay-Related Immune Deficiency. This stigmatization of the virus as being gay-related was one reason governments were slow to respond to its growing magnitude, or chose even to deny its existence, blaming it on "foreign" intrusions. Ignorance and irrational fears then helped to create an environment in which gay men were ostracized, blamed for their illness (the most prevalent view being that AIDS was a punishment from God for sinful behavior), and even physically attacked on suspicion of carrying the virus. In Brazil, in 1988, several gay men were found murdered, with notes attached to their bodies with such phrases as "Now I can no longer spread AIDS." In Cuba, the government instituted quarantine procedures for those infected with HIV, while in Warsaw, the city's only hospice for AIDS-infected persons was evicted from a neighborhood amid threats of being put to the torch. At the same time, gay groups throughout the world, with the support of concerned others, have begun and are continuing to wage campaigns to improve the situation of those infected and disseminate prevention information.

The three articles that follow offer different accounts about AIDS and its consequences for gays. In the first, a gay youth from Mexico tells of his experience after being diagnosed with the disease. Incompetence and insensitivity by medical personnel deny him the understanding and the support he needs to make important decisions as to treatment. At the same time, his situation as a gay man in a homophobic society makes his struggle even more difficult. In the second selection we learn how the Soviet press initially denied the seriousness of the disease in the USSR, warning instead of the danger of contact with foreigners. HIV-infected persons have met there with widespread discrimination, ranging from loss of employment to verbal and physical harassment. Lack of sufficient supplies of disposable needles and condoms has further hampered AIDS prevention efforts. In the third article, activist Herbert Daniel of Brazil shares with us his understanding of AIDS from a political perspective. Having been forced to confront his own mortality due to AIDS, the author refuses to succumb to being a "victim" and chooses life and hope above all.

MEXICO

"From The Yucatán to Being Alive"
by J. as told to Walt Senterfitt, from *Being Alive*
(September 1990).

[Note: A few months ago, Fred Clark met J. and was astounded at the story of his treatment by health care providers in a major Mexican city. "Why don't you do an article for the newsletter?" Fred asked. "I think a lot of people would be interested." Though these events took place in Mexico in 1989, the ignorance and lack of support from the health care system are typical in the lives of thousands of PWAs around the world in 1990, even in many communities in the United States. We share our story in solidarity with the struggle for access to decent care and support for ALL PWAs, and in memory of Fred, who so frequently reached out, almost casually, to give empathy, recognition, and support to fellow fighters.]

I lived all my life in Mérida, capital of the Yucatán state in south-eastern Mexico. It's a large but laid-back city, near the Gulf of Mexico and major Mayan ruins.

Being gay there, though, is pretty difficult, despite the presence of a major university, several other colleges, and a steady stream of tourists. I was not part of a gay community. There IS no public, organized gay community there. Underground, informal communities revolve around the one bar and private friendship networks, especially among men old enough and well off enough to have their own homes or apartments. Like nearly all younger men who aren't married, I lived at home. The traditional family and the Catholic Church are very important. The culture of machismo is strong. Being "out" as a gay man is almost impossible. My awareness of

SIDA or AIDS was very vague, based only on word-of-mouth rumors. I did not see any pamphlets, posters, or flyers about AIDS and HIV until Walt sent me some from the United States in early 1989. There was no mention of HIV transmission or safe sex on radio or television. Two friends who regularly read newspapers told me that there were only occasional news articles, reporting numbers of cases, and often with incomplete and inaccurate information. Mostly, I heard only rumors told with nervous laughter, like "Be careful of the tourists because those gringos all have SIDA."

In retrospect, my first hint of my own diagnosis came in August 1988, but I didn't know it at the time. My mother was having surgery and my brothers and sisters and I went to the hospital to donate blood. Three or four days later, a public health nurse came to my house and asked me to come talk to the doctor at the Preventive Medicine Clinic at the IMSS [the Mexican Social Security Institute, which is a public agency providing HMO-type medical services to those people who are regularly employed and choose to have payroll deductions]. The doctor asked me a number of questions without telling me why, such as "Have you been out of the country lately? Do you use drugs? Are you gay? Do you have sex frequently? Do you know your sex partners?" I basically answered them all negatively. He told me then, "We're not going to use your blood, because there's something wrong. I want to take some more and send it to Mexico City for analysis. When the results come back, I'll call you again." After asking me if I had any current illness or physical problems (I did not, at the time), he sent me away. I never heard from him again.

In December and January 1988–89, I came down with what turned out to be a bad case of herpes zoster. The IMSS doctor told me the name of it, said there was no cure, gave me Tylenol, and sent me home. As the pain got worse and worse, I went to a private dermatologist who was upset at my previous treatment. She agreed there was no cure, but gave me more effective pain relievers and lotions to help the lesions. Still no word of any connection to HIV.

In May 1989, the owner of the restaurant where I worked appeared with a public health nurse and said everyone who worked in a hotel or restaurant is required to take a blood test for hepatitis and SIDA. The Chamber of Commerce had insisted on it, and the health authorities were complying. [Note: This compulsory screening of food service workers and in fact any worker in the tourism industry is apparently a national policy, which Mexican AIDS activists are trying to eliminate, thus far unsuccessfully.] Three days later, my boss called me and told me she was taking me to the IMSS doctor. She didn't say anything of what this was about, but she was very nervous. We engaged in strained, unreal conversations during the drive and wait, which was unusual, as we were fairly close friends. The first doctor I saw asked my boss, "Did you tell him?" "No, you're the doctor." The doctor then said, "Well, you have AIDS. To be absolutely sure, we're going to take another blood test." He sent me down to the Preventive Medicine division, where a doctor asked me a bunch of similar questions as a year earlier.

Then he told me point blank, "You have AIDS. You are going to live only two years or less. There is no cure. We don't have anything for you." Period. He asked me again if I knew people I had had sex with; he wanted their names. He also told me that I was infected at the time I tried to give blood to my mother, and he didn't know why I was not told then. He told me to come back in two or three days for the results of the repeat blood test. (I'm not being careless when I quote everyone I dealt with as referring only to SIDA or AIDS. No one, no doctor or nurse or anyone else, ever referred to HIV, or explained any difference between being HIV positive and having full-blown AIDS. Just boom boom boom: "You have a positive blood test, you have AIDS, you're going to die soon.")

When I returned, the doctor was out. I spoke to the nurse, who seemed a little afraid of talking to me. By this time I had recovered enough to ask a few questions, mostly out of my extreme worry about infecting my family and others. No one had given me any information about how the disease is transmitted and what precautions I should take. I asked about going to the toilet, washing my clothes (which I usually did together with the laundry for the whole family), and continuing to play sports, as I was a member of a university track and field team. The nurse said I should wash my clothes separately from my family's, with a lot of bleach. She said I should also wipe the toilet carefully with bleach after each use. And I should not have any further contact with the athletic team because my sweat might infect other members. There was never any follow-up contact from this doctor's office either.

This was June 8, 1989. I was stunned and frightened. I quit my job. I quit the track team. I washed my clothes separately from the rest of the family's, and had to make up stories in answer to my mother's questions. I was careful not to touch the toilet. I continued to exercise, on my own, but carefully wiped up any sweat that spilled on the floor of my home. Once my neighbors saw me wash all the floors and then wash again very carefully a little while later after I had exercised. "What are you doing? You just washed that floor! Flies come in all the time so what's the big deal? Your sweat is sweet, anyway!" I laughed it off. There was no one I could talk to.

Later last summer, on my first visit to the United States, I went to a gay community health center in Boston for exams and tests. I found that I did not yet have AIDS, but did have some ARC symptoms and a T-cell count of 116. I also began to find out from the doctors there and from Walt that there are medications and many other things that I can do to fight this virus. I decided to move to L.A. I'm in an AZT/ddI study at UCLA. Most important, I have access to full information here in English and Spanish and to a whole support system and community. I'm a member of the Being Alive Tuesday night Spanish-speaking support group.

Deciding to leave my country was difficult. Should I stay in my hometown, with my family I love and who loves me, but where there is no help for HIV disease and much ignorance, passively waiting for a miracle? Or should I stay in a new city and country where there are people who can help me fight, with medications, and with all kinds of other support? I decided I wanted to stay where I can actively try to find the miracle, with help, and can also

be who I am, openly, without having to lead one life in the daytime
and another at night.

I feel a great concern for others like me who are still in Mérida
and similar Mexican cities. In terms of education and prevention,
things may be getting a little better. I saw and heard TV and radio
ads for the first time when I was home for a visit in September
1989. Conasida, the national government's AIDS agency, was spon-
soring a series of ads with educational songs and jingles by different
artists.

In terms of treatment and support, I'm afraid there has not been
much if any change. The health care system is poorly financed and
grossly understaffed; there isn't money for AZT, ddl, or Pentamidine
unless you're rich or have access to rare research settings. There are
some support services in the largest cities like Mexico, Guadalajara,
and Tijuana, but little or nothing elsewhere. Many of us here would
dearly love to help organize some services in other cities, but can't
—another rotten consequence of the anti-PWA and antigay border
and immigration policies of the U.S. government and the antigay
and anti-PWA sensitivities of most Mexican authorities.

SOVIET UNION

From "We Have No Sex: Soviet Gays and AIDS in the Era of *Glasnost*" by Masha Gessen, from *OUT/LOOK* (Summer 1990).

PATIENT N. AND THE SOVIET AIDS CRISIS

In the winter of 1982 a thirty-one-year-old man was rushed to the clinic at the Central National Research Institute of Epidemiology directly from the international airport in Sheremetevo, near Moscow. The man's symptoms—fever, seizures, and diarrhea—were attributed to mononucleosis, an abnormal increase in the number of mononuclear white blood cells. The man was treated at the clinic until his fever abated. "Patient N.," as he was later came to be known, was then transferred briefly to another hospital before returning to the provincial town where he lived.

In the summer of 1985 the Soviet press mentioned AIDS for the first time, in warnings against contact with foreigners who were arriving for the Moscow Youth and Student Festival. On October 30 of that year *Literaturnaya Gazeta* published an extensive article titled "Panic in the West; or The Secrets Behind the AIDS Scandal," by V. Zapevalov. At that late date the article defined people at risk for AIDS as Haitian immigrants, homosexuals, drug addicts, and vagrants, and advanced the hypothesis that AIDS was a result of CIA and Pentagon biological-warfare experiments gone haywire.

At the end of November, Valentin Petrovskiy, the president of the Soviet Academy of Medical Sciences and the director of the

Central National Research Institute of Epidemiology, held a press conference to announce that no cases of AIDS had been reported in the USSR.[1]

On December 7 an interview with V. M. Zhdanov, the director of the National Research Institute of Virology, appeared in the weekly *Sovetskaya Kul'tura*. Zhdanov acknowledged that there were people with AIDS in the Soviet Union but claimed that they were fewer than a handful.[2]

In a December 12 *Washington Post* article Moscow correspondent Gary Lee quoted several Western businessmen who had imported HIV testing equipment to the Soviet Union. These businessmen were confident that cases of AIDS inside Soviet borders numbered at least in the hundreds. Lee quoted Moscow gay men confirming this information.[3]

On December 11 *Literaturnaya Gazeta* printed an article titled "AIDS: The Panic Continues." Dr. S. Dorzdov, the director of the National Research Institute of Poliomyelitis and Viral Encephalitis, who was interviewed for the piece, no longer linked AIDS to chemical warfare but instead traced the syndrome's origins to "remote areas of Central Africa."

In 1986 the Ministry of Public Health unveiled so-called anonymous diagnostic sites and urged all people at risk for HIV infection to be tested immediately. Public health officials assured citizens that all test results would be kept confidential. People familiar with the Soviet health care system, however, assumed that the guarantee of confidentiality would apply only to those who test negative. They reasoned that when a person tested positive, the venereal disease surveillance system would immediately kick in, as it does with syphilis: The person's place of employment would be notified, his or her passport for travel within the country would be stamped "infected," and public health officials would set off in search of his or her sexual partners.

By March 1987 the country had established forty-five "anonymous diagnostic sites." Plans called for sixty operational sites by the end of the year, and three hundred in another year. None of the clients of the forty-five laboratories had tested positive yet. Also in 1987 the Ministry of Internal Security decided to "take necessary prophylactic measures to prevent the occurrence of AIDS in places of incarceration." These measures took the form of mandatory testing of all prisoners, including those awaiting trial as well as all persons temporarily detained for vagrancy and loitering.[4]

On March 4, 1987, a young provincial proctologist on a business trip in Moscow stumbled into a lecture for dermatologists. Vadim Pokrovskiy (Valentin's son), a senior research scientist at an HIV-testing laboratory in Moscow, was teaching dermatologists to recognize the symptoms of AIDS. The lecture reminded the proctologist of a patient whose strange set of symptoms she had been unable to diagnose. Back in her hometown the next day, the young doctor drew a blood sample from her mysterious patient and forwarded it to the HIV lab at the Institute of Epidemiology. The positive results came back late that night. The following morning the proctologist delivered her patient to the Institute clinic, where the department head—a specialist in "rare infectious diseases of tropical origin"—immediately recognized Patient N.

The first order of business was to locate Patient N.'s sexual partners. Within hours the younger Pokrovskiy himself arrived in N.'s hometown, accompanied by a team of medical technicians armed with HIV testing equipment. Over the next few days they located N.'s former partners and drew their blood "on location"— at their homes, or at their places of work when necessary. Four people tested positive and were immediately shipped to the clinic in Moscow, where they, like N., would remain indefinitely.

On March 16, speaking at an AIDS conference in Munich, Vadim Pokrovskiy informed conference attendees that the first Soviet person with AIDS had been identified just twelve days earlier. Two months later *Ogonyok* printed an essay titled "When Men Cry." This is how it began:

> I have seen him—our first, the one who brought us that frightening disease. Emaciated, with shoulder blades that stick

out, with red splotches on his face, he looks more like an infantile adolescent than a thirty-six-year-old man. He willingly showed himself to the many doctors, from this clinic and others, who had come to look—and in his very readiness to expose himself there was also something unnatural.... But the most incredible thing was, he seemed not to comprehend what he had wrought, what kind of grief he had caused, what kind of a loss to this society he was responsible for.[5]

Quest for Condoms

At the end of 1987 a gay French film director visited Leningrad. The day after he left the country, tells a Leningrad gay man, the approximately twenty men who had had sexual or social contact with the director were apprehended by the police. Samples of their blood were taken at the police precincts, where the men were held until the HIV test results arrived.

By the end of 1987 twenty-six people infected with HIV had been identified by the Soviet Union. None of them had been clients of the "anonymous diagnostic sites."[6]

During the first four months of 1988, according to *Ogonyok,* authorities identified thirty HIV-infected individuals, bringing the total to fifty-six.[7]

Early in 1988 a husband and wife tested positive for HIV. The news spread through their small town within days. The woman was forced to leave her job. The couple could not venture outdoors without being verbally and physically harassed. Residents mounted a campaign to pressure town authorities to quarantine the couple. Finally, local doctors decided to hospitalize the two and place them in an isolated unit for people with highly infectious disease. The couple spent the next several weeks in a small room with no windows but a glass door, through which journalists continuously snapped photographs. Upon learning about the couple, Moscow authorities had them transferred to the clinic at the Institute of

Epidemiology. Months later they returned to their hometown but were unable to find work there.

Around the same time *Ogonyok* received a letter to the editor that read as follows:

> I have tested positive for AIDS. I am twenty-six years old, and at this point perfectly healthy. I try not to think about what is going to happen to me. But sometimes I get very scared.
>
> I told my wife right away.... We went to the anonymous testing site. Fortunately, she tested negative. So now how do we live? . . .
>
> We decided to use condoms. But they did not have any at the drugstore. It's been a month now, and I still cannot find condoms in any drugstores in Riga [the capital of Latvia].
>
> My wife and I are young and in love. Once during the past month we simply could not restrain ourselves. I shook all night after that: What if I infected her?
>
> God, can it really be an impossible challenge for our great country to manufacture enough condoms? Or does somebody up there need people to keep infecting each other?

In July 1988 *Ogonyok* published a groundbreaking article by journalist Alla Alova titled "Life in the Age of AIDS: Are We Prepared?" A first for Soviet journalism in many respects, the article contained the stories of the quarantined married couple and the Riga letter-writer, along with interviews with Soviet health care officials and a sexologist. The article stated, as simple truths, some revolutionary ideas for Soviet society: that the notion that people should abstain from sex is absurd; that gay men constitute a sizable group (estimated by the sexologist at between 2 and 5 percent of the population) and that occasional same-sex sexual contact among adolescents is widespread; that sexual orientation is usually unchangeable; that heterosexuals are at risk for AIDS; and that the decadent Westerners, with their sexual permissiveness, are better able than their "morally superior" Soviet counterparts to change their behavior in order to avoid contacting HIV.

The article also contained some sobering statistics. Alova discovered that government experts had estimated the need for condoms in 1988 at 600 million—which would give every sexually active Soviet man (figuring that half of the population is male, and a third of the males are sexually active) approximately fifteen condoms a year. The agency responsible for manufacturing condoms, however, rejected the estimate and lowered the target production of condoms to 220 million—or about five per man. Explaining the agency's decision not to make up the difference by importing foreign-made rubbers, the director of the Drugstore Department of the Ministry of Public Health stated, "The main thing is not to have casual contacts. Then condoms wouldn't be necessary."

Alova also reported that disposable syringes were practically unheard of in Soviet medicine. And while all health care providers were required to sterilize reusable syringes in accordance with guidelines adopted during the 1978 outbreak of hepatitis B, many nurses did not have the education necessary to comprehend the instructions. As a result, while many conscientiously sterilized needles, they often did not bother with the syringes themselves. Others ignored the guidelines altogether. The country's total production of disposable syringes stood at 7 million, while the doses of injectable medication manufactured in the Soviet Union numbered 6 billion. While official plans called for 3 billion disposable syringes by 1991, there was no indication that the country's production capability would exceed one quarter of a billion. No plans to import disposable syringes existed. As for other disposable medical equipment—dialyzers, IV bags, and blood-storage containers, for example—the country had no capability for manufacturing these, and no new measures in this area were planned. Even the elder Pokrovskiy, when questioned by Alova, admitted that all was not well on the AIDS front and that the government-mandated testing of donated blood was performed strictly at the discretion of physicians.

A full year passed before Alova tackled the subject of AIDS again.

But in June 1989 she was no longer playing the inquisitive but removed journalist: She was mad as hell, and she vowed "not to write another article about why there is no domestic equipment for the manufacturing of disposable syringes. I will not go to ministry spokesperson after ministry spokesperson, each of whom will rightly blame the other, forcing me to wax melancholic and draw some profound conclusion about the ill health of the health care system. No, I have firmly decided to use my journalistic privileges to find a solution."[8]

With that, Alova became the first AIDS activist, and *Ogonyok* the first Soviet AIDS organization. For the conclusion of her article she proposed a radical solution: the Soviet Union's first private charity, a hard-currency fund that would be used by *Ogonyok* to purchase and distribute foreign-made disposable medical equipment and condoms.

Three weeks later Alova announced that "Account AntiSPID" (SPID is the Russian acronym for AIDS) had been opened at the International Bank of the USSR. The first contributors were Soviet writers, artists, and actors who had been paid in foreign currency. They were followed by Soviet émigrés in the West as well as some Western philanthropists.[9]

Two weeks later Alova declared that "AntiSPID has begun its work," with a contribution of 60,000 disposable syringes by a consortium of Japanese corporations. The syringes were immediately delivered to a children's hospital in Moscow.

The AIDS activist, whose new byline reads "Alla Alova, AntiSPID Coordinator," has continued to print updates on the work of the foundation at least monthly. In six months the foundation's contributions of disposable syringes totaled over a million—about ten times the country's production of disposable syringes that year. All the contributions—the bulk of which hailed from Western Europe —were forwarded to regional children's hospitals. The foundation's original commitment to soliciting and distributing condoms, however, seems to have dissolved along the way: The single contribution of a large number of condoms, a shipment of 50,000 from Bulgaria, was sold to three Moscow drugstores, and the money was used to buy more syringes for children.[10]

By early August 1989 eleven people, including four children, had been diagnosed with AIDS. Two of them had died. Thirty-two million people who had come to "anonymous diagnostic sites," or to whom an infected person had been traced, had been tested for HIV. Twenty million potential blood donors were screened as well. Two hundred eighty-nine individuals, including 115 children, had tested positive. Eight of them were identified through the screening of blood donors.[11]

As of January 15, 1990, the World Health Organization had learned of twenty-three cases of AIDS in the Soviet Union—signifying a threefold increase in six months. While this number is much lower than the numbers of cases in other countries affected by the epidemic, Soviet epidemiologists' projections far exceed any other government's worst-case estimate. By the year 2000, according to Alova, Soviet scientists expect to have logged 200,000 cases of AIDS and 15 million cases of HIV infections.[12]

The Backlash

While gay men now figure less prominently in media coverage of AIDS than they did three years ago, as long as AIDS stays in the news—as it will for many years—the Soviet public will not forget about the existence of homosexuals. Whatever the eventual outcome of the current political changes in the USSR, this generation of Soviets will probably be unable to pretend again that theirs is a sexless society.

Russian-speaking lesbians and gay men in the West have found the surfacing of the subject of homosexuality in Soviet society fascinating and exciting—in much the same way that Western Jews have taken pleasure in reading about Jews in the Soviet Union. But gays behind what used to be the Iron Curtain do not have the luxury of approaching the changes in their society and their lives as a curious phenomenon. Nor can they ignore the right-wing backlash that is gaining strength in the Soviet Union.

While U.S. public officials have hailed the liberation of some Soviet media outlets, and while the U.S. media have quoted generously from such sterling examples of *glasnost* as *Ogonyok* and *Argumenty i Fakty,* they have all but ignored the rise of right-wing media. With greater circulation, size, and resources than the relatively progressive press, these publications function as mouthpieces for the reactionary group *Pamyat* (Memory).

The stated objective of *Pamyat* and other Russian nationalist organizations is to return Russia to the Russians, a strong, beautiful, and most importantly, pure people. This means not only the end of Communist rule but also an end to all foreign influence on the Russian culture—an end to Satan worship, rock music, horror films, drug addicts, Jews, homosexuals, and all other sorts of decadents. And in a country where political reform has failed to improve the lot of the millions of people who have spent their entire lives in poverty, a group that places the blame on groups that are already perceived as privileged gains more sympathizers every day.

In keeping with the spirit of *glasnost,* the new right-wingers are refusing to temper their angers or to cushion their hatred in socially acceptable terms. Spurred by *perestroika,* they join reformers in exposing the old liars, who told them that everyone is equally equal, and the new liars, who tell them that everyone is equally free. And with all the pain and rage that lay dormant for seven decades, they point the finger at Jews, gays, and other perennial objects of Russian fury, the victims of all of Russia's bloody revolutions—including this revolution to openness.

EPILOGUE

The two years since this article was written saw some progress in the fight against AIDS in Russia, but much of the work that was done was too little too late. At the beginning of 1992, the "official" number of cases of AIDS on the territory of the Soviet Union was estimated at just under 700, most of them in Russia. But by this time officials including Vadim Pokrovskiy agreed that the real number of cases of AIDS was ten times the official estimate or more. The discovjery of several pockets of infection confirm this theory: For example, in 1991 it came to light that seventy-five children and fourteen of their mothers had been infected through unsterilized equipment in a children's hospital in Elista, the capital of the Kalmyk autonomous republic in Russia. "This tragedy can be repeated —and has been repeated—in other cities," writes Aza Rachmanova, chief epidemiologist of St. Petersburg and director of the city's AIDS clinic.

Rachmanova's clinic, a ward of St. Petersburg's infectious diseases hospital, is one of two places that provide the bulk of AIDS care in Russia. The other is a Moscow clinic run by Pokrovskiy. Both facilities suffer from chronic shortages of medication and basic supplies. Patients in the Moscow clinic complain of poor conditions, including bad food, a lack of medication (as basic as aspirin) and treatment on the part of the staff. In September 1991 a gay patient in the clinic, 21-year-old Gennady Roshupkin, declared a hunger strike to protest the conditions in the clinic. He called off the strike following negotiations with Pokrovskiy, who made several concessions, including a commitment to lobby for the repeal of Article 1231.

Pokrovskiy has kept his word, but he has also declared what is essentially a quarantine regime at the clinic, whereby patients, many of whom come to the clinic voluntarily, cannot leave without a doctor's permission.

In 1986 the Soviet of Ministers amended an existing law to criminalize sexual activity on the part of HIV-positive people, making it punishable by up to three years in prison, which rises to eight years if infection occurs. The first known case to go to trial under this law was still pending at the beginning of 1992. It involved a gay man who was accused of infecting his one-time lover, who had said that he didn't want to press charges. The existence of the law and Article 121 is probably one of the major reasons for the undercount —and undertreatment—of AIDS cases.

Testing sites are still open around the country, but supplies are hard to come by, and many sites operate sporadically, while others use unreliable testing technology without the confirmatory tests that are customary in the United States. The single organization that is probably in the best position to relieve some of the problems of AIDS diagnosis and treatment by supplying equipment and medication—Foundation AntiSPID Ogonyok—seems, meanwhile, to have been stricken with paralysis. The group's fund-raising efforts have raised enough money for a full-time staff of eleven and a number of commercial investment ventures, but in 1991 the foundation halted its only steady program: a 100-rouble monthly stipend provided to families of children with AIDS. None of the group's programs have benefitted adults with HIV or AIDS. And in an April 1991 conversation Alova told me that the foundation was literally sitting on $600,000 in hard currency because the board was deadlocked concerning potential uses of the money.

Small-scale efforts by activists have appeared here as they have in the arena of gay and lesbian liberation. At least two journals devoted entirely to AIDS—SPIDInfo, published by Pokrovskiy's organization, and SPID, Sex, Zdorovye (AIDS, Sex, Health), published by Rachmanova's group—are popular and available widely in the cities. Russian and American activists living in both Moscow and St. Petersburg are conducting AIDS education programs in the gay community. The World Health Organization donated over 40,000 condoms to one such group. But while such efforts inspire hope, only a large-scale effort that enjoys the support of both the Russian government and Western money can inspire faith in the country's ability to forestall a pandemic.

Masha Gessen
February 1992

Notes

1. Gary Lee, "Soviets Try to Quiet AIDS Fears," *The Washington Post* (December 12, 1985).

2. Knight-Ridder report, *The Washington Post* (December 8, 1985).

3. Gary Lee, "Gay Is 'Light Blue' at a Moscow Bar," *The Washington Post* (December 12, 1985).

4. V. Nikolayev in *Argumenty i Fakty*, No. 41 (October 14, 1989).

5. Galina Kulikovskaya, "No Backward Moves Allowed," *Ogonyok*, No. 19, (May 1987).

6. Alla Alova, "Life in the Age of AIDS: Are We Prepared?" *Ogonyok*, No. 28 (June 1988).

7. Ibid.

8. Alla Alova, "Just Put It Out of Our Minds?" *Ogonyok*, No. 26 (June 1989).

9. Alla Alova, "A Charitable Hard-Currency Account 'AntiSPID' Is Number 70000015 at the International Bank of the USSR," *Ogonyok*, No. 29 (July 1989).

10. Alla Alova, "A Chronicle of Foundation AntiSPID," *Ogonyok*, Nos. 31, 34, 40, 49 (July, August, September, and December 1989) and 2 (January 1990).

11. A. Kondrusyev, deputy minister of public health, in *Argumenty i Fakty*, No. 32 (August 12, 1989).

12. Alova, "Just Put It Out of Our Minds?" op. cit.

BRAZIL

"Above All, Life" by Herbert Daniel, translated by Elizabeth Station, from *Vida Antes Da Morte* = *Life Before Death* (1989).

> I burst
> at times just
> because I am alive. . . .
> —Gilberto Gil
> *(Brazilian composer and singer)*

I know that I have AIDS. I know what this means for me. I try not to have any illusions about it. Only I don't know what other people mean when they say that I have "AIDS." Most of the time they mean, "you are going to die" (but who isn't?). Other times, the more prejudiced say, "you are already dead" (my daily experience refutes that). Sometimes they sum it up by saying, "you've lost your resistance" (Not yet! Not yet . . . I indignantly resist). In the end, what AIDS is this? What's with AIDS?

1.

The concept of AIDS was constructed, in the last decade, in a worldwide political and ideological battle. The source of the problem lays in the medical definition of what is called, incorrectly, the AIDS epidemic. In fact, the epidemic was caused by several retroviruses called HIV (Human Immunodeficiency Virus), which were transmitted either sexually, through the blood, or vertically (from mother to fetus or baby). Meanwhile, world consciousness adopted the acronym AIDS (or SIDA) as a fact based on and transcending the technical and medical definition. Many different meanings nebulously crisscrossed in the dance of words that sought to define the new disease—or if not really new, at least new to contemporary minds and, certainly, a novelty as a worldwide epidemic.

From an exclusively medical standpoint, the definition of AIDS was pure fiction. The acronym very primitively referred to a set of signs and symptoms (that is, a syndrome, in medical terminology) which resulted from a deficiency in the body's immune system. This immunodeficiency was denominated "acquired" in order to distinguish it from similar congenital situations. However, "acquired" immunodeficiencies were also seen in radiation victims, in patients who had undergone certain types of chemotherapy (in preparation for transplants, for example, to avoid rejection of the transplanted organ), in certain leukemia cases, etc. The terms which composed the acronym were enormously uncertain. Explanations about the disease were still few and incomplete.

Even this layperson's analysis of the acronym shows that it is obviously the systematization of some early generic observations about the disease. If rigorously scrutinized, the acronym certainly reveals how little was known about the disease at that time. Lack of knowledge is less than it was ten years ago, but it still exists today. Meanwhile, the acronym stuck. The problem is to define that to which it refers, considering the complex context of individual or collective infection by HIV.

The expression "acquired immunodeficiency syndrome" is as pompous as it is vague. Solemn words that try to say too much say nothing, in the end. Surely we have before us a formidable display of medical rhetoric. We all know how this rhetoric rushes to cover up, with rebounding erudite words, the gaping hole of its own ignorance. Where doubt and uncertainty throb, arrogant jargon soothes the unrest with an expression that tries to stand for truth, or a personal embodiment of truth. A word, fragile veil of uncertainty, becomes a truth in itself, an ether filling the emptiness that totalitarian knowledge so abhors.

Because it did not refer to anything in particular, the word "AIDS" began to slide over available significants, thereby producing a signifier for social fissures which previously had no exact expression. AIDS became, in fact, the syndrome of our days (in Portuguese, by the way, *dias*—days—is an anagram of AIDS—an illuminating coincidence).

It is curious to remember that at the time of its discovery, the disease was called GRID—Gay-Related Immunodeficiency. It is remarkable that medical jargon should have produced the expressions "gay plague" or "gay cancer," which later would become so widespread. Even more notable is the use of the word "gay" rather than the more erudite term "homosexual," a clear indication of profound changes in the medical view of homosexuality, no doubt as a result of the gay movement's political importance, especially in the United States. A new age is blowing in the wind. Medicine no longer sees homosexuality as an illness but instead subtly begins to consider it the source of illness: No longer a pathology, it has become a pathogenic condition. A change indicative of a ferocious ideological battle, whereby the medicalization of sexuality is part of an ominous strategy.

Medical discourse, with generalizing definitions that take on airs of definitive truths, has drawn upon established taboos to produce the idea that AIDS was either a fatality or a fatal mystery. Yet while much about the disease remains unknown, accumulated knowledge does allow the assertion that at least AIDS is not a mystery. It is a challenge, yes, but there is nothing magical or fantastic about it. In the end, AIDS is an illness like other illnesses. But because medical science knows no more about the disease than the classification of the sexuality of those who have it—understanding nothing of homosexualities—this only results in throwing more wood on the bonfire of prejudice. While still no more than a concept, the contagiousness of AIDS, expressed by the ambiguity of the word "acquired," was conceptually contaminated with the taboos that envelop homosexuality, making the disease a scandal, a terror, and a fascination. And because medical science cannot admit, on ideological principle, the idea of death, an intrinsic incurability was invented for the disease. Medical incompetence became AIDS's own destiny, as if its incurability was of a sacred nature laden with ulterior motives.

At present, all public disclosure about the disease has focused on three aspects: it is contagious, incurable, and fatal. In fact, these three myths engender the most distorted and distorting views of the epidemic. Along with the viruses identified as causal agents of the epidemic, an ideological virus has spread in a more generalized and unrestrained manner.

Without resorting to metaphors, it can be said that our society is sick with AIDS. Sick with panic, disinformation, prejudice, and immobility before the real disease. Effective measures against the HIV epidemic must begin with concrete measures to combat the ideological virus. This means correct information, efficient action, demystification of fear, removal of prejudice, and permanent exercise of solidarity.

For the person who has AIDS or is HIV-positive, living with the consequences of the mythologies produced by the ideological virus is a tragedy. Objectively, mystification kills. As much as or more than cellular immunodeficiency. Some dramatic consequences of mystification include the inability to fight back the disease, failure to get treatment, the increase of "miracle" cures and charlatanism, and violence against people with AIDS and the HIV virus. Two others are the solitude and secrecy with which people with AIDS often feel forced to survive.

At the root of the mystifications about AIDS are a series of half truths based on apparently "objective" facts resulting from "scientific" observations. The "fact" that the disease is contagious, incurable, and fatal has become, thanks to a rigorously inexact simplification, part of the minimum operational definition society uses to deal symbolically with the disease. Deep prejudices directed to already marginalized groups (principally homosexuals) reemerge and are reinstated. Worst of all, the person with AIDS or the HIV virus is declared dead while still alive. Before his or her biological death, he or she suffers civil death, which is the worst form of ostracism that a human being is forced to bear.

2.

Yet there are still other problems with the definition of AIDS, which reveal distinctive types of prejudice. I have observed that the disease's definition was based on its evolution in the United States and Europe. The fundamental "model" was First World. Third World models were the "exceptions to the rule." The "African model" (where transmission is basically heterosexual) serves as a counterpoint rather than a starting point for understanding the global problem of this pandemic. The racism of this ethnocentric view has had a devastating effect.

In Brazil, where studies about the disease are still insufficient, Ministry of Health bureaucrats remain fascinated by these "chic models." All too often we see how hard they try to demonstrate that a "North American pattern" should also fit us. This has two results: (1) to disseminate the idea of an elite disease coming to our privileged classes from the "developed world" (an idea which those who actually work with the disease have proven untrue); (2) to disguise characteristics of the disease that are unique to Brazil, such as the question of transmission through contaminated blood transfusion. (Blood continues to be a scandalous issue in our country—genocide is being committed against hemophiliacs and others who need blood transfusion.)

It becomes evident that in Brazil the disease will reach predominantly poor people. This is because the majority of our population is poor, and any epidemic affects real people in a real country. AIDS is not a foreign disease. The virus is here among us; it is "ours."

And it does not distinguish sexual orientation, gender, race, color, creed, class, or nationality.

The epidemic will develop among us according to our specific cultural characteristics—our sexual culture, our material and symbolic resources for dealing with death and disease, and our prejudices and capacity to exercise solidarity. AIDS inscribes itself upon each culture in a different way. Each culture constructs its own particular kind of AIDS—as well as its own answers to the disease. Today these answers largely depend on civil society's capacity to mobilize itself against AIDS and force the government to assume its responsibilities. The current Brazilian government is still not aware of the epidemic's importance. Actually, it isn't aware of anything. This government is only a death rattle, ridiculous in its mediocrity, of the authoritarian system which it perpetuates. At present there is absolutely nothing that looks like a national program to control and prevent the HIV epidemic. As a result, AIDS in Brazil will have the same dimension as the government's incompetence.

I know I have AIDS. I know what it means for me to have AIDS in this country. I don't have any illusions about it, even though I am a person with privileges. I am also dying because of it. We all will die because of it. I know very well what so many living dead mean. I know that I want to shout with them: We are alive. In the end, what AIDS is this which has diseased this (which?) country?

3.

They foretold my death, naming it with an acronym whose four letters don't spell the word love. They are the letters which spell the word *dias* (days) in Portuguese—days that we live, or that we survive. I don't want those days; I will not accept a predetermined death. AIDS is no more than an illness of our time, like any other, and I cannot agree to their making it a synonym for the final day.

AIDS is no more than a viral infection that caused an epidemic which we will defeat. With all the letters that spell love: solidarity.

The days hurt, the last one kills, cautions an old proverb. Thus I am not a survivor. An AIDS sufferer tends to be referred to as a terminal patient with a short survival period. I'm as terminal as a bus station, full of hopeful arrivals and departures to the most incredible and exciting roads that lead to the living. I don't have a survival period; I have a surplus of life, the only one which I can use to leave the trace of a passion that always moved something immobile in me, rooted in a place which I used to call my breast, but which I know reaches beyond any heart. The body, in the end, is disorganized—and AIDS, poor thing, is just an affliction of the organs. Desires are organic disorders. It won't be AIDS that makes me lose my appetite. AIDS only places me, like an explosion of a corporeal truth, in a state of impermanence. Something I always was lived, but never felt.

Let all my days hurt, all of them up to the last, as they say of a finger striking the strings of a guitar during a dance.

There, where a truth explodes, passion commands. I am certain that most people with AIDS begin to live passionately from the moment they learn they are ill. Many people very naively believe that this passion comes with the explosion of death's truth. As if all that was left for the sick person was the last cigarette before the guillotine falls or before the shot of mercy is fired. Death is not a truth. Death is nothing. The truth which explodes, in this curious discovery of our mortality—a futile and obvious discovery, although the obvious has become obscure in this alienated world—the truth which bursts forth, is the significance of life. Before death.

4.

The World Health Organization created one of the first logos for an AIDS campaign, depicting two romantic, interlocking red hearts with an unfortunate skull and crossbones drawn between them. (I won't try here to discuss the quality of this inspiration.) The artist attempted to summarize the two earliest and best-known clichés about AIDS, associating—as the modern world has come to do—sex with death. Yet, instead of producing an image to describe the new social phenomenon, the HIV-caused epidemic, he created a symbol of prejudice of utmost gravity generated by AIDS: the contagiousness of loving contact, the incurability and fatality of the disease.

This minimal and operational definition of AIDS was the favorite phantom of the 1980s and will probably haunt us for many years to come. The broad social impact of this oversimplification must be countered with efforts directed to AIDS education and information, using the voices of those who are seropositive or present full-blown symptoms. Their vital experience resoundingly contradicts the "minimum definition" and clashes with old prejudices and new forms of discrimination.

This is why I am talking about my illness—in an attempt to demystify a terrible disease that is a threat to the world's public health. It is also my contribution to the effort to disseminate correct information about the disease.

The disease surreptitiously created a mythology so complex that people who have it are seen as special beings, called "aidectics," in Brazil. Consequently, many people have told me that I have accepted or "assumed" my AIDS. I find it funny, this business of "assuming"—an act of will which implies admitting that something exists. What I have done in fact is to assume my place at the door of the world, in order to say: I'm alive; all this talk about my death is an outright lie.

People with AIDS must come forward to destroy the misunderstandings created by a corrosive ideology of condemnation followed by pity which has created a melodrama where a tragedy is unfolding. Undeniably, AIDS is a modern tragedy. It has quickly dismantled the medical and moral assumptions of bourgeois rationality. It reminds us all that pain, suffering, and death—as well as pleasure—

are integral parts of the world and that no pleasure survives far from the shadow of pain.

The world of melodrama, which extinguishes the conflict of tragedy in order to impose a false egalitarianism in the face of death, can only offer counsel, consolation, or consumption: the counsel of a pacification-by-passivity before death; the consolation of forgiveness, only possible if the sinner admits his guilt; the consumption of soothing therapies that render fat profits to laboratories and other charlatans. The dead—above all, those who have suffered civil death—may no longer be productive, but they aren't entirely unprofitable.

5.

For years I lived undercover in Brazil, while fighting against the dictatorship. At the time, I kept my sexuality a secret. They were hard times. Because I fought for freedom, I was persecuted by the police force. And during the fight, I thought that being a guerrilla was incompatible with being homosexual.

Later I learned that one can't fight for half liberties and that there is no freedom without sexual freedom. Many years ago I came to understand that living my sexuality openly meant demanding citizenship for everyone, not just those who are, or are said to be, homosexual.

To this day, even in large cities and in the most liberal circles, homosexuality is lived either in complete or partial secrecy. AIDS has revealed the most tragic aspect of this situation of living in the shadows. For many, the worst thing is not the disease, it is having to reveal that one is gay. Pathetically, the person with AIDS is forced to reveal how he was contaminated. The diagnosis is transformed into a denunciation. So much so that people who don't get AIDS through sexual contact feel compelled to repeatedly and per-

manently "differentiate" themselves, so as not to be confused with
those who have . . . the very same illness they have!

I know many people with AIDS. Homosexual or not, their greatest suffering comes from prejudice. It means not being allowed to
just be sick, but having instead to bear the stigmata of being an
"aidectic." It means feeling fear due to the frequent yet invisible
social pressures (the worst prejudices aren't always necessarily direct
discrimination). It means panic at the thought that their sexual and
emotional lives may be over. It means the constant presence of
those who seem to be just waiting to carry your coffin. It means the
invisible web of oppression created by family members, sometimes
doctors, priests, and even friends.

In the face of all this, the most frequent choice is to go undercover—a way of fleeing in order to die, since death is the only kind
of life that society seems to offer the sick person. The issue is not
finding better conditions for living. Concealment is proof of society's
inability to live with the disease. It is a testimony to its bankruptcy.

Many people live with AIDS secretly in Brazil, from those who
die without knowing they have the disease to those who are killed
by discrimination. Sick people who remain anonymous are not able
to impede the cruel march that pillages our citizenship from us.

To satisfy this spoliation, tinged by the morbidity of a distorted
curiosity, people with AIDS are shown in the shadows, their faces
darkened, principally on TV. This is not a way to preserve the sick
person's privacy—which, by the way, is an essential right. It is
instead a way of depicting a depersonalized destiny. Of fumbling
around in a region where we all live, unknowingly—a darkness that
tests our civil rights.

The person with AIDS has become someone without a name or
a history. We must take him out of the darkness of concealment so
that he can say, in the light of the day: "This is my name, this is my
story." Much more than "assuming" a "state of being" or a "condition," this action will be a collective way for us to write, more
democratically, our history.

6.

Nothing has changed in its impermanence. *Sic transit.* The experience of finitude is one of the many which weighs upon all mortals. Knowing oneself to be finite is not exactly a novelty. Accepting the body's mortality is more difficult. This is a lesson that the illness brings and—it seems to me—no belief in the immortality of the soul can console the clay which has just discovered its destiny of dust. Certainly, the disease does lead us to discover something fragilely different, with a certainty that is anchored in our most intimate depths: Life continues. That is, life continues now. There is no death before death. Despite the fact that they may already be preparing our funeral, despite the condemnations repeated in the official propaganda.

Much remains to be said about this death before death called AIDS, according to the most prejudiced and discriminatory definitions. To speak is to shout long live life. Long live life!

I have spoken unceasingly of life. With unfounded optimism. In the end, my well-founded pessimism says that life is no good and never has been. It is difficult to imagine a day without atomic terror, without class exploitation, without the assassination of forests, rivers, and people, without fear, without guilt, without shame— shamelessly just life. Yet there is no other way to find pleasure; we must not only tolerate life but sustain it. And make life a tingle, a jingle, a song. More metaphors! But life is also a poor metaphor. A metaphor for survival in spite of everything. Still, I have always believed, even when I doubted it, that life is the invention of life, the pure creation of the world of humans: To live is not only to transform the world; it is to make it become more beautiful. We haven't been too fortunate in this venture. But I do think that one day we will succeed—who knows?

One day, one day . . . I mean to say another day. A new one.

People come through and stay a little while. They leave ashes, footsteps, behind. Not always so memorable. It would be better to leave behind only what we would have liked to have done to ourselves.

Yet we are what we have done with ourselves. We are what we are made of, this material of time. Of this time. And many revolutions can mature in this flesh of ours that passes.

My time, my substance, this thing that we have been, myself and I, has not been what I wanted to call life. But it so tempts me that it happens like a precocious pleasure, inevitably. Something contagious, mortal, and very dangerous inside me, called life, throbs like a challenge.

To change, to remodel—one of those verbs or its synonyms—has always stirred inside me, a ravenous thing that has eaten me from within. This was hope. Hope. This that I always had, in the plural: selves, ourselves, agents of the chaos of light.

THE GAY GHETTO

An issue of major concern to many gay movements, especially in Europe and Latin America, has been the ghettoization of homosexuals. Gays, as is argued in the following article, taken from the Catalan magazine *La Pluma,* have been disenfranchised from any positions of power within the society and have become marginalized, not unlike Jews, Gypsies, Blacks, and the Aged. This has led to the appearance of gay ghettos. First, there are the "golden ghettos," usually areas of a city with a high concentration of gay clubs, bars, and saunas, where gays can feel relatively secure and socialize openly. Then there are the "other ghettos," the public parks, lavatories, and movie theaters where men, most likely those who are still secretive or "closeted" about their homosexual feelings, can congregate to "cruise," or meet one another for sex or possible friendship. The two types of ghettos, the author continues, need to be viewed critically. Both are economically exploitative of gays and serve chiefly as safety valves to prevent more meaningful challenges to societal oppression. The task, then, is for gays to make a break with the ghetto and the illusory freedom it offers, and to raise issues of sexuality in their everyday lives—at work, at school, and in the neighborhoods. Only by encouraging all people to reexamine their attitudes and behaviors regarding sexuality and the socially imposed norms of heterosexuality and machismo will marginalization come to an end.

It should be noted that the ghettoization of gays as described in the following article is a phenomenon characteristic of many countries. "Golden ghettos" are found, for example, in communities as diverse as San Francisco, Paris, Madrid, and Mexico City. Parks, movie houses, and public lavatories serving as furtive outlets for men to express their homosexual desires can be found even more universally—from Casablanca to London to Lima to Tel Aviv, Istanbul, Des Moines, Athens, and Taipei. As the repeating pattern of African-American ghettos throughout the United States is testimony to the pernicious effects of white racism, so the ubiquity of our ghettos throughout much of the world is evidence of the damaging consequences of heterosexism found in scores of countries.

SPAIN

"Contradictions and Miseries of the Gay Ghetto" by Dario, from *La Pluma* (February 1980).

To talk about the gay ghetto is to talk about all of the ghettos that exist or have existed throughout history and within this society. And this includes all sectors of society that have suffered the weight of oppression and exploitation and found themselves marginalized from (political) power and thus needing to search within their own ghettos for a place where they can collectively take shelter from the aggression perpetrated by the Establishment.

Included are the labor associations that emerged at the birth of capitalism, religious minorities, racial minorities (Gypsies, Blacks, Puerto Ricans), Jews, beggars, delinquents. Included also are those in asylums, old-age homes, day care and youth centers, institutions for the handicapped, mental hospitals, prisons, bars and cruising areas for homosexuals, lesbians, and transvestites, drug rehabilitation centers, red-light districts, etc.

These are all ghettos that the system, with all its contradictions, promotes as a means of dividing the population and as a safety valve to prevent these groups from using their oppressive situation as a weapon against it. Today our society, more than ever, is like an immense prison with many isolated, tiny compartments—all normalized and disciplined. And the gay ghetto is an example, consisting not only of the bars and clubs (what has come to be called the golden ghetto) but also the pickup places in parks, movie theaters, public lavatories, etc.

THE ILLUSION OF THE GOLDEN GHETTO:
A PLACE OF MARGINALIZATION/
INTEGRATION/EXPLOITATION

Bars, clubs, discotheques, saunas—a mosaic of shiny decor to attract fags, lesbians, transvestites, people from every background in order to create an illusion of perfect harmony. Golden cages where all of our needs as homosexuals seem to resolve themselves in an environment of music, color, and false intimacy. A sense of security in a world filled with insecurity, within our reach. The misery that derives from concealment and the unnerving sensation that this is not exactly what we were searching for, but the only outlet permitted. At least it is not the everyday type of aggression, the emptiness, the search for connecting with another person on the streets where everyone appears to be normal and is a (potential) cop. The embarrassing realization of our inability to fight this situation, the search for escape, the not knowing why to keep fighting for our collective freedom when it is said that our personal freedom is to be found in the bars and clubs, relating to those who find themselves in the same situation that we are. It is the comfortable escape of accepting tolerance toward us and our marginalization.

It is true that the development of our ghetto is the result of our struggles and the acceptance of our existence on the part of Society. It is a recognition by Society that it is impossible to end homosexuality with the weapon of repression. In the golden ghetto we are at least left alone, as homosexuals. We can meet peacefully and when we desire. But the ghetto is essentially a place of reclusion for homosexuals, a point of integration for channeling those who might present a threat to the system. To prevent us from using our situation as a starting point in the struggle against the cause of our oppression. To put to sleep our desire to once and for all put an end to our oppression.

Ghettos, including the homosexual one, have never been a point of rupture with any system of oppression but have served simply as a means of regulation, successfully channeling away all those sectors of society that could question its function and limitations.

The golden ghetto, then, is a point of self-repression for the homosexual movement, in which gays restrict themselves to those areas designated for them by society. It is a point of integration by which the system can show its acceptance—though only when all focus is limited to cruising and is confined to the ghetto environment. It is a point of integration in that it allows the homosexual to be open in only the appropriate places; during the rest of his everyday life, he needs to appear as a normal citizen. In this sense the golden ghetto is a brake in the development of the homosexual movement's struggle.

The ghetto is also an important place for the exploitation of homosexuals. The capitalist system is not satisfied with only repressing and integrating us, but would also take advantage of our situation for the benefits that can be obtained from our exploitation in the bars, clubs, saunas, and discotheques. Exploitation resulting from the high prices we must pay to frequent such places. This is the monetary price that we must pay to be tolerated within our golden cages.

If it is the system that, in the last instance, reaps the benefits of such exploitation, its agents are those homosexuals who take advantage of our situation to enrich themselves. And to top it off, they use the excuse that their "work" aims at benefiting all homosexuals, in providing quiet and beautiful places where we can find refuge and meet one another. Poor charitable souls who sacrifice themselves for all of us. We have never asked them for any such "sacrifice." Their role within the effort to integrate homosexuals is very clear, as is their collaboration with the system in maintaining the alienating character of the ghetto and its oppressive function.

WHY DOES THE HOMOSEXUAL TAKE REFUGE IN THE GOLDEN GHETTO?

Answering this question helps us to understand why a majority of homosexuals, lesbians, and transvestites frequent the golden ghetto despite its alienating character. The tendency to create one's own ghetto comes almost as a given, with the rejection of gays found at the workplace and in the neighborhood. The same marginalization that we experience as homosexuals in our everyday lives, in the streets, in our relations with our neighbors, companions, friends, and family necessitates our taking refuge in places where we do not feel marginalized. The solitude, the isolation, the obstacles in starting friendships with people who desire to develop a sexuality like ours tend to group us into the ghettos. These are places where we know such rejection does not exist and where everyone is searching for the same thing, where we can relate to one another openly as homosexuals. The golden ghetto is an "apparent" refuge, a suitable place for our solitude as homosexuals, a place where there is no doubt as to the sexuality of the people found there. And it is a place where our condition as homosexuals is reinforced and where in a way we can act as we want.

The false security that the four walls of the golden ghetto project is another of the elements that lead a homosexual to frequent it, especially in face of the insecurity created by this same system that has created the ghetto. The police repression in the streets when we are openly gay. The constant roundups carried out in public meeting places by the police, who use as excuses charges of "delinquency" or the need to safeguard public morals. The dangers of gang aggression against gays. The generalized rejection of gays by certain sectors of the population. The dangers involved in meeting someone on the streets, in the neighborhood, or at work. So many elements that necessitate our finding our desired "security" in the bars and clubs. Still, the golden ghetto is a false outlet that only

deepens our oppression and impedes us from confronting directly
the true causes of our oppression, and working against the "norm"
and the Establishment.

THE INTERIOR OF THE GOLDEN GHETTO

If the ghetto is a defensive response in face of the system's aggression, it is also the approved culture medium for introducing into
the minds of homosexuals all of the normalizing elements of the
system. Let's see how. . . .

We have spoken before of the exploitation that is found in the
bars and clubs by the mere fact of our frequenting them. But there
is another element at play here as well: the motivation to consume.
The golden ghetto is a center for the promotion of consumption on
a large scale. First there is the direct consumption carried out within
the bars themselves and which serves as a basis for their very
existence and growth. Essentially, every ghetto tends to promote
the consumption of all those products that confer on it all its
particularities—for example, the music and clothing that become
its characteristic elements. This development of consumerism falls
well within the tendencies that today define the development of
capitalism with its emphasis on image and (material) success.

These ghettos are constructed in such a manner to allow for the
removal of the homosexual from his own natural environment, from
the everyday misery. This is achieved through the creation of a
plastic, luxurious environment, imitative of bourgeois values. Everything tends to be stereotyped, regulated according to the norms of
the dominant class, with its emphasis on being well dressed, well
mannered, discreet, well educated, successful. It is an escape, pure
and simple, from everyday mediocrity. But there is a cost for homosexuals in achieving such an appearance. The burden of daily
frustration is replaced by an easy smile, by the suggestive diversion
and vitality of dance music. In this manner we find ourselves being

slowly incorporated into exactly the same consumer dynamic, which is both alienating and imitative.

The relationships that are established among those who gather in the golden ghetto are thus conditioned by the social environment that surrounds them. The pressures of the existent norms and public image are so strong that they come to easily influence our thinking. We will all be fags, lesbians, and transvestites, but the norm is still being imposed, albeit a more liberal norm.

The manner of socializing and of cruising are a vulgar copy of the relations established outside the ghetto with respect to the population at large. Today the interior of a homosexual bar is of the same appearance, more or less, as any other pickup bar. Machismo and the normalization of the new man have a strong foundation in the ghetto and within the homosexual movement. If at one time the golden ghetto was an important meeting place for the homosexual movement, today it is only another center of integration and a new source of burden, because we are slowly discovering that it can never be an escape. Along with the everyday misery is now added on the misery of the golden ghetto.

THE OTHER HOMOSEXUAL GHETTO

The homosexual ghetto does not start or end in the bars, clubs, etc.; it is wider than that. Other meeting and pickup places exist for homosexuals. We could name a number of parks, squares, movie theaters, public lavatories, areas of the city or city streets—places that even though they are used by homosexuals for cruising, are also frequented by other types of people. But cruising in these places is hidden and discreet. These are also dangerous places because of police actions, aggressive gangs of heterosexuals, and because of societal rejection in general.

These are places that, despite their public character, mask homosexuals from the rest of the population. The cruising and relationships established there are burdensome. Nonetheless, these places approximate the reality of the homosexual vis-à-vis the rest of Society. However, they are not a point of integration/alienation/ exploitation of the same intensity as that found in the golden ghetto.

The issue is not trying to decide if this other ghetto is better or worse than the golden ghetto. Both, in the last instance, enclose within them all the positive and negative aspects of any other ghetto, and because of that they can never become a point of rupture for questioning the oppression gays suffer. But it is necessary to point out an important difference. In the golden ghetto, the homosexual desire, the need for the realization and liberation of sexual relationships, is sheathed by normalizers and alienizers that become an essential part of the relationships that are formed between the people who frequent the place. In this way free sexuality is covered with a new outfit, but one that is just as oppressive as all those we have tried to escape. But in the other ghetto, the one of public places, pure sexual necessity does not appear at any time covered, it is right before the eyes of homosexuals as well as others. It is open, shown to all the world. Because of that, it is the most repressed ghetto, and is rejected by everyone, even those who accept and frequent the golden ghetto, weighted down by their bad conscience and their fear of homosexuality getting a bad reputation with the rest of the population.

CONFRONTING THE HOMOSEXUAL GHETTO

It is an essential task for the homosexual movement and, of course, any movement to break away from any form of ghettoization. How to achieve this is one of the most important problems we face if we want to change our present condition. For, today, the issue is not about enclosing ourselves within ghettos. It is about showing clearly what homosexuality means to all the world. To question in our workplace, our neighborhoods, our schools, and, of course, the streets, all the mechanisms by which we suffer. To question hetero-sexuality and machismo as the imposed norms. To clearly show ourselves for what we are, making people question themselves and their attitudes and their own behavior regarding sexuality. Today the issue is to keep fighting openly against everything that oppresses us, to fight against our own ghetto, to fight against the dangers created by the system—without enclosing ourselves in the ghetto's false security. Ultimately we must assert ourselves and fashion from our homosexuality one more weapon with which to destroy the system.

IDENTITY POLITICS

Within academic circles concerned with issues of lesbian and gay identity, a battle is now waging between two sets of proponents: Essentialists and Constructivists. According to Essentialist theory, there have always been people throughout history who could properly be called "homosexual." Their stories, along with their cultural expression, form part of our lesbian and gay legacy. Constructivist theory insists that identity is culturally based and that a "homosexual" identity dates only from nineteenth-century Europe. Before this time, each instance of homosexual expression needs to be examined within the specific context of the society in which it emerged. No doubt there is validity in both these approaches to history. The debate, however, points to the importance of "naming." What we are called as lesbians and gay men by the society at large and how we choose to identify ourselves are areas of enormous importance.

"Homosexual" was a term coined in the nineteenth century to designate a person who exhibited homosexual desires or behavior. Before that time, in the United States, for example, anyone was seen as capable of practicing sodomy, and the Salem witch-hunters would probably not have characterized any one group of persons as sodomites by nature.* Later, lesbians and gays chose the term "homophile" as more appropriate, since it did not focus solely on the sexual aspect of same-sex relationships, as did "homosexual." By the time of the Stonewall uprising in 1969, "gay" had become the term of preference by both lesbians and gay men. When lesbians

* David F. Greenberg, *The Construction of Homosexuality* (Chicago: The University of Chicago Press, 1988), p. 344.

began to follow their own political agendas, however, "gay" came to signify males only, while gay women were more often called "lesbians." Today the term "queer" is challenging "gay" and "lesbian" for dominance. Queer is a more inclusive term, able to serve as an umbrella for gay males, lesbians, bisexuals, transvestites, and transsexuals. It is also of particular interest because, as with the terms "dyke" and "faggot," it exemplifies how a term used to stigmatize a group can be subsequently reclaimed by that group and used proudly, as an act of assertiveness, by them.

The dynamics of naming for North American English speakers are not the same, of course, as what may be occurring, with all the concomitant nuance, among gay speakers of other languages. In the traditions of southern Europe, for example, as in much of Latin America, a male who plays the inserter role in a sexual relationship with another male still identifies himself as a heterosexual "man," while his partner is stigmatized by being labeled a "bitch" or "queen." However, since the advent of Gay Liberation, which has challenged the rigid dichotomization of sex roles, the term "gay" has entered other languages, including Spanish, where it has often come to denote both inserter and insertee, as well as the person who plays both roles. In the first selection that follows, the author examines the meaning of the term "gay" vis-à-vis its spreading usage in Latin America.

The second selection is taken from the Polish gay magazine *Inaczej* (On the Other Hand). In "Notes of a Malcontent," Sławek Starosta raises several issues concerning identity politics. First he criticizes *Inaczej*'s self-defined role as mouthpiece for the homosexual community, when only token recognition is afforded to lesbians and lesbian concerns. He then argues for the adoption of the word *pedał* (faggot) in much the same way as the gay community in the United States did when reclaiming the derisive word "faggot" as a badge of pride. Euphemisms such as "sexual minorities" or "those who love differently," he points out, serve only to reflect the insecurity of the gay community and its need to prove its worthiness both to itself and to the heterosexual majority.

In his letter of response to the Malcontent, Carpentarius pleads for more tolerance and appreciation of the diversity to be found among Polish gays. As a minority, he argues, gays cannot afford to be insensitive to society's perceptions of them. Being needlessly provocative can only result in damage to one's goals.

Within this polemic can be found issues of identity politics similar to those experienced by gays in Western Europe and North America: a homosexual movement that is comprised mostly of men and that pays scant attention to lesbian concerns; the cautious approach adopted by the homophile movement in seeking tolerance and social acceptance, versus the so-called radical approach to politics, which emphasizes the sexual aspects of what makes gays different; and the struggle for reclaiming once-stigmatizing epithets as one's own, whether it be *pedał,* "faggot," or, more recently in the United States, "queer."

LATIN AMERICA

**"Stigma Transformation and Relexification:
'Gay' in Latin America"
by Stephen O. Murray and Manuel Arboleda G.,[1]
from *Male Homosexuality in
Central and South America* (1987).**

The term "gay" diffused rapidly in urban Latin America during the
late 1970s and early 1980s, raising the question whether use of the
term reflects changes from a "gender" to a "gay" organization of
homosexuality. The latter was characterized by (Adam, 1979, p. 18)
as one in which

> people meet and form enduring social networks only because of
> mutual homosexual interest, (2) there is a sense of peoplehood
> and emerging culture (Murray 1979a; Levine 1979), and (3) there
> is the possibility of exclusive (nonbisexual) and egalitarian (not
> rolebound) same-sex relations.

In North American cities a shift—albeit one that is not complete
even now—has occurred. Formerly, the man who took only the
inserter role in homosexual coitus (termed "trade" in the homosexual subculture which preceded "gay community") was not identified
and did not identify himself as homosexual. Only (some of) those
regularly taking an insertee role ("queens") did.[2] Under the aegis of
"gay"—an aggressively stigma-challenging label (Goffman 1963)
without the negative connotations of "queer" or "queen"—a shift,
from what might be considered an exogamous system of sexual
exchange in which those identifying themselves or fantasized by

their partners as "straight" ("trade") were sought, to an endogamous system in which both partners identify themselves as "gay" has occurred in Anglo North America. This change has brought ideal norms closer to behavior patterns,[3] and ontogeny has recapitulated phylogeny in this transformation to mutual definition by both partners (Miller 1978; Humphreys and Miller 1981).

When the word "gay" was unknown in Latin America, which was as recently as the mid-1970s, homosexual identification was analogous to the pregay pattern in Anglo North America: Those whose homosexual behavior was confined to the *activo* (inserter) role did not consider themselves defined, nor even implicated by such behavior. Neither did their *pasivo* partners. *Activos* were simply *hombres* (men—unmarked), quite regardless of the sex of the persons who received their phallic thrusts. Even those persons who switched roles tended to identify themselves by one role designation or the other and to attempt to constrain any publicity about the other, although there were terms—*moderno* in Peru and *internacional* in Mesoamerica—for such dichotomy, transcending conduct.[4]

In Lima in 1976 the term "gay" was not used, and was known only to a very few Peruvians who had traveled to Europe or North America. By 1980, however, the term was widely known and was preferred above the previously standard term *entendido* (in the know) by most informants, both self-identified *pasivos* and *activos*. Although outside homosexual networks "gay" was an unfamiliar locution, in October 1980 the popular magazine *Gente* ran a cover story titled "Los Gays Peruanos Son Libres" (Peruvian Gays Are Free). The article itself oscillated between linking "gay" with effeminacy and using it in the stigma-challenging sense common in North America. That it was used at all to refer to a group usually invisible in respectable publications and completely stereotyped in tabloids in Latin America (see Taylor 1978; Murray 1980a) was remarkable. By 1982 "gay" had entirely replaced *entendido* as a self-designation, but in some cases the spelling pronunciation (gal) was used rather than the phonetic realization borrowed from French or English—that is ge(y).[5]

In Guatemala in 1978 two of five *pasivos* interviewed offered "gay" as a term for men who chose other men as sexual partners. The three *pasivo* informants who reported not having friends with similar preferences nor any involvement in settings where such persons congregated were not familiar with the term. Both those persons who identified themselves as *internacional* (and were much-traveled) used "gay" and remarked that the term was achieving ever wider currency in their country. Of the *activos* from whom lexical data were elicited, one did not know the word, one knew it but did not apply it to himself, and one both knew it and applied it to himself.[6]

Words that are borrowed do not necessarily retain the same meaning they had in the source language. For some of our informants "gay" seemed to be used as a fashionable (new and foreign) term that simply replaced *entendido* or *de ambiente* in an unchanged conception of homosexuality—that is, relexification of the preexisting conceptual order. For others, however, the new word seemed to reflect a new conception of homosexuality, paralleling the stigma transformation involved in replacing "queer" and "homosexual" with "gay" in Anglo North America. Table 1 shows which of these models was held by informants varying in (self-reported) role preference.

Those who answered "No" to the ritualized cruising question *"¿Eres activo o pasivo?"* rather than one or the other, invariably considered those who are *activo* to be gay, as well as those who are *pasivo*. For more than a third of those who identified themselves as *activo* and more than half of those who identified themselves as *pasivo* and who were familiar with the word, "gay" was a new word for the already existing conception of homosexuality. Interestingly, those who are stigmatized by this concept are less likely than those who seemingly profit in social esteem by it to embrace the wider conception of who is "gay." A number of explanations (including false consciousness, covert prestige among the stigmatized, cognitive dissonance, and/or ambivalence on the part of heavily involved *activos*) might be proffered, if this pattern holds up for larger samples. Here we are concerned with the more certain change over time observable among both *activos* and *pasivos* than with the tenuous differences by sex role.

Although we claim to have observed change in process,[7] it bears emphasizing that all three models in Table 1 represent the conception of some men involved in homosexuality in Latin America. Some still use the old word(s), others have borrowed the word "gay" but simply replaced *entendido* with it in the same slot (relexification); but for some others, "gay" refers to a "new man" who can **enact** *(estar) pasivo* behavior without **being** *(ser) un pasivo.*

This change parallels the earlier Anglo North American one (which is presumably the source of prestige for the label "gay"). Nonetheless, some caution is in order before concluding that the development of a stigma-challenging gay community in Anglo North America provides a blueprint of stages that will be copied elsewhere in the world. Although homosexuality in Latin America has been gender defined, just as it was earlier in Anglo North America, residence patterns, censorship of materials that can be interpreted by individual policemen or judges as politically subversive or incitements to vice, the absence of religious pluralism with its concomitant traditions (and freedoms) of voluntary associations, and other factors that may have been crucial to the history of gay institutional elaboration in Anglo North America but are quite different in Latin America (Taylor 1978; Murray 1980a; Lacey 1983) may shape different developments to different ends there (and elsewhere). Mexican liberation organizations eschew the term "gay" because their leadership do not consider Anglo gay culture to be what they aspire to emulate. They are also sensitive about "cultural imperialism" from the North and the elitism of expensive local replicas of Anglo gay bars. Moreover, cultures in which homosexuality is age defined, such as Islamic, Amazonian, and Melanesian ones (see Murray 1991, Herdt 1981, 1984) defy any scheme of unilinear evolution to the "gay" organization of homosexuality even more clearly than the stirring of change in Latin America (see also Wooden 1982; Kutsche 1983).

TABLE 1

Frequency of Conceptions of *Un hombre que prefiera los otros hombres* by Place/Time and Sex Role

Locale/Year of Elicitation Reported Role	Model 1	Model 2	Model 3
Guatemala City 1978			
activo	1	1	1
pasivo	3	2	0
internacional	0	0	3
Lima 1979			
activo	4	2	2
pasivo	7	3	1
Mexico City 1981–83			
activo	9	6	8
pasivo	5	3	5
internacional	0	0	10
Lima 1982–83			
activo	0	0	5
pasivo	2	3	6
moderno	0	0	4

Totals				(N)
activo	36%	23	41	(39)
pasivo	43%	28	30	(40)
moderno/internacional	0%	0	100	(17)
late 1970s	50%	27	23	(30)
early 1980s	24%	18	58	(66)

REFERENCES

Adam, Barry D. 1979. "Reply." *Sociologists Gay Caucus Newsletter* 18:8.
Akinnaso, F. Niyi. 1980. "The sociolinguistic basis of Yoruba personal names." *Anthropological Linguistics* 22:275–304.

—————. 1982. "Names and naming in cross-cultural perspective." *Names* 30:37–63.

Arboleda, Manuel. 1980. "Gay Life in Lima." *Gay Sunshine* 42:30.

Carrier, Joseph M. 1975. "Urban Mexican Male Homosexual Encounters." Ph.D. thesis, University of California, Irvine.

—————. 1976. "Cultural factors affecting urban Mexican male homosexual behavior." *Archives of Sexual Behavior* 5:103–24.

Chauncey, George W., Jr. 1985. "Christian brotherhood or sexual perversion? Homosexual identities and the construction of sexual boundaries in the World War One era." *Journal of Social History* 19:189–211.

Goffman, Erving. 1963. *Stigma.* Toronto: Prentice-Hall.

Herdt, Gilbert H. 1981. *Guardians of the Flutes.* New York: McGraw-Hill.

—————. 1984. *Ritualized Homosexuality in Melanesia.* Berkeley: University of California Press.

Humphreys, Laud. 1971. "New styles of homosexual manliness." *Transaction* (March): 38–65.

—————. 1975. *Tearoom Trade.* Chicago: Aldine.

—————. 1979. "Exodus and identity." In M. Levine (ed.), *Gay Men.* New York: Harper & Row.

Humphreys, Laud, and Brian Miller. 1981. "Satellite cultures" in J. Marmor (ed.), *Homosexuality.* New York: Basic Books.

Itkin, M-F. 1971. "On terminology." *Gay Sunshine* 7:2.

Kutsche, Paul. 1983. "Situational homosexuality in Costa Rica." *Anthropological Research Group on Homosexuality Newsletter* 4, 4:8–13.

Labov, William. 1972. *Sociolinguistic Patterns.* Philadelphia: University of Pennsylvania Press.

Lacey, E. A. 1983. *My Deep Dark Pain Is Love.* San Francisco: Gay Sunshine Press.

Levine, Martin P. 1979. *Gay Men.* New York: Harper & Row.

Miller, Brian. 1978. "Adult sexual resocialization." *Alternative Lifestyles* 1:207–33.

Murray, Stephen O. 1979a. "The institutional elaboration of a quasi-ethnic community." *International Review of Modern Sociology* 9:165–77.

—————. 1979b. "The art of gay insults." *Anthropological Linguistics* 21: 211–23.

—————. 1980a. *Latino Homosexuality.* San Francisco: Social Networks.

————. 1980b. "Lexical and institutional elaboration: The 'species homosexual' in Guatemala." *Anthropological Linguistics* 22:177–85.

————. 1991. *Oceanic Homosexualities.* New York: Garland.

Murray, Stephen O., and Robert C. Poolman, Jr. 1981. "Folk models of gay community." *Working Paper of the Language Behavior Research Laboratory* 51.

Reiss, Albert J. 1961. "The social integration of 'queers' and 'peers.'" *Social Problems* 9:102–20.

Taylor, Clark L. 1978. "El Ambiente." Ph.D. thesis, University of California, Berkeley.

Weinberg, Thomas S. 1978. "On 'doing' and 'being' gay." *Journal of Homosexuality* 4:143–56.

Wolf, Deborah G. 1983. *Growing Older Gay and Lesbian,* manuscript.

Wooden, Wayne S. 1982. "Cultural antecedents of gay communities in Latin America." Paper presented at the American Sociological Association meetings, San Francisco.

NOTES

1. Earlier versions of this paper were presented at the 1982 Pacific Sociological Association meetings in San Diego and the 1982 American Sociological Association meetings in San Francisco. The authors would like to acknowledge the encouragement of the session organizers, Wayne Wooden and William Devall, respectively; and also that of Niyi Akinnaso, John Gumperz, and Amparo Tuson.

2. See Reiss (1961); Humphreys (1975); Murray (1979b); Murray and Poolman (1981); Chauncey (1985).

3. See Humphreys (1971, 1979); Murray (1984); Murray and Poolman (1981); Weinberg (1983); Wolf (1983).

4. Murray and Dynes, "Hispanic Homosexuals: Spanish Lexicon," in *Male Homosexuality in Central and South America,* ed. Stephen O. Murray (GAU-New York: New York, 1987).

5. Wooden (1982) reports the other solution to the problem of borrowing a word that is spelled in a way other than the one pronounced, for example, changing the spelling, in Colombia and Venezuela.

6. See Murray (1980b) for a description of the elicitation procedures and social characteristics of this sample. Subsequent waves of repression in Guatemala prevented return fieldwork, as well as driving underground a previously emerging subculture.

7. Although structuralist linguistic orthodoxy held that linguistic change is too slow to observe, Lavov (1972) provided refutation. Generational differences in bounding "gay community" were found in the semantic work in San Francisco of Murray and Poolman (1981). The example of not merely observing but also explaining linguistic change as reflecting significant social change which has particularly influenced the work presented here is Akinnaso's (1980, 1982) work on Yoruba naming.

POLAND

"Notes of a Malcontent: Remember the Butt" by Sławek Starosta, translated by Jolanta Benal, from *Inaczej* (March 1991).

Today we will kick around "our" press—that is, the gay press, or to put it even more directly, the faggot press. (Of course, certain ever-ambitious publications try to be for all homosexuals without regard to gender, and from time to time they insert two lesbian verses and one notice of a lesbian event, but as far as I'm concerned that doesn't change their fundamentally masculine character.) What mainly disgusts me about the faggot press of Poland's Third Republic is that for the most part it's phony and untruthful. I realize that this is the result of feeling inferior and of the need to present ourselves to the general public, and also to ourselves, as healthy, normal, and worthy people. This is certainly the reason for those deadly serious, deathly boring installment biographies of well-known and not-so-well-known (usually, alas, the latter) fags. And those mile-long translations of educational articles asserting (with the help of some pretty convoluted language) that a fag is no worse than a hetero—quite the contrary, in fact. And the advice from "enlightened" indigenous sexologists who have lots of experience in solving fags' problems, unfortunately in theory and from a distance. And the "news" from around the world, mostly about where a guy can marry another guy, and where the possibility is just being discussed. And so on and so forth.

God, how boring. It's more like the propaganda leaflets the Allies dropped on Iraq than it is like a community press. I don't know who can stand it, apart from liberal straights and insecure people with lots of complexes. At least the latter can go on to revel in personals à la "I'll stay with that one man my whole life" or "I'm looking for a true friend."

None of these magazines is even aimed at fags, homosexuals, or gay men. No, they're for "sexual minorities" (of which there must be a dozen), or for "men" (of whom there are 19 million), or maybe for "those who love differently" (and what shall we do for those who love the same?). Are the editors ashamed of themselves, or of their readers?

The fundamental difference between Poland and Western Europe or the United States is that in those places you find several hundred homosexual publications instead of several, and several thousand bars, restaurants, dance places, baths, and other similar hangouts for gays and lesbians, which in our country you can easily count up on the fingers of your two hands. In Poland we have not yet created a fag culture—or subculture. There are few gay institutions like the ones I mentioned. But these are essential to the growth of a sense of community, to self-awareness, and to self-acceptance—everything that falls under the rubric of "gay consciousness." I will say nothing of [the Warsaw group] Lambda or its local affiliates, because the utter feebleness of that organization is a direct result of the lack of consciousness in gay men and lesbians, trying to take any action for whom is like rolling Sisyphus's rock up the hill. Groups and organizations usually spring up in an already developed community. In Poland the situation's reversed: The organization tries to create a community (with mediocre results). In such a situation, how can the faggot press produce a less nightmarishly didactic and moralistic impression?

My proposal is a simple one. Let us stop pretending, dear editors, that we're better than we really are. Let's stop expecting our readers to be bigger prudes than the heterosexual majority that surrounds us. Let our magazines be homo-sexual, not homo-asexual. After all, our sexuality is exactly what the general so-called public won't accept—so maybe it's time we paid it some attention. If our fag world really does revolve around the butt, then maybe instead of pretending that nothing could be farther from the truth, we might find it worth our while to start writing about that.

In closing, I should say that I don't want to be taken for an idolatrous worshiper at the shrine of pornography and sex. But (especially for us) these things make up a hell of an important part of life. And I am decidedly opposed to forgetting that. So—while not forgetting all the rest—let's remember the butt.

Translator's notes:

The preceding article, unlike Starosta's other installments of "Notes of a Malcontent," appeared with a disclaimer: "The opinions presented under the preceding title do not reflect those of the editors."

Sławek Starosta is one half of the rock group Balkan Electrique. (The other half is Wiolka Najdenowicz.) With Jarek Ender, Starosta founded the anti-AIDS education organization *Kochaj nie zabijaj* (Love, Don't Kill), whose name is taken from the title of one of Balkan Electrique's hits. He is also the founder of the Warsaw gay service group Pink Service.

"In Reply to the Malcontent" by "Carpentarius," translated by Jolanta Benal and Alicja Benal, from *Inaczej* (May 1991).

I've carefully read Sławek Starosta's "Notes of a Malcontent," which *Inaczej* furnished with a cautious disclaimer. The "Note" is angry, rude, ill-articulated, and confused; but, on the other hand, it strikes the reader with its impatience and candor, it desperately seeks that elusive thing, authenticity. But people shouldn't spout such ill-thought-out reasoning. It's easy to damage oneself in spite of one's best intentions—to damage not only oneself but also that aspect of the truth that one rightly wishes to demonstrate. For Sławek Starosta is right in some ways. But he forgets a thing or two.

He attacks our magazines (including *Inaczej*) on the ground that "for the most part they're phony and untruthful"; our organizations, such as Lambda, on the ground that they don't yet represent a fully developed community but rather try ("with mediocre results") to create one.

Indeed, these things are true to a degree—many of us feel it—but it's worth making oneself aware of why this is so, and worth asking if and how we can change it, in the mere year since censorship and government restrictions were lifted, and in the face of the rising tide of national piety that has replaced the facade of Communist prudishness. What can we do? Nothing? That would be easiest. We've waited forty-five years; we can wait a little longer, till economic transformation permits the legal and financial independence of those "thousands of bars, restaurants, dance places, baths, and other hangouts," till figures such as Messrs. Herzog, Jurek, Łopuszański, and Niesiołowski[1] disappear from public life—in a word, till our fusty Polish morals are blown away by the cosmopolitan wind. That'll take years, dear Malcontent, long years.

Certainly, we all know that from Constantine (A.D. 326) to Hitler, even the death penalty has been unable to change our nature, and we lived, somehow or other (rather well, in certain epochs and certain countries) despite repression and social ostracism. But coming out, which is the Malcontent's point (and ours), need not, should not, signify provocation. How can we change the fact that we don't live in a vacuum, that we've always been and still are a minority? A minority that today rightly demands tolerance and for that very reason shouldn't make light of other people's convictions, shouldn't attack the majority's sensibilities: To do so is to strike blows against ourselves. Whether one likes it or not, having our publications, our coffeehouses, our restaurants is a public act and produces a public judgment. And in what other ways would the Malcontent suggest that we show the world—sorry, but this is his word—our bare butt?

It's not true that "we are more prudish than the heterosexual majority that surrounds us." Nor are we afraid of nudity (in any case, Article 173 of the Penal Code binds us as well as them); and we publish more sexually realistic work than was formerly possible in this country. (It's impossible to doubt the sincerity and authenticity of the diverse matter published.) And real literature need no longer back away from any description or idea. Homosexuality isn't the only field in which there aren't enough good writers. Certainly there exist intimate recesses of our passions and fascinations, of which we're a little ashamed even among ourselves, to say nothing of how we feel in the presence of outsiders. But this was always so, and not only in matters of the closet. Does the Malcontent judge that every fifty-year-old man is ready to freely acknowledge to everyone his taste for fifteen-year-old girls? For that we need the talent of a Nabokov.

I don't see that we question or heavily camouflage our sensual characters, or particular aspects (for example, promiscuity) of our erotic life. It wouldn't make any sense to do so; it's quite impossible; in the end, our erotic character is what makes us different. But really, the erotic isn't limited to what happens in bed—or in the public john.

The Malcontent writes sarcastically of articles in which "with the help of some pretty convoluted language" someone supposedly opines that "a fag is no worse than a hetero—quite the contrary, in fact." I don't get his point; surely he also believes that we're no worse. And if we're as good as they are, then let's behave at least as well as they do; let's not fall into sexual monomania, blind to all other values that can protect us from loneliness better than passions that are transitory by nature.

Are we fakers? Everybody everywhere wants to show himself in the best light. After all, that's only normal. Surely it would be unfair to demand that we ourselves exhibit the evidence of our emotional and intellectual poverty—as we would if we occupied ourselves exclusively with the "butt." Homosexuality—for many people, I think—isn't only a physical attraction to people of one's own sex; it's first of all a different "social optics," a different way of seeing culture.

Finally, let's not forget that by no means do we form a harmonious, homogeneous group. To see this, just skim the ads. What connects, for example, a "highly specialized" young man for whom even a really handsome and well-endowed guy of twenty is too old, with an ex-priest longing to make the acquaintance of an older man who has a beautiful soul, or with a married fifty-year-old bisexual seeking a similar partner of the same age, "looks irrelevant, but must be discreet"? What joins us is only this: We're struggling together against a hostile environment. As for everything else, it's often easier for us to come to an understanding with an open-minded member of the "normal" majority.

I think that each of us ought to be able to find something that suits him in the gay press—but we should also expect from everyone acceptance of people's different standards, their preferences, and even their inhibitions, however incomprehensible these may seem to us.

The homosexual subculture of the West arose over half a century, and I don't need to remind anyone how many pioneers enabled the postwar-era gay revolution to occur. If we don't get knocked on the head first [omitted here is a reference to an earlier article by Starosta], little by little we'll take the same road. The magazines that the Malcontent criticizes are just taking shape, so perhaps we can allow them some time to accomplish that; and above all we should acknowledge that without them our chances of emerging into Polish society would be much slimmer. Their mistakes, which also—let's be honest—show a degree of courage, only reflect the real situation, which the printed word alone can't change.

As for the biographical and historical material that finds its way into these pages from time to time, [even the young will always encounter an unfriendly or hostile majority. Their freedom will be, first, an inner freedom. That's why it's useful to reach into the past at times, to inform oneself of the deep, historically documented roots of the psychological and physical inclination toward one's own sex, no matter how it has been hidden. . . . Without knowing that history, we'll never be completely sure of our identity and our rights, and we'll never leave the ghetto we've been in for fifteen centuries and in which we are kept to this day.] .[2]

And one more, marginal point on which I have some doubt. Would it really be to the Malcontent's liking to hear the hostility of the ignorant bursting forth with the vulgarisms "faggot" and "faggy"? If we want to revive the beautiful original meaning of the Greek word *paiderastia*[3] ("love of youths"), then maybe we ought to keep our distance from the guys who hang out on the corner drinking beer.

NOTES (OF TRANSLATORS)

1. Herzog, formerly the first deputy of the Polish Ministry of Justice, lost his job after making antihomosexual remarks. Jurek, Łopuszański, and Niesiołowski are members of the Sejm (Polish Parliament).

2. The material in brackets is taken from Carpentarius's column in issue No. 7 of *Inaczej,* to which he refers readers for an explanation of the importance of studying gay history.

3. The Polish *pedał* (fag) and *pedalski* (faggy) are derived from this.

MAN-BOY LOVE

One of the most sensitive issues with which gays have had to contend, both vis-à-vis heterosexual society and within the gay movements, is that of man-boy love. There are few charges that can be leveled at gays that have as powerful a negative impact as that of "corrupting" minors. Whenever the issue comes to public attention, as it has in Canada, the United States, Britain, and West Germany, it is almost a foregone conclusion that media-provoked hysteria will hamper any rational or critical discussion of the topic. Even within many gay movements, men who have identified themselves as "lovers of boys" have often been censored or ostracized.

The following article, taken from *Gay Left* of London, affords us an opportunity to examine man-boy love in several of its dimensions. Related questions are raised concerning homosexual identity, age of consent, childhood sexuality, and young people's rights, which provide us with a far broader perspective than that usually found. Interestingly enough, where age of consent laws have been lowered to 15 or 16 years of age and made equal for both heterosexuals and homosexuals (Netherlands 1971, Denmark 1976, Sweden 1978, France 1982), many of the issues surrounding man-boy love have ceased to exist.*

* Barry D. Adam, *The Rise of a Gay and Lesbian Movement* (Boston: Twayne Publishers, 1987), p. 152.

GREAT BRITAIN

"Happy Families? Pedophilia Examined" by the Gay Left Collective, from *Gay Left: A Gay Socialist Journal* (Winter 1978–79).

THE CHALLENGE

It is striking that over the past two or three years conservative moral anxiety throughout the advanced capitalist countries has switched from homosexuality in general to sexual relationships between adults and young people. Anita Bryant's antihomosexual campaign began as a crusade to "Save Our Children"; *The Body Politic* in Canada was raided following an issue on pedophilia; in France and elsewhere a moral panic has been stirred up over the issue of child pornography and "exploitation." And in Britain this has led to the rapid passage through Parliament of a restrictive Child Pornography Bill, which received no scrutiny and very little principled libertarian opposition from lawmakers. Even the recent *Gay News* trial had as a significant undercurrent the issue of pedophilia, a topic and stigma with which the prosecution made strenuous efforts to tar *Gay News.* The attacks on lesbian parenthood are obviously related to similar questions, while those organizations which counsel young homosexuals and help them to meet one another seem to be coming under increased surveillance.

There has, it seems, been a clear extension of concern from adult male homosexual behavior, which dominated debates of the '50s and '60s following the Wolfenden Report, to the question of pedophilia and childhood. In 1952 the *Sunday Pictorial* published a series of articles on adult homosexuality called "Evil Men." By 1972 "The Vilest Men in Britain" (*Sunday People,* May 25, 1975) were members of the Paedophile Action for Liberation (PAL), and the *News of the World* in 1978 (June 11) enjoined the members of PIE (Paedophile Information Exchange) to "Keep Your Hands Off Our Children: We expose the truth about this pack of perverts." "Child molesters" and "exploiters of children" are the new social monsters.

Why is this so? Realistically, the moral right wing cannot get much support out of campaigning against homosexuality as such. But they *can* hope to build up a new moral consensus around the issue of protecting childhood, particularly in the context of the current political emphasis on the family. Adult homosexuals can be dismissed as unfortunate historical deviations to be pitied, with all efforts being put into preventing any more children from "falling" into such a life. Here they can build out from their traditional evangelical core, which rejects all sex outside of marriage, building a coalition with various people from disillusioned libertarians to confused progressives.

Moral reactionaries can serve their cause better by building alliances on easy issues such as the protection of childhood. Their success in pushing through the Child Pornography Act in Britain is one proof of this. At the same time, gay opposition is minimized because of the wish to disassociate ourselves from the traditional public image of being "dirty old men." A moral panic can be drummed up over childhood because it *is* an area of such easy controversy. If, as bourgeois morality informs us, "the child is the father of the man," then it is of major concern to a conservative stratum that children are protected, cosseted, and channeled in the right direction—toward heterosexual familial patterns. We have all been brought up from infancy in such patterns, and know the scars we suffer in endeavoring to emerge with our own gay identities. Childhood is a battlefield that gay militants have to be concerned with. And to that degree, the moral Right is correct. Homosexuals *are* a threat; we can, in their language, "corrupt." Gay socialists cannot afford to avoid these issues.

PEDOPHILES, PARENTS, AND POWER

The question of pedophilia raises a multitude of issues, from those of simple civil rights to matters of sexual theory. As socialists we must join with other libertarians in defending the right of pedophiles to associate and organize to raise social awareness about the issue without harassment from press or police, or violence from the right.

The *Gay Left* Collective, like many others in the gay movement, has had many discussions about pedophilia. We do not feel it would be a justified position to discuss adult/child sexual relationships simply on libertarian grounds. It is no good merely to say, people feel like that, feeling is valid, let it all happen, right on. We know that feelings are socially constructed and we must view all feelings with great suspicion and scrutiny.

There is an argument that has developed from some quarters of the gay movement and the left which suggests that children are sexual beings like adults; and that since they are oppressed by parents, teachers, etc., and no pedophile experience could be any more harmful, pedophile relationships are therefore all right. This is a false and idealist argument. It likens childhood sexuality to the experiences of adult sexuality, an equation that cannot be made, as children cannot be read back as small adults. Pedophile relationships raise the question of power too sharply for us to treat them glibly. A radical approach to the question can only come through the interrogation of two areas:

1. The question of the dominance in our culture of certain categories of sexuality, of which "homosexuality" and "pedophilia" are examples. Is it, in other words, valid to think through the questions of sexuality as if these are pregiven, determined, and firm? Do they

clearly enough embrace the varieties of behavior which they seek to pull together within rigid definitions?

2. The question of childhood sexuality specifically, the real focus of the debate and the key to the issue. Conservative thought dismisses any idea of childhood sexual feelings and experiences, and much public opinion is reticent in acknowledging their existence. At the other extreme are those who see childhood sexual feelings as being identical to adult ones. Both are wrong. We began our discussion of this area with Freud's essays on children's sexuality. Whatever the limitations of Freud's categories, they are valuable in indicating the existence and diversity of childhood sexuality. But our present limited knowledge of children's sexual development still makes discussion of pedophile relations very difficult.

WHAT IS PEDOPHILIA?

One definition would embrace all sexual activities between "adults" and those under the age of consent. In countries like ours, however, where the age of consent for male homosexuals is so high (21), such a definition would be meaningless. An age of consent, in theory at least, would seem to be meaningful only in the context of an entry into social and sexual maturity, which in turn suggests a relationship to puberty. The problem is that puberty is a process rather than a particular age, occurring roughly between the ages of eleven and fourteen, though individuals differ greatly in their physical and emotional development at this time. Together with the sexual development of the body, puberty implies a growing awareness of the social world, particularly through greater contact with peers and older children as sources of education and experience. Most of the *Gay Left* Collective recognize that puberty is a useful framework. For convenience we define a pedophile as someone who is emotionally and sexually attracted toward children, that is, toward prepubertal people.

In their pamphlet *Paedophilia: Some Questions and Answers,* the Paedophile Information Exchange (PIE) defines it as "sexual love directed toward children," and they refer to "children" "both in prepuberty and early adolescence." In practice they state that the age group that attracts pedophiles is "usually somewhere in the 8–15 range." From our definition it is clear that we find this equation of adolescence and childhood confusing. Another issue with which we have to deal is that sexual/emotional relations between adults and children need not be between members of the same sex. In fact, the majority of such relationships are heterosexual, and in practice, between heterosexual men and young girls, usually in the context of the family. But it is also true that the (relatively tiny) number of people who have identified themselves as pedophiles are usually male and boy lovers. The vast majority of members of pedophile organizations seem to fall into this area. This already suggests the complexity of the issue: A yawning distinction between behavior and identity immediately appears. But once we recognize the very different context in which heterosexual and homosexual sexual relations take place, and the traditional invisibility of female sexuality, the "yawning distinction" becomes yet another example of the inequalities of conventional roles and relationships. The Collective feels that male heterosexual and homosexual pedophilia raise different questions.

The whole imagery of adult/child relationships is fraught with contradictions which reveal the symbolic differentiations between men and women, adults and children in our society. Whereas a male homosexual is invariably seen as a potential child molester, and a lesbian pedophile identity is socially nonexistent because it presupposes an autonomous female sexual identity, the image of an older woman initiating young men fits in with traditional male fantasies of woman. At the same time, the deflowering of the young virgin has a special place in male mythology. Given these factors and conditions, it is not surprising that the less common forms of adult/

child relationships, involving homosexuality, receive wider publicity and hostility than the much more common heterosexual pattern. And it is for this reason that a distinct male pedophile identity emerges within the range of homosexualities.

Pedophilia centrally touches on the question of homosexuality precisely because of the question of "corruption." The terror of homosexuals corrupting minors into their way of life has been a subtext of opposition to adult homosexuality at least since the nineteenth century, and behind it, of course, has been the terror of homosexuality. In certain ways homosexuality greatly overlaps with the heterosexual norm—that is, loving relations of "equals," living in types of relationships different from but not alien to heterosexuals. Children have been seen as needing protection from going down the homosexual road because of the potent challenge it poses to the family, and to protect them a whole battery of ideological devices has been employed. The major one has been the notion of corruption, of forcibly diverting the innocent child from the paths of righteousness to those of deviance. The use of this imputation has been an important method of control of adult homosexuality. We can already see that the campaigns such as those of Anita Bryant and Mary Whitehouse, ostensibly for the protection of children, become vehicles for assaults on all lesbians and gay men.

THE HOMOSEXUAL CATEGORY

The category of the "homosexual" is, as we have argued before, a historical creation, a cultural attempt to describe and control a variety of sexual behaviors between members of the same sex. The emergence of love or sexual desire by one person for another is pretty near universal. The attempt to describe this within rigid categories is relatively new, and did not take off dramatically until the late nineteenth century. The definitions of homosexuality have varied during the last hundred years; its origins variously described (genetic, environmental, "corruption"); its manifestations outlined (abnormal-sized bottoms, wide hips, inability to whistle); its likely effect delineated (unhappiness, suicide). But those thus defined have fought back. We have created our own sense of identity or identities; we have begun to assert and impose our own sense of ourselves, our own definitions ("gay"). The gay movements throughout the West, the great subcultural expansions, are all part of this process of self-definition. But even today a high proportion of those who engage in some form of homosexual activity (e.g., in public lavatories) do not define themselves as gay. And many would fall into the cultural category of "heterosexual" by their usual patterns of behavior (marriage, etc.).

These cultural categories are, in other words, arbitrary, only partially describing what they are supposed to, and are artificial divisions of sexual desire. They have a reality because they have social institutions backing them (the family, the law, medicine, psychiatry) and because they set the parameters within which we set out to live our various lives. But even for those of us who define ourselves as gay there is no essential identity, no single identifying pattern of behavior. There is not a single "homosexuality" but various "homosexualities." It is politically vital for gay people to organize to defend our rights to our own sexualities, but we should be clear that a radical perspective does not mean defending a gay ethnicity (the equivalent of a national or racial identity). It means defending the validity of homosexuality and, beyond that, the many-faceted nature of sexuality in general. It is not so much an oppressed minority that the gay movement is about as an oppressed sexuality. Freedom for gay people will not come simply when we have better facilities, freedom to marry or inherit property; it will develop as rigid cultural categories are broken down. It is a paradox that the only way for this to happen is through using these categories, organizing within them, and bursting their bonds.

THE PEDOPHILE CATEGORY

Pedophilia, like homosexual behavior, has existed universally and has been variously treated in different societies. "Boy love" particularly has often played an important and even socially approved role in some cultures—for example, pedagogic relationships in ancient Greece and puberty rites in various societies. In the nineteenth century it was possible even in Britain to have sentimental and even physical contact with children without social disapproval. During the past century the category of the corrupter emerged, so that today almost any nonfamilial contact between adult and child can become suspect. Partly as a defensive measure, pedophiles themselves have begun in recent years to assert their identity, a few openly in organizations such as PIE and other equivalents in Europe and America. But just as there is little uniformity in adult homosexual behavior, there is also little for pedophiles. Pedophilia in many cases is a matter of identity rather than actual sexual activity, and many of those adults who have sexual experiences with children would not in fact identify themselves as pedophiles. For instance, a German survey suggested that among 200 cases of men sentenced for indecent assault on children "there was not even a single one preferring children to adult partners." (Quoted in *Childhood Rights,* Vol. 1, No. 2, published by PIE.)

Just as assault or rape by a man on a woman cannot be defended, so no pedophile would defend assault or rape of children, or any alleviation of laws relating to these. Nor would they approve of the conscious use of power to "persuade" children. (PIE, for instance, apparently disapproves of parent/child incest.) The issue then comes down to the question of an *affectionate* relationship between a child and an adult that involves sex.

Three issues immediately emerge: first, the legitimacy of childhood sexuality; second, the adult fetishization of a particular age group; and third, the changing meaning and significance given to different parts of the body throughout an individual's life. The problem in discussing pedophile sexual relationships revolves around the prioritization of certain parts of the body along adult lines in relations with prepubertal children who may not have such priorities. Can pedophile relationships ever be justified, and what should the attitude of socialists and feminists be to them?

Some issues seem fairly clear. It seems unlikely that youthful sexual activity rigidly determines later orientation (object choice and emotional structuring seem to take place much earlier in life), and we see a homosexual choice as equally valid as a heterosexual one. We must reject the dominant idea that it is an issue whether a child is influenced into a homosexual rather than a heterosexual life. We must demystify sex. The notion that sex is the great secret, the ultimate mystery, is at the root of the worship of childhood innocence. It is the puritans who elevate sex into the embodiment of holiness. We should argue for sex as pleasure, not sacrament. If it is pleasurable, on what grounds can we deny it? We must also recognize that it is often the young person who initiates sexual activity. It is the intrusion of the law or panic-stricken parents which often causes misery and guilt in the child in a caring pedophile relationship rather than the relationship itself.

But, of course, there are difficulties. There are practical questions such as potential early pregnancy in girls, and the problems connected with venereal disease. A more rational attitude in society toward contraception, a realistic attitude toward VD, and better sex education would help. But it still leaves the question as to whether children have the emotional resources to deal with pedophile relationships and the emotional crises that can happen. It is important to stress that the pedophile issue is not one of molestation. No one can defend sexual violence in any situation in which one party is unwilling. It is in a crucial sense an issue of consent—an appallingly difficult concept to define in this particular context. This raises two related issues. In the first place, "consent" has different meanings for children and for adults and takes different forms. And second, specific sexual acts have different meanings, and a specific sexual act will have a different meaning for the adult and the young person. In this context what does it mean for a "child" to "consent" to "sex" with an "adult"?

Fundamentally, these are issues of disparity of experience, needs, desires, physical potentialities, emotional resources, sense of responsibility, awareness of the consequences of one's action, and, above all, power between adults and children. This is the crux of most opposition by feminists and gay socialists to pedophilia.

CHILDHOODS

We must recognize that "childhood" is itself a historical category, and like other cultural categories we have mentioned, is a fairly recent one (its evolution is traced in *Centuries of Childhood* by Philippe Aries). Only since the eighteenth century have we reified the position of young people into our particular embodiment of "innocence." The intervention by the State to "protect" children often flowed from economic and political pressures, leading to laws that controlled child labor and extended the period of schooling, for example. But it was also tied to concern with the family, and so laws controlling prostitution and homosexuality contained age of consent regulations. This all aided in the construction of the longer period of "childhood" we know today. Emotional relationships have been largely confined within the family, and the independence of the young has been seen as a threat.

Only since the last century have we so paradoxically both denied the existence of childhood sexuality *and* been preoccupied with curbing its manifestations, such as childhood masturbation and sexual games. Even today, while our moralists rush to protect children, the capitalist system they support constantly incites sexuality (including childhood sexuality) at all levels to sell its wares. But people will say that there is a difference between a child having sexual experiences with someone of the same age and having them with a more experienced, potentially exploitative adult. There probably is, but how is this difference to be recognized. Should a line be drawn, and, if it is, how should it be enforced? A legal age of consent is an arbitrary fiction. Emotional ages vary, and someone of 10 might be more able to "consent" than someone 16. An age of consent in law does not prevent the sexual activity from taking place; and it serves to perpetuate the myth that most, if not all, adults can *and always do* "consent."

Sexual expression between adults and children need not be harmful, and so it cannot be condemned just because it takes place. But it is problematical because it raises issues of disparities of power. How can we safeguard the child's right to consent? PIE (in its publication *Some Questions and Answers*) answers this question in four ways:

1. By suggesting that we overdramatize the question of moral choice involved in accepting a pleasurable act. "All that matters is whether the act is pleasurable."

2. The child is quite capable, from infancy, of showing reluctance. "If the child seems puzzled or hesitant, rather than relaxed and cheerful, he [the adult] should assume that he hasn't [gotten the child's consent]."

3. The best way to encourage choice is by encouraging different attitudes to sex. "A healthier attitude would make it easier for the child to speak up, without feeling embarrassed about it."

4. If the adult persists and enforces his will on the child, "the adult should then be liable to legal action and social condemnation."

It seems to us that (1) and (2) are vague and circular. Enjoyment is not necessarily a sign of having consented (an argument often used against raped women), and it is not a justification in itself for accepting a particular act. One may be hesitant but consenting. An adult can manipulate consent almost unconsciously.

Points (3) and (4) are the keys, but they need to be closely defined. This means two strategies which need to be developed and discussed in the gay movement. First, we need to be clearer about the implications of using legal action. We need to find the means of protecting young people's rights which do not patronize, introduce the arbitrariness of an age of consent, or destroy with a blunderbuss.

At present we have a situation in which adults have supreme power over children—economic, physical, intellectual, and emotional. So it is at least problematical whether in this situation relationships of some equality can be formed which involve sexual expression. In an ideal situation, in which relationships took place in the context of mutual agreement and without major social consequences for both parties, this may be possible. But some pedophiles stress that the sort of relationships they want with children can take place in the existing framework.

However, we have to take account of the real social situation in which we live, of the vulnerability of children and the relatively effortless way in which adults can manipulate in pursuing their desires to the point of ignoring the interests, wishes, and feelings of children. Children may not be equipped, either experientially or physically, for adult-defined sexuality. Children are very sensual and enjoy physical contact, but they may not have the same conceptual categories as adults about sex. With children's autonomy and awareness at such a low level, their ability to say no should not necessarily be taken as agreement. For this reason it would seem that pedophile relationships are likely to be unequal, though in this they only parallel other adult/child relationships in our society.

To sum up this point, it would appear that the criteria exist for recognizing the validity of relationships when there is some approximation of meaning. This does not imply identity of age or interest, but it does imply an ability on the part of the child to recognize some of the significance in social and sexual terms of his/her actions. We are inclined to believe that this does not usually happen before puberty. The problem becomes, then, how do we socially recognize this?

In the present climate some members of the Collective support proposals that the "age of consent" should be reduced to 14 as the only realistic possibility and that this age should be enforced outside of criminal law in special children's courts. These courts would deal with all sorts of children's rights outside the bureaucratic disaster of present legal interventions in this area.

Other members of the Collective, believing that any age of consent is unjust and unworkable, want the repeal of all legislation relating to the age of consent in the field of sexuality. Offenses would be considered on the basis of the use of violence, force, or pressure rather than an arbitrary age. The concept of consent would have to be used on a pragmatic basis, each case being judged on its particular circumstances rather than within the straitjacket of present legislation. This would mean removing criminal sanctions from nonviolent sexual activity while providing the maximum social means for protecting the child. In this situation the responsibility of pedophiles would have a major part to play.

CARE AND CONTROL

As a long-term issue we have to debate the whole question of changing attitudes toward sexuality. We can all agree that we need better sex education, advice on contraception and VD, etc. But how do we fundamentally transform social mores? How do we ensure that in the end the young person is allowed to grow at his or her own pace, untrammeled by overrigid categorization of childhood, protected from abuses of power, and yet able to grow in caring relationships with other (perhaps older) people?

Part of the difficulty is in the way we have defined and constructed the problem. If we ask, "How can we safeguard the child's right to consent?" we are already relegating to second place, if not totally ignoring, the ability of the child to safeguard that right for himself or herself. At present we find ourselves as third parties entering into a dialogue between unequal sides. The dialogue is one-sided because the children involved or potentially involved are not seen or felt capable of presenting their own case. In intervening, moral crusaders, and even people like ourselves, may serve not to decrease the power imbalance but to perpetuate it by totally excluding children from the debate. Adults are responsible for recognizing the limitations of children's ability to be responsible for themselves and for acting accordingly. But children still need to gain more autonomy within new social relations in which adult responsibility is not synonymous with parental authority. An important step toward this would be the strengthening of organizations such as the National Union of School Students and School Kids Against the Nazis. It is there, as well as in the sphere of adult life, that issues such as children's sexuality and their rights should be discussed and fostered.

It is paradoxical that it is in the area of sexuality that there is so much uproar about the power imbalance between adults and children. Where is the debate around the gross economic differences between adults and children, the intellectual and physical advantages adults have, all of which can and are used to exploit and "corrupt" children? It is paradoxical because it is in the sphere of sexual/physical pleasure that children could have the relatively lesser disadvantage. It is the one currency of social relationships that children are best versed in—we operate on the "pleasure principle" from birth. We do not deny that even on this level there are difficulties. But it is crucial that the debate has centered on child *sexuality* to the exclusion of other aspects of adult/child relations. What we must avoid is a totally "adult-centered" solution.

SADISM AND MASOCHISM

A variant of gay sexuality that tends to be more hidden from the public eye is S&M, or sado-masochism. It is a practice by which the giving and receiving of pain by consensual partners leads to erotic gratification. Fantasy usually plays a large role in its practice, as can bondage and the use of leather apparel or implements (whips, dildoes, etc.). Many large cities, especially in northern Europe and English-speaking countries, such as the United States, Britain, and Canada, have bars or clubs that cater to those interested. Reactions to S&M practice differ sharply. Critics associate it with perversion and human debasment, and liken the fascination with uniforms and leather to authoritarian and fascistic tendencies. Adherents, on the other hand, argue its merits with every bit as much conviction. The practice, they say, is by definition consensual and thus bears no comparison with cruelty or violence. On the contrary, it provides pleasure to both participants. From a more political perspective, advocates contend that S&M affords a means of exposing and exploring the underlying power discrepancies found in all of our relationships. In this latter sense, sado-masochism is but an exaggerated form or dramatic playing out of the dominant and submissive patterns into which we have all been socialized as men and women.

In the first of the following two articles, Italian writer Mario Mieli argues that we need to liberate the sadistic and masochistic components within us as part of our quest for self-realization. The many forms in which S&M manifests itself today, in his view, are but grotesque distortions, reflective of the alienating and dehumanizing capitalist system in which we live.

The second article, taken from the German magazine, *Schwuchtel*,

is rather cleverly written as a form of dialogue "Don Poofke" has
with himself. Here the suggestion is made that S&M practices are
not as out of the ordinary as one might think. Witness society's
obsession with sexual violence, or the rigid dichotomization of sex
roles, which encourages one partner to act dominant and aggressive
and the other passive and submissive in "normal" relationships.
When Don comments that his fantasies of rape contradict his
equally strong desires for a sexuality free of domination, Poofke
interjects that force need not be equated with oppression. Though
more issues are raised by the article than resolved, every person, it
concludes, should be encouraged to come to terms with his or her
sadistic and masochistic urges if new forms of behavior are ever to
emerge.

ITALY

From *Homosexuality and Liberation: Elements of a Gay Critique* by Mario Mieli, translated by David Fernbach (1980).

The achievement of homosexual awareness and the liberation of the gay desire break open the closed world of the traditional heterosexual couple, and above all dispel the murky fog of possible betrayals, infidelities, and jealousies that weigh upon it, poisoning it day and night. Jealousy, too, therefore, is based on a serious misunderstanding of the homosexual desire. It gnaws at the liver of the heterosexual male if his woman gets off with another man, because he is unaware that if he, too, were to make love with this other man, with other men in general, then he would have taken the most important step toward overcoming his tribulations and transforming jealousy into enjoyment. It may well be true that jealousy today often involves an indirect expression of masochist tendencies, and thus in a certain respect is a pleasure in itself. But it is also true that masochism can be enjoyed in a more satisfactory, conscious, direct, and communicative way.

Giuliano De Fusco has pointed out to me that a person aware of his masochism exerts himself to bring out the "contradiction" in his partner, by which he means the inhibited sadism, or, in the wider sense, the sadistic and masochistic impulses of those who do not recognize their own sado-masochistic propensity. The true masochist is adept at including his partner to liberate his aggression and become aware of it. This involves an increase in emotion and enjoyment for both parties, and the masochist ultimately manages to see the person as he "really" is, uninhibitedly. In a love relation, the genuine masochist sees himself the object of an amorous aggression, permitting him to directly and openly enjoy the pleasure of jealousy; "betrayal" becomes an act of love, since it reveals aggression and hence enhances pleasure and passion.

But conscious sado-masochism is certainly not the same thing as the sado-masochism implicit in the "normal" couple. As Giuliano De Fusco observes, this relationship reflects the alienated and alienating sado-masochism with which capitalist society is permeated, which is authoritarian and repressive, and which, by negating the human being, sadistically negates also his sadism, imposing on him a subhuman and humiliating condition, and debasing his masochism.

Just as a loving desire for people of the other sex is today reduced by the system to a stunted and phallocratic heterosexuality, while desire for people of the same sex is severely repressed by a society that transforms this into an instrument of capitalist power by forcing it to remain latent or desublimating it in an alienating manner, in the same way the sadistic and masochistic tendencies are divided and repressed, and exploited by capital, which distorts them so as to make them serve its own rule. The revolution will also involve, among other things, the positive liberation of sadism and masochism, and a free community in which masochistic and sadistic desires will find open expression and take on a new and transformed form, quite different from the "sado-masochism" of today. With masochism and sadism, too, the revolutionary critique also attacks the prejudice that sees sadism and masochism as simply "perversions," mere distortions of Eros, denying their intrinsic importance, their ability to bridge the gulf between Eros and Thanatos, between good and evil, and to overcome—in practical and emotional life—the dichotomy of opposites that is based on repression.

GERMANY

"Don Poofke Has a Serious Discussion With Himself," translated by Marilyn Kaiser-Lilly, from *Schwuchtel: Eine Zeitung der Schwulenbewegung* (June–August 1976).

POOFKE: Tell me about your latest difficulties.

DON: You have most likely heard about people who connect sexuality with pain. Don't you think that that falls a bit out of the framework of normality?

POOFKE: Which framework? Our society is boiling over with drives, whereby sexual violence is the most prominent.

DON: But there are only a few who are called sadists or masochists.

POOFKE: Even so, it appears to me that the desire for sexual violence or for sexual domination is fairly widespread. Take, for example, your parents' relationship? Isn't your mother subservient to your father? Isn't she economically dependent upon him?

DON: You could interpret such a relationship as a master/slave relationship. But isn't that different from sadistic sexual practices?

POOFKE: Consciousness of the enjoyment of pain is only an arbitrary criterion for sadistic sexuality. Sadism or masochism is sanctioned a thousand times over. Most people enjoy it in one form or another. At least for a short time. There is no qualitative distinction between sadistic and normal sexuality. But what is bothering you?

DON: I can no longer distance myself from sadists and masochists.

POOFKE: How does that manifest itself?

DON: Once I observed two prostitutes in a fight. I have to confess it turned me on. Once I flirted in the subway with a guy. He wore leather pants, which I liked so much that the very next day I had to buy a pair. I dreamed of raping and being raped. I didn't want to slowly slide my penis into the anus, and then tenderly fondle my men, because I was really in the mood to grab and ram them.

POOFKE: What prevented you from giving in to your desire?

DON: I'm not sure. Barriers are raised in my head, and this kicks in often while screwing. That is my problem. Then I don't want to be violent. There's nothing I hate more than domination, and that is not an arbitrary statement, there are experiences to support it. Every gay must hate domination, because he has experienced oppression. My wish for sexuality free of domination is not a demand, it is a need, just as strong as the need to be in charge.

POOFKE: I see the conflict, it goes right to the core. You must reject the violence that you have experienced, but you cannot suppress the desire for domination because it returns then through the back door and exacts a terrible revenge. But don't you think that you are too quick to equate force with oppression? Isn't every emancipation movement forceful when it hits the target? Doesn't that hold equally so for the class war? Isn't every change in general accompanied by force? What does it mean, then, when you don't dive in, and forgo grabbing your man roughly, when you instead fondle him gently with consideration? You respect that he is autonomous, you put up with your and his isolation, you accentuate his untouchability, in that you handle him with more care than you would an ordinary object.

DON: In this case, I agree with you. But what about my other needs? If I go and rape a man, I rob him of his freedom. It will hurt him, and I can neither assume that he enjoys it nor that the situation is communicative. He will then start to really withdraw.

POOFKE: You will also have difficulties if you attempt such a thing. You will want it and not want it. I don't believe that in this conflict you can throw all the experiences and insights into domination and violence overboard, nor can you minimize them. Just for that reason, the leather scene is not the place for you to learn to fulfill your desires, or if it should become necessary, where you learn to assimilate them in a different way. Most assuredly, that is important for you. It is important for everyone to come to terms with sadistic and masochistic sexuality. This should not take place in the repressed way that most people handle this. It is important for each person to establish his own personal point of reference. If this is not accomplished, the discussion is pointless and not even worth pursuing. The discussions will change our behavior, and out of this will arise new aspects and new perspectives on sadistic sexuality. Of this I am quite certain.

CHAPTER FIVE

LIVING OUR LIVES

There is perhaps no better indication of the monumental changes taking place worldwide in regard to the development of a modern gay consciousness than in the examination of our daily lives as lesbians and gay men. Ultimately it is not to the legal status of gays, or the ideologies espoused by organized movements, but rather to the details and incidents that are the weave of our daily existence where we find the most insight.

The seven selections that follow reflect the lives of gay men and lesbians from a wide variety of backgrounds, including Afro-Caribbean, Kenyan East Indian, Mexican, Canadian, Native American, Turkish Cypriot, and East German. Both men and women are represented, the physically able and disabled, the young and the elderly, Caucasians and People of Color, and citizens of the First and Third worlds. What connects these individuals together in common bond —despite their enormous cultural differences—is their awareness of being attracted to members of the same sex and their struggles to incorporate their sexuality into their everyday lives without shame or stigma.

All of the men and women whom we meet have experienced living secret, closeted lives due to homophobic prejudice within their respective societies. Pedro from Mexico and Zahid Dar, the East Indian from Kenya living in England, both recall being driven farther into isolation and feelings of loneliness when their search for validation of their homosexual feelings in books led only to same-sex love being portrayed as "disease" or "sin." Richard, a blind gay Canadian, finds his sexuality negated in the ubiquitous messages he receives that "Blind men don't fuck." Zerrin, a Moslem woman,

comments once feeling as an adult that she "has no sexuality," so
strong has been the negation of female sexuality, not to speak of
lesbianism, in her particular experience. Likewise, Makeda Silvera,
an Afro-Caribbean, can speak of the "invisibility" of lesbians both
in her native Jamaica and her adopted homeland of Canada.

Coming out, or the process by which a homosexual person comes
to accept and positively affirm his or her sexuality, is another experience that is shared by these same individuals. For some, the
process was relatively quick, for others it entailed prolonged periods
of self-doubt, anguish, and anger. With the possible exception of
J.A.W. of East Germany (now Germany), all have subsequently
channeled their energies into working politically for social change.
Most also have had to struggle as minorities within a minority, due
to their ethnic, racial, or disabled status within the larger gay or
lesbian movements. Though political goals have varied, the demand
for recognition of gay rights and the freedom to express one's
sexuality without impunity has remained constant.

The search for roots has played a prominent part in at least two
of the following accounts. M. Owlfeather is painfully aware of the
proud status many Native American nations had given to tribal
members with homosexual inclinations before the White Man's
incursion. His dream is to revitalize this tradition and restore to the
Native American peoples the special vision gay Native Americans
have to offer. Makeda Silvera, in exploring her Jamaican cultural
background, is able to connect the rampant homophobia and sexism
of recent generations to the experience of slavery and national
oppression to which her people were subjected.

The individuals who speak to us in the following pages would
not ordinarily be thought of as exceptional human beings—there
are no scholars, scientists, or national leaders among them. Yet, as
lesbians and gay men who have known oppression firsthand, survived, and struggled for a more honest and meaningful life—for
themselves and others—they are truly extraordinary. It is common
people such as these who hold the key to the world's future in their
hands.

CANADA

The three Canadians we meet in the following article are all gay or bisexual men who are physically disabled. Each of them has had to cope with being marginalized by society on multiple levels. As persons with disabilities, they have met with patronizing attitudes within institutional settings, and discriminatory practices in public. At the same time, as members of sexual minorities, society has denied them recognition, and institutional staff, due to their own discomfort, have routinely ignored or downplayed their sexual needs.

Even within the gay ghetto, as the article points out, the disabled are often unwelcome or, equally as disconcerting, treated in a patronizing or insensitive manner. What becomes evident is the need for more education and a heightened awareness by more privileged gays toward all minorities, whether they be People of Color, the aged, the economically disenfranchised, or the disabled. Hannon's article and the day-to-day struggles of the three men we meet provide a valuable contribution to this effort.

"No Sorrow, No Pity: The Gay Disabled" by Gerald Hannon, from *Flaunting It! A Decade of Journalism from "The Body Politic."* Mr. Hannon is a writer and prostitute from Toronto.

Richard was a premature baby. Fifty years earlier he might have died at birth. But this was 1953, and little baby Richard was placed lovingly in an incubator of reputable American make. No one would know for many, many months, but some of the machines did not work very well, and babies across North America were quietly breathing an oxygen mixture so rich that their retinal tissue slowly burned away. "I was one of the lucky ones," Richard told me. "Some grew up with really horrible brain damage. I just grew up blind." Richard is officially a handicapped human being. He is one of an estimated two hundred thousand disabled persons in Toronto alone—though numbers are hard to come by because nobody's counting. The conventional wisdom is that the handicapped represent 14 percent of the population—one in seven. But however many there are, the numbers, according to an article in *Physiotherapy Canada,* are growing. The "new paraplegics of Canadian society," it says, "are young people between the ages of fourteen and nineteen" —smashed up in car accidents, snowmobile disasters, even run-ins between ten-speed bicycles.

For Richard, an excess of oxygen slowly burned away his vision. For Scott McArthur, born in 1952, there were a few struggling moments in the throes of birth when oxygen was cut off, and in those minutes brain cells died like lights going out in a panicked and desperate city. His intelligence was not affected, but Scott grew up with a condition known as cerebral palsy—CP. His days are spent in a wheelchair. His speech is distorted and labored; anyone unused to it will find him very difficult to understand. His movements appear spastic and uncoordinated. If he is not careful, he will drool.

Like Richard, Scott McArthur is gay.

People like Richard and Scott have not been figures in our landscape. I know. I know that there are gay men and women everywhere—that they are single, that they are married, that they appear at every economic level and in every race and nationality, but . . . Maybe it's our dogged insistence on our essential health as gay people, on our persistent view of ourselves in our own media as whole, active, healthy, bright, and beautiful. Maybe that's it. But I feel that somehow, way at the back of our first closet we have built another one, and into it we have shoved our gay deaf and our gay blind and our gay wheelchair cases, and we've gone on with the already difficult enough problems of living as gay people.

If we've built that second closet, society has made it easy for us. We are not likely to meet the disabled in the workplace—of the employable blind, for example, 80 percent are unemployed. The general employment rate among the handicapped is usually given as 50 percent. And as for socializing—next time you're at your favorite gay spot, count the stairs.

The lives of many disabled gay people are passed in institutions. Scott McArthur lives in one—he asked me not to name it because he has to continue living there. When it was built, it was widely seen as a progressive and innovative institution. But when Scott moved in five years ago, residents were forbidden to shut their doors if they had a visitor of the opposite sex. That rule has changed, but even today there are no rooms that can accommodate couples, and it is generally expected that visitors will leave by midnight. No overnight guests are allowed.

Scott has known institutions most of his life, and this is not the worst of them. But in none of them has leading a sexual life been very easy.

"I can remember being interested in men since I was ten years old," he told me. "When I got into my teens, I began paying other boys in the hospital for sex. My parents gave me spending money, and I spent it paying the other kids to jerk me off. A few years later I was spending close to two hundred dollars a year for sex. But I didn't call myself gay—I didn't know what it meant. But I know I wanted men."

Scott was caught, of course—one thing almost no one has in any institution is privacy. He was told it was bad to have other boys jerk him off. He tried to talk to the staff psychologist about his mysteriously developing sexuality, but it didn't work. He went back to paying the other boys. Shortly after that his parents received a letter saying that Scott was ready to be discharged.

As Scott said, "It was a nice way of kicking me out."

He stayed in his parents' home in Nova Scotia for five years. Not

very much happened. Once, with the conniving of a sympathetic
housekeeper, he managed to order some porn from the States.
Shortly thereafter a letter from Canada Customs arrived—his
mother was the first to read it—informing him that copies of *Hot
Rod* and *Circumcision: A Study in Pictures* had been seized as "immoral
and indecent." Scott was handed the letter, told it was obviously
some business of his, and there the matter lay.

We who are able-bodied remember what coming out was like. It
was not easy, it required privacy, a chance to surreptitiously look
things up in books and magazines, a chance to get out alone for a
while and maybe "accidentally" wander by that place you'd heard
"those" people went to. Maybe, if you were lucky, you found
somebody sympathetic to talk to. All of the people I talked to for
this article have spent part or all of their lives in institutions where
privacy is almost nonexistent, and where the administration, acutely
aware of its dependence on "public money," has been quite frankly
terrified of the topic of sexuality.

"Blind people don't fuck." That is Richard's summation of the
attitudes of not only the School for the Blind in Brantford, but a lot
of the gay people he runs into.

Richard went through grade twelve at the blind school. Every
second Friday there was a very carefully chaperoned dance with the
blind girls to which the blind boys dutifully went, and from which,
before midnight, they were efficiently hustled back to their own
residence. "I used to suck off one of my roommates," Richard said.
"And I used to hear a lot of other people's doors opening and
closing after everyone was supposed to be in bed. We had no
privacy, though—anybody could come in or out because we
weren't allowed to lock anything. We used to call the place 'The
Zoo'—there'd always be people coming on tours to see the 'poor
blind kids.' "

Nothing was ever said about sexuality. Blind people don't fuck.
For Richard, the rationalization that he was sucking off his room-
mate because women were unavailable was beginning to wear a

little thin. "Anyway," he said, "from as far back as I can remember
I loved being with men. I used to have this great crush on my old
man. I loved climbing in bed with him when I was still a kid and
we both had our underwear on."

Again, the institution. The Canadian National Institute for the
Blind—the CNIB, "snib," as Richard calls it—is one of the powerful ones. Richard is not very happy with snib. "Having your life
run by the CNIB is like having your life run by a church group," he
says. "They're arbitrary, they provide 'services,' they have a custo-
dial attitude." BOOST (Blind Organization of Ontario with Self-
help Tactics), of which Richard is a member, says that fewer than a
third of the people on CNIB's board are blind, and that they've
ensured, in fact, that the blind *can't* have control. Richard simply
snorted when I asked him if the CNIB was a place for the blind to
turn to for information on sexuality. I went to check.

I had to because the CNIB has basically cornered the market on
information for the blind. Their Braille and "talking book" library
in Toronto is the blind person's national library. I spoke to the
CNIB's Pat Trusty who, if she is nonplussed by my probing questions about the availability of adequate sex information for the gay
blind, does not show it. She promises she will check their holdings.
I ask about pornography; she promises she will check that, too. In
the meantime she lends me a great stack of catalogues giving a
partial list of titles. Leafing through them, I discover they have *The
Joy of Sex*—but not the gay male and lesbian versions.

Trusty, who is nothing if not cooperative, calls back in a week
and says yes, the library does have one title. It is *The Gay Theology*. I
do not tell her it is a dreadful book. There are, however, eight more
titles in the United States that would be available on interlibrary
loan, if requested. There are some good titles—Peter Fisher's *The
Gay Mystique,* for example, or Wainwright Churchill's *Homosexual
Behaviour Among Males*. There is nothing specifically about lesbians,
and nothing published in the last five years. There are no gay
liberation periodicals. There are, however, volumes by those twin

quacks of psychoanalysis, Irving Bieber and Edmund Bergler. There is also the temptingly titled *Homosexuality: Its Causes and Curses*. And no, there is no available pornography.

Trusty assures me, however, that a selection committee of the CNIB will consider any request for the conversion of printed material to Braille or talking book. Fat chance. "Sighted" people may cruise a gay magazine for weeks before they dare pick it—even in the relative anonymity of a newsstand. It doesn't seem very likely to me that a gay blind person will put him- or herself on the line before an unknown quantity like a "selection committee"—no matter how badly the material may be wanted.

Richard, or course, had access to no information at all. Richard had to slowly stumble out of the closet. He called a gay counseling line a few times, but got nervous and hung up. And because he couldn't see, and because he had no access to any written materials on gayness, he developed some very peculiar ideas about what gay people were like. All he had to go on was voice—and for him, gayness became the stereotyped lisping, mannered male voice. *He* wasn't like that, but somehow it was all wrapped up in a man who would be taller than he and have a deep, resonant voice and a furry, muscular arm—something he could get to check, by the by, since it happens to be perfectly okay for a blind man to take another man's arm when walking.

He went looking for that man at The Barn, a Toronto gay bar. And there he ran into some of the same paternalistic attitudes that enraged him at "snib." "One man came up and asked if I knew what kind of bar this was. I said sure, it's a gay bar. He said you mean you go home with people? And I said no, I simply stand around all night like a statue." Richard says he also got *very* tired of people saying "isn't that too bad." Or people yelling in his face because they feel he must be a little dim as well. Or people who want "to look after me." Now, he says, he gets a lot of the initial tension out of the way by introducing himself as "that weird blind person who may fall over you."

You get to say something like that, of course, only if you happen to have a pretty good self-image. That wasn't always the case for Richard, but it helped to discover he could pick up two or three people a week at The Barn during what he now terms his "whoring phase." A phase now over—he's involved in a relationship, has a job with BOOST, and plans to keep plugging away in the fight for disabled rights. "It means more to me than the gay struggle," he says. "I have more to gain for one thing—like a job somewhere other than BOOST, and independence."

Independence. Like most everyone else, the disabled want to control their own lives. And if they must live in institutions, they want to control those institutions and make them responsive to their real needs.

John Kellerman has been fighting that battle—until recently, a rather lonely one—for twelve years. When he tried to move back into a group home he'd left a year and a half earlier, he was told he couldn't because he "raised too much shit. And I thought I was doing everything I could to make it a better place by organizing the residents and so on."

Like Scott, John Kellerman has CP. It hits people in many different ways, though, and John can walk (although very awkwardly), while Scott can't. But John's speech seems to have been affected much more, and I find him more difficult to understand. He's patient enough to repeat everything five or six times if that's what it takes, and I'm persistent enough to keep asking, so we struggle through.

John defines himself as bisexual. He has fantasized about having sex with women, but remembers how he used to love to watch construction workers in the summer even when he was just a kid, how he was fascinated by their bodies. "I used to be afraid," he says, "of being condemned by gay people for wanting both. But it hasn't really happened—mostly it's having been brought up in a society that says we have to love one or the other."

John says that he was so desperate for information on sexuality that he helped organize one of the earliest conferences on the topic just so he'd finally learn something. "I went to Queen's Park in

1974 and got two thousand dollars and we actually got something going. I felt ecstatic—I'd been so hung up about organizing and about sex generally. But the conference was great."

That hadn't been his first effort, however. In the early seventies he helped found a group called ALPHA, Advancement League for the Physically Handicapped, and that group successfully lobbied the city for the grading of sidewalks and the initiation of Wheel-Trans, the transit commission's project for the physically disabled. More recently he has organized a citizens' committee to plan activities for 1981—the International Year of the Disabled. "One thing that sort of frightens me," he said, "is that we'll be inundated with do-gooders. That scares the hell out of me."

John Kellerman is an activist, but every activist has a private life. Or tries to. "I'm very lonely," he says. "I want to develop a relationship with someone, but nothing much has happened with either men or women. I've often wanted to go to the baths, but I'm afraid to because I'm afraid they wouldn't let me in. I went to two in Winnipeg, and they wouldn't let me past the door. I don't go to many bars because I have a real complex about going, though I haven't had any problems in the gay bars I've gone to here. It's been worse in straight bars and restaurants. Sometimes they ask me to leave. Sometimes they allow me to stay, but then I just sit there and nobody ever serves me. I was physically removed from the Hotel Toronto last September—nobody gave me any reason. I was just there in the lobby waiting for a friend."

The worst incident he remembers occurred when he left a friend at a street corner and hailed a cab. When he got in, the driver took a good look at him and refused to drive off. John refused to get out. The driver, in desperation, began offering money to passersby if they would take John off his hands. He was offering two dollars. John says it was the most humiliating experience of his life.

I think John would call that taxi driver a "normal" person, and he does not have a very high opinion of normality. "Normal persons are very frightened persons," he wrote in a short essay. "They are frightened of themselves, and of people who are different, or who have different ideas, so why should we as disabled people try and degrade ourselves even more by becoming normal? Why not change the world . . . ? Normal people need a purpose for living, and we need people to help us. They need people to look up to. Could we be them?"

In those thoughts, John is beginning to reconceptualize the very categories into which our thoughts are straitjacketed. Already we have come some way from the times when a Sunday afternoon's entertainment was a trip to Bedlam to watch the mad cavort. And I suppose even that was an improvement over Justinian's Byzantium, where those born deaf were deprived of their civic rights. (Justinian was the emperor, though, who thought homosexuality caused earthquakes. Not a very scientific regime, that one.)

But we are still some way from seeing that to be handicapped means simply to be human in a slightly different way. UNESCO has published a paper which outlines the stages through which public attitudes develop with reference to the handicapped. There is the philanthropic stage, the public welfare stage, the stage of fundamental rights, the stage of the right to equal opportunity, and finally the stage of the right to integration. In that final stage, it is the very notion of norms and normality that is called into question. Suddenly one is faced with questioning whether there is very much difference between an individual with a baby carriage facing a staircase, and someone in a wheelchair facing a telephone booth. In both cases, the problem is not the "handicap." The problem is the telephone, or the stairs. "The difficulties of the disabled often reveal difficulties experienced by all," notes the UNESCO report, and cites the example of an American university where "the abolition of architectural obstacles for six handicapped students made life better for all the students."

Every one of us begins life as a disabled person. We don't ordinarily think of infancy in quite that way, but it is a period during which we are entirely helpless and dependent. For many of us, old age has some of the effects. And almost everyone, at some point in his or her life, will be briefly bedridden, or have a limb in a cast, or need psychiatric help. That is certainly not the same as spending your life blind or deaf or in a wheelchair, but it does indicate that we are talking about a spectrum here, not discrete and mutually exclusive groups. We are talking about ways of being fully human.

Sex is a fully human need. Sex that is masturbation, sex that's just a quickie with no names exchanged thank you very much, and sex that takes place as part of some broader relationship. Many disabled have known only masturbation. Not a few find even that impossible.

Scott McArthur works for the MCC as a referral person when that church gets calls from the gay disabled. "Someone called me last week," Scott told me. "He was desperate. He told me he couldn't even masturbate. Where could he go, he asked me, where could he go? I had to tell him there was nowhere he could go."

It's the big taboo. The disabled are supposed to have "more important" things to think about. A report from the Sex Informa-tion and Education Council of the United States notes that "in the name of benevolence and protection, many people still take the position that sex information would 'hurt' the disabled. Why should Pandora's box be opened to a person who is unable to use what is there? . . . After all, disabled people are fragile and not expected to take care of themselves." As one straight woman said at a Sex and the Disabled conference a few years ago, "I had come out of the rehab center and after twenty-two months of hospitalization we had never discussed the word sex, except among us, as paraplegics and quadriplegics. We were taught repression. We were taught that if we couldn't have something, don't rock the boat."

Blind people don't fuck, as Richard would say. But if the disabled do, or want to try, or—God forbid—if they're disabled enough to need assistance, then most of our institutions would really rather not hear about it. The public—not to mention Mom and Dad— might not be quite ready to hear that part of little Johnny's or Mary's physical therapy includes lessons on how to masturbate.

The topic, however, is finally beginning to surface among profes-sionals at least. I spoke to Michael Barrett of the Sex Information and Education Council of Canada (SIECCAN). He has long been an advocate of sexual rights for the disabled—you're unlikely to find a seminar or conference on the topic which doesn't feature him either as an organizer, chair, or speaker. I ask about sex and the gay disabled, and he admits that he has run into almost nothing on the topic. He is a very gay-supportive individual though, and makes sure the topic is raised whenever he gives a workshop or seminar. He sends me a package of materials to look through, and it is depressing. I think homosexuality was mentioned twice—once in passing, and once thus: "When the patient's sexual activity is homosexual or otherwise variant, physician-patient communication is ordinarily further restricted." Indeed.

I did a bit of checking—again with institutions, because institutions are so frequently "home" for so many disabled. The general reaction might best be described as cautious. And where gay sexuality is concerned, a kind of benign neglect seems to be the rule.

Mrs. Ann Pahl is the administrator of Participation House, a permanent residence in Markham for the multihandicapped. There have been two marriages at Participation House. She says there is no problem with casual sexual encounters, but the individuals would probably have to ask the staff for assistance, at least out of their wheelchairs, and it would be given. There can be no overnight visitors though—if residents want that sort of thing they're expected to book into a motel. She was quite frank when I asked whether a gay couple could set up house: "I certainly wouldn't be shocked, but to protect myself I'd have to present it to the Board for approval. I'm afraid we couldn't take it lightly; we're dependent on the community and the government for volunteers and funds. We're all very conscious of our community image, and we're closely watched by Queen's Park. People might be critical of anything that isn't pretty mainstream."

I was pleasantly surprised though, that Pahl was equally frank about how the needs of those who can't masturbate are met. "Staff might help if requested," she said. "Some staff might be comfortable with this, others might not, and only those who can handle it get involved. We don't use mechanical sex aids yet, but that may come."

Ms. Margaret Graeb, the administrator at Bellwoods, a residential center for handicapped adults, is rather more cautious. She is "not sure" whether any of the residents would be completely unable to masturbate, and on the topic of staff participation says, "We're not ready for that yet. I'd be concerned about the kinds of relationships that might develop. I'd be worried about how other residents might feel. I guess I'm not prepared to see that happening yet."

Asked if homosexuality was part of general discussion of sexuality, she said she thought it was "touched on."

The situation isn't much better out there in the great wide world of the "gay ghetto." Everyone I talked to had a horror story to tell. Deaf men will have someone come into their room at the baths, begin to have sex with them, discover they're deaf—and get up and leave. Scott has been told to get out of the Parkside Tavern— or face the cops. Told he would not be allowed in Charly's, a local disco, without an escort. At gay dances he *can* get to, the music is usually so loud that anyone unused to his speech problems will find him impossible to understand. Richard has heard people say, loudly enough for him to hear, "Why does *he* have to come to a place like this?"

As disabled activist Pat Israel said at a workshop on sexuality, "Everyone's handicapped, only some people's wheelchairs are on the inside, not on the outside where you can see them."

Then there's the emphasis on youth and beauty—an obsession that pervades the entire culture, and one the gay world certainly shares. "It's one that *I* share," Scott told me. "I want an attractive man."

None of this is very easy for anybody. Disabled people used to make me unbearably uncomfortable. If I saw a wheelchair coming my way, I would make some excuse to cross the street. I spoke about this to Tom Warner, a gay activist who's been involved with handicapped groups in the Coalition for Life Together. "I have two disabled relatives as well," he told me, "so I should be used to it.

But one night I got picked up by a man in a car, and it was only after I got in that I noticed the wheelchair in the back. I went home with him and we went to bed and it didn't really work out. I think he was quite depressed. But his legs were so cold, I flinched every time they touched me and of course he sensed it. But I couldn't help it."

None of this is going to be easy. But change is coming—partly because the disabled themselves are pushing against every constraint society has managed to put in their way, and not a few of the people doing the pushing are our gay brothers and sisters.

"Talk to us," Scott says. "If you see somebody in a wheelchair, talk. If you can't think of anything to say, go over and say, 'I've never talked to anybody in a wheelchair before, and I don't know what to say.' Maybe it'll get something going."

"I want to see more cooperation between minorities," says John Kellerman. "We have to understand our commonalities and differences. We have to talk, we have to discuss problems and tactics."

"Solidarity," said André Malraux, "is the most intelligent form of egoism."

They do not want pity. They say listen, and understand. They do not want help. They say cooperate. To be handicapped is one way of being human. They say that they are all that men and women *can* be.

CYPRUS–GREAT BRITAIN

Very little has been written and/or translated into English concerning homosexuality in contemporary Islamic culture. In the West, gross generalizations such as "all Moslem men are bisexual," or stereotypes of the submissive and veiled Moslem woman still abound. The following interview affords us the opportunity to meet a Moslem lesbian mother of Turkish Cypriot background who at present resides in England. Zerrin's story is one of a courageous individual who refuses to be channeled into traditional roles that are oppressive to her as a woman and who, in the end, comes to accept a lesbian identity against many odds.

The situations Zerrin confronts along her life's journey are difficult ones: incest, fixed marriage, being a woman of color in a racist society, the need to define her sexual identity, homophobic attitudes, and lesbian motherhood. Her experiences in coming to terms with each of these issues serve to strengthen her resolve and, ultimately, enable her to emerge from her many closets into a more fulfilling self-realization.

"Zerrin," interviewed by Liz Fletcher (March 1986)
for *Inventing Ourselves: Lesbian Life Stories*
by the Lesbian Oral History Group of the
Hall Carpenter Archives (1989).

I was born in Cyprus in a very small village in 1956. My memories of being a child are either very positive or very negative. In Cyprus I had a lot of freedom when I was young because my mother went out to work and my sister looked after us. I was allowed to play and climb trees and I would run wild. We lived in a village up to the age of six, then we moved to Limassol.

Most of the summer evenings people would sit outside under the jasmine tree. I remember one of the neighbors buying a television and inviting people around to watch it. We would sit in the garden, the television would be in the doorway, and you'd get loads of kids sitting in a row watching.

I remember not having hot water, so every time we wanted a bath we used to leave a big container of water outside and the sun would heat it up. In our garden—well, it was more like a backyard —we had an apple, a lemon, a date, and an almond tree, and I remember I was always a good climber. I could climb up but I would never be able to get down. I used to eat the dates when they were all green and horrible so we could make something with the pits like a necklace. I remember picking jasmines to make necklaces to sell, as that was the only way I was going to get any money to buy pencils and rubbers and things like that. We'd pick tiny little flowers in the early evening and by the time it was eight or nine o'clock they would have blossomed. We'd go over to the park and sell them. I used to always get into trouble for that because my mom thought that was begging.

I think that in 1963 the conflict began in Cyprus. The island wasn't divided then, but I remember having things drummed into my head about not playing with the Greek children. We were told not to pick any fruits off the trees in case they were poisoned, and that they were trying to kill us. We still did it as it made it more exciting thinking that it was forbidden.

I started school at the age of six. The schools were very strict and getting things wrong meant you were going to get hit. The thing that struck in my mind was the uniform: red and white gingham dresses, which reminded me of the flag: its red background and white moon and star.

Around twice a year we had special days off, such as Ramadan. The children would celebrate it more because they'd actually go around visiting the elders getting sweets and money, and whenever Ramadan came around I'd have a new frock. Sometimes when you visited really poor and elderly people they'd say a prayer in front of you, and I thought, "I don't want this, I want money." You'd have a competition: who could get the most money, pennies really. You'd be visiting very early in the morning, about half past five. Sometimes if it were a certain festival we'd have henna on our hands. My mother would put it on her hair but I wasn't allowed to because I wasn't a woman. I could have it on my hands and maybe I could have a moon and a star. They could call me a woman as soon as I started my period. Mind you, when I did start it I got a slap in my face. I didn't know why. Speaking to other Turkish girls I found that their moms slapped their face as well. I thought, "Is this my fate for being a girl?"

I remember periods being quite negative and being told to shave. In England I was given a razor blade and told to go to the bathroom to shave. I never talked to my eldest sister about it, because of the way we had been brought up. Periods and sex were things you didn't talk about. I didn't know what sex was. We didn't have sex education and I didn't know where babies came from. I remember giggling when watching films and seeing couples kissing. I remember going under my bed and doing the same things with a friend, you know, kissing. They're my first memories of physical contact. I remember saying to my friend that when I had a baby she would be allowed to feed it and I would breast-feed her baby. In some way I thought that would make them sisters and quite close: I'd seen other women doing it. When I was born my mom said that, because she had to go out to work, the neighbor would feed me because they were having babies at the same time. That was done a lot at the time. You didn't do it for money, you looked after each other's children as a way of supporting each other.

I felt everything that I learned came through women and I remember my looking up to how strong they were. I used to think there was this burden on us, that because we were born female we were inferior, but at the same time I saw strong women around me.

I saw my mother going out to work from half-past five, so to me she wasn't weak, she was the breadwinner.

I think around that time I started asking my mom, "Why do boys get treated differently?" She would say, "Because they are boys." She'd make no secret about it, that because they were boys they were stronger. What would I be doing? I'd be getting an arranged marriage and having children. The only thing I had to do was to have children and to learn how to knit and sew and make dresses. That would be it.

Q: You've touched on the positive aspects. Perhaps now you could say something about the bad times?

I don't mind. For years I didn't talk about the negative experiences in my childhood. I had been silenced. I think the most disturbing thing that ever happened to me was incest, and it wasn't until five years ago that I actually starting talking about it. I don't mind talking now, as I feel it helps me and it may help other women.

It started when I was six. I don't really remember what was happening to me, because as far as I was concerned all fathers might be like that. I thought because he wasn't a stranger it meant that it was OK. I didn't really think about it then, but when I was eleven I remember feeling quite powerless. I didn't want this thing to carry on but it was still happening to me. It wasn't so much that I consented to it, rather it was that I didn't have the power to stop it. I couldn't talk to my mother.

I remember an incident that happened when I was about ten and my mother going mad and having a big argument because my father tried to do it to a neighbor's daughter. She really hit the roof. I remember thinking, "Why don't you do something about it happening to me? Why go mad because it happened to a stranger? I'm your daughter." But I couldn't really say it to her because as far as I was concerned my mom loved me. I remember when it actually came out into the open she started locking the bedroom door, and around that time she started planning to leave Cyprus. It was her way of escaping. She had the power then because she had a British passport and he didn't. She worked for the British at an army base. I think it took two years before she had enough money to pay for the fares for all of us. I think that was one of the most wonderful moments of my life, being told that we'd be leaving in August. This was 1968.

I remember seeing my father off at the harbor. I was really happy. I remember my mom saying, "Give him a last kiss," and I thought, "No, I don't want to kiss him," and I remember seeing tears in his eyes. I felt nothing. The community felt sorry for him because he was going to be left without any family, but I didn't. I knew why and my mom knew why and I admired her because she had made the decision to leave.

I remember in the boat I was so sick but persevering because it would be all right once I got here. We ended up in Dover, then we got a train to Victoria. My uncle came to pick us up. I imagined he would have a massive house, but it was two-story with one family living at the bottom. It was rather shocking to me that housing conditions were so bad: damp walls, a horrible floor and kitchen. It wasn't at all what I imagined it to be. I'd imagined it to be a really beautiful house with a beautiful garden, because back in Cyprus, when I went to visit my mom at work, all the British lived in beautiful houses with carpets and had green gardens. So it was quite a shock to find some British people living in poverty. This was Battersea. We didn't live there long. I didn't go to school there because we moved to Forest Hill. My mom got this job finishing off garments and my sister worked in the same factory, sewing, and my brother, pressing clothes. They told me I was lucky because I was going to make it to school, a white British school.

I remember my first day in school, being introduced to another girl who was Turkish, but she didn't look Turkish to me. They said she would take care of me because I couldn't speak English. This girl really didn't want to be lumbered with me. I was determined to learn. I wasn't going to be dependent on this girl.

Once I spoke English I found it easy to make friends. I started mixing with lots of Black girls in the school and there were a few times when they said, "How come you can't speak English properly and we can and we're Black?" They were the same color as me and I felt, this is where I belong. But then there was the culture difference between us, as they were mostly born over here and I didn't feel English. I think there was a point in my life when I started denying that I was Turkish Cypriot. I actually said I was British because I could speak English and there was no way you might guess that I was Turkish Cypriot. I said I was a Black girl born here.

There were some staff who said we were lucky to be there getting an education as where we came from we might not have the chance. I remember being told that we smell and we were dirty; this came mostly from white girls in the school.

I just couldn't wait to leave school. I wasn't encouraged, nobody actually said to me, "Listen, you're like this because of the language barrier and not because you're thick," as I sat exams but didn't get anything. I didn't even go to see the Careers Service. The option I had was going into the factory because my family was there and I'd be quite safe among the Turkish community. I rebelled against that, and although I still feel I didn't have a good choice, I went into an office to do filing. I found that really boring.

One of the things I did was to have my hair short. I wanted to be grown up and I started plucking my eyebrows and wearing makeup. My mom didn't mind that, but she minded me wearing miniskirts as I was a Moslem girl and she didn't want me to wear tight trousers as they showed off my figure. I started asking for freedom to go out with my friends to discos. I remember being beaten up by my brother because I asked to go to a disco. I remember my mother nagging at him to take me out but he used to say, "No, I'm not dragging her along with me." I think that was one of the reasons I thought about marriage as an option to get out.

My family had mentioned that I was coming up to an age where they would be thinking about arranged marriages, because sixteen, to them, is quite a good age to get married. I was told that soon people would be coming just to meet me and I would be expected to behave in a certain manner, sit there like a lady and after fifteen minutes get up and make the tea without them telling me to. They told me I was not to look at the boy too much. I would make the tea and bring it in on a tray and start offering it to the eldest one in the room—that didn't include my mother—and end with the boy. I wasn't to look at him or smile or laugh because that meant I wasn't a good girl. That never did happen, as I didn't see why I should go through all that. As far as I was concerned I was capable of arranging my own life, whether it meant going out to find him, but I wasn't going to have someone tell me this was the guy I was going to marry and actually say to someone, "Come and look at me and buy me." I didn't tell them that, though. I just said, "Yeah, maybe you're right, but not yet." The only excuse I could give was that I wanted to work a bit more and buy more clothes before I got married.

I'd met this boy who lived in the same street and I was quite friendly with him, so rather than them arrange a marriage, I thought, "There's someone that actually likes me" and I liked him, so I started sneaking out with him and not going to work sometimes, and told Mom that I was working overtime when I was meeting him. He was Asian and seventeen. I think all I wanted was freedom. I didn't really want to get married but when they found out about us, they were either going to stop me from seeing him or make me marry someone else. My mother asked if we'd been sleeping together and I said, "No." She said, "You'd better tell the truth," or my brothers would take me to the doctors to have a test to see whether I was a virgin or not. At that time I *had* started sleeping with him. I was sixteen and really scared. Two days later I ran away with him because I thought they might find out.

We were on our way to Gretna Green but never made it. We got to North London, where we had some friends. We decided to stay there for a week. He phoned his parents and they said, "Come back, come and live here: she can live here, too." I actually lived there for a couple of months without being married but we weren't allowed to sleep together. After a couple of months I went through a ceremony where I had a Moslem marriage, and then I had to go to the registry office and get married again, as a Moslem marriage didn't really count in this country.

When I got married I was three months pregnant. I lived with his parents. I'd have done anything not to be sent back home, so I was under their thumb. My relationship with his parents wasn't that close because I couldn't speak Bengali and they couldn't speak English well. They owned a restaurant so were away most nights. It wasn't until I'd actually had the baby and was going to the restaurant to give them a hand that I became closer to them. They were really happy because the baby was a boy, the firstborn a boy. After having my first child I got pregnant again after two months and had another boy.

After four years I wanted us to live on our own. I don't think I actually ever enjoyed being married. I spent all four years really working. I used to feel exhausted and I had no social life. We were still without any kind of money and independence because he was studying and I was earning the money, so we applied for a council house. We got a place but after three weeks he'd left and gone back to his mom. He didn't want to be married anymore. I realized I wasn't ready for marriage but I wasn't going to walk out because I had two children and there was no way I could leave them. I had my pride and wasn't going to follow him around. It didn't work, so I was going to prove that I could survive on my own. I was twenty.

I'd patched up the relationship with my mom, thank God, because she was really supportive. I thought she would say to me, "Look, you made your own bed, you lie in it; I didn't ask you to marry him." I lived on my own for a year, then went to live with my mom. I was accepted back into the home. I still feel that it's through this that I've got quite close to her, because she'd actually been divorced twice and had two young kids. We had this in common. At that time everyone had married so there was just me and her and my two children. By this time Mom had retired so she looked after the children and I went to work in a factory.

When I was twenty-two I had a relationship with a woman.

While I was going to work I started socializing and going out. The first time that I actually went into a pub I met a woman there, and we started off by being friends and got closer. My mom went back to Cyprus for a holiday and this woman came around to stay and we started a relationship. We didn't talk about it, we just started doing it: it wasn't a big issue. I think that after three months I felt really guilty that I was actually having this relationship with a woman. I felt that if I was ever found out I'd be in disgrace. If the social workers ever found out my kids would be taken away and I felt really afraid that my kids may discover. So I told this woman that I wasn't a lesbian, that I could be bisexual, but I wasn't a lesbian because I'd been married. I told her to go. I told her that I was sorry but I didn't want to see her, and I even told her that I might go back to my husband.

I spent the next five years celibate, thinking, "Am I a lesbian, am I not?" I was really confused, because as far as I was concerned I didn't *have* sexuality. For five years I felt, well, I definitely wasn't heterosexual, but was I lesbian? I also felt that because I spent four years being married I couldn't possibly be a lesbian.

Around that time, 1979, I started being quite active in women's groups. It was a women's health group and wasn't political as such. It wasn't that the word "sexuality" was never used, but it was about relationships with men all the time, straight sex. I mentioned that I'd not had a relationship since I got divorced and it was looked on as something wrong. People would say that you need to lose weight, that's why you're not going out to meet men. You haven't got the confidence in yourself. But I knew I wasn't shy. It was because I didn't want a relationship. I never dared open my mouth and say I'd had a relationship with a woman.

I wanted at one time to talk about incest, but there was no way I was going to open a discussion because I didn't want them to think, "She's an incest survivor," and expose myself. I wanted everyone to be concerned about the issue. Most of my friends were women and straight. Some of them were really racist. They always said to me, "You're not Black, you're not like the rest of them," trying to console me.

When I started to be active, helping women and migrant people to claim benefits, they used to say to me, "If they don't like it here they should go back home and not come and get money from us." I never used to challenge this as they were my friends, and although they were racist I did have support from them, like there were times when I didn't have any money and they would give or loan money to me. So I felt really obliged. I didn't dare say, "Look, that isn't fair what you're saying: You're being racist."

About 1982 I set up a Turkish women's group while I was attending other groups like photography and women's drama. I decided that all those other groups weren't catering to women from other backgrounds. They were mostly set up by white women and attended by white women. I knew many Turkish women living on the estate and thought there was a point where they could come together. Three or four years ago, for Turkish women to organize separately was quite a task, as it meant that you had to get permission from their men before they could attend a women's group.

There were around twelve women between the ages of eighteen and sixty. A Turkish Women's Day that followed was organized by myself, the Turkish women, and some of the community workers on the estate. It was well attended by about fifty women, but I was thinking to myself, there's about forty white women (although at that time I called them English) and ten Turkish women. I wanted it to be the other way around, but I think we were lucky to get ten Turkish women there. When our group met we would discuss things like our position in this country as second-class citizens. We'd talk about the difficulties in getting benefits, anything.

Q: *Did you ever discuss lesbianism?*

No. God! No way. Although I didn't use the word "feminism," I was actually becoming quite a radical feminist, and I took on issues like Greenham. I started visiting Greenham and started talking about artificial insemination by donor. I was saying there were other ways of having babies, you could choose alternative ways, but never quite saying there are lesbian women who could start a family if they wanted to. I don't know how that would have gone down, I probably would have got stoned to death.

I started talking to the white workers on the estate about sexuality. I was visiting Greenham, 1983–84, and many of the women I was friends with kept saying to me that at Greenham they were all lesbians and I mustn't go because I would be affected. I kept saying, "Look, what makes you think I'm not a lesbian now?" and they said, "Of course you're not; you're a victim of circumstances, looking for somewhere to belong."

It was in the Greenham group and at Greenham that I met lots of lesbians. I came out to a man at one of the user groups on the estate and he was quite supportive. My friend started crying and said I was lying; she couldn't accept the fact that I was lesbian. Another woman that I'd been quite close to said it was just something I was going through and I'd just been unlucky with men. I told them that I'd had a relationship when I was twenty-two but they didn't believe me. This time I was ready. I was going to be quite open about it and if they didn't like me that was their problem. I was still the same person, I just preferred women. They kept saying, "What would your boys think of you?" and it wouldn't be fair to them. They were nine and ten. I said, "It wouldn't be fair on me if I hid it until they left home; I'd be denying myself so much and I've denied six years anyway." So I started openly saying I was a lesbian. People kept saying to me, "You're not having a relationship with a woman, so how can you be a lesbian?" They couldn't understand.

I think it wasn't until I got to Greenham that I actually realized that I had a sexuality. I could talk about whatever I wanted to talk about and I started talking about being an incest survivor and felt that I wasn't the only one. There were so many around me being so close to other women that it just felt the right thing to do. Greenham gave me a lot of courage to openly say that I was a lesbian.

Nobody was going to say, well, you're not having a relationship, because there was so many lesbians there not in a relationship. However, I wasn't not with a woman out of choice or politics but because I was quite shy and I wasn't going to make the first attempt to sleep with somebody. I was looking at women and finding them attractive but there was no way I was going to make the first move. I felt that if I found the right woman I would have gone ahead.

I started going to lots of women's socials and clubs and getting into the scene. After a while I had a relationship with a woman and then I met the woman who I first went with. I hadn't seen her for five years or so and I started seeing her again. The relationship didn't last long, though; I'd moved on and she didn't have any political interest at all so we split up.

I've now been having a relationship with my lover for the last ten months, but we've been friends for two years. I think I was looking for someone to fall in love with, and I wanted her to be someone who would actually understand where I was coming from and had gone through something like I had, someone that didn't have it easy. Both of us are incest survivors so I can freely talk about it to her and she can talk to me. I feel it's really important for us to have a relationship, a good friendship whether we're lovers or not, because of so much we share together. My children know; they've accepted it but I still feel there's a long way to go because they are boys and I'm doing my best to bring them up in a way so they don't oppress women. I know they're never going to be proud of me for being a lesbian, but they accept the situation. They get involved in our conversations and in our arguments. They know about sexism and racism. They accept my relationship with my lovers, although sometimes I feel there is jealousy between them and I get stuck in the middle. I wish that my sons would grow up with the possibility of having an option about their sexuality. I live in a women's housing co-op, so that's good for two boys to be living around and learning from women.

Although at times I still organize with white women I feel the need to organize separately with Black women because there are certain things we can discuss. I'm involved in the co-op so I think that's all I can manage at the moment, having a full-time job, two children, and a relationship.

A group of us started a lesbian group for Turkish women two weeks ago and now there's eight of us. I mean at one time I used to think I was the only one, the only Turkish Cypriot lesbian. I feel I've achieved a lot, I've moved a lot.

POSTSCRIPT

It was important for me to do this interview. I feel that I have contributed to lesbian history, and the anthology will show that it is not just a white history and will shatter the myths about lesbianism and motherhood.

My children, thirteen and fourteen, now live with their father during the week. I faced the fact that he had a responsibility toward them and I needed the space to think about my life. I had to understand that this was not selfish and irresponsible, as I have been made to feel by "society." In fact, this move has allowed me and the boys to enjoy each other more.

I now use my birth name and not my English name I took on. I've reached a point where I know who I am and I am no longer willing to compromise. I am proud to be a Turkish Cypriot lesbian mother.

MEXICO

The following selection includes the coming-out stories of two young Mexican men. In their accounts, we can see reflected the importance Mexican culture attributes to gender roles. As in many Latin American, southern European, and Middle Eastern cultures, it is not so much the sex of the person with whom one relates that defines one's sexual identity, as the role—active or passive—one plays with that person. At first glance this distinction seems illogical: Certainly the fellator is much more "active" in a sexual encounter than the fellatee generally is. More basic, then, is the identification of the insertee roles with women. And, given that the position of women in Judeo-Christian and Islamic societies is devalued, a man who demonstrates behavior assigned to women is consequently scorned. It is in this sense that we understand Pedro, who though accepting of his gay identity, feels very uncomfortable at the idea of ever playing a passive anal role. José's case is different, but it still reinforces the same antifemale bias. Though he is accustomed to being anally receptive, José wants his partners to be exclusively "active." If José were to learn that a person with whom he is involved has also been anally receptive, he feels that his sexual attraction to that person would immediately dissolve. His partner's "manhood" would be irretrievably compromised.

We might also note the significance Pedro attaches to his period of coming out. It is as if his life could be easily divided into "before" and "after." Gays in many different societies share this experience. An early awareness of same-sex attraction results in feelings of being different, while negative messages about homosexuality emanating from the media, religion, family, and peers make one fearful of having his or her feelings discovered. It is only in the process of "coming out of the closet," of finding validation for one's feelings and the support needed to be who one is, that most gay persons finally come to accept themselves. Evidence the widespread use of the terms "coming out" and "in the closet," which have been translated verbatim and are being used in many non–English-speaking cultures today.

From "Gay Liberation and Coming Out in Mexico" by Joseph M. Carrier, Ph.D., from *Journal of Homosexuality* (1989).

GAY LEADER'S COMING OUT

Pedro was born in the fall of 1956 to relatively prosperous parents in an upper-middle-class neighborhood of Guadalajara. He has an older brother and sister, and three younger brothers. At the age of 25 he became a leader in the gay rights movement and a candidate for the National Chamber of Deputies. He has a college degree in economics. Until he lost his job as a result of his gay activism, he was a secondary-school teacher. His father is a well-known lawyer.

Pedro is a brawny, good-looking young man, slightly taller than average (about 5′10″), with long dark black hair and a large mustache. He speaks in a masculine way, with a deep, resonant voice. Based on his physical appearance, most Mexicans would be surprised to learn that he is gay. As a child, he remembers himself as being like all the other boys his age.

Pedro divides his life into two phases: before and after "coming out of the closet" *(salir del closet)*. In recently reflecting on coming out, he was aware that although it happened several years ago, the pain of it lingers. He remembers the events leading up to it with great clarity. In talking about it, he divides the world into two groups: the straight *(buga)* and the gay. To him, the *buga* world is heterosexual and macho, and naive about homosexuality. The gay world, on the other hand, is revolutionary and allows him the freedom to follow his true sexual orientation.

Before coming out in his early twenties, Pedro thinks that, like most Mexicans who suppress their homosexual feelings, he was anguished and frustrated:

> I was going through life with a heterosexual mask, knowing that deep down I had incomprehensible desires and emotions that, in some way, should give a man pleasure. This caused me such distress, and was such a threat to my emotional equilibrium that it repressed me and put me low spiritually. I was living a life like that of any straight person. But, in my case, I was an anguished straight person *(buga angustiado)* because I did not understand what was going on inside me.

A long time before he came out, Pedro knew he was different from others his age. Since kindergarten he remembers:

> I knew already a profound, profound attraction—I don't think sexual, but, yes, of pleasure—to be with my little boy companions, with other boys. In my mind, clearly, I didn't yet think myself to be a homosexual but neither did I think myself odd *(raro)* feeling that. Yet I didn't sufficiently swallow the heterosexist education that was subsequently given me and that made me feel different and like something apart.

As time passed, gradually, from 17 to 23, Pedro began to learn about the homosexual world and how he might be related to it; much of what he learned made him feel bad about himself. Referring to what he had read about homosexuality, he reports:

> That was my first contact, I identified myself with what was being said in books—even though many things I read were venomous. For example, they say in encyclopedias that the homosexual is sick, dirty *(lugarcete comun),* you understand, and

specifically that homosexuality is a perversion. And in medical books they give all kinds of explanations that make you feel bad.

During his twenty-third year, Pedro went through a homosexual panic. He describes it as follows:

> I thought myself very bad, and many times I was at the point of suicide. I don't know if I really might have killed myself, but many times I thought about it and believed it was the only alternative. This caused me problems with many friends. I felt they thought me to be different, homosexual, and really sick. It made me separate from them. I felt myself inferior and thought I was the only one these things happened to.
>
> Some weeks before I left the closet, I went into a terrible panic. A panic that overwhelmed me above all, I was hysterical, psychotic. One morning I woke up yelling . . . in a cold sweat, stiff, eyes rolling. My family came into my room and asked me: What happened? What's going on? There were no medical explanations. And no other kind of explanation other than the strong anguish I felt over being what, at that moment, I did not want to be; and that I was rejecting . . . a product of the education I had received.
>
> I had an enormous fear that they might discover me . . . that my family or a friend might *know* something about me. Many times in the few family reunions I used to go to, talk would always turn to the subject of the *joto,* the homosexual, or something related, and I was forced to conceal myself. Everyone was saying bad things about homosexuals. I used to stay quiet then, distressed.

Pedro overcame his bad feelings about being homosexual, just as he had overcome his feelings of being "an anguished straight person, a heterosexual who did not know what was going on inside." It came about in part as a result of telling a heterosexual childhood friend of his dilemma of being a homosexual. His friend gave him some positive articles to read about gay people. Referring to them, Pedro recalls:

I remember reading in *El Viejo Topo* some articles by Carlo Forti, and others in *Sábado de Uno Más Uno,* that were truly revelatory. I was able to identify myself and know more of myself. They were excellent, and permitted me to know my homosexuality from a political point of view. I knew I didn't have to reject myself just for being gay.

Pedro still had another problem to surmount: coming out sexually. Although at some level he could accept being gay, as an ordinary masculine person he had not been able to face the trauma of physically acting out his inner sexual longings with other males. He had masturbated since puberty and once told a priest in the confessional about it. But

clearly I never told him that the fantasies which stimulated my masturbation were homosexual. I simply told him I masturbated, and he almost laughed. So I then told him my masturbation was obsessive. But I thought to myself what really was obsessive was my inability to touch and explore another masculine body.

In finally coming out to himself, Pedro started looking for homosexual encounters in the street *(el ligue en la calle)*. He remembers his first attempts to find sexual partners as excruciating experiences. He knew the special signals, "intense looks, lustful ones that say something." And he knew where to go to find them. "I knew that things happened in the center of Guadalajara . . . that here in this city the zone most open for an encounter is the street; there are very few places for gay people here."

He describes the very first time he set out to look for a sexual companion:

The first time I tried to make it with someone was horrible. I crossed Avenida Juárez and in a dark side street found a *chavo,* very feminine for sure. I saw him and said to myself: Fuck my prejudices, fuck my education, fuck everything. I want to go to bed with a man now, and I'm going to do it.

He, she, was a *loquita,* and I was standing close to her. But it was difficult for me to approach. With every step I took, I was feeling more flushed in my head and felt it growing. I was very nervous because I didn't know what to say to the *chavo,* I didn't know how to begin the conversation. The only thing I could think to say was hey, "carnal." I thought the word "carnal" was also used between homosexuals. He turned around. I looked at him but couldn't say another word. My jawbone was paralyzed. I wanted to say something strong, to express how I felt, but I couldn't. My brain thought I was saying things, but I couldn't hear anything. No sound left my mouth. A horrible sensation. For fractions of seconds, of course, but they seemed like long ones. I felt bad, my head was going around. And then what I did was to go running. I was running desperately, like a *loca!*

Pedro's first homosexual affair was with an older American professor who worked in Guadalajara in the summertime. It lasted for several years, and he felt very comfortable with the sexual part of it because it involved only fellatio. Although he has tried receptive anal intercourse a few times since becoming sexually active, Pedro generally prefers fellatio or playing only the *activo* sex role. Even now he is unable to deal with the psychological dissonance that results from his playing the *pasivo* role.

Pedro's final coming out was to his family, who he believed were not aware of his homosexuality, or at least who knew or were suspicious but never mentioned it. This changed dramatically during the latter part of his twenty-third year, when one of his younger brothers came home unexpectedly and found him having sex with a boyfriend. Both his father and eldest brother were told about the incident. A family crisis ensued, with lots of bitter remarks, tears, and rejection. But because by then Pedro had completely accepted himself as gay, he felt ready to confront his family. He first explained the situation to his father, then later to his brothers and sister as a group. Pedro, his father, and his brothers and sisters, however, decided to keep his homosexuality a secret from his mother, who was in Mexico City at the time. She did not learn of Pedro's homosexuality until two years later.

Pedro had decided not to tell his mother because she and his father were estranged and he did not want to burden her further. He felt very protective toward his mother then because his father treated her in such a chauvinistic way. Pedro deeply resented the way his father treated his mother, and he often upbraided him about it. In the fall of 1981, just one month prior to his twenty-fifth birthday, Pedro's father asked him to leave. Pedro claims, ironically, it had nothing to do with his homosexuality.

One of Pedro's younger brothers, who had gotten into some legal difficulties and become estranged from his father, joined him and they rented an apartment together. A short time later, their mother moved in with them on a temporary basis.

It was at this time that Pedro's mother discovered his homosexuality. In an interview several years later[1] she recalled to Pedro how she had had "small indications" that left her wondering and uneasy:

> Some telephone calls, some friends of yours who came to the house who I saw [as like] homosexual. Then I thought to myself . . . why do they visit my son? . . . Why do they call by telephone? Why? I wanted to cloud it over, it was not like you . . . not you. And I was rebelling and saying to myself, no! I looked for explanations . . . you were very sociable, you had all kinds of friends. When I finally realized, it was a tremendous shock for me.

Later in the interview, Pedro asked his mother, "What feelings or emotions did you experience when you discovered that a very beloved son of yours was a homosexual? Do you remember that day? Can you describe it?" She replied:

> Yes, son . . . I am never going to forget that day. Can you imagine . . . among my family I had discovered a homosexual . . . a son of mine . . . very dear, very special as you are . . . was homosexual. Given what I thought about homosexuality all of my

life, you must know how it shocked me and took me a long time to get over . . . a shock that included much rejection of you, very nearly . . . like . . . blaming you insofar as you might hurt me personally with this. And later I thought of you even as a cynic in the way you treated me. I don't know, son . . . I wished . . . maybe to attack you, beat you. How was it possible that you could be so bad, I thought to myself . . . because for me this was homosexuality. I was going through a terrible personal crisis when I discovered it. Then this came to give me yet more pain.

Pedro's mother then noted her eventual acceptance of her son's homosexuality: "At first I was very hard with you . . . severe. Later, little by little I began to understand you, I was . . . grasping it . . . I was understanding all that you had also suffered before. . . ."

Pedro overcame the final barrier to acceptance by his family in the spring of 1982, when he became a leader of the gay liberation movement and a candidate for the National Chamber of Deputies. The notoriety associated with these positions disarmed his family for a while. But believing in the cause he pursued, they set aside their fears and prejudices about homosexuality and accepted and supported him in his role as a leader of the movement. Pedro states that now "They do not just tolerate me . . . they admire me."

Since that time, Pedro has maintained a close relationship with his family, visiting them weekly. His mother and several of his brothers in turn visit him regularly at the Group Pride for Homosexual Liberation Movement's (GOHL) headquarters, a two-story rented house in the center of Guadalajara, where he lives, and they occasionally participate in some of the group's activities. They also know his current male lover. Antagonisms between Pedro and his father continue, but they relate mostly to the father's treatment of the mother.

Although disappointed that he lost his teaching position, Pedro has found that running a gay liberation organization is a full-time job. Maintaining an accommodation with the police in Guadalajara requires a continuing weekly dialogue with the relevant civil authorities and the chief of police. And on a daily basis, he must also oversee GOHL's gay support services and refreshment bar, and on weekends the operation of its disco, a major source of income for the organization.

Pedro feels strongly about the importance of the educational objectives of the gay liberation movement, and so maintains a telephone hot line to counsel youth having problems related to their homosexuality and coming out, and to provide information about AIDS. He also organizes semiannual gay pride week lectures and exhibits. He feels strongly about providing a place in Guadalajara for gay youth to congregate. Both the refreshment bar during the week and the disco on weekends fill this need.

Pedro's leadership role and living arrangement do not allow him a great deal of privacy. The inconvenience, however, is far outweighed, he feels, by GOHL's success.

JOSÉ'S COMING OUT

José was born in the fall of 1954 to relatively poor parents in an old lower-middle-class neighborhood of Guadalajara that has been continuously occupied since the city was founded by Spaniards in the sixteenth century. Located a short distance from the center of the city, the neighborhood is mainly made up of four- to five-room single-story Spanish-style adobe brick houses that adjoin sidewalks and have interior courtyards. Neighborhood youth socialize on the sidewalks in front of houses each evening, while buses, trucks, and cars rumble through the narrow streets. Many old customs are still followed. For instance, families give "sweet 15 parties" for their daughters, and boys serenade their girlfriends. Families also still worry about the virginity of their daughters and supervise as much of their behavior as possible, given the times.

Along with his mother, father, and 10 brothers and sisters, José has lived most of his life in the house where he was born. During his late teens and early twenties he lived on and off in the United States for five years, but moved back to live with his family in Guadalajara in 1978, where he has lived since then. Since he returned to Mexico he has held a number of different jobs. He worked several years in a well-known restaurant as a waiter and singer. He currently works as a tailor at his house and is employed part time with an *estudiantina* sponsored by the city.

At present José is a slim, nice-looking young man, about average in size (about 5'6" tall). He has maintained a trim physique all his life. Most people judge him to be much younger than he is. He dresses in a very flashy, sometimes feminine way, with skin-tight pants and blousy shirts. He believes his only obviously feminine trait, however, to be his manner of walking. Like Pedro, he speaks in a masculine way with a deep, resonant voice.

José established a gay identity in his late teens. Part of his motivation for going to the United States after "coming out" to himself, family, and friends at the age of 17 was to experience the freedom of living completely as a "gay" person in New York with a European male lover he had previously met in Guadalajara. After five years, however, his longing to be back with his family in his old neighborhood was so intense that, after breaking up with his lover, he returned home.

José explains his return:

> Even though I had a lot of gay and straight friends, a nice apartment, car . . . I was lonely. I'm sure it sounds crazy . . . to give all that up to come back to a poor family and share a small bedroom with two younger brothers. But my lover and I had broken up . . . and I really missed being with my family. Also, a neighborhood of straight young guys were back here waiting for me . . . available . . . most know I'm gay.

José's earliest homosexual experiences occurred prior to puberty, between four and 13 years of age, with neighborhood youths who were between 14 and 18. He remembers "sucking off" three teenage neighborhood brothers when he was four and being anally penetrated by a 16-year-old neighbor when he was six. He further remembers his initial anal experiences as being frightening and painful, and feeling disgusted with himself afterward for having allowed the older boy to do it to him.

Before reaching puberty at the age of 13, he also remembers being penetrated anally by several other neighborhood youth, but only a few times. He gradually became comfortable with the anal passive role and no longer felt repulsed by it. But he does not remember having a strong sexual role preference. He believes he ended up playing the passive role because he was sexually excited by the older neighborhood youth who would play the active role.

Reflecting on his masculinity, José reports that he has "always been in the middle, neither macho nor feminine." As a boy, he liked playing with both girls' and boys' toys, but when a teenager he mostly liked playing male sports. He acknowledges, however, that in his neighborhood he was probably viewed by many of his friends as being "slightly feminine." And when he was 16, his cousin of the same age told him that he "acted like a homosexual," which meant, José said, that he "was acting feminine."

José's first ejaculation occurred when he masturbated with some older neighborhood boys at the age of 13. He remembers his early mutual masturbatory experiences with considerable pleasure and little guilt.

During the first two years following the onset of puberty, José became actively involved in homosexual behavior. He established a pattern of weekly sexual encounters, generally with very masculine neighborhood youths whose ages ranged from 14 to 19. When first interviewed by the author at age 15, he remembered having homosexual encounters with 14 different youths the first year; 10 different ones the second year. Although on occasion he performed fellatio on some, it was only preliminary to the anal intercourse that he and his sex partners enjoyed most. He continued to play only the anal receptive role. During those two years, casual social contact with neighborhood youths led to most of José's homosexual encounters. He almost never went out deliberately looking for sexual partners in his neighborhood, but rather had sexual encounters with the same youth three or four times.

When he was 15 years old, José told the author that only a first cousin know about his homosexual behavior and that the rest of his family neither knew nor suspected anything. He worried a lot about their finding out. To cover himself, he had girlfriends in the neighborhood and made a point of introducing them to his family and friends. If his parents found out about his homosexuality, he said, "I would leave home at once and never return because I wouldn't be able to face the shame."

Two years later, when he was 17, José's family found out about his homosexual behavior. News about his homosexual contacts with neighborhood youths had finally reached his older brothers, and one of them told his parents. José's father was very angry with him, so he decided to leave forever. Although distraught about his homosexuality, his mother was not angry with him and did not want him to leave. He left believing he would never return. Not long after leaving, however, he learned through relatives that the family's furor over his homosexuality had subsided. He therefore decided to return home, hoping somehow he would be accepted by his family.

After being back home a while, his relationship with his mother, older sister, and six younger siblings returned to normal. He remained estranged from his three older brothers, however, and for several years his father and second oldest brother almost never spoke to him. His homosexuality was not mentioned by anyone. José started seeking sexual contacts with males living outside his neighborhood during this time.

A few months later, accepting that he had never had any real sexual interest in women and had no intention of getting married and having children, José decided that he was what he had known himself to be for a long time, a homosexual, and so should learn more about the "gay world." He envisioned the gay world as a place where he could be around people like himself and thus not have to put up a false front. José refers to the events of the following month as his "coming out of the closet" and establishing a "gay identity" *(los de Ambiente)*.

After coming out, José spent the next few months socializing with several young "queens" he had met in Guadalajara's only gay bar and adopted a feminine nickname, *la chepa*. He recalls his behavior during this time as being *muy loca* (extremely effeminate). He then met and started a sexual relationship with an older European man, became his lover, and decided to live with him in New York. José felt he could live there freely as a gay person. With his lover's help, he was able to enter the United States legally and get a job.

Although he enjoyed many aspects of his new life in the United States, José missed his family and neighbors. During his five years' residence in New York, he returned to Guadalajara every Christmas and on other occasions when possible to assuage his homesickness. His lover often traveled with him and became acquainted with his family. They knew the foreigner was José's lover, but nevertheless were hospitable, and no one confronted José about his homosexual relationship.

As time passed, José had a falling out with his lover. Though sexually compatible, he found his older lover to be possessive and jealous of his younger friends. Differences in social backgrounds and interests also contributed to the breakup. José's homesickness increased.

Shortly after breaking up with his lover, José decided to return home. On returning, except for his father and second oldest brother, he found his family delighted to have him home for good. He easily reintegrated himself back into family life, establishing a close bond with his mother and very warm relationships with his sisters and their husbands. Whenever he and one of his brothers-in-law got together, they often joked about his sexual availability.

After returning home, José's presentation of self to family and neighbors differed from before. He was still not blatantly homosexual, but he never denied being gay and was no longer ashamed of being gay.

He found few changes in his neighborhood, and resumed his old pattern of spending most of his free time socializing with neighborhood friends and having homosexual encounters with some of them. Shortly after his return, he started what turned out to be a long-term affair with a local youth who at the same time carried on active courtships with girlfriends. Both he and the youth were teased by neighborhood friends about their affair, but no one tried to break it up. The affair continued for many years, but tapered off when the youth became engaged and then married.

José was aware of the gay liberation movement from the time it started in 1981, but has never been an active participant. Some neighborhood youths had seen the first gay demonstration in the Umbrellas Plaza. They were curious and astonished, but not hostile. They questioned José as to what brought it on and wanted to know what he thought about it and why he had not participated. He said he told them, "I'm in favor of gay rights . . . gay people only have a few places they can go and be together, like Pancho's place, where I've taken some of you. But the police close down gay bars and extort and arrest lots of gay people for nothing."

José made no reply to them about not actively participating in the gay liberation movement. He prefers to spend most of his time socializing with neighborhood straight friends rather than with gay friends. He only occasionally goes to gay bars, and he finds all the sexual partners he wants among youths in his own neighborhood. Thus, although he supports gay rights, he has never felt involved enough in the struggle to become an active participant.

At present José is having an affair with an 18-year-old bisexual youth in the neighborhood. He maintains a close relationship with the youth and the youth's girlfriend, who lives next door. The girlfriend knows that José is gay and spends a lot of time with her boyfriend. She apparently does not mind sharing him with José. When she and her boyfriend are in the midst of a quarrel, she often approaches José as an intermediary.

José's boyfriend and some of his male cousins occasionally go to the gay disco run by GOHL, and have been seen in the neighborhood in the company of "queens." José is not at all pleased by this.

One of the major reasons José is attracted to his boyfriend is that he is, by José's standards, heterosexual. If the young man turns out to be gay, José is not at all sure he will continue to be interested in him sexually.

DISCUSSION

An uneasy accommodation now exists between gay people and civil authorities over gay rights in Guadalajara. Only after the election and change in city administrations in 1988 could it be known how long the accommodation would last. Gay leaders know they must continue to maintain vigilance over potential abuses by homophobic elements in their society. They are also aware of the continuing need to educate homosexual people and the general public about the positive aspects of being gay.

An ongoing problem *within* the gay liberation movement reflects differences between those homosexual males who are open and feminine and those who are not. Public demonstrations of feminine behavior by young gay males who consider it a basic part of their makeup is disturbing to those gay males who prefer to comport themselves in more masculine ways and thus be less obvious in straight settings.

Leaders of gay liberation must therefore deal with the need to accept the rights of young feminine gay males, who have provided major support for the gay rights movement, to behave in public as they want, as well as the right of other gay males to behave in public in more conservative ways, even stay in the closet if they choose to. Although attempts have been made in the gay liberation movement to get its more masculine members to view feminine male behavior in a more positive way, they have had little success.

The predicament has its roots in a rather pervasive cultural belief system. Although Mexicans are traditionally quite permissive about sexual behavior in private or in regulated urban zones *(zonas rojas),* as previously noted they have strong feelings against public displays of behavior which are considered immoral, scandalous, or publicly disturbing. Masculine gay males who are not out of the closet to family members, neighbors, or friends may thus be concerned about having their reputations burned by the "scandalous behavior" of young feminine gay males in public. They may participate in "campy" feminine behavior among themselves in private, but would only do so in public with great care.

Although differing considerably in the paths followed, Pedro's and José's biographies reveal that prior to coming out both were generally concerned about their families, neighbors, and friends finding out about their homosexual behavior. And even after coming out of the closet, they still carefully control their gay behavior at home and in public so as not to offend the sensibilities of others. For example, even though José is openly gay in his neighborhood, he still conducts himself "seriously " (meaning not in a campy gay manner) in the presence of his family, with whom he still lives, and in most social settings involving straight neighbors. Pedro also continues to conduct himself in a masculine way with his family and, as a leader of the gay liberation movement, with public officials and the general public.

A comparison of Pedro's and José's biographies further points out an important behavioral difference between young gay Mexican males: The amount of cognitive dissonance generated by being homosexual appears to differ considerably between them. Although some go through the kind of homosexual panic experienced by Pedro before coming out, many do not. José, for example, never really thought of himself as heterosexual prior to coming out, and so did not go through the kind of identity crisis that Pedro experienced.

Some critical variables related to cognitive dissonance generated when gay youth are contemplating homosexual or gay identities prior to coming out include (a) degree of masculinity, (b) heterosexual identity, (c) number of homosexual experiences, (d) age when first meaningful homosexual experiences occurred, and (e) sex role played.

Feminine male youth, who only play the *pasivo* sexual role (i.e., receptive anal intercourse in Mexico) and begin meaningful homosexual relations prior to puberty, appear never to think of themselves as being heterosexual, accepting homosexual identities in their early teens and thereby experiencing less cognitive dissonance. They appear to have fewer concerns with establishing gay identities and coming out.

Masculine male youth, on the other hand, who start out playing only the *activo* sexual role (i.e., insertive anal intercourse) and begin (or contemplate having) meaningful homosexual relations while adolescents, appear to think of themselves as being heterosexual and thus are more likely to experience considerable cognitive dissonance over their homosexual thoughts or behavior. They may reduce dissonance by having successful heterosexual intercourse or by limiting their homosexual contacts and by playing only the insertive sexual role. However, as Pedro's biography illustrates, sufficient dissonance may occur and homosexual panic generated when a youth with no sexual experiences just contemplates acting out homosexual desires and thus fears not being heterosexual. Another pathway involving panic occurs when a bisexual youth becomes increasingly involved homosexually and incorporates the receptive anal role into his sexual repertoire; that is, becomes an *internacional*.

Finally, the two biographies illustrate differences of opinion about gay liberation. Although José recognizes the need for a liberation movement for many gay people, he has not been an active participant and feels that, given *his* gay lifestyle, its outcome has no particular relevance to him. Pedro, on the other hand, as a gay activist believes the outcome is not only important to him but to all homosexually involved people in Guadalajara.

NOTE

1. Mother, "Confesiones de mi madre acerca de mi homosexualidad," *Crisalida: De y para la comunidad gay* (GOHL: Guadalajara, 1984), pp. A–D.

NATIVE AMERICA

Native American culture is one of many traditional cultures in the world in which same-sex relations have played an integral part. Among several Native American peoples, for example, berdaches, persons of one sex assuming the gender role of the opposite sex—including dress—were given special status, often as shamans or storytellers. With the arrival of the White man and the influence of Christianity, this tradition became nearly extinct.

Today many Native Americans view homosexuality with ridicule or scorn. Gay Native Americans living on reservations are likely to hide their feelings and lead double lives. Gay Native Americans outside the reservations often find alienating the homosexual lifestyles available to them in mainstream society. In the following selection, M. Owlfeather speaks of the need for Native Americans to reclaim more of their traditional ways, including the berdache tradition, and blend them with the new as a means of revitalizing Native American culture. After telling of his experiences as a gay Native American, both on and off the reservation, the author concludes that special recognition must once again be given to gay Native Americans and the unique vision they possess.

"Children of Grandmother Moon"
by Clyde M. Hall–"Owlfeather,"
from *Living the Spirit: A Gay American Indian*
Anthology, ed. Will Roscoe (1988).

Grandmother Moon comes slowly
    over the eastern hills.
Chanting a song, a song of a lost age,
    its meaning a mystery.
She comes dressed in orange calico.
Her hair wrapped in otter fur.
Her moccasins made of soft deer skin.
No one hears as she makes her journey
    to her lodge in the west.
Before her goes the owl, flying by night.
Singing, "Hush, respect your grandmother
    She is old and knows many things.
    Say nothing as she passes."
Sometimes she sends owl out, to warn her people
    of someone about to die.
He chants a verse, three times
    for three nights,
    before it happens.
This makes her very sad, her people are few.
You can tell she weeps
    because you find
    Her tears
On the grass and trees when she's gone.

The reservation where I live is a harsh place, situated on a high
plateau valley in the West. Most people wonder why anyone would
want to live here. The temperature ranges from one hundred degrees in the summer to forty below in the winter. Life is indeed
hard. It takes a certain kind of person, or people, to call this place
"home." Many people have lived in this place for many, many
generations and consider it more than home; it is the place from

where we come and to where we return. It is our mother and our special place in the world.

Many people ask me, "Why do you stay here? You have a good education, you have traveled the world and lived in many places, many different lives, so why return? There is no work here, little or no pride; there is depression, desolation, no hope. And for a person such as you, a gay Indian, what is there for you here, except perhaps criticism and humiliation?"

All of the above is true. But still I am here and surviving. I have a supportive group of friends, Indian and non-Indian, gay and straight. I hide my lifestyle and interests from no one. I participate in Indian traditional dances and religion. In a small town and in a tribal group of four thousand people nothing is hidden.

I returned to the reservation four years ago. I still remember a time when I vowed that I would never return. But despite all the situations listed above, the fact remains that I did return because there is something here that exists for an Indian person nowhere else: the sense of belonging, of family and of the land. You are not only a person, alone, but an extension of a family and a group of people, a "tribe," that has existed before the written word and history. It is a unique place and people, something that non-Indians cannot really imagine or feel. True, the culture is shattered, broken . . . and the people's lifestyle is in tatters and perhaps even still in culture shock to some degree. After all, my great-grandfather and great-grandmother saw the last of the buffalo killed. A lifestyle they knew and loved, with the rigors of moving camp and living in tipis, going anywhere they pleased, was destroyed.

Indian life and existence today is a paradox of the old and new. Christian beliefs are held along with native traditions. Western lifestyles are combined with traditional Indian lifestyles, and a number of people get hopelessly lost. Not respecting themselves or anyone else, some get angry, some get drunk, and some deny the Indian culture or anything Indian because they think it is useless in this present day and age.

No wonder a young man of nineteen years that I know and sleep with sometimes says to me, "I don't want to have people call me a queer or a faggot, but I want to be with you," or that I have a long-standing married lover who throws rocks at my window when the moon is full, wanting me to come out and play. He says, "I'm married, but I have always loved you and always will." Gay and bisexual Indian men and women are no different from anyone else in their fear of criticism. But I think it is more intense within a tribal structure, because our traditional way of correcting behavior is public chastisement and ridicule. And today, the view of the gay Indian man or woman has been twisted to fit the mix of Christian and Indian beliefs in contemporary tribal culture.

In the old days, during life on the plains, the people respected each other's vision. Berdaches had an integral place in the rigors and lifestyle of the tribe. The way they were viewed was not the same as the contemporary Indian gay lifestyle and consciousness that we have now—they were not fighting for a place in society to be accepted by that society. They already had a place, a very special and sacred place. They were the people who gave sacred names, cut down the Sun Dance pole, and foretold future events. They were renowned for their bead and quillwork and hide-tanning abilities and fancy dress. (Not all berdaches dressed in women's clothes; it depended on their vision.) It was considered good luck to have a berdache on a war party or on a horse-stealing raid. If a man wanted to, and had the ability to take a second or third wife, many times a man of the berdache vision would be chosen.

But all this changed with the coming of the reservation period in Indian history and the systematic crushing of all things Indian. The berdache visionaries were one of the outstanding targets, especially those who dressed and had the mannerisms of the opposite sex. (Some of these men were married to women but maintained the dress of their vision.) The last record of a berdache on my reservation was in the early 1900s.

You must understand that in the period of 1880 to 1910, if you were found or caught practicing Indian beliefs or dress, you could be jailed. Even if an Indian man wore his hair long, which was his pride, he could be jailed and punished. The great summer Sun Dance was suppressed. In one district of my reservation the dance was stopped by cutting down the Sun Dance pole in the midst of the ceremony. In another instance, the dance was held on a Mormon rancher's property where the government had no jurisdiction. So it was with little wonder that the vision of the berdache was forgotten or suppressed to the point that it was no longer mentioned and barely remembered. When it was mentioned, it was with shame and scorn, due to the influence of Christianity on Indian people. It is into this type of belief system and society that gay Indian men and women are born today.

On my reservation, it is traditional for the firstborn of a generation to live and be raised by the grandparents. They are called the "old peoples' children," and they are taught the knowledge, traditions, songs, and life ways of the tribe. Usually these people either become respected members of their community and tribe or turn out to be totally useless!

I was raised in this manner and lived a wonderful childhood. I was raised by my grandmother in a little one-room cabin that she and my great-uncle built in the 1920s. We had a wire strung for drying meat and hanging dish towels and clothing. In the center of the room we had a big round oak table covered with oilcloth. My grandmother's friends would come to visit and have coffee. Sometimes my great-aunts or great-uncles could come. I always knew my place, but would sometimes sit with them and drink coffee with lots of sugar and canned milk in it. I always enjoyed these visits and still feel more comfortable with Indian elders than with people my own age. I lived through their tales and my grandmother's own stories. In the winter she would tell "coyote stories." I felt very secure hearing those stories of our family and tribe and would listen very intently after the fire had burned down and everyone was bedded down for the night. The winter nights were wonderful when those stories were told, with the snow blowing around the edges of the cabin.

Our life was very simple by non-Indian standards. In the mornings when I was older I would chop wood and pump water—those would be my chores at the start of each day. After breakfast, which was either oatmeal or pancakes, my sister and I would venture forth to greet the day and many adventures.

My relationships with children my age were limited. Besides my sister and several cousins, I had very few young friends. Even at an early age I was attracted to members of my own sex. I was dreaming in my childhood. I knew that I was different in my attraction to other boys and men. I always had this dream in which a bearded man would open his arms to me and say "Come." When I was eight years old, I experienced my vision and found out how truly different I was.

It was during a hot, dry, and dusty Idaho summer, when I was eleven, that I had my first real contact with another male. I had more freedom then. I had both a pony and a red bicycle. With those possessions my circle of friends widened. I met a boy who lived a few blocks down from my grandmother's cabin. He was a local white boy some years older than myself. I admired his independent and cocksure ways. He seemed to be everything that I was not: good in sports and, above all, sure of himself in every situation. He had tousled brown curly hair and was somewhat stocky. He became my hero in the eye of my budding desire.

The local boys our age frequented several well-known swimming holes on the reservation. We always picked one that was well secluded with overhanging trees and green grass on the banks. One day toward the end of summer—on the kind of day when the light is hazy and diffused and the air is barely moving and heavy to breathe—my friend and I decided to have an impromptu swim before returning home. The water was cool and clear as we dove in. I came up from under the water first. He came up right behind me and reached around and into my shorts (we always swam in our undershorts). I noticed that he was hard, as he rubbed against my backside. As his hands reached around me . . . I became aroused and hard, too. It felt good and right, like something that was supposed to be. I knew then that this is what I had been waiting for and I have never looked back since.

After that summer and after many more rendezvous, my friend moved away. I was dumbstruck. I had found a companion, someone to share with and be my friend, closer than a brother or a buddy. But then he was gone. My young heart experienced for the first time the loneliness and the ache of missing someone that you love. Since that time I have found many more boys and men of all races in many different cities and countries and situations. But, of course, there is no time like the first time. It is something that is burned in my memory, like those hot Idaho August days so long ago.

It is unfortunate that among today's gay Indians the great tradition and vision of the old-time berdache has been suppressed and is nearly dead. Gay Indians today grow up knowing that they are different, act in a different way, and perceive things in a different light from other Indians. They know these things, but sometimes are afraid to act or acknowledge their gayness. If they do, they try to accept and emulate the only alternative lifestyle offered to them, that of the current gay society of bars, baths, and, until recently, numerous sex partners. It is no wonder that many succumb to alcohol or drug addiction and early death. Today I see so many of my Indian brothers and sisters with the same vision living a life that is damaging to themselves, denying or fighting against what they really are. I see and know many gay Indians on the reservation and elsewhere that think along the following lines: "It's okay for you to go to bed with me. I will talk to you in bars or when I want to fuck. But don't come around me in Indian society, at powwows, or other tribal functions. I don't want our people to know. Nobody knows my secret but everyone knows what you are and what you like to do."

To escape this kind of thinking and the oppressive lifestyle that gay Indians are often forced to live on the reservations, many go to the city and follow the way of the non-Indian gay society—taking up the latest trends in fashion, carrying on in the bars, or dancing the night away in discos and after-hours clubs and, of course, having sex, lots of it. I followed this way myself for many years, but in the end I became tired of it all. Deep inside I knew that, as an Indian, something else was needed—something more than poppers, drugs, booze, fashion, restaurants, bars, gay shops, cock rings, leather, drag, and the latest dance hits—especially for a person of substance and especially for an Indian person. Most Indian people, gay or straight, have been instilled with a respect for all things, a love for the earth and all things living. The current gay lifestyle, although it is an up-front gay existence, is not an Indian way. Most gay Indians become lost in it, not only to themselves but to their cultures, tribes, and sometimes families as well.

In the past ten years, however, efforts have been made by gay Indians who live in the cities to found support groups and social organizations for urban gay Indians as well as those across the country on reservations and in other rural areas. They are to be commended. Organizations such as Gay American Indians of San Francisco and the Native Cultural Society of Vancouver, British Columbia, are at least there to provide the positive statement and support needed by so many gay Indians. They exist to say, *"We are here, we exist, we are INDIAN and we are GAY!!"* That is very important, not only to those in the cities but also to the gay Indian living on the reservation. Many live in such isolation that they cannot react to other gay Indian people in a positive way and are afraid to associate with other gay Indians because of social ostracism or criticism.

In the old days, groups of berdaches lived on the outer edge of the camp. They lived together in a tipi or a group of tipis that were usually the best made and decorated in camp. The old-time berdaches had a pride in their possessions and in themselves. They knew who they were and what place they had in Plains Indian society.

I believe this is exactly what needs to happen again with gay Indians today. There is a need to take pride in one's self and to respect other gay Indian people. There is a need for a resurgence of that old pride and knowledge of place. Traditions need to be re-searched and revived. If traditions have been lost, then new ones should be borrowed from other tribes to create groups or societies for gay Indians that would function in the present. An example of this is the contemporary powwow that takes elements from many tribal groups and combines them into an exercise in modern Indian tradition and social structure.

I am not saying that we should all go "back to the blanket" or return to the reservation. But somehow there should be a blending of the old with the new, to develop more within ourselves and our consciousness—as a people living on the "outer edge," possessing a unique and valid vision and a place in the history and contempo-rary lifestyle of our country.

> When you are born into this world, you reach for either a bow and quiver, which is blessed and protected by the Sun, our Grandfather, or you reach for an awl and sewing bag, which is blessed by the Moon, our Grandmother. From that time on you will follow that vision and be blessed.
> —Traditional Indian belief and teaching

JAMAICA–CANADA

In the following selection, Makeda Silvera, an Afro-Caribbean lesbian, reminisces about her childhood in Jamaica, and examines her situation as a member of a visible minority living now in Canada. Using conversations she has held with both her mother and grandmother, she pieces together colorful portraits of the strong Black women, many of whom were lesbian, she admired while growing up.

As commonplace as many of these "Man Royals" or "Sodomites" were in her community, a veil of shame and silence has prevented any open recognition or validation of their specialness—even to this day. Ms. Silvera, then, gives voice to these once-invisible women. Importantly, she places the sexism and homophobia prevalent throughout her childhood within the context of her Afro-Caribbean culture, and the impact made upon it by slavery and imperialism. "Man Royals and Sodomites" is a significant contribution to the emerging literature of lesbian and gay life as experienced by Third World peoples.

**"Man Royals and Sodomites: Some Thoughts
on the Invisibility of Afro-Caribbean Lesbians"
by Makeda Silvera, from *Lesbians in Canada*, ed.
Sharon Dale Stone (1990).**

I will begin with some personal images and voices about woman-loving. These have provided a ground for my search for cultural reflections of my identity as a Black woman artist within the Afro-

Caribbean community of Toronto. Although I focus here on my own experience (specifically, Jamaican), I am aware of similarities with the experience of other Third World women of color whose history and culture has been subjected to colonization and imperialism.

I spent the first thirteen years of my life in Jamaica among strong women. My great-grandmother, my grandmother, and grandaunts were major influences in my life. There are also men whom I remember with fondness—my grandmother's "man friend" G., my Uncle Bertie, his friend Paul, Mr. Minott, Uncle B., and Uncle Freddy. And there were men like Mr. Eden, who terrified me because of stories about his "walking" fingers and his liking for girls under age fourteen.

I lived in a four-bedroom house with my grandmother, Uncle Bertie, and two female tenants. On the same piece of land, my grandmother had other tenants, mostly women and lots and lots of children. The big veranda of our house played a vital role in the social life of this community. It was on that veranda that I received my first education on "Black women's strength"—not only from their strength, but also from the daily humiliations they bore at work and in relationships. European experience coined the term "feminism," but the term "Black women's strength" reaches beyond Eurocentric definitions to describe what is the cultural continuity of my own struggles.

The veranda. My grandmother sat on the veranda in the evenings after all the chores were done to read the newspaper. People—mostly women—gathered there to discuss "life." Life covered every conceivable topic—economic, local, political, social, and sexual: the high price of salt fish, the scarcity of flour, the nice piece of yellow yam bought at Coronation market, Mr. Lam, the shopkeeper who was taking "liberty" with Miss Inez, the fights women had with their menfolk, work, suspicions of Miss Iris and Punsie carrying on something between them, the cost of school books. . . .

My grandmother usually had lots of advice to pass on to the

women on the veranda, all grounded in the Bible. Granny believed in Jesus, in good and evil, and in repentance. She was also a practical and sociable woman. Her faith didn't interfere with her perception of what it meant to be a poor Black woman; neither did it interfere with our Friday night visits to my Aunt Marie's bar. I remember sitting outside on the piazza with my grandmother, two grandaunts, and three or four of their women friends. I liked their flashy smiles and I was fascinated by their independence, ease, and their laughter. I loved their names—Cherry Rose, Blossom, Jonesie, Poinsettia, Ivory, Pearl, Iris, Bloom, Dahlia, Babes. Whenever the conversation came around to some "big 'oman talk"—who was sleeping with whom or whose daughter just got "fallen"—I was sent off to get a glass of water for an adult, or a bottle of Kola champagne. Every Friday night I drank as much as half a dozen bottles of Kola champagne, but I still managed to hear snippets of words, tail ends of conversations about women together.

In Jamaica, the words used to describe many of these women would be "Man Royal" and/or "Sodomite." Dread words. So dread that women dare not use these words to name themselves. They were names given to women by men to describe aspects of our lives that men neither understood nor approved.

I heard "sodomite" whispered a lot during my primary school years, and tales of women secretly having sex, joining at the genitals, and being taken to the hospital to be "cut" apart were told in the schoolyard. Invariably, one of the women would die. Every five to ten years the same story would surface. At times it would even be published in the newspapers. Such stories always generated much talking and speculation from "Bwoy dem kinda gal nasti sah!" to some wise old woman saying, "But dis caan happen, after two shutpan caan join"—meaning identical objects cannot go into the other. The act of loving someone of the same sex was sinful, abnormal—something to hide. Even today, it isn't unusual or uncommon to be asked, "So how do two 'omen do it? . . . what unoo use for a penis? . . . who is the man and who is the 'oman?" It's inconceivable that women can have intimate relationships that are whole, that are not lacking because of the absence of a man. It's assumed that women in such relationships must be imitating men.

The word "sodomite" derives from the Old Testament. Its common use to describe lesbians (or any strong, independent woman) is peculiar to Jamaica—a culture historically and strongly grounded in the Bible. Although Christian values have dominated the world, their effect in slave colonies is particular. Our foreparents gained access to literacy through the Bible when they were being indoctrinated by missionaries. It provided powerful and ancient stories of strength, endurance, and hope which reflected their own fight against oppression. This book has been so powerful that it continues to bind our lives with its racism and misogyny. Thus the importance the Bible plays in Afro-Caribbean culture must be recognized in order to understand the historical and political context for the invisibility of lesbians. The wrath of God "rained down burning sulfur on Sodom and Gomorrah" (Genesis 19:23). How could a Caribbean woman claim the name?

When, thousands of miles away and fifteen years after my school days, my grandmother was confronted with my love for a woman, her reaction was determined by her Christian faith and by this dread word "sodomite"—its meaning, it implication, its history.

And when, Bible in hand, my grandmother responded to my love by sitting me down, at the age of twenty-seven, to quote Genesis, it was within the context of this tradition, this politic. When she pointed out that "this was a white people ting," or "a ting only people with mixed blood was involved in" (to explain or include my love with a woman of mixed blood), it was a strong denial of many ordinary Black working-class women she knew.

It was finally through my conversations with my grandmother, my mother, and my mother's friend five years later that I began to realize the scope of this denial, which was intended to dissuade and protect me. She knew too well that any woman who took a woman lover was attempting to walk on fire—entering a "no-man's-land." I began to see how commonplace the act of loving women really was, particularly in working-class communities. I realized, too, just how heavily shame and silence weighed down this act.

A conversation with a friend of my mother:

> Well, when I was growing up we didn't hear much 'bout woman and woman. They weren't "suspect." There was much more talk about "batty man businesses" when I was a teenager in the 1950s.
>
> I remember one story about a man who was "suspect" and that every night when he was coming home, a group of guys use to lay wait him and stone him so viciously that he had to run for his life. Dem time, he was safe only in the day.
>
> Now with women, nobody really suspected. I grew up in the country and grew up seeing women holding hands, hugging up, sleeping together in one bed, and there was no question. Some of this was based purely on emotional friendship, but I also knew of cases where the women were dealing but no one really suspected. Close people around knew, but not everyone. It wasn't a thing you would go out and broadcast. It would be something just between the two people.
>
> Also one important thing is that the women who were involved carried on with life just the same, no big political statements were made. These women still went to church, still got baptized, still went on pilgrimage, and I am thinking about one particular woman name Aunt Vie, a very strong woman, strong-willed and everything, they use to call her "man royal" behind her back, but no one ever dare to meddle with her.
>
> Things are different now in Jamaica. Now all you have to do is not respond to a man's call to you and dem call you sodomite or lesbian. I guess it was different back then forty years ago because it was harder for anybody to really conceive of two women sleeping and being sexual. But I do remember when you were "suspect," people would talk about you. You were definitely classed as "different," "not normal," a bit of a "crazy." But women never really got stoned like the men.
>
> What I remember is that if you were a single woman alone or two single women living together and a few people suspected

this . . . and when I say a few people I mean like a few guys, sometimes other crimes were committed against the women. Some very violent, some very subtle. Battery was common, especially in Kingston. A group of men would suspect a woman or have it out for her because she was a "sodomite" or because she act "man royal" and so the man would organize and gang-rape whichever woman was "suspect." Sometimes it was reported in the newspaper, other times it wasn't—but when you live in a little community, you don't need a newspaper to tell what's going on. You know by word of mouth, and those stories were frequent. Sometimes you also knew the men who did the battery.

Other subtle forms of this was "scorning" the woman. Meaning that you didn't eat anything from them, especially a cooked meal. It was almost as if those accused of being "man royal" or "sodomite" could contaminate.

A conversation with my grandmother:

I am only telling you this so that you can understand that this is not a profession to be proud of and to get involved in. Everybody should be curious, and I know you born with that, ever since you growing up as a child and I can't fight against that, because that is how everybody get to know what's in the world. I am only telling you this because when you were a teenager, you always say you want to experience everything and make up your mind on your own. You didn't like people telling you what was wrong and right. That always use to scare me.

Experience is good, yes. But it have to be balanced, you have to know when you have too much experience in one area. I am telling you this because I think you have enough experience in this to decide now to go back to the normal way. You have two children. Do you want them to grow up knowing this is the life you have taken? But this is for you to decide. . . .

Yes, there was a lot of women involved with women in Jamaica. I knew a lot of them when I was growing up in the country in the 1920s. I didn't really associate with them. Mind you, I was not rude to them. My mother wouldn't stand any rudeness from any of her children to adults.

I remember a woman we use to call Miss Bibi. She lived next to us—her husband was a fisherman, I think he drowned before I was born. She had a little wooden house that back onto the sea, the same as our house. She was quiet, always reading. That I remember about her because she used to go to the little public library at least four days out of the week. And she could talk. Anything you want to know, just ask Miss Bibi and she could tell you. She was mulatto woman, but poor. Anytime I had any school work that I didn't understand, I use to ask her. The one thing I remember, though, we wasn't allowed in her house by my mother, so I used to talk to her outside, but she didn't seem to mind that. Some people use to think she was mad because she spent so much time alone. But I didn't think that because anything she help me with, I got a good mark on it in school.

She was colorful in her own way, but quiet, always alone, except when her friend come and visit her once a year for two weeks. Them times I didn't see Miss Bibi much because my mother told me I couldn't go and visit her. Sometimes I would see her in the market exchanging and bartering fresh fish for vegetables and fruits. I used to see her friend, too. She was a jet Black woman, always had her hair tied in bright-colored cloth, and she always had on big gold earrings. People use to say she lived on the other side of the island with her husband and children and she came to Port Maria once a year to visit Miss Bibi.

My mother and father were great storytellers and I learnt that from them, but is from Miss Bibi that I think I learnt to love reading so much as a child. It wasn't until I move to Kingston that I notice other women like Miss Bibi. . . .

Let me tell you about Jonesie. Do you remember her? Well, she was the woman who lived the next yard over from us. She is the one who really turn me against people like that and why I fear so much for you to be involved in this ting. She was very loud. Very show-off. Always dressed in pants and man-shirt that she borrowed from her husband. Sometimes she use to invite me over to her house, but I didn't go. She always had her hair in a bob cut, always barefoot and tending to her garden and her fruit trees. She tried to get me involved in that kind of life, but I said no. At the time I remember I needed some money to borrow and she lent me, later she told me I didn't have to pay her back, but come over to her house and see the thing she had that was sweeter than what any man could offer me. I told her no and eventually paid her back the money.

We still continued to talk. It was hard not to like Jonesie— that's what everybody called her. She was open and easy to talk to. But still there was fear in me about her. To me it seem like she was in a dead end nowhere to go. I don't want that for you.

I left my grandmother's house that day feeling anger and sadness for Miss Jones—maybe for myself, who knows? I was feeling boxed in. I had said nothing, I'd only listened quietly.

In bed that night, I thought about Miss Jones. I cried for her (for me) silently. I remember her, a mannish-looking Indian woman, with flashy gold teeth, a Craven cigarette always between them. She was always nice to me as a child. She had the sweetest, juiciest Julie, Bombay, and East Indian mangoes on the street. She always gave me mangoes over the fence. I remember the dogs in her yard and the sign on her gate. "Beware of bad dogs." I never went into her house, though I was always curious.

I vaguely remember her pants and shirts, though I never thought anything of them until my grandmother pointed them out. Neither did I recall that dreaded word being used to describe her, although everyone on the street knew about her.

A conversation with my mother:

Yes, I remember Miss Jones. She smoke a lot, drank a lot. In fact, she was an alcoholic. When I was in my teens she use to come over to our house—always on the veranda. I can't remember her sitting down—seems she was always standing up, smoking, drinking, and reminiscing. She constantly talked about the past, about her life. And it was always women, the fun they had together and how good she could make love to a woman. She would say to whoever was listening on the veranda, "Dem girls I used to have sex with was shapely. You shoulda know me when I was younger, pretty and shapely just like the 'oman dem I use to have as my 'oman."

People used to tease her on the street, but not about being a lesbian or calling her sodomite. People use to tease her when she was drunk, because she would leave the rum shop and stagger down the avenue to her house.

I remember the women she use to carry home, usually in the daytime. A lot of women from downtown, higglers and fish-women. She use to boast about knowing all kinds of women from Coronation market and her familiarity with them. She had a husband who lived with her, and that served as her greatest protection against other men taking steps with her. Not that anybody could easily take advantage of Miss Jones, she could stand up for herself. But having a husband did help. He was very quiet, insular man. He didn't talk to anyone in the street. He had no friends, so it wasn't easy for anyone to come up to him and gossip about his wife.

No one could go to her house without being invited, but I wouldn't say she was a private person. She was a loner. She went to the rum shops alone, she drank alone, she staggered home alone. The only times I ever saw her with somebody were the times when she went off to the Coronation market or some other place downtown to find a woman and bring her home. The only times I remember her engaging in conversation with any-body was when she came over on the veranda to talk about her women and what they did in bed. That was all she let out about herself. There was nothing about how she was feeling, whether she was sad or depressed, lonely, happy. Nothing. She seemed to cover up all of that with her loudness and her vulgarness and her constant threat—which was all it was—to beat up anybody who troubled her or teased her when she was coming home from the rum shop.

Now, Cherry Rose—do you remember her? She was a good friend of Aunt Marie and of Mama's. She was also a sodomite.

She was loud, too, but different from Miss Jones. She was much more outgoing. She was a barmaid and had lots of friends—both men and women. She also had the kind of personality that attracted people—very vivacious, always laughing, talking, and touching. She didn't have any children, but Gem did.

Do you remember Miss Gem? Well, she had children and she was also a barmaid. She also had lots of friends. She also had a man friend named Mickey, but that didn't matter because some women had their men and still had women they carried on with. The men usually didn't know what was going on, and seeing as these men just come and go and usually on their own time, they weren't around every day and night.

Miss Pearl was another one that was in that kind of thing. She was a dressmaker, she used to sew really good. Where Gem was light complexion, she was a very Black woman with deep dimples. Where Gem was a bit plump, Pearl was slim, but with big breasts and a big bottom. They were both pretty women.

I don't remember hearing that word "sodomite" a lot about them. It was whispered sometimes behind their backs, but never in front of them. And they were so alive and talkative that people were always around them.

The one woman I almost forgot was Miss Opal, a very quiet woman. She used to be friends with Miss Oliver and was always out of her bar sitting down. I can't remember much about her except she didn't drink like Miss Jones and she wasn't vulgar. She was soft-spoken, a half-Chinese woman. Her mother was born in Hong Kong and her father was a Black man. She could really bake. She use to supply shops with cakes and other pastries.

So there were many of those kind of women around. But it wasn't broadcast.

I remembered them. Not as lesbians or sodomites or man royals, but as women that I liked. Women whom I admired. Strong women, some colorful, some quiet.

I loved Cherry Rose's style. I loved her loudness, the way she challenged men in arguments, the bold way she laughed in their faces, the jingle of her gold bracelets. Her colorful and stylish way of dressing. She was full of wit; words came alive in her mouth.

Miss Gem: I remember her big double iron bed. That was where Paula and Lorraine (her daughters, my own age) and I spent a whole week together when we had chicken pox. My grandmother took me there to stay for the company. It was fun. Miss Gem lived right above her bar and so at any time we could look through the window and onto the piazza and street, which was bursting with energy and life. She was a very warm woman, patient and caring. Every day she would make soup for us and tell us stories. Later on in the evening she would bring us Kola champagne.

Miss Pearl sewed dresses for me. She hardly ever used her tape measure—she could just take one look at you and make you a dress fit for a queen. What is she doing now? I asked myself. And Miss Opal, with her calm and quiet, where is she—still baking?

What stories could these lesbians have told us? I, an Afro-Caribbean woman living in Canada, come with this baggage—their silenced stories. My grandmother and mother know the truth, but silence still surrounds us. The truth remains a secret to the rest of the family and friends, and I must decide whether to continue to sew this cloth of denial or break free, creating and becoming the artist that I am, bringing alive the voices and images of Cherry Rose, Miss Gem, Miss Jones, Opal, Pearl, and others. . . .

There is more at risk for us than for white women. Through three hundred years of history we have carried memories and the scars of racism and violence with us. We are the sisters, daughters, mothers of a people enslaved by colonialists and imperialists.

Under slavery, production and reproduction were inextricably linked. Reproduction served not only to increase the labor force of slave owners but also, by "domesticating" the enslaved, facilitated the process of social control. Simultaneously, the enslaved responded to dehumanizing conditions by focusing on those aspects of life in which they could express their own desires. Sex was an area in which to articulate one's humanity but, because it was tied to attempts "to define oneself as human," gender roles, as well as the act of sex, became badges of status. To be male was to be the stud, the procreator; to be female was to be fecund, and one's femininity was measured by the ability to attract and hold a man and to bear children. In this way, slavery and the postemancipated colonial orders defined the structures of patriarchy and heterosexuality as necessary for social mobility and acceptance.

Socioeconomic conditions and the quest for a better life have seen steady migration from Jamaica and the rest of the Caribbean to the United States, Britain, and Canada. Upon my arrival, I became part of the so-called visible minorities encompassing Blacks, Asians, and Native North Americans in Canada. I lived with a legacy of continued racism and prejudice. We confront this daily, both as individuals and as organized political groups. Yet for those of us who are lesbians, there is another struggle: the struggle for acceptance and positive self-definition within our own communities. Too often we have had to sacrifice our love for women in political meetings that have been dominated by the "we are the world" attitude of heterosexual ideology. We have had to hide too often that part of our identity which contributes profoundly to make up the whole.

Many lesbians have worked, like me, in the struggles of Black people since the 1960s. We have been on marches every time one of us gets murdered by the police. We have been at sit-ins and vigils. We have flyered, postered, we have cooked and baked for the struggle. We have tended to the youths. And we have all at one time or another given support to men in our community, all the time painfully holding on to, obscuring, our secret lives. When we do walk out of the closet (or are thrown out), the "ideologues" of the Black communities say, "Yes, she was a radical sistren but I don't know what happen, she just went the wrong way." What is implicit in this is that one cannot be a lesbian and continue to do political work and, not surprisingly, it follows that a Black lesbian/artist cannot create using the art forms of our culture. For example, when a heterosexual male friend came to my house, I put on a dub poetry tape. He asked, "Are you sure that sistren is a lesbian?"

"Why?" I ask.

"Because this poem sound wicked; it have lots of rhythm; it sounds cultural."

Another time, another man commented on my work, "That book you wrote on domestic workers is really a fine piece of work. I didn't know you were that informed about the economic politics of the Caribbean and Canada." What are we to assume from this? That Afro-Caribbean lesbians have no Caribbean culture? That they lose their community politics when they sleep with women? Or that Afro-Caribbean culture is a heterosexual commodity?

The presence of an "out" Afro-Caribbean lesbian in our community is dealt with by suspicion and fear from both men and our heterosexual Black sisters. It brings into question the assumption of heterosexuality as the only "normal" way. It forces them to acknowledge something that has always been covered up. It forces them to look at women differently and brings into question the traditional Black female role. Negative response from our heterosexual Black sisters, though more painful, is, to a certain extent, understandable because we have no race privilege and very, very few of us have class privilege. The one privilege within our group is heterosexual. We all suffered at the hands of this racist system at one time or another and to many heterosexual Black women it is inconceivable, almost frightening, that one could turn her back on credibility in our community and the society at large by being lesbian. These women are also afraid that they will be labeled "lesbian" by association. It is that fear, that homophobia, which keeps Black women isolated.

The Toronto Black community has not dealt with sexism. It has not been pushed to do so. Neither has it given a thought to its heterosexism. In 1988, my grandmother's fear is very real, very alive. One takes a chance when one writes about being an Afro-Caribbean lesbian. There is the fear that one might not live to write more. There is the danger of being physically "disciplined" for speaking as a woman-identified woman.

And what of our white lesbian sisters and their community? They have learnt well from the civil rights movement about organizing, and with race and some class privilege, they built a predominantly white lesbian (and gay) movement—a precondition for a significant body of work by a writer or artist. They have demanded and received recognition from politicians (no matter how little). But this recognition has not been extended to Third World lesbians of color —neither from politicians nor from white lesbian (and gay) organizations. The white lesbian organizations/groups have barely (some not at all) begun to deal with or acknowledge their own racism, prejudice, and biases—all learned from a system that feeds on their ignorance and grows stronger from its institutionalized racism. Too often white women focus only on their oppression as lesbians, ignoring the more complex oppression of non-white women who are also lesbians. We remain outsiders in these groups, without images or political voices that echo our own. We know too clearly that, as non-white lesbians in this country, we are politically and socially at the very bottom of the heap. Denial of such differences robs us of true visibility. We must identify and define these differences, and challenge the movements and groups that are not accessible to non-whites—challenge groups that are not accountable.

But where does this leave us as Afro-Caribbean lesbians, as part of this "visible minority" community? As Afro-Caribbean women we are still at the stage where we have to imagine and discover our existence, past and present. As lesbians, we are even more marginalized, less visible. The absence of a national Black lesbian and gay movement through which to begin to name ourselves is disheartening. We have no political organization to support us and through which we could demand respect from our communities. We need such an organization to represent our interests, both in coalition-building with other lesbian/gay organizations, and in the struggles that shape our future—through which we hope to transform the social, political, and economic systems of oppression as they affect all peoples.

Though not yet on a large scale, lesbians and gays of Caribbean descent are beginning to seek each other out—are slowly organizing. Younger lesbians and gays of color are beginning to challenge and force their parents and the Black community to deal with their sexuality. They have formed groups, "Zami for Black and Caribbean Gays and Lesbians" and "Lesbians of Color," to name two.

The need to make connections with other Caribbean and Third World people of color who are lesbian and gay is urgent. This is where we can begin to build that other half of our community, to create wholeness through our art. This is where we will find the support and strength to struggle, to share our histories, and to record these histories in books, documentaries, film, sound, and art. We will create a rhythm that is uniquely ours—proud, powerful, and gay. Being invisible is no longer. Naming ourselves and taking our space within the larger history of Afro-Caribbean peoples is a dream to be realized, a dream to act upon.

KENYA–GREAT BRITAIN

The following interview with Zahid Dar is one of fourteen interviews conducted by the Gay Men's Oral History Group in England for inclusion into the collection *Walking After Midnight*. The subject is a young man of Indian background who spent his early years in Kenya and Tanzania before moving with his family to England in 1963.

Aware of his attraction to the same sex at an early age, Zahid Dar finds life before his coming out very difficult. His mother is a devout Moslem, and his large family closely knit, allowing for little personal privacy. His homosexual inclinations have to be hidden, and this entails being less than honest with both family and friends. Even the simple act of purchasing a homoerotic magazine from a bookshop near his college is not without its trauma. Many readers, even those of markedly different backgrounds, will find resonating here echoes of their own days before "coming out." Later, after coming to terms with his own gayness, Zahid Dar commits himself to politics. The story of his struggles as a member of both sexual and racial minority groups brings to the fore several questions, at least one of which is pertinent today to many gays of color: Is it more important to identify and involve oneself politically as a Black person in gay politics or as a gay person in Black politics?

"Zahid Dar," interviewed by Will Todd (October 1985) for *Walking After Midnight: Gay Men's Life Stories* by the Gay Men's Oral History Group of the Hall Carpenter Archives (1989).

Both my parents were born in East Africa; their parents had migrated there early this century from India. My mother's father was a tailor and my father's father used to work on the railways and then, when he retired, he started tailoring as well. I was born in Nairobi, Kenya, in 1956. When I was about five we moved to Tanzania for a couple of years and then we moved back to Nairobi till I was eight.

I went to school in East Africa, starting when I was five, for about three years. When we were in Tanzania, my father worked in a gold mine, and one of his workmates used to teach me arithmetic. I remember our house and traveling to and from Tanzania to visit my grandmother. I remember my grandmother's house had a rocking horse in the garden. Up to when I was eight, I just used to enjoy going out, playing in the garden. In Tanzania I used to have a pet monkey, which we tied to the outside of the house and it could run on the roof and all around the garden. And we had a duck and chickens.

I remember I was afraid to go to school in Kenya because the teacher was frightening, very strict. I remember getting my knuckles rapped for getting the answer wrong. I had a woman teacher who I liked, who wasn't as strict. It was a boys' school and there was an Islamic girls' school nearby. The majority of pupils and teachers were Asian, and the areas we lived in were always populated by Asians. I used to have to go to the mosque to say my prayers and was taught to read the Koran in Arabic. My mother's very pious, but my father's not very religious—he follows, but he's a hypocrite. I thought about it when I was at college and decided I didn't believe in God, so I don't follow a religion.

My parents came to Britain in '63. Trouble had just started over the fact that Asians owned a lot of the shops and had Asian-only schools and Blacks wanted more control over the economy. It seemed that Asians had a lot of property and owned a lot of the businesses. So there was animosity between Blacks and Asians. My parents felt there was going to be a backlash toward Asians and so they left the country before they were expelled, before the real trouble started. One of my uncles had left and he told my parents, "Yes, it's a good life in Britain. You can get work," etc. So they left Kenya and came here. My father was a motor mechanic; his first job was in Walls, working in their garage, fixing trucks. My mother worked in a sweet factory in Hayes.

My secondary school was a boys' secondary modern in Hayes in Middlesex. I started in '69. I hated it; well, I was scared to go at first, but then I got used to it. I found it quite strange that you had different teachers for different classes; at primary school you had one teacher. But I started to enjoy it. I've got three younger brothers and a younger sister. We used to beat the shit out of each other, I recall. [Laughs.] I used to get angry very quickly. We never used to get on. When my parents bought a house in Hayes, there were five children, so there were seven of us in a three-bedroomed house. We always had other families living with us, so every room was a bedroom. And so I'm not surprised we used to get angry at each other. The visitors were my dad's brothers' or sisters' families. As people were coming over, they were staying with us first before they found their own accommodation. We had people staying with us for months and months at a time, before they settled down. All in all, about five or six families went through our house. I can remember it was quite nice having my cousins around because there were more of us to go out and play.

But I know there was always something going on between my parents. They wouldn't fight openly in front of us, but you could see there were tensions. There was always something in the air.

Q: Did you have any sex education in school or at home?

No, none at all. The only sex education we had in school was when we did the rabbit in biology and the teacher just threw in at the end of the lesson [laughs], "And that's how we have babies." It was really peculiar. I remember when I was at primary school, somebody told me babies are born and I wouldn't believe them. [Laughs.] I said, "No, you're lying."

Q: What about your own sexual feelings? Were you aware of having any?

I always fancied boys. I always got attached to someone in the class. I had a very good friend while I was at primary school, a boy who used to live near our home. We used to come back from school together. He was from a family of nine children. But he went to a different secondary school. We stayed friends because we lived close, but we didn't see each other as much as we used to. And he got a girlfriend at secondary school and I just made other friends, but I didn't have any sexual experiences at all. I was intrigued by other boys talking about their sexual experiences with girls, but I knew I didn't want to investigate sex like that—not with women —and I was frightened to do it with boys.

I remember I heard people talking about homosexuality when I was in the second or third year. I looked it up in the dictionary and thought about it. And I thought, "Yes, that's me." It described my feelings. I remember doing this for two or three years, because I wouldn't believe it at first. Then I remember looking up "homosexuality" in sociology or psychology books and all I could find was that it was a disease. So I was convinced that I had a disease, and that I mustn't ever tell anyone. It was just something that I didn't want to mention. I also read that it was just a phase that you go through. So I just thought, "I'll grow out of it, like everyone else." Like I was supposed to. So I forgot about it. I didn't want to do anything about it. And I repressed all my sexual feelings to the extent that when heterosexual porn was passed around the class, I used to say, "Yeah, it's really good."

It wasn't until I got to college in Manchester, in '76, that I decided I was going to buy gay porn because I didn't want to go out and have sex with someone. That was going too far. I hadn't accepted my sexuality. I remember near the coach station there used to be a gay bookshop called Gaze. I just happened to look in through the window and there was a calendar of a naked man. I'd never seen anything like it before. From then on, I always used to take that route into the town center. Then one Saturday I put on a long coat and a muffler so that nobody would recognize me, because the shop was near the poly campus. I walked into the shop and bought a magazine and left with it hidden in my bag. From then on, for three years while I was at college, I never mentioned it to anyone. But that's how I released my sexual frustration and I'd buy one magazine and keep it for a year. Then I'd throw it away when I used to have to go home for the summer vacation. If anybody ever found it, I would have just gone to pieces.

I played on the fact that I knew lots of women. In my final year I had an affair with a woman. Because we were always together, most people thought it was sexual, but it wasn't. I'd miss lectures for her. We tried to see each other at weekends and it was really wonderful. It was a relationship—without sex. I mean, I'd get annoyed if I saw her with someone else. She used to talk to me about gay characters in films, so I think she'd guessed, because I hadn't made any sexual advances toward her. I just changed the topic of conversation. I'd say, "It wouldn't matter to me if someone was gay; I think it's immaterial." It never came to me that I should accept it and say, 'Yes, I am gay.' I didn't want to. Other people were gay; I wasn't.

When I'd finished college I came back from Manchester and was staying with my parents. While I was a student, living away from home, I had independence so I could go out, see films, go to discos, cope with myself. But when I got back home my parents expected me to be like I was before I left, to have no friends outside the family. Because none of my brothers had been to college, I couldn't talk to them about the things I wanted to talk about. At college I'd been politicized to an extent because I'd joined the Students' Union and I was on the exec. I thought it was great being a student councillor, being on the Board of Governors as a student rep. There was more to life than just watching telly. And life got really boring when I got home because I couldn't talk to anyone. My father reads the *Sun* and my mother likes the *Daily Mirror*.

Having left college, my parents expected me to get married. And because I had this girlfriend in Manchester, I decided that, as they wanted me to get married, I'd like to marry her. From that time onward, when they were saying, "Yes, we'll go and ask her parents," I got really worried because I had to think about having sex with a woman. It dawned on me that I couldn't go through with it. How on earth was I going to do it? I started having sleepless nights and I couldn't eat, but her parents didn't agree to it. They wanted her to marry an accountant cousin of hers. When that fell through I breathed a sigh of relief and just thought, "I've got to do something because I can't go through this again."

My father kept saying to me, "Look, you can't just die over a woman like this. It's not right, son."

After that, I used to read *Time Out* and they carried an ad for Gay Icebreakers. For weeks and weeks I used to turn to this ad. Eventually I was alone one Saturday night and I phoned and I couldn't say a word. Whoever it was who answered said, "You don't have to say anything." And he just talked and talked and talked. He knew exactly what I was going through. Eventually I came out with it. I said, "Oh, I think I might be bisexual." I could only ring when everyone was out and I'd also said to this person that I'm going to have to put the phone down if someone comes through the door. Icebreakers invited me to their disco at the Hemingford Arms on a Friday night. I had to get home by eleven, and even that was late for my parents. This was when I was about twenty-two, twenty-three. After that, going to Icebreakers discos and their tea parties on Sunday afternoon, I became more politicized. I met another gay

Asian at an Icebreakers tea party, and we became very good friends. I've known him ever since, and I haven't looked back since [laughs].

When I first phoned Icebreakers in '80, I was working as a research assistant in Wembley for a tobacco company. I did that for two years and then the company folded and I took the redundancy. While I was doing that job I told my parents that I couldn't travel all that way every day and that my company wanted me to do an evening class, which was a lie, but I had to make something up. And so I rented a flat with a gay man, lived in Northolt, and it was near enough for work and I could still visit my family. So I moved out soon after I came out to myself.

I wanted to go on the scene. I'd learnt to drive and my brothers had got me a little Ford Escort, so I was able to drive to meetings and to clubs and pubs. Chatan, my gay Asian friend, and I used to go out nearly every night—Harpoon Louis, Wags. We used to meet at Bunjie's coffee bar and then go on to a gay bar. We used to go to Heaven, Scandals, Spats, and Bangs on a Monday night. There were a couple of discos in Tottenham that don't exist anymore. So we used to travel around.

After Icebreakers, Chatan wanted to start a group with gay Asians. We talked about it and I agreed with him that there was a need for a group. He wrote an article in the first issue of *Gay Noise;* I was very critical, but agreed with the gist of it. We asked Gay's the Word if we could meet at the shop and we advertised the Gay Black Group. Two or three people turned up, then four or five at the weekend. When it first started it was amazing the way people said, "Yeah, I felt like that." And talking about their family and how they felt about being gay, the pressures to get married. Explaining to their parents, if they had come out to them, what "gay" meant because such a term doesn't exist in Pakistani or Hindi. There was a lot of empathy in the group. We all understood and that made us feel really good. I'd talked in gay groups before about being Black and gay, with white people just nodding their heads and saying, "Yes, yes." There were also occasions where people would talk about the racist door policies of some clubs and none of the white gay groups would take that up as an issue.

I remember an incident in the Bell pub in King's Cross sometime in '83. On a Friday night there used to be a disco run jointly by the Icebreakers collective and the Nightworkers DJs. The Lesbians and Gay Black Group, as it had then become, used to go after the Friday evening meetings. Over a period of a few weeks, there was a marked rise in the attendance of skinheads wearing Union Jack T-shirts and British bulldog tattoos and some fascist regalia. The disco organizers were asked to refuse entry to these people as they offended most members of the LGBG. We were met with rhetoric about choice of one's dress, which had nothing to do with politics. The Lesbian and Gay Black Group continued to attend—as did the skinheads. Then one occasion I overhead one of the skinheads saying, "I don't like colored." This was not going to go unchallenged. I insisted he leave, but the incident went unchallenged by the organizers. The plugs had to be pulled to get the Nightworkers to make the announcement. This incident sparked off a series of letters in *Capital Gay*. The core of the debate was that Icebreakers could not impose a ban on "members of the gay community" because of their dress, whereas the LGBG—myself, in particular—felt that the ban was against gay racists and fascists. I should point out that not all members of the LGBG supported my views.

From '81, the Gay Black Group [later the Lesbian and Gay Black Group] just went on from strength to strength. We had lots of consciousness-raising sessions and lots of heated debates about various things: a recurrent one was about the cultural differences between Afro-Caribbeans and Asians and the fact that we called the group "Black." We would get Afro-Caribbeans coming to the group, saying, "You can't call yourself Black—Black means Afro-Caribbean"; and Malaysians saying, "I'm brown, I'm not black." But the political argument for calling the group "Black" was that it wasn't the color of your skin that mattered—it was the experience of imperialism and racism; people who had experienced that historical background.

Then there was always the debate about whether gay was more important than being Black. Or, as an identity, was being Black more important than being gay? Personally, I felt that you couldn't hide the fact that you were Black, but you could hide the fact that you were gay. All right, some of us couldn't [laughs], but we felt that our being Black was probably a larger part of our identity than being gay. And that, politically, we should try working within the Black community, strengthening our ties politically with Black activists and raising issues of sexuality within those circles, rather than the issue of racism within gay politics.

We got involved in campaigning for the Bradford Twelve and we used to take our Gay Black Group Banner with us on the marches. This campaign was defending twelve Asian youths in Bradford against charges of "conspiracy to riot," after buried petrol bombs had been found in the students' residential area. There had been warnings that fascists were going to be marching in Bradford like they had in Southhall. In particular, I remember the March '82 demo in Leeds. We used to go along to the Bradford Twelve's London Support Group meetings. I remember marching through the streets of Bradford and holding up the Gay Black Group banner, and people laughing and the crowds watching and saying, "Oh, look at that." [Laughs.] It wasn't terrifying, you know. Whereas the thought of doing it was terrifying. I thought people would react violently against us, but they didn't. Most of the people on the demo were quite supportive of us.

I left the group after two and a half years. Toward the end of '82. I began to attend less and less and only key meetings, such as the one in September with Paul Boateng about GLC grant funding for the Gay Black Group. People drifted in and out and I got to the point where I wasn't developing. I felt that whatever I was putting in was just out of guilt. I thought, "I don't need to do this. There are enough people in the group to carry on." So I left. After the Gay Black Group, I wanted to try working for Black campaigns. I did quite a lot with the Newham Eight campaign as a volunteer between August '83 and December '83. The Newham Eight had been charged with many things, including a conspiracy charge. The eight men charged had been variously involved in defending their brothers and sisters from racist attacks in school and on their way home. The police provoked an attack against these men and then arrested and charged them. A few were acquitted and a few convicted and sentenced to do community service. I went to most of the police-accountability meetings and distributed leaflets.

Straight after I left the Gay Black Group, I worked on the '82 Gay Pride Week committee for a year. Since coming out, I've always been involved in something politically.

In mid-'82 I went to a weekend of gay workshops at South Bank poly, where people were saying that what the gay community needed was a center as a focus point for the community; a while after that there was talk that the GLC were willing to fund one. When I went to my first meeting, I couldn't believe my ears. You know, at County Hall in November '82, people talking about a gay center. Somebody had drawn up a report about feasibility and aims of a center; I agreed, and I was elected on to the steering committee. I worked on that for three years as a volunteer, from '82 to '85. I've also worked for PDC, Publications Distribution Co-op, and after that at Gay's the Word, doing the mail order.

I still see my family quite regularly, but I'm finding it difficult at the moment because I'm nearly thirty and my parents are drawing the line—if I don't get married at thirty, nobody is going to look at me and people are going to talk. I'm finding it quite a strain at the moment, and I've decided not to see my parents as often as I used to because I can't cope with the pressure of constantly being reminded that I have to get married.

I've just started to live together with a group of Asians and Afro-Caribbeans: two gay men, including myself; one straight man; and two straight women. There's five of us. I like living communally. I think that's because of having lived in a large family and that's what I'm used to.

When I came out, Chatan and I went to all these gay places and I saw it as part of a gay lifestyle. But I don't see the need at the

moment. I don't want to be politically active, either. When I was
very politically active, going to nightclubs was like a release. That
was my way of coping with the stress of working—for example,
within the Newham Eight campaign. I'd rather use the gay commercial scene than go to a straight place, but it's just there for
people to make money. That's why I believe in the gay center. The
commercial scene is a meat market. Of course, I've met people on
the scene and had really nice discussions, but the majority of times
I've gone on the scene to pick people up and found it quite depressing because usually you don't pick people up. And I think now,
with the AIDS scare, that even on the commercial scene people are
beginning to drop the defense and actually talk to people other than
for sexual reasons.

I've had a few sexual relationships, but not many. The very first
one was important to me, when I first came out. I was very upset
when it broke up. I also had a relationship with a bisexual man, and
that was really traumatic. It meant a lot to me, and it still does.

I've recently been to India and, having come back from India,
going on the gay scene is not so important to me anymore. In India
there aren't any nightclubs. I was away three and a half months and
I saw that just because there were all these gay pubs and clubs, I
didn't have to use them just because I was gay. This visit was a
"soul-searching and discovering my roots" journey.

POSTSCRIPT BY ZAHID DAR, AUGUST 1988

Since my interview I have moved from the communal house in the
Elephant and Castle, have been a part-time and then full-time
worker at Gay's the Word, and am now a bookseller in a community
in Hackney. I have also been to India again and am now living with
my lover, Nick, in a flat we have bought together in Hackney. This
list is what I would call the high points of the last three years.

There have been low points, too, the most painful of which was the breakup with my closest friend, Chatan, the Gujarati man I talk about in the interview who I met in '80. We came out to our families during the same time. The communal house just wasn't the same for me after that breakup. I stayed on for two and a half years.

I visited India with Nick at the beginning of this year, which was a totally different experience than the first. We stayed with a gay friend's family in Bombay. We met many gay men. The network of gay men is getting larger, but there is still no political will to form any group or forum other than parties for socializing. There was, however, the first signs of a gay bar. It was almost like they didn't want to say it. As most bars are frequented by men in India, this one didn't stand out. But the reasons why clients came here wasn't because all the men were homosexuals but because their friends came here.

Some of the Indian gay men believe that AIDS isn't going to come to India and have frequent casual sex. This is despite the fact that some prostitutes HIV-tested in venereal disease clinics are positive. I acquired this information from a gay doctor and AIDS researcher on a visit from Australia. We met in the gay bar.

When I returned to India, I had to deal with my parents' renewed constant nagging about getting married. I then made a decision about not visiting even as regularly as three years ago. Now my mother has stopped asking me about marriage and asks about Nick. The family knows that we lived together and one of my aunts commented to my parents that what I was doing was not right, in particular that I was living with a heathen. To my surprise, my mother told her that I had my good points, for all my faults. I couldn't believe she had said that.

When we moved into the flat I asked the family to give me the equivalent of my wedding presents, as I wouldn't be getting married the traditional way. I received money from my brothers, and my brother-in-law has helped with the mortgage. All these events have made me feel I made the right decision about marriage. I know of Asian gay men who get married due to pressure from their parents and then regret it later.

My work at Gay's the Word's bookshop branch at the London Lesbian and Gay Center was important to me because of my involvement in the center's development. I feel disappointed at the lack of support the gay community has shown the center. In the present political climate the center should be used to the community's advantage. Moving on from the development work with the center to full-time work with Gay's the Word was a pleasant change because I came into direct contact with people. Gay's the Word is an excellent source of lesbian and gay literature, and I feel it will remain so.

The interview and this postscript are important to me because I feel that it contributes toward recording Black people's gay history in Britain. I remember hearing Audre Lorde speak at the Shaw. She said how important it was for all Black people to write about our lives and struggles; the more people did so, the more others may be encouraged to do the same.

EAST GERMANY

The fact that we have a life such as J.A.W.'s preserved in writing results in part from the heightened interest by gay communities to document stories of lesbians and gays who have lived in the decades before Stonewall. Collections of life stories have now appeared in, at least, France, Germany, Great Britain, and the United States.

Born in 1917, J.A.W. has borne testimony to a wide variety of homophobic manifestations in his native Germany: the ridicule he experienced as a child for being different; the severe repression of gays under the fascists, resulting in large numbers being physically exterminated; and the societal pressures exerted on gay acquaintances that led them into often disastrous marriages.

Though very much a survivor, the toll on J.A.W. has not been light. He tells of suppressing his sexual desires for years at a time, of the lies and deceits to which he has resorted to hide his secret longings, and the separation within him of sex from eros, which hinders him from becoming involved sexually on a long-term basis with other males. Yet there is little sadness evoked in listening to J.A.W. tell of his life. Somehow the "internal exile" of which he speaks has been at the same time a source of strength for him and enabled him to survive with self-respect and minimal compromise to his integrity.

"The Harlequin and the Faun" by J.A.W., from *Gay Voices from East Germany: Interviews by Jürgen Lemke* (1991). J.A.W., born in 1917, is a painter and art educator.

Back in the early twenties, in the train yards of old small-town railroad stations, there were these upright rollers with hemispheric tops. They were made of solid porcelain, around ten inches high, five inches in diameter, and had red and white stripes. They must have been part of the signal system back in the early days of the railroad: guideposts for the engineers when switching tracks. I wanted one so badly. I admired it the way I now like my East Asian figurines.

One hot summer day, my father and I were out walking. Mommy had dressed me up especially nicely, in white overalls with embroidery. At the train yards I spoke my wish: I'd really like to have one of those!

Father nodded, much to my surprise. What I'd expected was a stern no, stuffily proper and reproving. All right, just take it, he said.

Was I ever happy! Giving no thought to my white overalls, I got down on the gravel and went to work with my little hands. It was no use: The thing wouldn't budge. Solid, top-grade industrial porcelain. I refused to give up. At the very moment I was given permission, I was unable to do anything with it. I was getting worn out and disappointed, so I looked to my father for support and . . . found myself looking at a bemused face. He'd been just letting me root around like a dog in a molehill.

I've never forgotten that.

From the vividness of my account, you may detect how much that incident still preoccupies me, even now, a good sixty years later. I'm not criticizing him; he was also intelligent and a good man. But what immaturity this behavior shows. He was relishing an easy victory over a small, helpless boy. But the victory had its aftereffects. Often I felt he was treating me like some little dog, something you like for being funny and cute, but you don't take seriously. Even when I was a university student, something as crazy as this could still go on: I was on my usual weekend visit home and was having a conversation with my mother. We read a lot of the same things and would talk about them. Father walked in, broke into our conversation, and dismissed me with one sentence: And what, boy, makes you think you have anything to say?

That hit like a pail of cold water. After all, I was a student of probably twenty-two. I stormed out, slammed the door, and was livid. . . .

Fortunately, he left my day-to-day upbringing to my mother. He probably realized that she was better at educational matters, more empathetic.

My mother and I were a unit from early on. She was a real partner and treated her children as having equal rights. From my childhood right up to her death, I was joined with her by a deep and close friendship. As a child I was quite naturally jealous of my father, and it wasn't long until the effect became evident: a first-class Oedipus complex.

Back then, I didn't realize that my father was also involved in my intellectual development and was closely supervising it from a certain distance, as was often characteristic of fathers in that era. Both of my parents provided whatever I needed and could somehow manage to integrate in terms of my development. I didn't even notice how supplies for painting and sculpting simply materialized within my reach. When I first showed an interest in art as a twelve-year-old, I found a book about Dürer under the Christmas tree.

My father secretly participated in my artistic experiments, but sadly from such a distance that no father-son dialogue ever came about. Not later, either. I mustn't hold back one thing, however: As a sixteen- or seventeen-year-old, I violently rejected his initial attempt to reach out to me because it made me uneasy. That connection was never made.

He died at an early age, and I didn't fully realize until decades later just how much richer our lives might have been if we'd ever managed to find a common language. He himself had grown up without a father and had never learned to show love to his children. He was jealous of them because they put a claim on his wife, whom he evidently needed very much. He hid his intellectual cultivation from me behind cynical remarks and an ironic mask.

My father was born in 1885 to a teacher's family in the old town of Thorn on the Vistula River. He was entirely a product of late-nineteenth-century Prussia. As a state-employed civil servant in the customs division, he quickly reached a financial level to sustain a family. With a government-backed pension, of course. The total security and reliability of the civil-service hierarchy was the credo to which I was born.

On a material level, we could scarcely bear comparison with the average craftsman. The modest level we lived at is unimaginable today. But the Prussian civil servant knew how to compensate for a small income with a cultivated bearing and social dignity. The bookcase of such a family was a good measure. By the way, even today I still regard a person's bookcase as the best indicator of his character. Not his bank account, or even his car's horsepower. I learned at an early age that culture is not primarily a matter of material outlay but rather of intellectual and personal pride. It's interesting that the German language still separates the concepts of culture and civilization.

Self-control, a dignified bearing, sublimation—these were required of me at an early age, but they were also modeled in a way that gave them credibility. The sex drive was curbed by education and channeled as much as possible into other interests. Young people were supposed to get plenty of outdoor exercise, to postpone sexual gratification until later in life. I believe that this is one of the reasons I survived during the dangerous years from 1933 to 1945.

I was born in 1917. By one full year, I'm still a part of the lost German Empire. It's curious: I was one of the last to be enrolled in "One-Year Insurance." You have no idea what that means? Prussia had created the so-called One Year for the sons of its indispensable civil servants: a single year of military service instead of the usual three—an institution that, in its own way, helped divide society into upper and lower orders. In 1918, when Germany became a bourgeois republic, the One Year was done away with. Up to then it had existed as a privilege. One Years were to the manor born: They slept in separate quarters and were largely spared the indignities of military service. After cleaning weapons, regular recruits had to show they'd washed their hands before they entered the mess hall, whereas the One Years could walk through unchecked.

You could only become a One Year if you had reached a certain level in school: promotion to the senior level, which ended with the university admission exam. That cost money—tuition money—which the "lower" orders were able to raise only in exceptional cases. As a rule, the "simple boys" would enter an apprenticeship at age fourteen in order to start earning money as quickly as possible.

Yet the One Years had to cover all kinds of living expenses themselves, and they also had to pay for their expensive uniforms. Since this was beyond the means of many civil-service families, a fine and practical institution came into being: an insurance policy. If a newborn son of a civil servant promised to be sufficiently fit, his parents could enroll him in the One-Year Insurance.

Later, anytime I'd complain about the rough times in the Labor Corps or in the service, my father would remark dryly and tersely: "Well, One Years didn't have to worry about that."

In 1937, I took my university admission exam. It was grotesque when my final German literature teacher, a Nazi by temperament, replaced the classics with texts from Wagner operas. I couldn't take him seriously, and I was unwilling to parrot that vacuous Teutonic babble with its overwrought wording. It took a long time for me to develop anything like an unbiased relationship to Wagner. Concerning the Hitler Youth, I once stated publicly that I was not going to join "that group." That worked out rather poorly. A gang lay in wait for me, surrounded me, and beat me up.

Like my parents, I despised brutality and thus also hated those brown-shirted big shots who puffed themselves up so much. They were the antithesis of culture. We regarded them as preposterous, yet they soon turned out to be horribly real. We viewed what was happening without comprehending, flabbergasted: This can't go on for long—that's what we were thinking and hoping.

You know, the preconditions for being homosexual were evident in me from early on. Those around me figured out earlier than I did that I was different from them. I didn't see it; I didn't realize it for a long time. As a youngster I was often faced with people who laughed at me. I lacked a military bearing, didn't march as smartly as the others, couldn't handle a soccer ball properly. If anybody joked about the oddness of my way of walking, the others around me would smirk knowingly. I lived in constant fear that they would take me for a fairy, and that before I even knew what a fairy was. This was one of the most wrenching and crucial experiences of my life. I had to learn early on to put up with heartless ridicule. I could tell you a thing or two about what it's like to be the butt of jokes. I was forced to put up with it. I've never belonged to any crowd, never was a pillar of society. I've never felt I had the support of being in a majority. Early on I discovered for myself what was later called internal exile without ever having heard anyone use the term.

Allowing thugs to bash minorities with impunity is a feature of all fascistic systems. During my youth it was the "East European subhumans," the Jews, and the homosexuals who were in trouble. They were "degenerates" to be beaten up at will. Doing so, even the lowest, most rotten, pathetic thug could feel great.

At school I was given to understand in quite unmistakable terms that I could give up any hope of passing my university admission exam if I didn't wear the brown shirt in some form or other. So shortly before the exam, I had myself transferred from the civil defense league into the SA. I skipped duty as often as possible. During my university studies in G. and in M., I simply ignored my membership. I officially resigned two days before my army induction.

The Nazis had established compulsory military service, and like all my school classmates, I had "volunteered" for military service months before my exam. All the others were called up for active duty immediately after the exam; I was the only one who wasn't. I was waiting for that letter in fear and trembling. It never came. Somehow my petition must have gotten snagged in some office. Military service repelled me in the extreme, but I wanted to get it over with to avoid having to interrupt my university studies at some future point. My fellow students were rejoicing: They assumed they'd be able to study undisturbed and in peace once they finished their hitch in the service.

Not one of them was even able to start university study. What was waiting for them was the battlefield. They were mowed down in droves, for the war began two years after that exam.

Thanks to a private connection of my parents, I did, however, show up right on schedule for Labor Service in the filthiest and dampest area of East Prussia. The noncommissioned officer corps there was the dregs of the entire Prussian military and ranked even lower than the usual service. Anyone who got turned down by the regular military was sent to the Labor Service to try to make it there. And now there I was, smack in the middle of it.

Every Saturday afternoon, the command for base cleanup boomed out: College brains, fall out left; route step, march! Woe to the pivot man who didn't immediately turn in the direction of the latrine. That was our field of action. Quite a hilarious joke—the college-bound servicemen double-timing it right into the crap. They couldn't get enough of this regular Saturday gag, those Nazi Labor Service pigs.

For many years I was in a sort of sexual and erotic hibernation. For more than half a century I was successfully sublimating. Those were strangely amorphous, dead years—a time when I was blocking everything. Our bourgeois upbringing had put us through the wringer, cranking out a product that was expected to know what was respectable, what was seemly and proper, and what was to be rejected. After all, parents seldom realize how much their kids do realize or at least suspect, despite all attempts to shelter them—and why should they?

I can't have been more than six or seven when a gentleman whom I didn't pay too much attention to was visiting us in our apartment. I was playing quietly in my corner when suddenly I heard him say: "My man *(mein Mann)* is waiting for me."

It was an electric moment. Up to the present day, I still don't know what he meant. A business partner, a workout buddy in an athletic club—I just don't know. Since my parents reacted to this remark completely normally, it must have been insignificant. In a peculiar way, I became intensely preoccupied with this "my man" spoken by a man.

After finishing my stint in the Labor Services, I was allowed to attend the university for a while at the end of 1937. I'd received a provisional discharge. I began studying language and literature in K., where my older brother was starting a career after finishing an engineering degree. As is so often the case with brothers, we didn't really communicate with each other until we got older. We discovered each other as brothers during wonderful weekend outings in the countryside around K.

Once this happened: It was a spring day warm as summer, but for safety's sake we'd brought along our heavy jackets. He was carrying his, folded over his arm. My jacket was cheaper, more modest than his. In order to hide that, I threw it over my shoulder casually, and I kept it from sliding down by sticking my hand in a back pocket. So my cheap nothing became a little toga, a wrap that was "chic." My brother looked at me and said: God, the way you do that . . . He, the big, good-looking guy, gladly yielded to me: Without any apparent effort on my part, something worked for me that he was incapable of—me, the "little shrimp." He conceded this.

You know, one institution played an important part in my childhood: ballroom dance lessons. Without these dance classes I never would have overcome my deep, panicky shyness. During these months I received instruction on how to move in "society." I learned to walk across a polished hardwood floor and how to carry a chair across a dance floor. Just look at today's youngsters, the way they drag a chair across a disco. You have to learn how to make an entry. From the Renaissance up to the nineteenth century, the dancing teacher played an important role in the education of aristocratic children. Without learning how to walk, the women of earlier centuries couldn't even have worn their big crinolines. Those enormous masses of skirts would start swaying terribly if you walked in the normal way. A small intermediate step catches it, making it possible to sweep across the floor. Wearing the outfits of baroque lords also required such small touches. It must have been a splendid time for our kind of people, since they can generally do that sort of thing without lengthy training.

In short, I had this knack for staging a scene from early on, and the dance lessons were not without their use. I learned to cover up my shyness, lost my fear of socializing, and to top it off received the confirmation that I was quite an attractive, good-looking little fellow after all.

For many people, it takes an exhausting effort to change from insecurity to a self-assured manner. It's like learning to peak extemporaneously. It may well be that you have to learn to pull yourself up by your own bootstraps from the swamp of fear; incidentally, the same is true in bed.

My dance-lesson partner was a sweet, good girl, sadly not very attractive, tall and skinny, daughter of a silly, arrogant mother who worshiped her son and who must have been pretty herself once. This girl took after her father—which is why she was so homely. Well, this father, who had no power within his own four walls, loved his daughter very much. Naturally, the poor kid was overshadowed by the other girls, whom the young cavaliers swarmed around.

Then I began to look after this poor thing. I had found a meaningful task. I surrounded her with attention, which finally caused the others to take notice. She gained self-assurance, was happy not to be a wallflower anymore, and suddenly others were coming over, too, and asking her to dance. To a very small, modest extent she even became stylish. This girl, actually quite homely because of her skinny angularity, learned to smile and in her own way even became pretty. She came through the dance lessons well, and I came through the dance lessons well.

Every society has its rituals, and the entrance is of great importance. Anyone who is out of step from early on tends to keep on stumbling along.

What you in today's jargon call "coming out" or entering the gay scene happened to me very late. I was a university student and was on vacation at the seashore. At that very time, location shots were being filmed in our dunes landscape for a big Ufa movie, *U-Boats Westward*.[1] Movies were terrifically important at that time, especially in the small towns. Movies were the bridge to the wide world outside. People had their idols—for example, the young Wolfgang Liebeneiner, Hannes Stelzer, and others.

So there in the romantic isolation of the dunes came a man in a sailor's uniform who later turned out to be an actor from the theater world of Berlin. This sailor knew very well what effect his movie costume was having and wisely enough didn't pack it away after the day's shooting. I was the clear proof that the sailor gambit worked, even in remote East Prussia. This was my first lapse into sin.

From that time on, I would occasionally go to Berlin. After a short time, my sailor—a well-known habitué of the Kudamm—had directed me further. Not even discreetly so. My country innocence was savored as a delicacy; I was consumed for breakfast —but not for long. You know how things go in life: Having once been deceived, I learned to deceive. . . .

Certainly, the Nazis did drive our people even deeper into illegality. Many were murdered in their barbaric camps. Yet despite all that, there existed in that era what today is called a "scene." The sex drive can't be suppressed for long. Certainly not if you're young and good-looking and for a time seem to consist of nothing but sex drive. Besides, young people always think that the worst can only happen to the next guy.

In this web of experiences, one person suddenly turned up who was not like most others—my first great love. We've kept in touch up to today. He was the prototype of the cultivated homosexual—smart, subtle, playful, too. He had a beautiful baritone and could camp it up marvelously—and do it with charm. And—he was a decent guy. I loved him. He made me aware of the link between intellect and eros, and through that I learned to cope with my differentness.

A close relationship of trust arose between us, and that has continued even when we can't see each other for a long time. I could count our sexual contacts on the fingers of one hand. When we met again after the war was over, we did try it one more time. We cut it out right away; it was not more than a kind of politeness on both sides.

My real friendships usually entailed sex only in the beginning phase, and sometimes not at all. Long-lasting, erotic, and intellectual friendships would arise when the animalistic was excluded. Generally, a real bond didn't become possible until we were past sex.

I found out early on that sex and eros can never be harmonized for me. I have to get beyond sex, whereas I cultivate and honor the divinity of eros.

Now as in the past, I take care of my sexual business at places that, by the way, are not completely devoid of a certain romanticism. All you have to know is how to find them. One thing I do know: Beyond a certain stage of consciousness, any false sense of shame is ridiculous, a sham. What you do with full consciousness with another person cannot be "indecent." The desired body has no "pure" and "impure" zones.

I told you that I served as a medical corpsman throughout the war. I was stationed the longest period of time in G. There I met a fellow who opened up a whole new world for me. He was coming directly from the Eastern Front to spend a few days home on leave.

We found each other with the total absoluteness that is possible for our kind.

I'll never forget that summer night. He was just swept off his feet by our acquaintance, and up till then I'd never been able to give and receive such joy. We immediately made a date to meet the next day. I couldn't go—unexpectedly had duty; I was desperate. In the next days I tore through the town like a madman. He was nowhere to be found.

It's as if something in me snapped at that point. I believe the social pressures gradually produced in me a psychic response that left me unsuited for building up any firm, long-lasting love relationship. I don't know whether this human capacity can be destroyed, but if so, it happened to me back then.

There were encounters with other people. The word expresses it fully: We encountered each other and separated again. You'd schedule a get-together and then not show up. If you did show up, the other guy wouldn't. There was so much fear in us. It was a terrible, appalling time. As a corpsman I met a young physician in my unit, an oddly tormented individual. One day he disappeared—something not all that unusual in the middle of a war; I assumed he was probably transferred. So I didn't give him any more thought.

Months later I was on duty taking care of a simple medical treatment in a penalty stockade. And suddenly the two of us were standing facing each other; he was only a shadow of his former self, a skeleton. I was deeply shocked, in despair about not being able to help. I never saw him again. The linkage was fear—self-control—sublimation.

After all, what did I know at that time? To what extent did I think through what I occasionally heard and make connections? It's astonishing how little we knew in distant East Prussia about the development of things and what was going on. There weren't many Jews in our area; I had heard the term "concentration camp," but I didn't begin to imagine what it actually concealed. The inhumanity of the regime became apparent to me only gradually, like a puzzle; for a long time my experiences lay there next to each other like unsorted pieces, out of order; the real pattern remained hidden from me for a long time.

I got an idea of what had really gone on only in the very last weeks of the war. I learned the final story early in the summer of 1945, during an inspection of the concentration camp in Buchenwald.

You younger folks so enjoy handing out grades retrospectively for our behavior back then—usually in a reckless way, since you're overhasty to project later knowledge back into the past. Things you're not supposed to know—things you don't want to know: The origin of a lot of human tragedies and anxieties is located somewhere between the two, it seems to me. A lot of guilt came about because people knew, and yet so many ignored what was happening.

At the end of 1944, I was transferred to the Rhön Mountains. At the battleline you could no longer tell the front and the rear apart; everything was gradually crumbling. And then came May 8, 1945, and I saw more than a few men crying when they had to cut the braid off their uniforms. Even though everyone had figured that the end was coming, we were surprised when it really did arrive. The army was passé. . . .

The American prisoner-receiving camps were overfilled and wouldn't take us in. We made up what was called a precapture camp. Even in defeat we maintained order, that's how long we'd been drilled. For two weeks we vegetated, dozing away and just starving, until we were distributed to the surrounding villages. After two weeks of nettles, finally potatoes again.

My release came quickly, and I met my mother at the home of relatives in W. We were standing facing each other, what remained of our family. Father and brother dead, our possessions lost, no prospect of employment. But work squads . . . and hunger. That time has been described often enough.

Our situation turned catastrophic when the savings account passbooks from the former Eastern territories were devalued. Right at the beginning I had bought myself watercolors, remnants of which could be bought cheap in paper goods stores. In the summer I would sit with my painting stuff at the edge of a grain field, in autumn at the outermost furrow of a potato field. And, depending on the time of day, I'd paint sunrises or sunsets. In the evening, when the colors could no longer be distinguished, I would creep onto the field and collect whatever was growing on the soil and my pockets could hold. At home I would record the date and what I had harvested on the back side of my watercolors. The pictographs: cabbage, ears of grain, potatoes.

From an earlier visit in W., I remembered an antique store run by two charming older ladies. I went there, and they immediately recognized me. As usual, tales of tribulation were exchanged. When I told them that I was producing watercolors in my abundant free time, they told me firmly that I just had to bring some by—yes, people would buy them, precisely because the town was full of refugees who had money and nothing to spend it on.

The next day I put a portfolio together, *Goethe's Garden House* on top. I took the portfolio to the ladies, and from that hour on I made a big detour to avoid the shop. It simply didn't make sense to me that right now there should be an interest in my little pictures. Weeks later the two ladies called to me on the street: "Young man, why haven't you been by? We're waiting for you!" I was flabbergasted when they told me that one hundred marks were waiting for me for the first sheets sold.

One hundred marks! We were saved, and I could hope for even more. My commissions didn't stop. Among the refugees from Silesia the best selling were little pictures of saints and madonnas. I varnished them with clear nail polish and framed them.

The end of 1945. Of course, nothing was uncomplicated at that time. While filling out the endless questionnaires, I recorded, as called for, my membership in the SA. On doing so I was treated as if I had personally instigated the *Reichskristallnacht,* and it seemed as if I had been the only SA member far and wide. I owe it to two honorable and influential citizens that I was able to close the chapter titled "Denazification" in the autumn of 1945 and to begin studying at the conservatory of fine arts.

A very productive time was beginning for me. In my first pictures it became apparent that my mental-artistic and my erotic impulses made up a close unity, that they conditioned one another. My teachers, tactful and wise, didn't reproach me, but guided me and otherwise let me be.

To my own dismay, I would repeatedly arouse female interest; my polite helplessness vis-à-vis women encouraged them more than it frightened them. It has always pained me to stir feelings and desires I cannot reciprocate, to create expectations that a word might have dispelled. Might have! I couldn't say the word—what else could I do? I got accustomed to lying.

When the law was repealed, it never occurred to me to live in a substituted family with a man. It became ever clearer to me that coupling would be bought at the price of my intellectual existence. It has been wonderful in each of my digs: in a tiny student place or now in this roomy apartment. I need only spread out my beautiful objects—manifestations of my spiritual being—in order to be myself in complete composure, that is, be able to work. The knowledge of having friends and being able to count on their occasional closeness suffices for me and makes me calm and cheerful. I've never yet felt lonely. I do fear this scourge a bit in old age. But even now I've got to watch my appointments and commitments carefully; without an engagement calendar I'd be lost. My mother, whom I lived with until her death, warned me back then: "Boy, those friends of yours are eating you up. You're like a candle burning at both ends." I just laughed at her, which I could get away with.

During my conservatory years in W., I had a thoughtful circle of friends who exchanged views in a frank way. It was a time of change, of growth. Social and intellectual bonds have always taken priority for me—a lifestyle I've been able to maintain up until today. Sitting right here at my coffee table, many people have drawn strength from me; they've turned me and this table into their wailing wall and thus shown how much they respect us. I've learned that he who gives also receives. It almost sounds like a Bible verse, but why not? The people who visit here really open up and reveal themselves, just as I do. I haven't been at all religious in outlook from my boyhood on. Selfless I'm not, not by any means.

By and by, life became orderly again: university degree; my term as an academic assistant; my fourth decade was already beginning. Slowly I came to realize that living as a homosexual can lead to and produce that elusive quality of refinement and sophistication in intellectual matters. From that point on, I finally really accepted my destiny. Stigma, yes, but you can do something with it. The feeling of being an outcast, of being cheated, disappeared completely. On the contrary, now I sometimes had a twinge of conscience because it seemed I had an easier and more comfortable life than do others whose eros seems to be a huge burden for them to bear. Raising children—what an unimaginably huge responsibility. If you look at it that way, then we are parasites, just going after the beautiful everywhere and complaining even so. I "father" my sons wherever I may find them, and I give the best I have to offer to my friends. This willingness to give is actually a need on my part and thus no special achievement. It isn't really selfless. People who are stingy with themselves just don't know in what wonderfully surprising ways you'll get repaid if you are allowed to give.

Oh, yes, it was a real liberation, the repeal of the statute [against homosexuality in 1968], and before the other German state at that. For many long years that need to hide was an overriding pressure in my life. I suffered from having to lie and deceive—at work, everywhere. If I liked a man, I always waited for an opening. If it didn't come, I would withdraw. I think I can fairly say that I've never pushed myself on anyone. Without wanting to, people lived in illegality, beyond the law, in conditions of constant injustice, of constantly being vulnerable to prosecution and, worst of all, to ruthless blackmail. That state of affairs resulted in many crimes, a mass of horrible lies, and their consequences.

How many mistaken and unjustifiable marriages took place because of the law—marriages in which women stood facing their partners at a complete loss, wondering what was wrong with themselves. And usually an unwanted child would be born right before the final crisis. Those poor kids, who had to grow up between quarreling and mutually destructive parents. I've often had to observe dramas of this kind in my life. I have desperately advised young friends: Don't do it—it will be terrible for everyone involved. Any time I would meet a man and learn he was married, I would withdraw. By the way, one of the awful things I can't forgive our people is breaking up marriages. Earlier, in my time of torment, of suffering over my orientation, I envied the guys who could swing both ways. How well I could have concealed and camouflaged myself if I'd been able to do it. Only later did I realize what a gift of the gods it is to be absolutely and clearly aimed in one direction. I've learned to interpret the gaze of these self-proclaimed bi-men who respond to my imploring words by leaning back skeptically in their chairs, mulling over my words, and finally coming to the conclusion: They certainly aren't quite that queer—I use the word very consciously—quite as queer as I am. They'd work things out at home. What their marriages were like and where they finally ended up I don't need to tell you.

Each of us experiences the phase where people say vicious things about you behind your back, where the more or less subtle stabs of society cripple your soul. Weaklings tend toward shortsighted actions then, to panicked goofs, like that sort of marriage—or they kill themselves. They're still doing it. If we can manage to wait it out, the malicious interest of the conventional people will die down; they'll accept us, perhaps with certain reservations, but . . . the next attention-grabbing event is sure to come along. Nowadays many people behave weirdly, so that we with our fine feathers scarcely attract any notice. We "homos" are, after all, not the center of society.

Along with my professional activity, which I do very much love, my easel has been a dominant part of my intellectual life. Just as a musical person sits down at his piano or picks out a pretty passage while standing, that's how I treated my easel. Looking at pictures from twenty or more years ago places me back into experiences and circumstances from the time of their origin. Should I ever write my memoirs, I'd need only stroll through my pictures. Quite a bit would come back to me.

If I long sought to conceal my male-orientedness from the world, this character trait is expressed rather frankly in my pictures. The split between eros and sex that I established at such an early age has never been hidden, either. The pictures say it. I've never played at being a married couple in a canopied bed, not even with the one I called my great love. In my forties I once again tried a long-lasting relationship; it didn't work out. Evidently I just didn't want to accept that I was born to be a "single"—or did I turn into one? No, love relationships in the usual sense haven't happened for me; instead, I have a love for the male in general.

By the way, this chasm between eros and sex is a phenomenon that has shaped cultural history over entire epochs: In a real sense, the bordello was probably always the institutionalization of this split. The extreme sacralization of marriage obviously made this escape valve necessary.

Over and over again, you encounter in my pictures the harlequin and the faun. The harlequin is the thinking, conscious, and therefore suffering individual; for me, the faun means the vital-animal world. And then there are Ovid's metamorphoses: Artemis transforming the hunter Actaeon into a stag, who is then torn to death by his own dogs; Apollo losing Daphne, who has turned into a laurel. . . . I can't compete with Master Freud and wouldn't want to, but compared with this Artemis, the toughest feminists are gentle maidens. But enough of that—all these figurations are, naturally, a direct reflection of my world of experience and thus of my eros. My abstract works and my landscapes should also be included here. Over and over again you find grotesque, surreal elements in my work. For a time I was painting such scurrilous imagery that my mother began to fear I might be disturbed. So I said to her: "If these things stayed shut up inside me, if I couldn't get them out, then you'd have reason to be worried about me. This is the way I conjure up the uncertain, formulate it, and by capturing it in my pictures I can be rid of it."

Art is active meditation, a different form of attaining knowledge, and you cannot grasp the essence of art with rationality alone. There are two possible ways of acquiring knowledge: the meditative, which the early cultures largely relied on, and the empirical, which our world has taken to the atom bomb.

It was fate that granted me the ability to incorporate elements of figurative talent in my professional work. Professional and artistic ability were linked with each other, rather like the water level at two ends of a siphon hose—the one matched the other. I'm happy that I'm still of some use even now, that my advice occasionally still has some value.

The basis of this pretty assemblage of *objets d'art* around us was laid in my early years. Assemblage—you heard me right. My assemblage is no collection. In the time after 1945, you found the prettiest things literally on the streets, in trash cans. Goethe in his wisdom once said that what you've inherited from your fathers, you must make your own in order to possess it. You only own things if you grasp them, understand and love them. If you can afford valuable artworks, fine, but just by buying them, you haven't made them yours by a long shot. Incidentally, I'm of the opinion that things beyond a certain level of quality no longer belong in private hands.

I associate lovely memories with many of these objects, and I live with them.

At an appropriate time a man must adjust to his age. Lucky the man who succeeds at turning into a happy oldster. The misfortune of declining vital energies can be halted to a certain extent with consciousness, or so at least I hope.

The gods have been lavish with their gifts to me, and I needn't torment myself with regrets about sins I failed to commit. A smart friend once called me an attractive ugly person. Growing old is often a curse for beautiful people, while an attractive ugly person may be in a better position to grow old gracefully.

As a young man I wished to be beautiful in order to be able to turn heads. Woe to those who dazzle everyone in their youth, for what's to come later?

In order to deceive those around me, I wished I could love men and women. But I couldn't do it, and that kept calamity away from me and others. I also lacked that boundless, unlimited vitality that leads many people to neglect their own well-being. Anyone who has to work at staying healthy quickly learns to monitor his energies and to use them sensibly.

As I've grown older, I've gained the interest and even the friendship of some remarkable women. That always pleases me; the memory of my mother sets the standard here.

When I was stuck deep in my midlife crisis, a friendly older colleague at work drew me into a conversation and said: "You know, just wait till you turn fifty, and then everything will be fine again." How right he was.

Do I have a sense of humor? You'll have to ask my friends.

NOTE

1. The Ufa film studio in Babelsberg near Berlin was the leading German film studio up to 1945.

SELECTED BIBLIOGRAPHY

Adam, Barry D. *The Rise of a Gay and Lesbian Movement.* Boston: Twayne Publishers, 1987.

Altman, Dennis. *Coming Out in the Seventies.* Boston: Alyson Publications, 1981.

———— *Homosexual: Oppression and Liberation.* New York: Outerbridge & Dienstfrey, 1971.

Beam, Joseph. *In The Life: A Black Gay Anthology.* Boston: Alyson Publications, 1986.

Beck, Evelyn Torton, ed. *Nice Jewish Girls: A Lesbian Anthology.* Boston: Beacon Press, 1982.

Boyd, Clodagh, et al., eds. and comps. *Out for Ourselves.* Dublin: Dublin Lesbian and Gay Men's Collectives and Women's Community Press, 1986.

Brossard, Nicole. *The Aerial Letter.* trans. Marlene Wildeman. Toronto: The Women's Press, 1988.

Cant, Bob, and Susan Hemmings, eds. *Radical Records: Thirty Years of Lesbian and Gay History, 1957–1987.* London: Routledge, 1988.

Chebel, Malek. *L'Esprit de Sérail: Perversions et Marginalités Sexuelles au Maghreb.* n.p.: Lieu Commun, 1988.

Daniel, Herbert. *Vida Antes Da Morte = Life Before Death.* Rio de Janeiro: Escritorio e Tipografia Jaboti Ltda., 1989.

Dieckmann, Bernhard, and François Pescatore, eds. *Drei Milliarden Perverse.* Schwule Texte 5. Berlin: Verlag Rosa Winkel, 1980.

Dynes, Wayne R. *Encyclopedia of Homosexuality.* New York: Garland Publishing, 1989.

Enriquez, José Ramon. *El Homosexual Ante La Sociedad Enferma.* Barcelona: Tusquets Editor, 1978.

Fernbach, David. *The Spiral Path: A Gay Contribution to Human Survival.* Boston: Alyson Publications, 1981.

FHAR (Front Homosexuel d'Action Revolutionnaire). *Rapport Contre la Normalité.* Paris: Éditions Champ Libre, 1971.

Frieling, Willi, ed. *Schwule Regungen——Schwule Bewegungen.* Berlin: Verlag Rosa Winkel, 1985.

Gai Pied Hebdo. *Best 1979–1991.* Paris: Éditions du Triangle Rose, n.d.

Gauthier-Hamon, Corinne and Roger Teboul. *Entre Père et Fils: La Prostitution Homosexuelle des Garçons.* Paris: Presses Universitaires de France, 1988.

Gay Left Collective, ed. *Homosexuality: Power and Politics.* London: Allison and Busby, 1980.

Gays in Indonesia: Selected Articles from the Print Media. Fitzroy, Australia: Sybylla Press, 1984.

Gil, Manuel Soriano. *Homosexualidad y Represión: Iniciación al Estudio de la Homofilia.* Colección: Lee y Discute, No. 86. Bilbao: Edita Zero, 1978.

Girard, Jacques. *Le Mouvement Homosexuel en France 1945–1980.* Paris: Éditions SYROS, 1981.

GLHPQ (Groupe de Liberation Homosexuel——Politique et Quotidien). *Dossier de Press sur L'Homosexualité.* Paris: Savelli, 1977.

Grahn, Judy. *Another Mother Tongue: Gay Words, Gay Worlds.* Boston: Beacon Press, 1984.

Greenberg, David F. *The Construction of Homosexuality.* Chicago: University of Chicago Press, 1988.

Guerin, Daniel. *Homosexualité & Revolution.* Saint-Denis: Le Vent du Ch'min, 1983.

Hall Carpenter Archives, Gay Men's Oral History Group. *Walking After Midnight: Gay Men's Life Stories.* London: Routledge, 1989.

Hall Carpenter Archives, Lesbian Oral History Group. *Inventing Ourselves: Lesbian Life Stories.* London: Routledge, 1989.

Hinsch, Bret. *Passions of the Cut Sleeve: The Male Homosexual Tradition in China.* Berkeley: University of California Press, 1990.

Hockings, Jacqueline. *Walking the Tightrope: Living Positively with AIDS, ARC, and HIV.* Loughton, Eng.: Gale Centre Publications, 1988.

Hocquenghem, Guy. *Homosexual Desire,* trans. Daniella Dangoor. London: Allison & Busby, 1978.

Hocquenghem, Guy. *Race d'ep! un siècle d'images de l'homosexualité.* Paris: Éditions Libres-Hallier, 1979.

International Association of Lesbians/Gay Women and Gay Men (IGA). *IGA Pink Book 1985: A Global View of Lesbian and Gay Oppression and Liberation.* Amsterdam: COC—Magazijn.

International Lesbian and Gay Association. *Second ILGA Pink Book: A Global View of Lesbian and Gay Liberation and Oppression.* Utrecht Series on Gay and Lesbian Studies, No. 12. Utrecht: Interdisciplinary Gay and Lesbian Studies Department, Utrecht University, 1988.

Jackson, Ed and Stan Persky, eds. *Flaunting It! A Decade of Journalism from "The Body Politic."* Vancouver, B.C.: New Star Books, 1982.

Jackson, Peter A. *Male Homosexuality in Thailand: An Interpretation of Contemporary Thai Sources.* Elmhurst, N.Y.: Global Academic Publishers, 1989.

Johnson, Cary Alan. "Male Homosexuality in Africa: An Overview." Master's thesis, Columbia University, 1991.

Johnston, Jill. *Lesbian Nation: The Feminist Solution.* New York: Simon & Schuster, 1973.

Kinsman, Gary. *The Regulation of Desire: Sexuality in Canada.* Montreal: Black Rose Books, 1987.

Lemke, Jürgen. *Gay Voices from East Germany,* ed. with English introduction by John Borneman. Bloomington: Indiana University Press, 1991.

Lumsden, Ian. *Homosexuality, Society and the State in Mexico.* Toronto: Canadian Gay Archives, 1991.

Malinowsky, H. Robert, comp. *International Directory of Gay and Lesbian Periodicals.* Phoenix: Oryx Press, 1987.

Mieli, Mario. *Homosexuality and Liberation: Elements of a Gay Critique,* trans. David Fernbach. London: Gay Men's Press, 1980.

Moraga, Cherrie, and Ana Castillo, eds. *Esta Puente, Mi Espalda: Voces de Mujeres tercermundistas en los Estados Unidos.* San Francisco: Ism Press, 1988.

Moraga, Cherrie, and Gloria Anzaldua, eds. *This Bridge Called My Back: Writings by Radical Women of Color.* Watertown, Mass.: Persephone Press, 1981.

Murray, Stephen O. *Male Homosexuality in Central and South America.* GAI Saber Monograph 5. San Francisco: Instituto Obregón, 1987.

Naerssen, A. X. van, ed. *Gay Life in Dutch Society.* New York: Harrington Park Press, 1987.

Nicolas, Jean. *La Cuestión Homosexual.* Barcelona: Editorial Fontmara, 1978.

Penelope, Julia and Sarah Valentine, eds. *Finding the Lesbians: Personal Accounts from Around the World.* Freedom, Calif.: The Crossing Press, 1990.

Perez, Alfonso Garcia. *La Rebelión de Los Homosexuales.* Madrid: Pecosa Editorial, 1976.

Perrin, Elula. *So Long As There Are Women,* trans. from the French by Harold J. Salemson. New York: William Morrow & Company, 1980.

Pezzana, Angelo, ed. *La Politica del Corpo: Antologia del "Fuori," Movimento di Liberazione Omosessuale.* Rome: Savelli, 1976.

Praunheim, Rosa von. *Army of Lovers.* London: Gay Men's Press, 1980.

Ramos, Juanita, comp. and ed. *Compañeras: Latina Lesbians (an Anthology).* New York: Latina Lesbian History Project, 1987.

Richmond, Len, and Gary Noguera, eds. *The Gay Liberation Book.* San Francisco: Ramparts Press, 1973.

Roscoe, Will, ed., and Gay American Indians, comps. *Living the Spirit: A Gay American Indian Anthology.* New York: St. Martin's Press, 1988.

SAMOIS, ed. *Coming to Power: Writings and Graphics on Lesbian S/M.* Boston: Alyson Publications, 1982.

Schifter, Jacobo. *La Formación de una Contracultura: Homosexualismo y Sida en Costa Rica.* San José: Ediciones Guayacan, 1989.

Smith, Michael J., ed. *Black Men/White Men.* San Francisco: Gay Sunshine Press, 1983.

Stone, Sharon Dale. *Lesbians in Canada.* Toronto: Between the Lines, 1990.

Sylvestre, Paul-François. *Propos pour une libération (homo)sexuelle.* Montreal: L'Aurore, 1976.

Tatchell, Peter. *Europe in the Pink: Lesbian & Gay Equality in the New Europe.* London: GMP Publishers Ltd., 1992.

Thompson, Denise. *Flaws in the Social Fabric: Homosexuals and Society in Sydney.* Sydney: G. Allen and Unwin, 1985.

Trevisan, João S. *Perverts in Paradise,* trans. Martin Foreman. London: GMP Publishers Ltd., 1986.

Tsang, Daniel, ed. *The Age Taboo: Gay Male Sexuality, Power, and Consent.* Boston: Alyson Publications, 1981.

Walter, Aubrey. *Come Together: The Years of Gay Liberation (1970–73).* London: Gay Men's Press, 1980.

Watanabe, Tsuneo and Jun'ichi. *The Love of the Samurai: A Thousand Years of Japanese Homosexuality,* trans. D. R. Roberts. London: GMP Publishers, 1989.

Whitam, Frederick L., and Robin M. Mathy. *Male Homosexuality in Four Societies: Brazil, Guatemala, the Philippines, and the United States.* New York: Praeger Publishers, 1986.

Young, Allen. *Gays Under the Cuban Revolution.* San Francisco: Grey Fox Press, 1981.

STEPHAN LIKOSKY currently works for The New York Public Library as a Correctional Services Librarian. He was born and grew up in Burlington, Vermont. He holds Masters Degrees from Harvard University in Slavic Languages and Literatures and from Simmons College in Library Science. Other publications include *Connections/Conexiones,* a job search guide for prison ex-inmates. Mr. Likosky has been involved in the Gay movement and with issues of sexual politics for many years. In 1989, he was recipient of the "World of Difference" Award, presented by the Mayor of the City of New York in recognition of his work to combat ethnic, racial, and religious bigotry and to celebrate difference.